Valuing Environmental and Natural Resources

NEW HORIZONS IN ENVIRONMENTAL ECONOMICS

Series Editors: Wallace E. Oates, *Professor of Economics, University of Maryland, USA* and Henk Folmer, *Professor of General Economics, Wageningen University and Professor of Environmental Economics, Tilburg University, The Netherlands*

This important series is designed to make a significant contribution to the development of the principles and practices of environmental economics. It includes both theoretical and empirical work. International in scope, it addresses issues of current and future concern in both East and West and in developed and developing countries.

The main purpose of the series is to create a forum for the publication of high quality work and to show how economic analysis can make a contribution to understanding and resolving the environmental problems confronting the world in the twenty-first century.

Recent titles in the series include:

International Climate Policy to Combat Global Warming
An Analysis of the Ancillary Benefits of Reducing Carbon Emissions
Dirk T.G. Rübbelke

Pollution, Property and Prices
An Essay in Policy-making & Economics
J.H. Dales

The Contingent Valuation of Natural Parks
Assessing the Warmglow Propensity Factor
Paulo A.L.D. Nunes

Environmental Policy Making in Economics
with Prior Tax Distortions
Edited by Lawrence H. Goulder

Recent Advances in Environmental Economics
Edited by John A. List and Aart de Zeeuw

Sustainability and Endogenous Growth
Karen Pittel

The Economic Valuation of the Environment and Public Policy
A Hedonic Approach
Noboru Hidano

Global Climate Change
The Science, Economics and Politics
James M. Griffin

Global Environmental Change in Alpine Regions
Recognition, Impact, Adaptation and Mitigation
Edited by Karl W. Steininger and Hannelore Weck-Hannemann

Environmental Management and the Competitiveness of Nature-Based Tourism Destinations
Twan Huybers and Jeff Bennett

The International Yearbook of Environmental and Resource Economics 2003/2004
A Survey of Current Issues
Edited by Henk Folmer and Tom Tietenberg

Valuing Environmental and Natural Resources

The Econometrics of Non-Market Valuation

Timothy C. Haab
The Ohio State University

Kenneth E. McConnell
University of Maryland at College Park

NEW HORIZONS IN ENVIRONMENTAL ECONOMICS

Edward Elgar
Cheltenham, UK • Northampton, MA, USA

Published by
Edward Elgar Publishing Limited
Glensanda House
Montpellier Parade
Cheltenham
Glos GL50 1UA
UK

Edward Elgar Publishing, Inc.
136 West Street
Suite 202
Northampton
Massachusetts 01060
USA

Paperback edition 2003

A catalogue record for this book
is available from the British Library

Library of Congress Cataloguing in Publication Data
Haab, Timothy C., 1969–
Valuing environmental and natural resources: the econometrics of non-market valuation / Timothy C. Haab, Kenneth E. McConnell.
p. cm. – (New horizons in environmental economics)
Includes bibliographical references and index.
1. Natural resources–Evaluation. 2. Environmental economics.
I. McConnell, Kenneth E. II. Title. III. Series.
HC21.H32 2002
333.7–dc21 2002018956

ISBN 1 84064 704 3 (cased)
1 84376 388 5 (paperback)

Printed and bound in Great Britain by MPG Books Ltd, Bodmin, Cornwall

For Beth, Abby, Maddy and Drew
T.C.H

For Ginny, John, Maggie and Maryanna
K.E.M

Contents

List of Tables

List of Figures

Preface

This book has a limited aim: to make available empirical approaches to non-market valuation in a single location. We cover the two major areas of non-market valuation: stated preferences and behavioral approaches. The breadth and rapid expansion of methods have forced us to choose our coverage carefully. We have opted for depth in the more frequently applied methods, wanting the book to serve as a source for the popular and established models of non-market valuation. We have provided a portal to the literature for methods that we have not covered.

The spirit of the book is empirical modeling. We focus on how observations on behavior or responses to questions can be used to recover measures of willingness to pay. This is not a strictly econometric book. We provide the basics of models but space and time constraints prevent us following many otherwise compelling questions. It is not a book on the theory of non-market valuation either. But we think the book will help in both directions.

The motivation for writing the book has come from many encounters with able economists and students who want to do non-market valuation, but have not yet been exposed to the methods. For them we hope this book will make some parts of the enterprise easier. Almost everything in the book can be found somewhere in the literature. In some cases, we have simply transcribed models. In other cases, we have engaged in simplification or exposition.

Non-market valuation employs microeconomics, welfare economics, and econometrics. Readers will need some knowledge of each to profit from the book. Three books that are especially valuable in these areas are Just, Hueth and Schmitz on welfare economics, A. Myrick Freeman's book on valuation, and the volume edited by Joe Herriges and Cathy Kling, also published by Elgar. Most models applied to valuation use maximum likelihood methods. For readers not familiar with these methods, we have provided a brief review in Appendix A. The books by Maddala and by Ben-Akiva and Lerman are good sources for the econometric issues associated with maximum likelihood estimation for discrete choice methods.

While the book deals with the empirical approaches to valuation, we do not want to leave the impression that this role dominates. Valuation stretches from defining the problem, to formulating the economic model, to questionnaire design and then estimation. This books focuses principally on the last part, the estimation of models for non-market valuation. It will have implications for the other tasks, for it is not really correct to separate the components of research. Econometric model formulation is part of questionnaire design. This is especially true for contingent valuation. One needs to be armed with a sense of good questionnaire design and practice, such as one can find in Mitchell and Carson's book, *Using Surveys to Value Public Goods*, Carson's paper 'Contingent Valuation: A User's Guide' (2000) and Carson's forthcoming book *Contingent Valuation: A Comprehensive Bibliography and History* published by Elgar.

The options for software for estimating maximum likelihood models are growing. Increasingly many researchers write their own estimation routines using packages like Gauss or Matlab. We develop models and methods principally for programs like LIMDEP and SAS. And for the most part, we limit our model to development to those that can be estimated by researchers without writing their own maximum likelihood routines. We write the likelihood function for each model in a way that should allow one to program the function. Researchers writing their own programs probably don't need our help.

We have received help and encouragement from many. Kerry Smith wrote an encouraging review and provided his own disproportionate contribution to the literature on all of the chapters. John Loomis read parts of the contingent valuation chapters and provided the dataset used in Chapters 2-5. John Whitehead also read parts of the early chapters and gave us access to several datasets. Cathy Kling read parts of the chapters on travel cost models. Brent Sohngen lent us a dataset used in Chapter 7. George Parsons provided us with the dataset for logit model estimation of Chapter 8. Nancy Bockstael, Chris Leggett and Ray Palmquist read the hedonic chapter. Part of the data for the hedonic models was also provided by Nancy and Chris. Charles McCormick provided the other part. Virginia McConnell provided encouragement and a thorough reading of the first chapter. Margaret McConnell did extensive work on the references. Graduate students in the Department of Agricultural and Resource Economics at the University of Maryland and in the Department of Agricultural, Environmental and Development Economics at The Ohio State University read various draft chapters of the book and provided valuable comments on clarity and exposition. We thank them for their comments and willingness to help with data. In short, we thank all who helped directly as well as all contributors to the literature whose results we have used. And we accept full responsibility for the remaining errors, omissions and misuse of data.

1

Welfare Economics for Non-market Valuation

1.1 The Background for Valuation

Over the last five decades, economic analysis has spread from its traditional market orientation to such esoteric areas as crime and punishment, family planning, the disposal of nuclear wastes, and drug use. This seeming imperialistic tendency of economics is a consequence of the logic of resource allocation. The notion of an efficient allocation of resources that has emerged from economic theory is a powerful idea. Coupling this idea with empirical techniques, economists have devised and refined methods for measuring whether and to what extent resources are being allocated efficiently. Measurement is an essential part of the approach because it allows the idea of efficiency to be applied to an array of resources, and it serves as the basis for decisions that can improve resource allocation.

The role of measurement in the efficient allocation of resources is especially important in cases of public goods. Markets cannot efficiently allocate public goods or resources with pervasive externalities, or for which property rights are not clearly defined. Examples of these market failures abound. Commercial harvesters of fish have no stake in the future of the individual fish they catch and so they tend to harvest inefficiently large quantities. Automobile drivers don't account for the negative effects of auto emissions when they make driving decisions. The market provision of protection against infectious diseases does not account for the public protection provided by each private decision. These examples have the characteristic that there are gains or losses that extend beyond the private individuals making the decisions.

The principle that public goods and goods with externalities are not efficiently allocated by the market suggests the possibility of improvement by public action. But whether the public action in fact yields net benefits requires measurement. An improvement in resource allocation requires that the benefits of a decision exceed its costs, which in turn requires the measurement of benefits and costs. Whether the issue is public regulation of private actions that have externalities, or the provision of public goods, measurement is the key. To meet the demands for measurement, economists have devised a variety of empirical tools for estimating the benefits and costs of public actions. These tools are typically called valuation methods, and this book deals with their implementation. For public goods and pervasive externalities, implementation involves data collection, model specification and econometric estimation. This book is concerned with the specification and estimation.

Much legislation and many governmental practices give benefit-cost analysis an important role in the public sector. For the US government, Executive Order 12291 states that for each major federal project, the benefits and costs of the project must be measured. Other important legislation includes the Clean Water Act, the Comprehensive Environmental Response, Cleanup and Liability Act (CERCLA), and the Oil Pollution Act. In addition, benefit-cost analysis is a routine procedure for the approval of public projects supported by multilateral international banks. When banks lend for environmental projects such as water treatment systems it is critical to know whether the country has the aggregate willingness to pay for the project supported by the loan.

Measurement of benefits and costs often plays a role in debates about resource allocation even when there is no formal requirement to measure benefits and costs. For example, the study of prairie potholes by Hammack and Brown measured the unforeseen costs resulting from agricultural practices that removed nesting grounds for migratory waterfowl. Unregulated farming practices regarded only the agricultural production from these wetlands. Measuring the economic gains from preserving wetlands required valuation methods, and the measures themselves helped in the public debate about converting wetlands to cultivation.

Benefit estimation plays an important role in lawsuits to compensate the public for private actions that injure public resources. This is its essential role in CERCLA and the Oil Pollution Act. For example, the Oil Pollution Act states

> The valuation approach requires that trustees determine the amount of services that must be provided to produce the same value lost to the public. The approach relies on the idea that lost value can be determined using one of a variety of possible units of exchange, including units of resource services or dollars. The valuation approach requires that the value of lost services be measured explicitly and that the compensatory restoration alternative provide services of equivalent value to the public.

The practice of measuring benefits and costs extends back at least five decades. In the US, the Army Corps of Engineers has a long history of measuring the costs and benefits of dams. The pressure to derive logically consistent measures is relentless. These measures have been applied to national parks, oil spills, acid rain, waiting time at hospitals, endangered species, sewer connections in developing countries, risk of disease, and many other areas. Methods are constantly being developed, refined, tested, rejected and revised.

This book deals with the empirical issues that arise in the estimation and calculation of benefits for public goods, environmental amenities and natural resources. Researchers use two basic approaches for benefit estimation: indirect or behavioral methods and direct or stated preferences methods. With behavioral methods, the researcher observes individual behavior in response to changes in public goods, and from this behavior attempts to infer the value of changes in public goods. Stated preferences is an omnibus name for a variety of approaches. The most prevalent is contingent valuation. Others include contingent ranking, contingent choice and conjoint analysis. In the stated preferences approach, researchers pose contingent or hypothetical questions to respondents, inducing responses that trade off improvements in public goods and services for money. From the responses, one can infer preferences for or the value of changes in public goods.

The need for statistical inference and econometrics arises because individual actions, whether behavior that is observed in quasi-market settings or responses to hypothetical questions, almost never reveal precisely the economic value that a researcher wishes to measure. Such data are typically two steps removed from measures of benefits or willingness to pay. First one infers a preference function such as a utility function, or behavioral relation such as a demand function, and then one calculates benefit measures such as willingness to pay. Randomness enters through uncertainty about the nature of preference functions and via errors in estimation.

Stated preference methods are a more recent development than behavioral methods. Economists initially viewed the former, especially in their contingent valuation form, as inferior to behavioral methods. The idea that one could learn about values except from what was revealed by behavior had seemed foreign to economists. However, in recent years, stated preference techniques have become more accepted. The debate about valuation by stated preferences is over, with the possible exception of its use in eliciting existence values. Contingent valuation has proved to be no less reliable than behavioral methods in a variety of tests. In an early example, Brookshire *et al.* (1982) showed that contingent valuation and hedonic models yielded similar magnitudes for the willingness to pay for improvements in air quality in Los Angeles. In more recent research, Carson, Flores, Martin and Wright (1996) assembled evidence that contingent valuation and behavioral methods gave similar results across a variety of environmental improvements. As Randall (1998) has argued persuasively, looking for a single test of the validity of stated preferences is a poor research strategy. Further, there is no good reason to accept behavioral methods as the truth in testing stated preferences versus behavioral methods. Stated preferences is a class of methods that is generally acceptable, and one wants to know for any particular application whether the method works. We are not concerned with whether stated preferences work better or worse than behavioral methods, or whether stated preferences measure true values, but given that one has chosen an approach, how the data should be handled to ensure defensible valuation estimates.

This book covers the empirical methods for estimating benefits for non-market goods and services. These methods include contingent valuation and the related approaches of stated preferences, travel cost models, random utility models, and discrete-continuous recreation demand models. Our purpose is to provide guidance to the solution of empirical problems that arise in the estimation and calculation of benefits. This guidance will stem from our reading of the consensus of researchers, when such a consensus has been achieved. In the absence of consensus, we will present the issues for making an informed judgement. The emphasis will be on the practical use of estimation techniques rather than the conceptually correct concepts that have less applicability in the routine estimation benefits. We have attempted to provide guidance for the most commonly used methods.

1.2 The Theoretical Background

In this section we provide a brief synopsis of the results of welfare economics that are employed in the remainder of the book. This skeletal presentation of the basic welfare economics serves two purposes: it can guide the reader back to the literature when the concepts are not clear and it can satisfy the informed reader that the appropriate concepts are employed. More complete background in the welfare economics can be found in Freeman and in Just, Hueth and Schmitz.

1.2.1 The Value of Public Goods

The idea of a potential Pareto improvement provides the rationale for public intervention to increase the efficiency of resource allocation. If the sum of benefits from a public action, to whomever they may occur, exceeds the costs of the action, it is deemed worthwhile by this criterion. The sum of the benefits entails two kinds of information: knowledge of the individual benefits and a means of expanding the benefits to the relevant population. Econometric practice is typically applied to obtain individual benefits. Knowledge of the number of individuals who benefit, while not necessarily inferred from econometric work, is nevertheless an essential ingredient in determining the benefits.

The process of benefit estimation begins with the desired measurement for an individual: the net change in income that is equivalent to or compensates for changes in the quantity or quality of public goods. The process is complete when the net income changes are expanded to the relevant population. The theory of measurement of net income changes for individuals is a well developed area. (See Just, Hueth and Schmitz, or Freeman.) In this section we provide a brief survey of this theory as a basis for the estimation that follows.

We begin with the preference function for an individual. (For the most part, we ignore the distinction between household and individual. See, however, the recent work by Smith and van Houtven.) Let $u(\mathbf{x}, \mathbf{q})$ be the individual preference function, where $\mathbf{x} = x_1 ... x_m$ is the vector of private goods, and $\mathbf{q} = q_1 ... q_n$ is the vector of public goods, which may also be characteristics of private goods. (Throughout the book, we use bold to denote vectors and matrices. If there is potential for misinterpretation, we specify whether the vector is a row or column.) The distinction between $\mathbf{x}$ and $\mathbf{q}$ rests on whether the individual controls the quantity, not whether there is a market. Individuals choose their $\mathbf{x}$ but their $\mathbf{q}$ is exogenous. For example, the individual chooses x_i, how much water to draw from a tap; the public determines q_j, the quality of the water.

The $\mathbf{x}$ are assumed available at parametric prices, $p_1, ..., p_m = \mathbf{p}$, which may or may not be market-determined. The individual maximizes utility subject to income y. The indirect utility function, $V(\mathbf{p}, \mathbf{q}, y)$, is given by

$$V(\mathbf{p}, \mathbf{q}, y) = \max_{\mathbf{x}} \{u(\mathbf{x}, \mathbf{q}) | \mathbf{p} \cdot \mathbf{x} \leq y\}.$$

The minimum expenditure function $m(\mathbf{p}, \mathbf{q}, u)$ is dual to the indirect utility function

$$m(\mathbf{p}, \mathbf{q}, u) = \min_{\mathbf{x}} \{\mathbf{p} \cdot \mathbf{x} | u(\mathbf{x}, \mathbf{q}) \geq u\}.$$

The indirect utility and the expenditure function have well known properties. The derivative of the expenditure function with respect to price gives the Hicksian or utility-constant demand, where the subscript indicates a partial derivative:

$$x_i^u(\mathbf{p}, \mathbf{q}, u) = m_{p_i}(\mathbf{p}, \mathbf{q}, u).$$

The negative of the ratio of derivatives of the indirect utility function with respect to price and income gives the Marshallian or ordinary demand curve:

$$x_i(\mathbf{p}, \mathbf{q}, y) = -V_{p_i}(\mathbf{p}, \mathbf{q}, y)/V_y(\mathbf{p}, \mathbf{q}, y).$$

Further, when $u(\mathbf{x}, \mathbf{q})$ is increasing and quasi-concave in $\mathbf{q}$, $m(\mathbf{p}, \mathbf{q}, u)$ is decreasing and convex in $\mathbf{q}$ and $V(\mathbf{p}, \mathbf{q}, y)$ is increasing and quasi-concave in $\mathbf{q}$.

The indirect utility function and the expenditure function provide the theoretical structure for welfare estimation. For stated preference approaches, one needs the changes in these functions. Contingent valuation can be viewed as a way of estimating the change in the expenditure function or the change in the indirect utility function. For pure public goods, such as those providing existence value, only the expenditure functions or the indirect utility functions are relevant. There is no area under demand curves that corresponds to the change in the expenditure function. For behavioral methods, one needs a conceptual path from observations on behavior to these constructs. Behavioral methods lead to areas under demand or marginal value curves, or to indirect utility or expenditure functions from which welfare measures can be directly computed.

There are two equally valid ways of describing money welfare measures: one is with the ideas of compensating and equivalent variation and the other is with the ideas of willingness to pay and willingness to accept. They measure the same phenomenon–the increment in income that makes a person indifferent to an exogenous change, where the change might be price change, a quality change, or a change in some public good. Willingness to pay is the maximum amount of income a person will pay in exchange for an improvement in circumstances, or the maximum amount a person will pay to avoid a decline in circumstances. Willingness to accept is the minimum amount of income a person will accept for a decline in circumstances, or the minimum amount a person will accept to forego an improvement in circumstances. Compensating variation is the amount of income paid or received that leaves the person at the initial level of well-being, and equivalent variation is the amount of income paid or received that leaves the person at the final level of well-being. Willingness to pay and willingness to accept relate to the right to a utility level, as implied by their nomenclature. When one is required to pay to maintain current well-being or achieve a higher well-being, the right to that level of well-being lies elsewhere. When one must be paid to accept a worse situation, the right to the current level of well-being adheres to the individual who accepts payment. Equivalent and compensating variation rely on the initial versus final well-being for their distinction. Compensating variation decomposes in the following way: when the final well-being is worse than the initial well-being, it is willingness to accept but when the final well-being is better than the initial well-being, it is willingness to pay. Equivalent variation is just the opposite: willingness to accept for situations where well-being is improved and willingness to pay when well-being declines.

The relationship is shown in Table 1.1. Although the definitions are

TABLE 1.1. The Relationships among CV, EV, WTP and WTA

	Equivalent Variation	Compensating Variation
Utility Increases	WTA	WTP
Utility Decreases	WTP	WTA

fully consistent, and the variation ideas older, recent practice has tended to adopt the willingness to pay and willingness to accept terms, chiefly because contingent valuation surveys have used this language. (Hanemann (1999a) has explored the topics of WTA and WTP at length, though his conclusions about the use of the concepts differ from ours somewhat.) We begin by defining these more intuitive measures. We based the definitions on changes in $\mathbf{q}$, though we could equally well change $\mathbf{p}$. For an individual, willingness to pay (WTP) is the amount of income that compensates for (or is equivalent to) an increase in the public good:

$$V(\mathbf{p}, \mathbf{q}^*, y - WTP) = V(\mathbf{p}, \mathbf{q}, y) \tag{1.1}$$

when $\mathbf{q}^* \geq \mathbf{q}$ and increases in $\mathbf{q}$ are desirable ($\partial V/\partial q_i > 0$). The changes in $\mathbf{p}$ can be valued by evaluating the indirect utility function at a new price vector $\mathbf{p}^*$. We can also define willingness to pay with the expenditure function:

$$WTP = m(\mathbf{p}, \mathbf{q}, u) - m(\mathbf{p}, \mathbf{q}^*, u) \text{ when } u = V(\mathbf{p}, \mathbf{q}, y) \tag{1.2}$$

and assuming that we start at the same place, $y = m(\mathbf{p}, \mathbf{q}, u)$. Willingness to pay is the amount of income an individual would give up to make him indifferent between the original state: income at y and the public good at $\mathbf{q}$ and the revised state: income reduced to $y - WTP$ and the public good increased to $\mathbf{q}^*$. The WTP for a price change (let the price vector decline) is defined analogously:

$$WTP = m(\mathbf{p}, \mathbf{q}, u) - m(\mathbf{p}^*, \mathbf{q}, u) \text{ when } u = V(\mathbf{p}, \mathbf{q}, y). \tag{1.3}$$

Willingness to accept (WTA) is the change in income that makes an individual indifferent between two situations: the original public good $\mathbf{q}$, but income at $y + WTA$ and the new level of the public good, $\mathbf{q}^*$, but income at y. It is defined implicitly in the following equality:

$$V(\mathbf{p}, \mathbf{q}, y + WTA) = V(\mathbf{p}, \mathbf{q}^*, y). \tag{1.4}$$

It is given explicitly by the expenditure function:

$$WTA = m(\mathbf{p}, \mathbf{q}, u^*) - m(\mathbf{p}, \mathbf{q}^*, u^*) \tag{1.5}$$

where $u^* = V(\mathbf{p}, \mathbf{q}^*, y)$. By this definition, $WTA \geq 0$ when $q^* \geq q$. The definitions of WTP and WTA correspond to the positive parts of the Hicksian measures. As Table 1.1 shows, WTP is the positive part of equivalent variation and WTA is the positive part of compensating variation. In practice below, we will calculate welfare measures as only willingness to pay. These measures will sometimes be negative, meaning that this is the amount that the individual would pay to prevent the proposed change. A positive WTP measure has the standard meaning of the willingness to pay rather than go without the change.

1.2.2 Willingness to Pay versus Willingness to Accept

There is a well known empirical anomaly that has persisted over roughly three decades of experimental and contingent valuation research. It is common to find that for the same goods in the same setting, WTA exceeds WTP by an amount that seems intuitively far too much even for goods and services with quite small nominal values. In a summary of 45 studies, Horowitz and McConnell find the mean ratio of WTA to WTP to exceed 5. The anomaly is accentuated by the empirical results obtained from behavioral models, where one typically finds no meaningful difference between willingness to pay and willingness to accept.

Two explanations have been offered for the experimental finding. The first exploits a psychological model such as prospect theory or loss aversion in which individuals base their decisions on the net change relative to the status quo, not on their well-being before and after a change. This explanation abandons the neoclassical utility function as a basis of choice and posits the difference between willingness to pay and willingness to accept as an attribute of preferences. The alternative, based on the neoclassical utility function and articulated most clearly by Hanemann (1991), explains the difference between willingness to accept and willingness to pay as the inability to substitute between public and private goods. This explanation may work for many public goods but does not seem to account for the divergence between WTA and WTP for such mundane goods as mugs and pens. Further, there is field evidence that the divergence declines as respondents become familiar with the process. List (2001) has ongoing field experiments that reach this conclusion.

Regardless of the explanations of the anomaly, we will emphasize the role of willingness to pay and for the most part, ignore willingness to accept. Several factors motivate this decision. First, the absence of evidence of differences between WTA and WTP from behavioral methods, despite several decades of looking, lends support to the choice of WTP. Second, there is widespread belief that stated preference approaches cannot be used to measure willingness to accept because they are not incentive-compatible for this measure. Related support for the role of WTP comes from the NOAA Blue Ribbon Panel on contingent valuation, which recommends that researchers measure willingness to pay, not willingness to accept. Consequently, circumstances suggest that with behavioral methods, one cannot find differences between willingness to accept and willingness to pay, and that stated preference measures cannot or should not be used to measure willingness to accept. The reasonable path, at least where the focus is on empirical methods, is to concentrate on willingness to pay.

While for most valuation issues, the changes in services are by themselves small enough for researchers to work with willingness to pay, one must avoid the temptation to think that this is always the case. In some individual cases, when the change from public goods or natural resources causes a large change in services, there may well be a difference between WTP and WTA. The Brookshire *et al.* (1985) hedonic model of earthquake insurance is a good example of this, because in some outcomes, there could be quite large differences in utility. And in very poor countries, changes in access to natural resources can induce large changes in income, and lead to substantial differences in WTA and WTP.

The decision to focus on willingness to pay is a compromise, reflecting the unsettled state of research. But it leaves an asymmetry in the theoretical constructs for behavioral and stated preference approaches. In behavioral approaches, empirical evidence supports the idea that willingness to pay equals willingness to accept, and so the logical next step is to adopt the most observable measure, consumer surplus. This we will do, and call it willingness to pay.

1.3 Theoretical Support for Behavioral Methods

The theoretical expressions defining willingness to pay (equations 1.1 and 1.2) and willingness to accept (1.4) are very general. They require only that individuals have preferences over $\mathbf{x}$ and $\mathbf{q}$. We have assumed that utility is increasing in $\mathbf{q}$, but it is easy to modify the theory to account for a $\mathbf{q}$ (such as pollution) that reduces utility. It is not necessary to know how behavior adjusts to apply contingent valuation, although most changes in $\mathbf{q}$ would cause people to adjust their behavior. For example, a decrease in pathogens in drinking water might reduce illness and decrease both losses in work and time spent boiling water. Sometimes changes in $\mathbf{q}$ cause no meaningful adjustment in behavior. For example, the planting of wildflowers in median strips of highways seems likely to induce only the slightest adjustment in driving. Yet the flowers themselves could be valued via stated preference approaches. (For example, see Smith 1996.) Whether $\mathbf{q}$ represents wildflowers in median strips or pathogens in drinking water, the theoretical constructs in equations (1.1) and (1.2) provide a basis of measurement that is sufficient support for stated preference approaches.

However, when behavioral methods are used, it is necessary to trace the influence of the public good on behavior, and behavior on welfare. For this tracing, one must impose some structure on the preference function. There are two types of changes that lead to welfare measures: price changes and quality changes. Each requires some kind of restrictions. For price changes, we assume that the approximate measure from a Marshallian demand curve equals the more exact Hicksian measure. The principal restriction for quality is weak complementarity, an assumption about an individual's preference function that permits the value of changes in public goods to be traced to private behavior. The intuitive content of weak complementarity links a private good and a public good such that, if the private good is not consumed, then the public good is not valued. For a detailed explanation of weak complementarity and its implications, see Smith and Banzhaf.

To develop the theoretical basis of weak complementarity, partition $\mathbf{x}$ into x_1, $\mathbf{x}_{-1}$ where x_1 is the purchase of a private good and $\mathbf{x}_{-1}$ the remainder of the private goods, and suppose that q is a scalar. (When there are several commodities in the partition being analyzed, one must be concerned with the conditions for integrability of the incomplete system. For the most part in this book, we will not deal with such systems. But see LaFrance and von Haefen for more details.) Let the price of x_1 be p and the prices of $\mathbf{x}_{-1}$ be a vector of ones. (In a slight abuse of notation, we now let $V(p, q, y)$ be the indirect utility function with all other prices set to one, and $m(p, q, u)$ as the corresponding expenditure function.) The Marshallian demand for x_1, the quantity that would be observed, is given by Roy's identity:

$$x_1(p, q, y) = -V_p(p, q, y)/V_y(p, q, y) \tag{1.6}$$

when the subscripts on the indirect utility function denote partial derivatives. The Hicksian (or utility-constant) demand can be derived via the envelope theorem from the expenditure function:

$$x_1^u(p, q, u) = m_p(p, q, u). \tag{1.7}$$

Let p^* be the minimum price that induces zero consumption—the choke price:

$$x_1^u(p^*, q, u) = 0.$$

Then there are three equivalent ways to define weak complementarity:

$$\begin{aligned} \partial m(p^*, q, u)/\partial q &= 0 \\ \partial V(p^*, q, y)/\partial q &= 0 \\ \partial u(0, \mathbf{x}_{-1}, q)/\partial q &= 0. \end{aligned}$$

The first two expressions state that the expenditure function and the indirect utility function are constant with respect to q if the price is so high that x_1 is not consumed. The third states that direct utility does not change when q changes if x_1 equals zero. Each makes intuitive sense. Suppose that x_1 is drinking water from a river and q is the number of pathogen-free days in the river water. Then weak complementarity implies that the individual does not care about pathogens in the river when he does not drink water from the river. This is a meaningful restriction, because there are at least two other ways of getting utility from the river: swimming in the river or the altruistic value of others' use of the river.

Weak complementarity implies that the value of (or willingness to pay for) changes in the public good equals the change in the value of access to the private good. By definition, the willingness to pay for a change in a public good is given by equation (1.2):

$$WTP = m(p, q, u) - m(p, q^*, u).$$

To demonstrate weak complementarity, suppose we have estimated the Hicksian or utility-constant demand $x_1^u(p, q, u) = m_p(p, q, u)$. The value of access to this good (an individual's willingness to pay for the right to consume, given p, q, and u) is the area under the demand curve from the current price p to the choke price p^*:

$$\begin{aligned} WTP(\text{access}) &= \int_p^{p^*} x_1^u(p',q,u)dp' = \int_p^{p^*} m_p(p',q,u)dp' \quad (1.8) \\ &= m(p^*,q,u) - m(p,q,u). \end{aligned}$$

In some cases, this measure holds interest in itself. That is, one could seek to measure the willingness to pay for access to a public good such as a natural resource, where an individual must spend part of his income to obtain access. Researchers frequently measure willingness to pay for access to a recreational resource, because policy decisions may entail an all-or-nothing choice between recreational and competing uses of the resource.

In practice, one observes the income-constant demand curve, not the utility-constant demand curve, and so it is relevant to ask the connection between the two measures. Is the consumer surplus, that is, the area under an income-constant demand curve, substantially different from the area under utility constant demand curve over the same price change? There are three ways to address the question. The first, an inexact but relevant response, comes from Willig (1976), who demonstrates that for price changes the difference between the areas under a Marshallian (income-constant) and Hicksian (utility-constant) demand curve can be approximated with knowledge of the budget share of the good, the income elasticity, and the consumer surplus:

$$\frac{CV - CS}{CS} \approx \frac{\eta CS}{2y} \approx \frac{CS - EV}{CS}$$

where η is the income elasticity, CV is compensating variation, CS is consumer surplus–the area under the Marshallian demand curve, and EV is equivalent variation. (See Just, Hueth and Schmitz, p. 378.) For recreational cases, the deviations are quite small, certainly smaller than the many kinds of measurement errors that confound econometric analysis. For example, an income elasticity of 0.5, consumer surplus estimate of 200, and an income of 20000 would create a deviation of 0.0025. This means that we could approximate CV by $(1.0025)CS$, quite an acceptable approximation.

Hanemann (1980) and Hausman (1981) provide a second means to answer the question: use information in the Marshallian demand curve to derive the Hicksian demand curve. Essentially one 'integrates back' from the Marshallian to the expenditure function, and then uses the Hicksian demand curve to calculate the appropriate area. Integrating back is enabled by recognizing that along an indifference curve utility is constant, so that (holding q constant):

$$\frac{\partial V(p,q,y)}{\partial p}\frac{dp}{dt}+\frac{\partial V(p,q,y)}{\partial y}\frac{dy}{dt}=0. \tag{1.9}$$

Using the implicit function theorem yields $\frac{dy}{dt}\div\frac{dp}{dt}=\frac{dy}{dp}$ or expressed in terms of the expenditure function, $\frac{dy}{dt}\div\frac{dp}{dt}=\frac{dm}{dp}$. Using these relationships when solving equation (1.9) gives

$$\frac{dm}{dp}=-\frac{\partial V(p,q,y)}{\partial p}/\frac{\partial V(p,q,y)}{\partial y}=x_1(p,q,y).$$

The right hand side is the Marshallian demand curve. When we let income equal expenditure ($m=y$), we recognize this as a first order differential equation. This equation can be solved when $x_1(p,q,y)$ is given suitable functional form. Subsequent work using the integrating back has failed to reveal noteworthy differences between the areas under the Hicksian and Marshallian demand curves. The Hanemann-Hausman approach requires that one specify a Marshallian demand curve that can be integrated back. This effectively excludes some flexible forms.

But in the third approach, Vartia provides a numerical method that allows one to compute the Hicksian area given any Marshallian demand curve. Essentially these careful investigations have made researchers more comfortable in using the areas under Marshallian demand curves as close approximations of the more exact areas under Hicksian demand curves. At least for applications to the demand for recreation, the budget shares are small and the income elasticities are low, making the Willig bounds quite tight.

The preference restrictions for using behavioral models to measure the welfare effects of quality changes are more severe than for price changes, but equally plausible. To employ weak complementarity, we ask the willingness to pay for access to x_1 changes when q changes. Suppose q increases to q^*. The increase in willingness to pay for access is

$$\int_p^{p^*} x_1^u(p',q^*,u)dp' - \int_p^{p^*} x_1^u(p',q,u)dp'. \tag{1.10}$$

This is of course just the change in the area under the utility-constant demand curve. Because such demand curves are derivatives of the expenditure function with respect to price, by integrating we can express this change as

$$m(p^*,q^*,u)-m(p,q^*,u)-[m(p^*,q,u)-m(p,q,u)]. \tag{1.11}$$

Weak complementarity implies that $m(p^*, q^*, u) = m(p^*, q, u)$. With a price of p^* or higher, changes in q don't shift the expenditure function. Combining equations (1.8), (1.10) and (1.11) leads to the weak complementarity result:

$$\int_p^{p^*} x_1^u(p', q^*, u)dp' - \int_p^{p^*} x_1^u(p', q, u)dp' = m(p, q, u) - m(p, q^*, u). \tag{1.12}$$

The change in the willingness to pay for access to the private good equals the willingness to pay for changes in the public good. Weak complementarity offers a way of measuring willingness to pay for changes in public goods by estimating the demand for private goods. Note that the left hand side of equation (1.12) can be represented graphically as the change in areas under two demand curves.

The development of the theoretical implications of weak complementarity assumes the knowledge of a utility-constant demand function. Naturally if such demand curves are available, then the exact analysis can be carried out. Typically, one observes only income-constant demand curves. One might be tempted to reason that if the area under a utility-constant demand curve can be approximated by the area under a Marshallian demand curve, then one can simply approximate twice, using the result in equation (1.12). This, however, is not true. The reasoning is as follows. To approximate a Hicksian area with a Marshallian area, both demand curves must start at the same price, quantity point, which they do before the quality change. However, after the quality change, the demands are no longer equal at the given price, unless the income effect is zero.[1] Once again, practice has demonstrated that the income effects are not big enough to create a wedge between the Hicksian and Marshallian areas for quality changes, despite the potential for differences based on duality results.

The role of exact measures is critical when there is a difference between willingness to pay and willingness to accept. In such cases, initial endowments and entitlements can influence resource allocation. When there is negligible difference between willingness to pay and willingness to accept, the exact measures lose their significance. However, since we have limited our analysis to willingness to pay for stated choice methods, we can likewise dispense with the distinction between willingness to pay, willingness to accept and consumer surplus for behavioral methods. This modus operandi implies that we can work with the Marshallian, or income-constant demand curve, and calculate changes in the value

[1] See Bockstael and McConnell for the full analysis of this idea.

of access from this demand function. Empirical evidence strongly supports the idea that willingness to pay and consumer surplus differ by negligible amounts. However, if the circumstances suggest that there is a substantial difference between WTA and WTP, then one can use numerical methods such as Vartia's algorithm to obtain utility-constant demand curves and WTA and WTP.

The assumption of weak complementarity has the added virtue of helping determine the extent of the market as well as characterizing the path from behavior to welfare effects of public goods. Extent of market describes a means of thinking about the number of people who would be willing to pay for changes in the public good. The total benefits of improvements of the public good are the sum across individuals with positive willingness to pay. The extent of the market defines households who may have positive willingness to pay. And when positive willingness to pay requires some use, the extent of the market is limited to users. This contrasts with valuation not necessarily connected with use. In this case, the extent of the market may be more difficult to determine.

Weak complementarity, while an important assumption for behavioral analysis, cannot be tested with behavioral data. The assumption of weak complementarity would be violated if one of the three conditions could be proved wrong. But because the three conditions require stationarity of a value function when there is no relevant behavior, they are typically not testable. Especially when the relationship between the public and private good is limited for practical purposes to only one private good, there is no empirical test based on behavior of the assumption that when the private good is zero, changes in the public good are not valued. Instead, weak complementarity should be thought of as an assumption that makes sense in some cases but not in others.

1.4 Conclusions

There is sufficient theoretical support for the task of measuring the economic value of non-market resources. This theory is quite general but provides support for stated preference and behavioral approaches to non-market valuation. The theory seems to imply a straightforward approach to valuation. However, most applications involve creative blending of theory with the practical problems of the immediate application. In the remainder of the book we engage the issues that emerge when researchers build the empirical models that form the basis for welfare measurement.

2

Parametric Models for Contingent Valuation

2.1 Introduction

In this chapter we describe the basic econometric models for responses to dichotomous contingent valuation (CV) questions. CV is a method of recovering information about preferences or willingness to pay from direct questions. The purpose of contingent valuation is to estimate individual willingness to pay for changes in the quantity or quality of goods or services, as well as the effect of covariates on willingness to pay. Although economists were slow to adopt the general approach of CV, the method is now ubiquitous. It is used on virtually any kind of public good or service imaginable. Journals are filled with papers on CV. Carson (forthcoming) has an extensive bibliography and history of CV. This chapter considers parametric models of the standard discrete response of CV. Chapter 3 explains the use of distribution-free models for analyzing CV data. Chapter 4 deals with the statistical distribution of willingness to pay estimates, while Chapter 5 investigates some more specialized topics that arise in the application of parametric models. The general approach of conjoint analysis and attribute-based stated preferences, covered in detail in Louviere, Hensher and Swait, is addressed briefly in Chapter 10.

The lure of providing numerical results not otherwise available overcame economists' reluctance to rely on evidence not backed by behavior, and hence accounts for the growth of CV. Certain classes of goods or services cannot be valued with behavioral methods under any circumstances. Passive use value, also known as existence value or non-use value, is the willingness to pay for the preservation or improvement of natural resources, without any prospect or intention of direct or in-situ use of the resource. Such values cannot be recovered with behavioral methods because by definition they do not motivate behavior and hence have no underlying demand curves. Even when demand curves exist in principle, CV methods may provide the only hope for valuing certain services. For example, the willingness to pay for improved water quality in a lake that has a long history of severe pollution probably cannot be estimated with behavioral methods because the lake may not have had any previous use. Contingent valuation offers great flexibility compared with behavioral methods. For example, the value of a government program to provide malaria control for children of different ages in a developing country is amenable to CV analysis, but would require considerable resources for estimation via behavioral methods.

The essential and most important task of CV analysis is the design of questionnaires and survey procedure. It is worth stating the obvious: no amount of careful data handling and econometric analysis can overcome a poorly designed questionnaire. Mitchell and Carson[1] provide a thorough analysis of the process and issues in the development of questionnaires and sampling. A CV question asks a respondent about monetary valuation of a service that is meaningful to the respondent. The service must be limited geographically and temporally and be defined in terms of characteristics that can reasonably enter a respondent's preference function. For example if studying willingness to pay to avoid exposure to PCBs, the service should be described in terms of health risk commonly understood by the general public, not ambient concentrations of PCBs. The second element of the CV question is the method, or vehicle, for paying for the service that links the payment with the service such that without the payment, there would be no service. A common and natural method is to link public good services with tax payments, but other methods, such as payments on utility bills, are used. Acceptable vehicles provide a clear link, one that implies the necessity of payment to receive the service. Further, the time dimension of the payment must not be ambiguous. An immediate, one shot increase in taxes is clear while an increase in a periodic payment is open to several interpretations. Questions that rely on voluntary contributions are fraught with difficulty, because of the implicit free-riding problem.

The final element of a CV scenario is the method of asking questions. This part of the questionnaire confronts the respondent with a given monetary amount, and one way or the other induces a response. This has evolved from the simple open-ended question of early studies such as 'What is the maximum amount you would pay for...?' through bidding games and payment cards to dichotomous choice questions, which are the subject of this chapter. The literature on CV is replete with terms for survey practice and econometrics. Here are the basic approaches to asking questions that lead directly to willingness to pay or provide

[1]Mitchell and Carson (1989). This book is an invaluable source for contingent valuation. A more recent, updated, but abbreviated companion to contingent valuation is Carson (2000).

information to estimate preferences.

Open Ended CV: A CV question in which the respondent is asked to provide the interviewer with a point estimate of his or her willingness to pay.

Bidding Game: A CV question format in which individuals are iteratively asked whether they would be willing to pay a certain amount. The amounts are raised (lowered) depending on whether the respondent was (was not) willing to pay the previously offered amount. The bidding stops when the iterations have converged to a point estimate of willingness to pay.

Payment Cards: A CV question format in which individuals are asked to choose a willingness to pay point estimate (or a range of estimates) from a list of values predetermined by the surveyors, and shown to the respondent on a card.

Dichotomous or Discrete Choice CV: A CV question format in which respondents are asked simple yes or no questions of the stylized form: Would you be willing to pay $t?

The dichotomous choice approach has become the presumptive method of elicitation for CV practitioners. The other three methods have been shown to suffer from incentive compatibility problems in which survey respondents can influence potential outcomes by revealing values other than their true willingness to pay. The dichotomous choice approach has become quite widely adopted, despite criticisms and doubts, in part because it appears to be incentive-compatible in theory.[2] When respondents do not give a direct estimate of their willingness to pay, they have diminished ability to influence the aggregate outcome. This gain in incentive compatibility comes at a cost however. Estimates of willingness to pay are not directly revealed by respondents and as such, it is necessary to develop means for analyzing dichotomous choice responses. These methods are the focus of this and subsequent chapters.

To execute the dichotomous choice approach, the researcher provides the respondent with a payment that must be made. Hence the payments, or bid prices, are an important part of the survey design. In this chapter we assume that the bid prices are given. In Chapter 5, we take up the

[2]For a debate on the incentive compatibility of dichotomous choice CV questions see Cummings *et al.* (1997); Haab, Huang and Whitehead (1999) and Smith (1999).

more difficult problem of choosing these prices. The design of good questionnaires is a skill learned from experience but requires expertise in survey research. Economists have learned that other social sciences, social psychology and sociology, frequently are better prepared for the design of questionnaires and survey procedures.

A lingering controversy is whether CV provides reliable estimates for passive use value. This controversy stems in part from the damage settlement for the Exxon Valdez oil spill. State and federal trustees of natural resources sued Exxon for damages to the resources. The state settled for damages of approximately $1 billion. This damage settlement was supported by a CV study of the passive use values of Alaskan natural resources.[3] The size of the settlement spawned a lengthy debate about CV, especially its role in estimating passive use values. The initial debate about passive use values centered around a conflict in a simple version of the scientific method. Valid scientific conclusions require some means of disproof. A CV study that estimates the value of clean air in Los Angeles can in principle be disproved by a combination of behavioral studies. But a CV study that estimates willingness to pay for preserving pristine wilderness for its own sake is not subject to disproof, at least through behavioral means. There are no behavioral implications of passive use value, and hence no alternative means to disprove CV. The basic scientific issue has not disappeared, but more knowledge of and confidence in the method have dampened the controversy. And of course, research with behavioral methods has turned out to be not more disprovable than CV, in large part because of the extensive series of assumptions and judgments that must be made to use behavioral functions.

One consequence of the Exxon Valdez controversy was an attempt to determine the validity of the CV method, especially applied to non-use values. A series of studies critical of the method was edited by Hausman (1993). This was followed by the so-called Blue Ribbon Panel. This group, assembled by the National Oceanic and Atmospheric Administration (NOAA), did not finally resolve the question of whether CV can be reliably used to estimate passive use values. But it performed a far more valuable task in essentially establishing good practices for CV. These practices, which almost constitute a protocol, should be carefully considered for every CV study. Not all of the guidelines have proved to be essential, but the presence of the guidelines has helped unify the practice of contingent valuation.

---

[3] See Carson, Mitchell *et al.* (1992).

2.1.1 NOAA Panel Guidelines for Value Elicitation Surveys

The following guidelines[4] are met by the best CV surveys and need to be present in order to assure reliability and usefulness of the information that is obtained. The guidelines are designed for contingent valuation questions to be posed after an oil spill. All parts are obviously not relevant for all CV settings, but the general sense of careful and thorough survey design and testing is relevant.

1. *Conservative Design*: Generally, when aspects of the survey design and the analysis of the responses are ambiguous, the option that tends to underestimate willingness to pay is preferred. A conservative design increases the reliability of the estimate by eliminating extreme responses that can enlarge estimated values wildly and implausibly.

2. *Elicitation Format*: The willingness to pay format should be used instead of the compensation required because the former is the conservative choice.

3. *Referendum Format*: The valuation question should be posed as a vote on a referendum.

4. *Accurate Description of the Program or Policy*: Adequate information must be provided to respondents about the environmental program that is offered. It must be defined in a way that is relevant to damage assessment.

5. *Pretesting of Photographs*: The effects of photographs on subjects must be carefully explored.

6. *Reminder of Substitute Commodities*: Respondents must be reminded of substitute commodities, such as other comparable natural resources or the future state of the same natural resource. This reminder should be introduced forcefully and directly prior to the main valuation question to assure that respondents have the alternatives clearly in mind.

7. *Adequate Time Lapse from the Accident*: The survey must be conducted at a time sufficiently distant from the date of the environmental insult that respondents regard the scenario of complete restoration as plausible. Questions should be included to

[4] *Federal Register*, **58**(10), 4601-14 January 15, 1993.

determine the state of subjects' beliefs regarding restoration probabilities. This guideline is especially relevant for natural resource accidents but may not be relevant for many other more mundane types of studies.

8. *Temporal Averaging*: Time dependent measurement noise should be reduced by averaging across independently drawn samples taken at different points in time. A clear and substantial time trend in the responses would cast doubt on the 'reliability' of the finding. This guideline pertains to natural resource accidents that have a high public awareness, such as oil spills.

9. *'No-answer' Option*: A 'no-answer' option should be explicitly allowed in addition to the 'yes' and 'no' vote options on the main valuation (referendum) question. Respondents who choose the 'no-answer' option should be asked to explain their choice. Answers should be carefully coded to show the types of responses, for example: (i) Rough indifference between a yes and a no vote; (ii) inability to make a decision without more time and more information; (iii) preference for some other mechanism for making this decision; and (iv) bored by this survey and anxious to end it as quickly as possible. Subsequent research has concluded that 'no-answer' responses are best grouped as 'no'.

10. *Yes/no Follow-ups*: Yes and no responses should be followed up by the open-ended question: 'Why did you vote yes/no?' Answers should be carefully coded to show the types of responses, for example: (i) It is (or isn't) worth it; (ii) Don't know; or (iii) The polluters should pay.

11. *Cross-tabulations*: The survey should include a variety of other questions that help to interpret the responses to the primary valuation question. The final report should include summaries of willingness to pay broken down by these categories. Among the items that would be helpful in interpreting the responses are: Income, Prior Knowledge of the Site, Prior Interest in the Site (Visitation Rates), Attitudes toward the Environment, Attitudes toward Big Business, Distance to the Site, Understanding of the Task, Belief in the Scenarios, Ability/Willingness to Perform the Task.

12. *Checks on Understanding and Acceptance*: The above guidelines must be satisfied without making the instrument so complex that it poses tasks that are beyond the ability or interest level of many participants.

Some of these guidelines, such as photos, adequate time lapse, etc., pertain to specific kinds of natural resource damages such as oil spills. But the general idea here is that one invests a substantial portion of one's research resources in the development of a survey instrument. And much of this development involves iterative revisions of questions with feedback from potential respondents. These guidelines were also supplemented by additional criteria for a good survey. One prominent criterion was the testing for scope effects. The idea is that a good survey will show that respondents are sensitive to significant and substantive differences in the public good. A split sample, in which different respondents are offered different amounts of public good, should be used to demonstrate scope effects.

Example 1 *Carson, Hanemann et al. (1994)*[5]

We illustrate the nature of a CV dichotomous choice question from a natural resource damage case in which trustees of marine resources in Southern California sued principal responsible parties for damages from the deposition of PCB and DDT in the Southern California bight. Chemicals were deposited on the ocean floor off the coast of Los Angeles through several outfall pipes. Very few of the thousands of CV studies have been carried out under the stringent control of this study. In-person interviews were conducted with residents of California, and the survey was carefully designed to comply with the NOAA guidelines. The instrument includes maps and cards for illustrating different points. After an extensive explanation of the problem, which included reproductive difficulties with two species of fish, the instrument provides a solution in the form of four feet of clean sediment that would render harmless the residual PCBs and DDTs. This is called a speed-up program because it speeds up the natural process of sedimentation. Then the respondent is given the CV question. Here is one version of the question. It gives the nature of the question but not the very rich context of the interview (Carson, Hanemann *et al.* 1994, Volume II, Appendix A, pp. 15-16).

> I mentioned earlier that the State has asked people about various types of new programs. We are now interviewing people to find out how they would vote if this program was on the ballot in a California election. Here's how it would

[5] See Carson, Hanemann, Kopp, Krosnick, Mitchell, Presser, Ruud and Smith 'Prospective Interim Lost Use Value due to DDT and PCB Contamination of the Southern California Bight', Volumes I and II, National Oceanic and Atmospheric Administration, September 30, 1994.

> be paid for. California taxpayers would pay a one time additional amount on their next year's state income tax to cover the cost. This is the only payment that would be required. It would go into a special fund that could only be used for the program to cover the contaminated sediment. The program would only be carried out if people are willing to pay this one time additional tax. There are reasons why you might vote for the speed-up program and reasons why you might vote against. The speed-up program would make it possible for the two fish species to reproduce normally in the place near Los Angeles 10 years earlier than if natural processes take their course. On the other hand, this deposit does not harm humans and the two fish species will recover anyway in 15 years. Your household might prefer to spend the money to solve other social and environmental problems instead. Or, the program costs more money than your household wants to spend for this. At present, the program to speed up the covering of the contaminated sediments is estimated to cost your household a total of $80. Your household would pay this as a special one time tax added to next year's California income tax. If an election were being held today and the total cost to your household would be a one time additional tax of $80, would you vote for the program to speed up recovery or would you vote against it?

The respondent is given the option of voting for, against, or being uncertain. The yes-no response and the required payment, as well as questionnaire and individual, form one observation in a CV study.

2.2 Parametric Models for Dichotomous Choice Questions

The goal of estimating parametric models from dichotomous choice CV responses is to calculate willingness to pay for the services described. In addition, parametric models allow for the incorporation of respondent characteristics into the willingness to pay functions. Understanding how willingness to pay responds to individual characteristics allows the researcher to gain information on the validity and reliability of the CV method, and to extrapolate sample responses to more general populations. Further, a richer set of explanatory variables that conforms with expectations makes the contingent valuation application more convincing. There are two distinct but linked parts to the task of estimating parametric models for dichotomous choice contingent valuation questions: estimating the part of the preference function that allows the calculation of willingness to pay, and calculating willingness to pay given the estimated parameters.

We first take up the task of parameter estimation, utilizing the random utility model. Estimating parametric models is not a necessary step in the calculation of willingness to pay. We show how to calculate nonparametric estimates of willingness to pay in Chapter 3. The desire to estimate covariate effects on dichotomous responses reflects a natural interest in learning more about the influence of these covariates. Part of the impetus for covariate effects stems from testing CV. For example, testing for scope, price, income and other socioeconomic effects helps describe behavioral or preference tendencies that make intuitive sense. In their Exxon Valdez study, Carson, Mitchell *et al.* (1992) show the effects of fourteen socioeconomic variables on the response. Covariate effects sometimes help with benefit transfers because response tendencies can be adjusted to different populations and local conditions by estimating the probability of yes as a function of exogenous variables. It is not necessary to estimate covariate models to expand a sample mean to a population. But models with covariates can facilitate the expansion of a sample to a population if the sample is not representative of the population in a way that can be corrected by exogenous variables. The downside of parametric models lies in the risk of misspecification. If the estimated model differs radically from the true-but-unobservable model, then the covariate effects can be wrong in magnitude and size, and hypothesis tests will not be valid.

2.2.1 The Random Utility Model

The basic model for analyzing dichotomous CV responses is the random utility model. Although Bishop and Heberlein employed a dichotomous question for CV responses, Hanemann (1984) constructed the basic model. Utilizing the random utility framework that McFadden[6] had developed, Hanemann rationalized responses to dichotomous CV questions, putting them in a framework that allows parameters to be estimated and interpreted. In the CV case, there are two choices or alternatives, so

---

[6]McFadden's work on the random utility model is published in a series of papers and books. See, for example, McFadden (1974).

that indirect utility for respondent j can be written

$$u_{ij} = u_i(y_j, \mathbf{z}_j, \varepsilon_{ij}) \tag{2.1}$$

where $i = 1$ is the state or condition that prevails when the CV program is implemented, that is, the final state, and $i = 0$ for the status quo. The determinants of utility are y_j, the jth respondent's discretionary income, $\mathbf{z}_j$, an m-dimensional vector of household characteristics and attributes of the choice, including questionnaire variations, and ε_{ij}, a component of preferences known to the individual respondent but not observed by the researcher. The $u_{ij} = u_i(y_j, \mathbf{z}_j, \varepsilon_{ij})$ function is written with only the subscript indicator i and the random component of preferences changing. All we know is that something has been changed from the status quo to the final state. It could be a measurable attribute–e.g. a quality indicator q could change from q^0 to q^1 so that utility for the status quo would be $u_{0j} = u(y_j, \mathbf{z}_j, q^0, \varepsilon_{0j})$ and utility in the final state would be $u_{1j} = u(y_j, \mathbf{z}_j, q^1, \varepsilon_{1j})$.

Based on this model, respondent j answers yes to a required payment of t_j if the utility with the CV program, net of the required payment, exceeds utility of the status quo

$$u_1(y_j - t_j, \mathbf{z}_j, \varepsilon_{1j}) > u_0(y_j, \mathbf{z}_j, \varepsilon_{0j}). \tag{2.2}$$

However, researchers do not know the random part of preferences and can only make probability statements about yes and no. The probability of a yes response is the probability that the respondent thinks that he is better off in the proposed scenario, even with the required payment, so that $u_1 > u_0$. For respondent j, this probability is

$$\Pr(yes_j) = \Pr(u_1(y_j - t_j, \mathbf{z}_j, \varepsilon_{1j}) > u_0(y_j, \mathbf{z}_j, \varepsilon_{0j})). \tag{2.3}$$

This probability statement provides an intuitive basis for analyzing responses, and can be used as the starting point for non-parametric approaches. But it is too general for parametric estimation. Two modeling decisions are needed. First, the functional form of $u(y_j, \mathbf{z}_j, \varepsilon_{ij})$ must be chosen. Second the distribution of ε_{ij} must be specified. Virtually all approaches begin by specifying the utility function as additively separable in deterministic and stochastic preferences:

$$u_i(y_j, \mathbf{z}_j, \varepsilon_{ij}) = v_i(y_j, \mathbf{z}_j) + \varepsilon_{ij}. \tag{2.4}$$

Indirect utility is the sum of a deterministic component that has the arguments that are important to the CV scenario and to the individual, and the stochastic component. The $v_i(y_j, \mathbf{z}_j)$ is sometimes written with an explicit argument about quality or characteristics of the CV scenario: $v_i(y_j, \mathbf{z}_j) = v(y_j, \mathbf{z}_j, q_i)$. With the additive specification of equation (2.4), the probability statement for respondent j becomes

$$\Pr(yes_j) = \Pr[v_1(y_j - t_j, \mathbf{z}_j) + \varepsilon_{1j} > v_0(y_j, \mathbf{z}_j) + \varepsilon_{0j}]. \tag{2.5}$$

This probability statement is still too general for parametric estimation, but it leads to all of the utility-based parametric models discussed in this chapter. Once utility is specified as the sum of random and deterministic components, the differences in the random components between the status quo and the CV scenario cannot be identified, and so there is no reason not to write the random term as $\varepsilon_j \equiv \varepsilon_{1j} - \varepsilon_{oj}$, a single random term. Then let $F_\varepsilon(a)$ be the probability that the random variable ε is less than a. Hence the probability of a yes is

$$\Pr(yes_j) = 1 - F_\varepsilon[-(v_1(y_j - t_j, \mathbf{z}_j) - v_0(y_j, \mathbf{z}_j))]. \tag{2.6}$$

No further progress in estimation is feasible now without specifying a parametric version of the preference function. Equation (2.5) represents the point of departure for all of the random utility described below. We begin with the simplest and most commonly estimated function, the linear utility function.

The Random Utility Model with a Linear Utility Function

The linear utility function results when the deterministic part of the preference function is linear in income and covariates

$$v_{ij}(y_j) = \boldsymbol{\alpha}_i \mathbf{z}_j + \beta_i(y_j) \tag{2.7}$$

where y_j is discretionary income, $\mathbf{z}_j$ is an m-dimensional vector of variables related to individual j and $\boldsymbol{\alpha}_i$ an m-dimensional vector of parameters, so that $\boldsymbol{\alpha}_i \mathbf{z}_j = \sum_{k=1}^{m} \alpha_{ik} z_{jk}$. A CV question induces the respondent to choose between the proposed conditions at the required payment t, and the current state. The deterministic utility for the proposed CV scenario is

$$v_{1j}(y_j - t_j) = \boldsymbol{\alpha}_1 \mathbf{z}_j + \beta_1(y_j - t_j) \tag{2.8}$$

where t_j is the price offered to the jth respondent. The status quo utility is

$$v_{0j}(y_j) = \boldsymbol{\alpha}_0 \mathbf{z}_j + \beta_0 y_j. \tag{2.9}$$

The change in deterministic utility is

$$v_{1j} - v_{0j} = (\boldsymbol{\alpha}_1 - \boldsymbol{\alpha}_0)\mathbf{z}_j + \beta_1(y_j - t_j) - \beta_0 y_j. \tag{2.10}$$

A reasonable assumption is that the marginal utility of income is constant between the two CV states, unless the proposed CV scenario provides a substantial change. Hence $\beta_1 = \beta_0$ and the utility difference becomes

$$v_{1j} - v_{0j} = \boldsymbol{\alpha}\mathbf{z}_j - \beta t_j \tag{2.11}$$

where $\boldsymbol{\alpha} = \boldsymbol{\alpha}_1 - \boldsymbol{\alpha}_0$ and $\boldsymbol{\alpha}\mathbf{z}_j = \sum_{k=1}^{m} \alpha_k z_{jk}$. With the deterministic part of preferences specified, the probability of responding yes becomes

$$\Pr(yes_j) = \Pr(\boldsymbol{\alpha}\mathbf{z}_j - \beta t_j + \varepsilon_j > 0) \tag{2.12}$$

where $\varepsilon_j \equiv \varepsilon_{1j} - \varepsilon_{0j}$ as defined above.

To proceed in estimating the parameters of the utility difference, it is necessary to specify the nature of the random terms. The assumption that the ε_j are independently and identically distributed (IID) with mean zero describes most distributions used. Given that the error is IID with mean zero, two widely used distributions are the normal and logistic. The normal distribution for the difference $\varepsilon = \varepsilon_1 - \varepsilon_0$ would result if ε_1 and ε_0 are each independent normal. The logistic can be derived as the difference of two extreme value distributions. Both the normal and the logistic are symmetric, which facilitates model estimation from packaged programs such as SAS or LIMDEP.

Thus the probability of yes for respondent j can be estimated as

$$\begin{aligned} \Pr(\boldsymbol{\alpha}\mathbf{z}_j - \beta t_j + \varepsilon_j &> 0) = \Pr(-(\boldsymbol{\alpha}\mathbf{z}_j - \beta t_j) < \varepsilon_j) \\ &= 1 - \Pr(-(\boldsymbol{\alpha}\mathbf{z}_j - \beta t_j) > \varepsilon_j) \\ &= \Pr(\varepsilon_j < \boldsymbol{\alpha}\mathbf{z}_j - \beta t_j). \end{aligned} \tag{2.13}$$

The last equality exploits the symmetry of the distribution. For symmetric distributions $F(x) = 1 - F(-x)$. Suppose that $\varepsilon_j \sim N(0, \sigma^2)$. To use typical software packages, it is necessary to convert $\varepsilon \sim N(0, \sigma^2)$ to a standard normal ($N(0,1)$) variable. Let $\theta = \varepsilon/\sigma$. Then $\theta \sim N(0,1)$ and

$$\begin{aligned} \Pr(\varepsilon_j &< \boldsymbol{\alpha}\mathbf{z}_j - \beta t_j) = \Pr(\theta < \frac{\boldsymbol{\alpha}\mathbf{z}_j}{\sigma} - \frac{\beta}{\sigma} t_j) \\ &= \Phi\left(\frac{\boldsymbol{\alpha}\mathbf{z}_j}{\sigma} - \frac{\beta}{\sigma} t_j\right) \end{aligned} \tag{2.14}$$

where $\Phi(x)$ is the cumulative standard normal, i.e. the probability that a unit normal variate is less than or equal to x. This is the probit model. Note that the probability is now in terms of parameters divided by an unknown variance. This is a fundamental characteristic of dichotomous dependent variables. The parameters can only be estimated up to a scalar multiple, because the dependent variable, taking a value of zero or one, has no scale in it.

When ε is distributed logistic, it has mean zero and variance $\pi^2\sigma_L^2/3$. Normalizing by σ_L creates a logistic variable with mean zero and variance $\pi^2/3$. I.e. if ε ~logistic $(0, \pi^2\sigma_L^2/3)$ then $\varepsilon/\sigma_L = \theta$ ~logistic $(0, \pi^2/3)$. The standard logistic has a variance $\pi^2/3$ times the standard normal and so will have parameters $\pi/\sqrt{3}$ ($\doteq$ 1.814) times the probit parameters.

One of the traditional appeals of the logistic distribution is the closed form solution for the cumulative distribution. The probability that a variate distributed as a standard logit is less than or equal to x equals $(1+exp(-x))^{-1}$. Then the probability that respondent j answers yes is

$$\Pr(yes_j) = [1 + \exp(-(\boldsymbol{\alpha}\mathbf{z}_j/\sigma_L - \beta t_j/\sigma_L))]^{-1}. \qquad (2.15)$$

This is the logit model. However, the advantage of a closed form solution over an iterated solution has lost any real significance with the increase in computing power.

Practically, the estimation of parameters comes from the maximization of the likelihood function. Suppose the sample size is T and let $I_j = 1$ if respondent j answers yes. The likelihood function becomes

$$L(\boldsymbol{\alpha}, \beta|\mathbf{y}, \mathbf{z}, \mathbf{t}) = \prod_{j=1}^{T}\left[\Phi\left(\frac{\boldsymbol{\alpha}\mathbf{z}_j}{\sigma} - \frac{\beta t_j}{\sigma}\right)\right]^{I_j}\left[1 - \Phi\left(\frac{\boldsymbol{\alpha}\mathbf{z}_j}{\sigma} - \frac{\beta t_j}{\sigma}\right)\right]^{1-I_j} \qquad (2.16)$$

for the probit and when the logit is estimated

$$[1 + exp(-(\boldsymbol{\alpha}\mathbf{z}_j/\sigma_L - \beta t_j/\sigma_L))]^{-1}$$

is substituted for $\Phi\left(\frac{\boldsymbol{\alpha}\mathbf{z}_j}{\sigma} - \frac{\beta t_j}{\sigma}\right)$.

Typically the differences between probit and logit models are slight. Both distributions are symmetric. The logit has thicker tails, which can be seen from the fact that logistic density at zero is smaller than the normal. The standard logistic density at zero is $\frac{e^{-x}}{(1+e^{-x})^2} = 0.25$ at $x = 0$ while the standard normal density at zero is $(2\pi)^{-1/2}e^{-\frac{1}{2}x^2} \doteq 0.399$. The densities intersect at variate values of 1.3245 and -1.3245. Over this range, 90.73% of the normal area can be found, while only 57.98% of the logistic area lies between the two values. Hence the probability that a standard logistic variate falls into one of the tails is 41.02%, while a normal variate falls into these areas with a probability of 9.67%. Despite this fairly significant difference in the tails, the distributions typically yield similar ratios of parameter estimates.

Maximum likelihood routines use the log of the likelihood function to calculate the maximum likelihood estimates. Maximum likelihood estimation is discussed briefly in Appendix A. For the models discussed above, the log likelihood function is

$$\begin{aligned}\ln L(\boldsymbol{\alpha}, \beta|\mathbf{y}, \mathbf{z}, \mathbf{t}) &= \sum_{j=1}^{T} I_j \ln \left[\Phi\left(\frac{\boldsymbol{\alpha}\mathbf{z}_j}{\sigma} - \frac{\beta t_j}{\sigma}\right)\right] \\ &+ (1-I_j)\ln\left[1-\Phi\left(\frac{\boldsymbol{\alpha}\mathbf{z}_j}{\sigma} - \frac{\beta t_j}{\sigma}\right)\right] \quad (2.17)\end{aligned}$$

for the probit, or

$$\begin{aligned}\ln L(\boldsymbol{\alpha}, \beta|\mathbf{y}, \mathbf{z}, \mathbf{t}) &= \sum_{j=1}^{T} I_j \ln \left[\left(1+e^{-\left(\frac{\boldsymbol{\alpha}\mathbf{z}_j}{\sigma} - \frac{\beta t_j}{\sigma}\right)}\right)^{-1}\right] \quad (2.18) \\ &+ (1-I_j)\ln\left[1-\left(1+e^{-\left(\frac{\boldsymbol{\alpha}\mathbf{z}_j}{\sigma} - \frac{\beta t_j}{\sigma}\right)}\right)^{-1}\right]\end{aligned}$$

for the logit. It is well known that these functions are concave in parameters. Maximization of the likelihood functions yields unique estimates of the parameter functions $\boldsymbol{\alpha}/\sigma$, $-\beta/\sigma$. Defining a new $1 \times (m+1)$ parameter vector $\boldsymbol{\beta}^* = \{\boldsymbol{\alpha}/\sigma, -\beta/\sigma\}$ where m is the number of covariates in $\mathbf{z}$ including the constant, and a new individual-specific $1 \times (m+1)$ data vector $\mathbf{X}_j = \{\mathbf{z}_j, t_j\}$, the log likelihood function for the linear random utility probit becomes:

$$\ln L(\boldsymbol{\beta}^*|\mathbf{y}, \mathbf{X}) = \sum_{j=1}^{T} I_j \ln[\Phi(\mathbf{X}_j\boldsymbol{\beta}^*)] + (1-I_j)\ln[1-\Phi(\mathbf{X}_j\boldsymbol{\beta}^*)] \quad (2.19)$$

and for the logit model becomes:

$$\begin{aligned}\ln L(\boldsymbol{\beta}^*|\mathbf{y}, \mathbf{X}) &= \sum_{j=1}^{T} I_j \ln[(1+e^{-(\mathbf{X}_j\boldsymbol{\beta}^*)})^{-1}] \\ &+ (1-I_j)\ln[1-(1+e^{-(\mathbf{X}_j\boldsymbol{\beta}^*)})^{-1}]. \quad (2.20)\end{aligned}$$

Equations (2.19) and (2.20) represent the standard forms of the probit and logit log likelihood functions estimated by most econometric packages. A lower bound of the variance-covariance matrix $[\mathbf{V}(\boldsymbol{\beta}^*)]$ for the maximum likelihood parameter estimates can be found by inverting the negative of the expected value of the matrix of second derivatives of the log likelihood function evaluated at the parameter estimates

$$\mathbf{V}(\boldsymbol{\beta}^*) = \left[-E\left(\frac{\partial^2 \ln L(\boldsymbol{\beta}^*|\mathbf{y},\mathbf{X})}{\partial\boldsymbol{\beta}^* \cdot \partial\boldsymbol{\beta}^{*\prime}}\right)\right]^{-1}. \tag{2.21}$$

The maximum likelihood parameter estimates obtained by maximizing (2.19) and (2.20) are asymptotically normal with expectation equal to the true parameter values, and variance-covariance matrix as defined in equation (4.13) (see Appendix A). A closed form for the expected value of the matrix of second derivatives is often not available, so the variance-covariance matrix typically must be approximated. Standard computer packages typically use two methods, depending on the algorithm used to calculate the maximum likelihood estimates.

Method 1: Invert the matrix of second derivatives evaluated at the maximum likelihood estimates

Using Slutsky's theorem (see section A.3.1 in Appendix A) and the knowledge that under typical conditions maximum likelihood estimates are consistent estimates of the true parameters, one sees that evaluating the actual matrix of second derivatives at the maximum likelihood estimates provides a consistent estimate of the expectation of the matrix of second derivatives. The difficulty here lies in the derivation of the matrix of second derivatives. This matrix is often a complicated nonlinear function of the parameters and as such calculation of the matrix of second derivatives is time-consuming.

Method 2: Calculate the outer product of the maximum likelihood gradient vector

Because the matrix of second derivatives is difficult to calculate, many statistical packages will instead rely on the vector of first derivatives to calculate the variance-covariance matrix. The outer product of the vector of first derivatives of the log likelihood function represents a first order Taylor-series approximation to the matrix of second derivatives.

Procedure for Estimating a Random Utility Model with Linear Utility Function

1. *Define the yes/no responses to the contingent valuation question such that yes is coded 1 and no is coded 0.*

2. *Define the data matrix* $\mathbf{X}$ *so that it contains the concatenation of the covariate matrix* $\mathbf{z}$ *and the offered fee vector* $\mathbf{t}$.

3. *Using any standard statistical software, run a probit or logit model with the 1/0 yes/no responses as the dependent variable, and the matrix* $\mathbf{X}$ *as the matrix of right hand side variables.*

4. *Recover the reported parameter estimates. The coefficients on the variables in the matrix* $\mathbf{z}$ *represent estimates of* α/σ. *The coefficient on the offered fee is an estimate of* $-\beta/\sigma$.

Example 2 *Estimating a Linear Random Utility Model*

To illustrate the random utility model with a linear in income utility function, we estimate a model from a CV study in Colorado.[7] This is a study of the water use in the South Platte River. The respondents are interviewed in person. The CV question relates to their willingness to pay an increment to their water bill to restore recreational services provided by the river. After a lengthy description of a proposal to restore part of the South Platte, the respondent is asked the following question.

> If the South Platte River Restoration Fund was on the ballot in the next election, and it cost your household $__ each month in a higher water bill would you vote in favor or against?

The $__ was filled in with one of the following amounts: 1, 2, 3, 4, 8, 10, 12, 20, 30, 40, 50, 100. Table 2.1 describes the independent variables and gives the means. The specification follows the original model,[8] and uses the variables in this table.

In this and following sections and chapters, we estimate various models using this data to illustrate the workings of different types of econometric models for CV. Table 2.2 gives the parameter estimates when the linear random utility logit and probit models are fitted. The statistical properties of the estimated parameters depend on their being maximum likelihood estimates. The parameters are asymptotically normally distributed, with the lower bound of the variance-covariance matrix given by equation (4.13) involving the matrix of second derivatives of the log likelihood function. The ratio of estimated coefficient to standard error is asymptotically N(0,1) under the null hypothesis that the coefficient is zero and standard hypothesis testing applies. In Table 2.2, all of the

---

[7] We thank John Loomis, who generously gave us access to this very well-behaved dataset.

[8] See Loomis, Kent, Strange, Fausch and Covich (2000).

TABLE 2.1. Means of Variables for South Platte River Study

Variable	Description	Mean (n = 95)
t	Increment to water bill	\$14.78
hhinc	Household income from all sources (before taxes) for 1997	\$54175
unlimwat	Farmers entitled to unlimited water?*	0.45
govtpur	Believes government should purchase land on South Platte*	0.78
environ	Member of a conservation group*	0.19
waterbil	Average water bill for community*	\$35.80
urban	Lives in a large city*	0.75

*Equals 1 if true, 0 otherwise.

coefficients except the constant are significantly different from zero at the 95% level of confidence.

The quantity $-2\ln(L_R/L_U)$ reported in the table represents a full-model test of significance (see Appendix A). The null hypothesis is that the parameters β and α_1 to α_5 are equal to zero. The test statistic is constructed from the value of the log likelihood functions, where the R indexes the restricted log likelihood function under the null hypothesis and U indexes the unrestricted model. Under the null hypothesis, the tabled Chi-squared for six degrees of freedom (the number of restrictions) at the 95% confidence level equals 12.59, so that the hypothesis is rejected. The signs on the coefficients all make intuitive sense. The probability of a yes declines with increases in the bid, and the household's water bill, and when the household supports unlimited water access for farmers, a proxy for opposition to river conservation. The probability of a yes increases when the household belongs to an environmental group, supports government purchases of water, and lives in an urban area. The last column of the table presents the ratio of the logit parameter estimates to the probit estimates. Because each of the parameter estimates is normalized by the standard deviation of the distribution, we would expect the ratio of the parameter estimates to be roughly equal to the ratio of the standard logistic and standard normal distribution scales $(\pi/\sqrt{3} \doteq 1.814)$.

Calculating Willingness to Pay with the Linear Random Utility Model

The ultimate goal of most practical dichotomous choice CV studies is to calculate willingness to pay and the effects of covariates on WTP. The

TABLE 2.2. Binary Discrete Choice Model Estimation

$\Pr(\theta < (\alpha_0 + \alpha_1\text{unlimwat}+\alpha_2\text{govtpur}+\alpha_3\text{environ}+\alpha_4\text{waterbil}+\alpha_5\text{urban}-\beta t)/\sigma))$			
	θ logistic Parameter est. (Std. Error)	θ normal Parameter est. (Std. Error)	$\frac{\theta\ logistic}{\theta\ normal}$
β^a/σ	0.14 (0.03)	0.08 (0.02)	1.8
α_0/σ	[b]2.44 (1.48)	1.41 (0.83)	1.7
α_1/σ	−1.47 (0.74)	−0.81 (0.41)	1.8
α_2/σ	1.84 (0.75)	1.11 (0.44)	1.7
α_3/σ	3.37 (1.18)	1.89 (0.64)	1.8
α_4/σ	−0.06 (0.03)	−0.04 (0.02)	1.5
α_5/σ	1.82 (0.71)	1.12 (0.41)	1.6
Log-likelihood	−34.8	−34.6	–
$-2\ln(L_R/L_U)$	56.5	56.5	–

[a]Note that this is the parameter on $-t$.

[b]All parameters different from zero at 99% level of confidence except for this parameter.

calculation of willingness to pay uses estimated parameters, depends on the covariates chosen, and is also a function of the random component assumed for preferences. The presence of two sources of uncertainty–parameters and preferences–and the additional source of variation, individual covariates, causes a good deal of confusion in calculating willingness to pay. In general, willingness to pay is the amount of money that makes the respondent indifferent between the status quo and the proposed CV scenario. For the linear random utility model defined in equations (2.11) and (2.12), WTP can be defined as

$$\boldsymbol{\alpha}_1\mathbf{z}_j + \beta(y_j - WTP_j) + \varepsilon_{j1} = \boldsymbol{\alpha}_0\mathbf{z}_j + \beta y_j + \varepsilon_{j0}. \tag{2.22}$$

Solving this equation for WTP yields

$$WTP_j = \boldsymbol{\alpha}\mathbf{z}_j/\beta + \varepsilon_j/\beta. \tag{2.23}$$

Here we see the two sources of randomness and the potential for variation across individuals. We list here briefly these three sources of variation in WTP, and in Chapter 4 we pay more attention to the distribution of willingness to pay from CV estimates, and explicitly discuss these three sources of variation.

- uncertainty from randomness of preferences: ε_j/β has mean zero and variance σ^2/β^2, given the parameters;
- uncertainty from randomness of parameters: because the parameters are maximum likelihood estimates, they are asymptotically distributed:

$$N(\boldsymbol{\alpha}, \beta; \left[\frac{-E\partial^2 \ln L(\boldsymbol{\beta}^*|\mathbf{y},\mathbf{X})}{\partial\boldsymbol{\beta}^* \cdot \partial\boldsymbol{\beta}^{*\prime}}\right]^{-1});$$

- variation across individuals in the sample: the expression for WTP can be calculated for any set of independent variables, or we could calculate the sample mean, which would have its own measures of dispersion, such as the sample variance. It is important to distinguish between the variation across individuals in the sample with randomness from preference or parameter uncertainty.

In dealing with the willingness to pay, we initially assume that the parameters are given, and look for measures of central tendency over the distribution of preference uncertainty. The literature has focused on two measures of central tendency with respect to preference uncertainty. One is the expectation of willingness to pay with respect to preference uncertainty (ε):

$$E_\varepsilon(WTP_j|\boldsymbol{\alpha}, \beta, \mathbf{z}_j) = \frac{\boldsymbol{\alpha}\mathbf{z}_j}{\beta}. \tag{2.24}$$

The second measure of central tendency is the median or 50th percentile of the distribution with respect to preference uncertainty ($Md_\varepsilon(WTP_j)$). To solve for the median WTP, find the WTP that solves the expression that the probability that $u_1 > u_0 = 0.5$.

$$\Pr[\boldsymbol{\alpha}_1\mathbf{z}_j + \beta(y_j - Md_\varepsilon(WTP_j)) + \varepsilon_{1_j} > \boldsymbol{\alpha}_0\mathbf{z}_j + \beta y_j + \varepsilon_{0j}] = 0.5$$

$$= \Pr[Md_\varepsilon(WTP) > \boldsymbol{\alpha}\mathbf{z}_j/\beta + \varepsilon_j/\beta] = 0.5. \tag{2.25}$$

Since ε is symmetric with mean zero, this expression yields

$$Md_\varepsilon(WTP_j|\boldsymbol{\alpha}, \beta, \mathbf{z}_j) = \frac{\boldsymbol{\alpha}\mathbf{z}_j}{\beta}. \tag{2.26}$$

We introduce the notation E_ε and Md_ε for the mean and the median of the random preference term to emphasize the different sources of uncertainty. In the case of a linear utility function and a symmetric, mean zero error, the mean and median WTP with respect to random preferences are equal.

If the true parameters are known, then the only uncertainty that must be resolved when estimating WTP is the preference uncertainty. However, because the parameters are unknown and consequently must be estimated, parameter uncertainty must also be resolved. In the expression for mean and median, only the ratio of parameter estimates is required. From Slutsky's theorem on consistency (see section A.3.1 in Appendix A), the probit and logit maximum likelihood estimates for $\boldsymbol{\beta}^* = \{\boldsymbol{\alpha}/\sigma, -\beta/\sigma\}$ are consistent estimates. A consistent estimate of expected willingness to pay can be found by substituting the normalized parameter estimates into the expression for expected willingness to pay (equation 2.24):

$$E_\varepsilon(WTP|\boldsymbol{\alpha},\beta,\mathbf{z}_j) = [(\boldsymbol{\alpha}/\sigma)/(\beta/\sigma)]\,\mathbf{z}_j. \tag{2.27}$$

The same consistency holds for the median of WTP.

Note that in expressions (2.24) and (2.26), the expected value and median of WTP with respect to preference uncertainty, the estimate is subscripted j. Each respondent has an expected or median WTP with respect to preference uncertainty. There is also variation across the sample. One could calculate the sample mean of the expected WTP, the sample mean of the median WTP, and so forth. For sample expansion, an appropriate measure would be the sample mean. For the linear model of the CV study of the South Platte river, we calculate the expected willingness to pay based on the mean vector of exogenous variables.

$$E_\varepsilon(WTP|\boldsymbol{\alpha},\beta,\bar{\mathbf{z}}) = [(\boldsymbol{\alpha}/\sigma)/(\beta/\sigma)]\,\bar{\mathbf{z}}) \tag{2.28}$$

For mean $[(\boldsymbol{\alpha}/\sigma)/(\beta/\sigma)]\,\bar{\mathbf{z}} =$ \$20.70 for the logit model and \$20.40 for the probit model. As can be seen from the expressions for expected WTP, there are still major questions about the variation of WTP across the sample and randomness due to the randomness of parameter estimates. We explore methods for understanding the dispersion of WTP in Chapter 4.

The linear model is a mainstay for econometric applications to dichotomous choice CV questions. For most purposes it is a good approximation to any arbitrary utility specification. One drawback of the linear random utility model is that it eliminates income as a determinant of responses by assuming the marginal utility of income is constant across scenarios posed by the CV questions. In the following sections we discuss a variety of models that exploit differences in the marginal utility of income to explain responses to CV questions.

The Random Utility Model Log Linear in Income

Referring back to equation (2.5), the derivation of an estimable version of the random utility model begins with the probability statement:

$$\Pr(yes_j) = \Pr[v_1(y_j - t_j, \mathbf{z}_j) + \varepsilon_{1j} > v_0(y_j, \mathbf{z}_j) + \varepsilon_{0j}]. \tag{2.29}$$

Consider a utility function of the form

$$v_i(y_j, \mathbf{z}_j) + \varepsilon_{ij} = \beta \ln(y_j) + \boldsymbol{\alpha}_i \mathbf{z}_j + \varepsilon_{ij}. \tag{2.30}$$

This utility function relaxes the constant marginal utility of income across individuals implicit in the linear utility function. Differentiating with respect to income yields the individual-specific expression for marginal utility of income

$$\frac{\partial v_i}{\partial y_j} = \frac{\beta}{y_j}, \tag{2.31}$$

which is decreasing in income assuming $\beta > 0$. Note also that this form of the utility function allows the marginal utility of income to vary across utility states as money income changes.

Substituting the log-linear in income utility function into the random utility probability expression (2.29) and rearranging it, one sees that this form is compatible with the standard probit or logit estimation routines.

$$\begin{aligned}\Pr(yes_j) &= \Pr\left(\beta \ln(y_j - t_j) + \boldsymbol{\alpha}_1 \mathbf{z}_j + \varepsilon_{1j} > \beta \ln(y_j) + \boldsymbol{\alpha}_0 \mathbf{z}_j + \varepsilon_{0j}\right) \\ &= \Pr\left(\begin{array}{c}\beta(\ln(y_j - t_j) - \ln(y_j)) \\ +(\boldsymbol{\alpha}_1 - \boldsymbol{\alpha}_0)\mathbf{z}_j + (\varepsilon_{1j} - \varepsilon_{0j}) > 0\end{array}\right) \\ &= \Pr\left(\beta \ln\left(\frac{y_j - t_j}{y_j}\right) + \boldsymbol{\alpha}\mathbf{z}_j > -\varepsilon_j\right).\end{aligned} \tag{2.32}$$

Here $\boldsymbol{\alpha} = \boldsymbol{\alpha}_1 - \boldsymbol{\alpha}_0$, and $\varepsilon_j = \varepsilon_{1j} - \varepsilon_{0j}$. Assuming ε_j is distributed normally with mean zero and variance σ^2 results in the standard normal probability of a yes response:

$$\Pr(yes_j) = \Phi\left(\frac{\beta \ln\left(\frac{y_j - t_j}{y_j}\right) + \boldsymbol{\alpha}\mathbf{z}_j}{\sigma}\right) = \Phi(\mathbf{X}_j \boldsymbol{\beta}^*) \tag{2.33}$$

where $\mathbf{X}'_j = \left\{\mathbf{z}_j, \ln\left(\frac{y_j - t_j}{y_j}\right)\right\}$, and $\boldsymbol{\beta}^* = \left\{\frac{\alpha}{\sigma}, \frac{\beta}{\sigma}\right\}$.[9] The parameter vector $\boldsymbol{\beta}^*$ can be estimated by running a simple probit on the data matrix $\mathbf{X}_j$.

If ε_j is instead assumed to be distributed logistically, then the probability of a yes response becomes

$$\Pr(yes_j) = \frac{1}{1 + e^{-\mathbf{X}_j \boldsymbol{\beta}^*}} \tag{2.34}$$

and parameters can be estimated with a logit model on the no/yes responses with $\mathbf{X}_j = \left\{\mathbf{z}_j, \ln\left(\frac{y_j - t_j}{y_j}\right)\right\}$ as independent variables and $\boldsymbol{\beta}^*$ the parameters.

Example 3 *The South Platte River Study*

Continuing the previous example, we estimate probit and logit versions of the log-linear in income random utility model on the South Platte River dataset. The parameters are given in Table 2.3. The data differ from the previous example in two ways. The number of observations decreases by one because of a missing income variable. One of the exogenous variables changes from t, the bid, to $\ln((y - t)/y)$. Otherwise, the log-linear in utility random utility model is estimated in the same fashion as the linear random utility model. Comparing Tables 2.2 and 2.3, the parameter estimates for $\alpha_0/\sigma, ..., \alpha_5/\sigma$ do not change sign or magnitude appreciably, but the level of significance changes. Using a one-tailed test, because we have expectations on the sign of the parameter estimates, only three coefficients–*govpur*, *environ*, and the bid–are different from zero at the 95% level of confidence. The increase in variance of the parameter estimates is due to the more complicated form of the bid function, which includes income.

Procedure for Estimating a Log-linear in Income Random Utility Model.

1. *Define the yes/no responses to the contingent valuation question such that yes is coded 1 and no is coded 0.*

2. *Define a data matrix* $\mathbf{X}$ *so that it contains the concatenation of the covariate matrix* $\mathbf{z}$ *and the composite income term, which for a typical individual* j *is* $\ln((y_j - t_j)/y_j)$.

3. *Using any standard statistical software, run a probit or logit model with the 1/0 yes/no responses as the dependent variable, and the matrix* $\mathbf{X}$ *as the matrix of independent variables.*

---

[9] Programs typically insert a vector of ones so that a constant is estimated. In writing one's own likelihood function, this vector needs to be included in $\mathbf{X}$.

TABLE 2.3. Estimation with Logarithmic Utility

$\Pr(\theta < (\alpha_0 + \alpha_1\text{unlimwat}+\alpha_2\text{govtpur}+\alpha_3\text{environ}+\alpha_4\text{waterbil}+\alpha_5\text{urban}+\beta\ln\left(\frac{y-t}{y}\right))/\sigma))$		
	θ logistic	θ normal
	Parameter estimate (Standard error)	Parameter estimate (Standard error)
β/σ	2939.60	1546.50
	(901.30)	(458.00)
α_0/σ	1.08	0.61
	(1.24)	(0.74)
α_1/σ	−0.90	−0.55
	(0.59)	(0.34)
α_2/σ	1.54	0.97
	(0.66)	(0.39)
α_3/σ	1.96	1.08
	(1.03)	(0.55)
α_4/σ	−0.03	−0.02
	(0.03)	(0.01)
α_5/σ	0.96	0.60
	(0.64)	(0.37)
Log-likelihood	−42.90	−42.60
$-2\ln(L_R/L_U)$	38.33	38.28

Calculating Willingness to Pay Using the Log-Linear in Income Random Utility Model

The expression for willingness to pay can be found by equating utility in the improved state to utility in the status quo state and solving for the income difference (WTP) that equates the two utilities:

$$\boldsymbol{\alpha}_1\mathbf{z}_j + \beta\ln(y_j - WTP_j) + \varepsilon_{1j} = \boldsymbol{\alpha}_0\mathbf{z}_j + \beta\ln(y_j) + \varepsilon_{oj}. \tag{2.35}$$

Willingness to pay that satisfies this equality is

$$WTP_j(\varepsilon_j, \boldsymbol{\alpha}, \beta, \mathbf{z}_j, y_j) = y_j - y_j\exp\left(-(\frac{\boldsymbol{\alpha}}{\beta}\mathbf{z}_j + \frac{\varepsilon_j}{\beta})\right). \tag{2.36}$$

Willingness to pay in this expression depends on the same variables–the unobserved preference term, the estimated parameters and the exogenous variables–as in the linear utility case. Since the expectation of WTP is taken with respect to the unobservable error, and in this case, the error enters exponentially, the expected value of willingness to pay will depend on the distribution assumed for the error (and not simply rely on the mean zero assumption as in the linear models). The expected willingness to pay will not be the same for the logit and probit specifications as was the case for the linear utility function specifications.

Probit Model

If ε_j is assumed to be normally distributed with mean zero and unknown variance σ^2 then the expected value of willingness to pay is

$$E_\varepsilon(WTP|\boldsymbol{\alpha},\beta,\mathbf{z}_j,y_j) = y_j - y_j \exp(-\frac{\boldsymbol{\alpha}}{\beta}\mathbf{z}_j + \frac{1}{2}\frac{\sigma^2}{\beta^2}). \tag{2.37}$$

Because ε_j is a mean 0 symmetric random variate, the 50th percentile of willingness to pay (median willingness to pay) is found by setting $\varepsilon_j = 0$ in equation (2.36):

$$Md_\varepsilon(WTP|\boldsymbol{\alpha},\beta,\mathbf{z}_j,y_j) = y_j - y_j \exp(-\frac{\boldsymbol{\alpha}}{\beta}\mathbf{z}_j). \tag{2.38}$$

Returning to the South Platte River example, we find that for the sample mean individual (see Table 2.1), the median willingness to pay is estimated as

$$Md_\varepsilon(WTP|\boldsymbol{\alpha},\beta,\bar{\mathbf{z}},\bar{y}) = \bar{y} - \bar{y} \exp(-\frac{\boldsymbol{\alpha}}{\beta}\bar{\mathbf{z}}) = \$15.15.$$

We do not include the expected value of WTP because the ratio σ/β (see Table 2.3) is so small that the expected value of WTP is indistinguishable from the median.

Logit Model

If ε_j is assumed to be logistically distributed with mean zero and unknown variance $\frac{\pi^2\sigma^2}{3}$ then $\exp(-\frac{\varepsilon_j}{\beta})$ is distributed with mean $\frac{(\sigma/\beta)\pi}{\sin((\sigma/\beta)\pi)}$. The expected value of willingness to pay is:

$$E_\varepsilon(WTP|\boldsymbol{\alpha},\beta,\mathbf{z}_j,y_j) = y_j - y_j \frac{(\sigma/\beta)\pi}{\sin((\sigma/\beta)\pi)} \exp(-\frac{\boldsymbol{\alpha}}{\beta}\mathbf{z}_j). \tag{2.39}$$

Median willingness to pay is found by setting $\varepsilon_j = 0$:

$$Md_\varepsilon(WTP|\boldsymbol{\alpha},\beta,\mathbf{z}_j,y_j) = y_j - y_j \exp(-\frac{\boldsymbol{\alpha}}{\beta}\mathbf{z}_j). \tag{2.40}$$

The median value of WTP for the mean individual for the logit is \$15.15. Note that the medians are the same for different distributions of the unobservable error.

The Random Utility Model with Box-Cox Transformation of Income

The log-linear in income utility function above assumes a specific form for the marginal utility of income: i.e. the marginal utility of income is inversely proportionate to income (see equation 2.30). Further flexibility in the specification of the utility function with respect to income can be obtained by specifying a utility function that is linear in a Box-Cox transformation of income. Consider the simple Box-Cox transformation of income:

$$y^{(\lambda)} = \frac{y^{\lambda} - 1}{\lambda}. \tag{2.41}$$

Denoting $y^{(\lambda)}$ as the income term in the utility function, the random utility function becomes

$$v_i(y_j, z_j) + \varepsilon_{ij} = \beta y_{ij}^{(\lambda)} + \boldsymbol{\alpha}_i \mathbf{z}_j + \varepsilon_{ij}. \tag{2.42}$$

The Box-Cox transformation is a generalized functional form that has nested within a number of recognized forms depending upon the value of the transformation parameter λ: when $\lambda = 2$, $y^{(\lambda)} = \frac{y^2-1}{2}$ and utility depends on the square of income, when $\lambda = 1$, $y^{(\lambda)} = y-1$ and the utility function is linear in income, when $\lambda = 0$, $y^{(\lambda)}$ converges to $ln(y)$,[10] and the utility function is log-linear in income, when $\lambda = -1$, $y^{(\lambda)} = 1 - \frac{1}{y}$ and the utility function is linear in the inverse of income. The marginal utility of income in the Box-Cox income model is $\frac{\partial v}{\partial y} = \beta y^{\lambda-1}$. The Box-Cox transformation introduces flexibility in modeling the effects of income on indirect utility.

Assuming the Box-Cox transformation parameter is constant across utility states, the probability of a yes response is:

$$\begin{aligned} \Pr(yes_j) &= \Pr[\beta(y_j - t_j)^{(\lambda)} + \boldsymbol{\alpha}_1 \mathbf{z}_j + \varepsilon_{1j} > \beta y_j^{(\lambda)} + \boldsymbol{\alpha}_0 \mathbf{z}_j + \varepsilon_{0j}] \\ &= \Pr[\beta((y_j - t_j)^{(\lambda)} - y_j^{(\lambda)}) + (\boldsymbol{\alpha}_1 - \boldsymbol{\alpha}_0)\mathbf{z}_j + (\varepsilon_{1j} - \varepsilon_{0j}) > 0] \\ &= \Pr\left[\beta \frac{(y_j - t_j)^{\lambda} - y_j^{\lambda}}{\lambda} + \boldsymbol{\alpha} \mathbf{z}_j > -\varepsilon_j\right] \end{aligned} \tag{2.43}$$

where $\boldsymbol{\alpha} = \boldsymbol{\alpha}_1 - \boldsymbol{\alpha}_0$ and $\varepsilon_j = \varepsilon_{1j} - \varepsilon_{0j}$. Assuming ε_j is distributed normally with mean zero and variance σ^2 results in the standard normal

---

[10] This convergence can be seen by taking the limit of $y^{(\lambda)}$ as λ approaches 0: $\lim_{\lambda \to 0} \left(\frac{y^{\lambda}-1}{\lambda}\right)$. Applying L'Hôpital's rule, $\lim_{\lambda \to 0} \left(\frac{y^{\lambda}-1}{\lambda}\right) = \lim_{\lambda \to 0} \left(\frac{\partial(y^{\lambda}-1)/\partial\lambda}{\partial\lambda/\partial\lambda}\right) = \lim_{\lambda \to 0} \left(\frac{y^{\lambda}\ln(y)}{1}\right) = \ln(y)$.

probability of a yes response

$$\Pr(yes_j) = \Phi\left(\frac{\beta\left[\frac{(y_j-t_j)^\lambda - y_j^\lambda}{\lambda}\right] + \boldsymbol{\alpha}\mathbf{z}_j}{\sigma}\right) = \Phi(\mathbf{X}_j\boldsymbol{\beta}^*) \tag{2.44}$$

where $\mathbf{X}_j = \left\{\mathbf{z}_j, \frac{(y_j-t_j)^\lambda - y_j^\lambda}{\lambda}\right\}$, and $\boldsymbol{\beta}^* = \{\boldsymbol{\alpha}/\sigma, \beta/\sigma\}$. For a given value of λ, the parameter vector $\boldsymbol{\beta}^*$ can be estimated by running a simple probit on the data matrix $\mathbf{X}_j$. If ε_j is instead assumed to be distributed logistically, then the probability of a yes response becomes

$$\Pr(yes_j) = \frac{1}{1+e^{-\mathbf{X}_j\boldsymbol{\beta}^*}},$$

and the parameters can be estimated by running a logit model on the no/yes responses with $\mathbf{X}_j$ as independent variables.

This derivation assumes that the value of λ is either known, or has been pre-determined. However, the attraction of the Box-Cox model is its flexibility for different values of λ. Since the functional form of the utility function is at best an educated guess on the part of the researcher, it is desirable to treat λ as an unknown parameter. Direct estimation of λ requires a tailored likelihood function. Noting that the random utility difference is linear in a function of y and λ : $\frac{(y_j-t_j)^\lambda - y_j^\lambda}{\lambda}$, indirect estimation of λ can be accomplished through a one-dimensional grid-search on λ. A grid-search involves choosing a vector of potential values for λ (typically restricted to the range (-1,3), and estimating the random utility model for each value of the λ. The value of λ that maximizes the log likelihood function value from the models estimated is the maximum likelihood estimate of λ. The following procedure outlines the steps for estimating a Box-Cox random utility model.

Procedure for Performing a One-dimensional Grid Search for the Box-Cox Random Utility Model.

1. *Define the yes/no responses to the contingent valuation question such that yes is coded 1 and no is coded 0.*

2. *Define a K dimensional vector of possible values for the Box-Cox transformation parameter λ. These values should include, but should not be restricted to {-1,0,1,2,3}. For completeness, non-integer values within this range should also be considered. Index these values λ_k where $k = \{1, 2, ..., K\}$.*

3. *For the first value of* λ_k*, define a data matrix* $\mathbf{X}$ *so that it contains the concatenation of the covariate matrix* $\mathbf{z}$ *and the composite income term* $\frac{(y_j-t_j)^{\lambda_k}-y_j^{\lambda_k}}{\lambda_k}$.

4. *Using any standard statistical software, run a probit or logit model with the 1/0 yes/no responses as the dependent variable, and the matrix* X *as the matrix of independent variables.*

5. *Repeat steps 3 and 4 for all values of* λ_k.

6. *The maximum likelihood estimates of the parameter vector* $\boldsymbol{\beta}^* = \{\boldsymbol{\alpha}/\sigma, \beta/\sigma\}$ *are those estimates corresponding to the value of* λ_k *that maximizes the value of the log likelihood function. The associated value of* λ_k *is the maximum likelihood estimate of* λ.

The Box-Cox utility function can be expanded to include transformations of other covariates. Doing so represents additional degrees of flexibility for the model. However, unless the transformation parameter is assumed to be the same for all covariates, the estimation procedure involves a multi-dimensional grid search: i.e. all possible combinations of the transformation parameters must be considered. Such a procedure increases the number of models that must be estimated drastically. For example, if there are two transformation parameters that can each take on one of five values, the grid-search procedure would require the estimation of 25 different probit or logit models.

Example 4 *Box-Cox Transformation: The South Platte River Study*

To illustrate the Box-Cox transformation we return to the South Platte River study. The survey gathered household income by income categories. Income was then interpolated as the mid-point in the category. The model was specified as closely to the linear model as possible, with the only difference being the construction of the bid and income variable. The model was estimated by a grid search over λ over the $(-1, 3)$ range. The optimal value for λ was 0.83 for both the logit and the probit models. The parameters for the exogenous variables, given the optimal value of λ, are in Table 2.4.

Testing Functional Forms using the Box-Cox Model

The maximum likelihood estimate for λ gives the highest value of the likelihood function from all candidate values for λ. This value may not, however, be statistically different from some other standard values. It is worthwhile to test whether the maximum likelihood value of λ is

TABLE 2.4. Model Estimation: Box-Cox Transformation

$\Pr(\theta < (\alpha_0 + \alpha_1\text{unlimwat}+\alpha_2\text{govtpur}+\alpha_3\text{environ}+\alpha_4\text{waterbil}+\alpha_5\text{urban}+\beta[(y-t)^\lambda - y^\lambda]/\lambda)/\sigma))$		
For $\lambda = 0.83$	θ logistic	θ normal
	Parameter estimate (Standard error)	Parameter estimate (Standard error)
β/σ	0.92	0.53
	(0.21)	(0.11)
α_0/σ	2.80	1.61
	(1.54)	(0.86)
α_1/σ	−1.48	−0.81
	(0.74)	(0.41)
α_2/σ	1.79	1.08
	(0.75)	(0.44)
α_3/σ	3.31	1.86
	(1.18)	(0.64)
α_4/σ	−0.06	−0.04
	(0.03)	(0.02)
α_5/σ	1.69	1.05
	(0.71)	(0.41)
Log-likelihood	−33.80	−33.70
$-2\ln(L_R/L_U)$	56.39	56.74

significantly different from several strategic values of λ. Two common strategic values are $\lambda = 1$ for the linear model and $\lambda = 0$ for the log-linear utility function. The test for $\lambda = 1$ is interesting because it can be considered a test for whether a utility-consistent income effect should be part of the model. The appropriate test for all such hypotheses is the likelihood ratio test. The general form for the likelihood ratio test statistic is: -2(log likelihood value from the restricted model less the log likelihood value from the unrestricted model). This test statistic is distributed Chi-squared with degrees of freedom equal to the number of restrictions placed on the restricted model. The restricted form of the likelihood function is obtained by estimating the standard linear or log-linear in income models described in previous sections. Because only a single transformation parameter is estimated, the number of restrictions, and therefore the degrees of freedom for the likelihood ratio test, is one.[11]

To illustrate we test the Box-Cox against the linear and log-linear models of the South Platte River study. Table 2.5 gives the log likelihood values for probit and logit models for each of the three functional forms.

TABLE 2.5. Log-likelihood Values for Strategic Functional Forms

	Log-likelihood Values	
Functional form	Logit	Probit
Linear $\lambda = 1$	−34.81	−34.65
Log-linear $\lambda = 0$	−42.88	−42.91
Box-Cox $\lambda = 0.83$	−33.83	−33.68

The restrictions of course pertain to λ. First consider the Box-Cox versus the log-linear. The Chi-squared values, $-2(\ln L_{\lambda=0} - \ln L_{\lambda=0.83})$ $= 18.1$ for the logit and 18.46 for the probit, are greater than the critical value with one degree of freedom at the 95% level of confidence of 3.84. Hence we reject the log-linear in favor of the Box-Cox parameter value of $\lambda = 0.83$. Next consider the Box-Cox versus the linear. The Chi-squared values of $-2(\ln L_{\lambda=1} - \ln L_{\lambda=0.83})$ are 1.96 for the logit and 1.93 for the probit. Consequently we cannot reject the linear model in favor of the Box-Cox, for both of the calculated Chi-squared values are less than the critical Chi-squared values at the 95% level of confidence.

Procedure for Testing Functional Forms Using the Box-Cox Random Utility Model.

1. *Estimate the Box-Cox random utility model. Recover the log likelihood function value. This will represent the unrestricted log likelihood function value for the likelihood ratio test.*

2. *Estimate the random utility model under the null hypothesis. For the linear model the null hypothesis is $\lambda = 1$. For the log-linear in income model the null hypothesis is $\lambda = 0$. Recover the log likelihood function value. This represents the restricted log likelihood value for the likelihood ratio test. The restricted model has a number of restrictions equal to the number of transformation parameters that are being tested. For the simplest model, the number*

[11] If λ were to be estimated with continuous methods rather than a grid search, we would have a standard error and this test could be done with a t-test. See Chapter 9 for an example of this.

of restrictions is one representing the restriction on the transformation of income parameter.

3. *Calculate the likelihood ratio statistic:* $-2(\ln L_R - \ln L_U)$ *where* $\ln L_R$ *is the restricted log likelihood function value and* $\ln L_U$ *is the unrestricted log likelihood function value. This test statistic is distributed Chi-squared with degrees of freedom equal to the number of restrictions in the restricted model. Compare the test-statistic calculated to the critical value from a Chi-squared distribution for the desired level of confidence. For example, the 95% critical value from a Chi-squared distribution with one degree of freedom is* 3.84.

4. *If the test statistic is larger than the critical value then reject the restricted model as a statistically accurate representation of the random utility model. If the test statistic is less than the critical value then accept the restricted model.*

Calculating Willingness to Pay Using the Box-Cox Random Utility Model

The principles for calculating willingness to pay are the same as in any utility function. WTP satisfies the equality of utility expression

$$\beta(y_j - WTP)^{(\lambda)} + \boldsymbol{\alpha}_1\mathbf{z}_j + \varepsilon_{1j} = \beta y_j^{(\lambda)} + \boldsymbol{\alpha}_0\mathbf{z}_j + \varepsilon_{0j} \tag{2.45}$$

which is found by substituting the Box-Cox indirect utility function of equation (2.42) into the general expression for WTP from equation (2.22). Solving for WTP yields

$$WTP_j(\varepsilon_j, \boldsymbol{\alpha}, \beta, \lambda, \mathbf{z}_j, y_j) = y_j - [y_j^\lambda - \lambda\boldsymbol{\alpha}\mathbf{z}_j/\beta - \lambda\varepsilon_j/\beta]^{1/\lambda}$$

where $\boldsymbol{\alpha} = \boldsymbol{\alpha}_1 - \boldsymbol{\alpha}_0$. In this expression WTP is a non-linear transformation of the unobservable error ε_j so that the calculation of the expectation of WTP with respect to ε_j can only be done analytically for the strategic cases of $\lambda = 0$ or 1. It is always possible to calculate the mean by using numerical methods.[12] The median is easily computed by recognizing that ε_j is a symmetric mean zero variate and as such the median of WTP occurs where $\varepsilon_j = 0$:

$$Md_\varepsilon(WTP_j|\boldsymbol{\alpha}, \beta, \lambda, \mathbf{z}_j, y_j) = y_j - \left[y_j^\lambda - \lambda\boldsymbol{\alpha}\mathbf{z}_j/\beta\right]^{\frac{1}{\lambda}}. \tag{2.46}$$

[12] That is, $E_\varepsilon WTP_j(\varepsilon_j, \boldsymbol{\alpha}, \beta, \mathbf{z}_j, y_j) = \int_{-\infty}^{\infty}(y_j - [y_j^\lambda - \lambda\boldsymbol{\alpha}\mathbf{z}_j/\beta - \lambda\varepsilon_j/\beta]^{1/\lambda})f(\varepsilon_j)d\varepsilon_j$. With numerical methods, the integral can be approximated for any distribution of the error.

Returning once again to the South Platte River data set, for the Box-Cox parameters in Table 2.4, and the exogenous variables taken at the sample means, $Md_{\varepsilon}(WTP|\boldsymbol{\alpha},\beta,\lambda=0.83,\bar{\mathbf{z}},\bar{y}) = \$22.00$ for the logit and \$21.09 for the probit. This is quite close to the measures calculated for the other functional forms. In this case, the model is almost linear in income because λ is so close to one. Income has very little effect on willingness to pay. For example. suppose that we consider an individual who has the sample average independent variable values, but a much higher income = \$75000, a \$21000 increase over the mean in Table 2.4. Then $Md_{\varepsilon}(WTP|\boldsymbol{\alpha},\beta,\lambda=0.83,\bar{\mathbf{z}},\$75000) = \$22.70$ for the probit.

A Varying Parameter Specification

There are two different but related reasons for wanting to incorporate income in random utility models. Meeting the budget constraint is one reason. When the term income minus the cost of the scenario is included, then the model ensures that the budget constraint will be met. A second reason is that households with considerably different incomes may answer quite differently because income will be a proxy for other variables pertaining to economic status. When the term income minus the cost of the scenario is included in a linear random utility model, of course income drops out. When the term is included in a non-linear model, such as the log-linear random utility model, then the composite income less cost of the scenario term becomes one of the regressors. Because income is apt to be measured with a good deal of error, and because the payment is often a very small share of income, the arguments for including income non-linearly in the form of income minus the cost of the scenario are weak. For CV studies with a very low cost, it is not reasonable that the marginal utility of income varies with the income of a given respondent. A marginal utility of income that varies across individuals with different incomes is more plausible, however. One means of incorporating the effect of income, including allowing the marginal utility of income to vary across individuals, is to use income categories, and allow the coefficients to vary by income categories. This approach, illustrated below, avoids the effect of errors in the measurement of income, while at the same time capturing some of the differences among individuals because of income differences.

To relax the assumption of constant marginal utility of income β, we can assume that the marginal utility of income from the linear model for $u_{ij} = \beta_j y_j + \boldsymbol{\alpha}_i \mathbf{z}_j + \varepsilon_{ij}$ (the utility of individual j, scenario i) varies across individuals such that

$$\beta_j = \delta(w_j) = \delta_0 + \delta_1 w_{1j} + \delta_2 w_{2j} + \ldots + \delta_K w_{Kj} = \boldsymbol{\delta}\mathbf{w}_j, \qquad (2.47)$$

where w_j is a vector of individual specific covariates and where

$$\begin{aligned}\boldsymbol{\delta} &= \{\delta_0, \delta_1, ..., \delta_K\}\\ \mathbf{w}_j &= \{1, w_{1j}, ..., w_{Kj}\}.\end{aligned}$$

Substituting into the linear utility function results in the linear utility function

$$\begin{aligned}u_{ij} &= \delta_0 y_j + \delta_1 w_{1j} y_j + ... + \delta_K w_{Kj} y_j + \boldsymbol{\alpha}_i \mathbf{z}_j + \varepsilon_{ij}\\ &= (\boldsymbol{\delta}\mathbf{w}_j) y_j + \boldsymbol{\alpha}_i \mathbf{z}_j + \varepsilon_{ij}.\end{aligned} \tag{2.48}$$

This specification can give a variety of different models. We can let the $\mathbf{w}_j$ be a vector of indicator variables, telling whether income lies within a specified income group. That is, suppose we have a set of K income categories, $c_1, ..., c_K$. Then we can classify household income y_j as follows:

$w_{1j} = 1\ if\ y_j < c_1; 0$ otherwise;
$w_{2j} = 1\ if\ c_1 \leq y_j < c_2; 0$ otherwise;
$w_{Kj} = 1\ if\ y_j \geq c_K; 0$ otherwise.

With these categorical variables, each group has its own marginal utility of income. This formulation can also be modeled by including the constant δ_0 and omitting one of the income groups.

For the general model the marginal utility of income is

$$\frac{\partial u_{ij}}{\partial y_j} = \boldsymbol{\delta}\mathbf{w}_j. \tag{2.49}$$

By way of example, suppose we think that the marginal utility of income is different for individuals with income above the sample median income than for individuals below the sample median income. Let w_{kj} be the indicator variable defined by $w_{1j} = 1$ when household income is less than the sample median and $w_{2j} = 1$ when household income is greater than median income.

$$u_{ij} = \delta_1 w_{1j} y_j + \delta_2 w_{2j} y_j + \boldsymbol{\alpha}_i \mathbf{z}_j + \varepsilon_{ij}. \tag{2.50}$$

The estimated parameter δ_1 represents the marginal utility of income for those individuals with income below the median, and the estimate of δ_2 represents the change in the marginal utility of income for those individuals with income above the median. A test for the equality of δ_1 and δ_2 is a test of the hypothesis that the marginal utility of income is the same across income classes. In this model the marginal utility of income varies across households but is constant with respect to a given household's income. Further, the marginal utility of income does not vary between CV scenarios. Hence the income variable itself will not be an argument in the probability model.

More flexible specifications can be created by refining the income categories (including more income dummies), or by including continuous covariates in the varying parameter vector w_j. With this model the probability of a 'yes' response becomes

$$\begin{aligned}\Pr(yes_j) &= \Pr(\delta_1 w_{1j}(y_j - t_j) + \delta_2 w_{2j}(y_j - t_j) + \boldsymbol{\alpha}_1 \mathbf{z}_j + \varepsilon_{1j} \\ &> \delta_1 w_{1j} y_j + \delta_2 w_{2j} y_j + \boldsymbol{\alpha}_0 \mathbf{z}_j + \varepsilon_{0j}) \\ &= \Pr[-\delta_1 w_{1j} t_j - \delta_2 w_{2j} t_j + \boldsymbol{\alpha} \mathbf{z}_j < \varepsilon_j] > 0. \qquad (2.51)\end{aligned}$$

When the unobserved error is transformed to a unit variance error, this model becomes a simple logit or probit.

Example 5 *Varying Parameters Model: The South Platte River Study*

To illustrate a model with varying marginal utility of income we return to the South Platte River study. With the same specification for non-income variables as in the previous models, we now introduce two income coefficients, one for household income less than or equal to \$45000 and one for household income greater than \$45000. Table 2.6 gives the estimated models.

Estimating Willingness to Pay in the Varying Parameters Model

Equating utility in the improved state (u_{1j}) to utility in the status quo state (u_{0j}) gives an implicit expression for willingness to pay:

$$\begin{aligned}&\boldsymbol{\delta}\mathbf{w}_j(y_j - WTP_j(\varepsilon_j, \boldsymbol{\alpha}, \boldsymbol{\delta}, \mathbf{z}_j, y_j)) + \boldsymbol{\alpha}_1 \mathbf{z}_j + \varepsilon_{1j} \\ = \;& \boldsymbol{\delta}\mathbf{w}_j y_j + \boldsymbol{\alpha}_0 \mathbf{z}_j + \varepsilon_{0j}. \qquad (2.52)\end{aligned}$$

Solving for the willingness to pay yields

$$\begin{aligned}WTP_j(\varepsilon_j, \boldsymbol{\alpha}, \boldsymbol{\delta}, \mathbf{z}_j, y_j) &= \frac{(\boldsymbol{\alpha}_1 - \boldsymbol{\alpha}_0)\mathbf{z}_j + (\varepsilon_{1j} - \varepsilon_{0j})}{\boldsymbol{\delta}\mathbf{w}_j} \qquad (2.53) \\ &= \frac{\boldsymbol{\alpha}\mathbf{z}_j + \varepsilon_j}{\boldsymbol{\delta}\mathbf{w}_j}.\end{aligned}$$

Since ε_{1j} and ε_{0j} are both mean zero errors with unknown variance, ε_j is likewise mean zero with unknown variance. The expected value of willingness to pay taken with respect to the random error is therefore

$$E_{\varepsilon}(WTP|\boldsymbol{\alpha}, \boldsymbol{\delta}, \mathbf{z}_j, y_j) = \frac{\boldsymbol{\alpha} z_j}{\boldsymbol{\delta}\mathbf{w}_j}. \qquad (2.54)$$

TABLE 2.6. Varying Parameters Model

$\Pr(\theta < (\alpha_0 + \alpha_1\text{unlimwat}+\alpha_2\text{govtpur}+\alpha_3\text{environ}+\alpha_4\text{waterbil}+\alpha_5\text{urban}-\delta_1 w_{1j}t - \delta_2 w_{2j}t)/\sigma))^*$		
	θ logistic	θ normal
	Parameter estimate (Standard error)	Parameter estimate (Standard error)
δ_1/σ	−0.13	−0.08
	(0.03)	(0.02)
δ_2/σ	−0.16	−0.09
	(0.04)	(0.02)
α_0/σ	2.30	1.32
	(1.48)	(0.82)
α_1/σ	−1.43	−0.79
	(0.74)	(0.41)
α_2/σ	1.83	1.10
	(0.75)	(0.44)
α_3/σ	3.35	1.90
	(1.17)	(0.64)
α_4/σ	−0.06	−0.04
	(0.03)	(0.02)
α_5/σ	1.82	1.13
	(0.71)	(0.41)
Log-likelihood	−34.40	−34.20
$-2\ln(L_R/L_U)$	57.41	56.54

$^*w_{1j} = 1$, income $\leq \$45000$; 0 otherwise; $w_{2j} = 1 - w_{1j}$

Median willingness to pay can be found by substituting $\varepsilon_j = 0$

$$MD_\varepsilon(WTP|\boldsymbol{\alpha}, \boldsymbol{\delta}, \mathbf{z}_j, y_j) = \frac{\boldsymbol{\alpha}\mathbf{z}_j}{\boldsymbol{\delta}\mathbf{w}_j}. \tag{2.55}$$

As in the other models, the parameters $\{\boldsymbol{\alpha}, \boldsymbol{\delta}\}$ are unknown. A consistent estimate for expected or median willingness to pay can be found by substituting consistent estimates of the parameters $\{\boldsymbol{\alpha}, \boldsymbol{\delta}\}$ into the expressions for expected and median willingness to pay. Using the South Platte River estimates from Table 2.6, we find that an individual with the sample mean independent variables but income below the median has an expected willingness to pay $E_\varepsilon(WTP|\boldsymbol{\alpha}, \boldsymbol{\delta}, \bar{\mathbf{z}}, y_j < \text{median } y) =$ \$18.90. The same individual with income above the median would have expected willingness to pay $E_\varepsilon(WTP|\boldsymbol{\alpha}, \boldsymbol{\delta}, \bar{\mathbf{z}}, y_j \geq \text{median } y) = \$22.90$.

Both of these estimates are for the probit. The absence of a large difference is consistent with the earlier finding of an income effect not different from zero.

2.2.2 *The Random Willingness to Pay or Expenditure Difference Model*

Rather than modeling the indirect utility function and then deriving the appropriate willingness to pay measure, various researchers, beginning with Hanemann and Cameron, have emphasized directly modeling the willingness to pay function for dichotomous choice CV questions. The basic idea is that willingness to pay is a well-defined concept by itself. The dichotomous CV question can be interpreted as the question of whether willingness to pay exceeds the price that is posed to the respondent. The willingness to pay function is more transparent than the utility difference, and can lead to more plausible distributions. In contrast, some quite simple utility differences may imply unacceptable distributions of willingness to pay. Although willingness to pay does not need a utility function for its derivation, it is useful to show that it can be derived from the indirect utility function. From this derivation we can see that for certain functions, the models that start as random utility models or random willingness to pay models really are the same. This result holds for the dichotomous choice models but not the multiple choice models that arise in conjoint analysis or site choice models. By the definition in equation (2.22), the willingness to pay for the CV scenario relative to the status quo is defined as

$$v_1(y_j - WTP(y_j, \mathbf{z}_j, \varepsilon_j), \mathbf{z}_j) + \varepsilon_{1j} = v_0(y_j, \mathbf{z}_j) + \varepsilon_{0j}. \tag{2.56}$$

WTP is the amount of income that makes the respondent indifferent between the status quo and the final state. Solving this equality for WTP defines WTP as a function of income, covariates and the unobserved random preferences (where in general, $\varepsilon_j = f(\varepsilon_{1j}, \varepsilon_{0j})$, and in the case of additive errors, $\varepsilon_j = \varepsilon_{1j} - \varepsilon_{0j}$). A respondent answers yes when willingness to pay exceeds the required payment:

$$WTP(y_j, \mathbf{z}_j, \varepsilon_j) > t_j. \tag{2.57}$$

This will be true if

$$v_1(y_j - t_j, \mathbf{z}_j) + \varepsilon_{1j} > v_0(y_j, \mathbf{z}_j) + \varepsilon_{0j}.$$

If equation (2.56) defines WTP as an equality, then any amount less than WTP will make the left hand side of equation (2.56) greater than the right hand side, because utility is increasing in income. Consequently, we can make the equivalent probability statements:

$$\begin{aligned} \Pr[WTP(y_j, \mathbf{z}_j, \varepsilon_j) &> t_j] = \\ \Pr[v_1(y_j - t_j, \mathbf{z}_j) + \varepsilon_{1j} &> v_0(y_j, \mathbf{z}_j) + \varepsilon_{0j}]. \end{aligned} \quad (2.58)$$

Either the utility difference or the willingness to pay function provides the basis for modeling responses to dichotomous choice CV questions, as Hanemann originally recognized. However, in some situations currently, researchers are exploiting techniques based on conjoint analysis, in which the respondent chooses among more than two alternatives. In the more than two alternatives choice, the utility function approach offers the only consistent means of modeling responses.

The connection between WTP and the utility difference can be made more explicit. Let $\Delta u = \Delta v + \varepsilon$ where $\varepsilon = \varepsilon_1 - \varepsilon_0$ and $\Delta v = v_1 - v_0$. The probability of responding yes is modeled with a distribution function for ε. Let F_ε be the distribution function for ε, so that $F_\varepsilon(x)$ is the probability that the variate ε is less than the number x. Then for $F_\varepsilon(x)$ symmetric

$$\Pr(yes) = \Pr(\Delta v + \varepsilon > 0) = F_\varepsilon(\Delta v). \quad (2.59)$$

If we solve equation (2.56) for WTP we get (the dependence of WTP on y and $\mathbf{z}$ is suppressed for notational convenience):

$$WTP(\varepsilon) = y - v_1^{-1}(v_0 - \varepsilon). \quad (2.60)$$

The probability statement in (2.59) can be transformed from Δv to WTP but we can see from (2.60) that these are equivalent only when v_1^{-1} is a linear transformation. Noting that the derivative of $v_1^{-1}(v_0 - \varepsilon)$ with respect to utility is the same as the derivative with respect to ε (except for sign) provides for the change of variable in integration to transform the change in utility expression to a willingness to pay expression in equation (2.59). This derivative is the marginal cost of utility and it is the reciprocal of the marginal utility of income. Hence when the marginal utility is constant, WTP will have the same family of distributions as the utility difference. When v_1^{-1} is a nonlinear transformation, we can derive the distribution of WTP applying the transformation in (2.60), but the distribution will not be the same as the utility difference. And in the case of a nonlinear transformation, the WTP function will not be the sum of stochastic and deterministic parts. In fact, one will not be able to separate the known and deterministic parts from the unknown and random to the researcher parts.

The Linear Willingness to Pay Function

Let the willingness to pay function be linear in attributes with an additive stochastic preference term:

$$WTP(\mathbf{z}_j, \eta_j) = \gamma z_j + \eta_j \tag{2.61}$$

where η_j is symmetric, IID with mean zero, and γ and $\mathbf{z}_j$ are m-dimensional vectors of parameters to be estimated and covariates associated with respondent j. The respondent answers yes to a required price of t if willingness to pay exceeds t. The probability of a yes response is

$$\begin{aligned} \Pr(yes_j) &= \Pr(WTP > t_j) = \\ \Pr(\gamma\mathbf{z}_j + \eta_j &> t_j) = \Pr(-(\gamma\mathbf{z}_j - t_j) < \eta_j) \\ &= \Pr((\gamma\mathbf{z}_j - t_j) > \eta_j). \end{aligned} \tag{2.62}$$

The last statement follows only for symmetric η_j. When η is $N(0, \sigma^2)$, the problem can be converted to a standard probit by dividing by σ. Then

$$\Pr(\gamma\mathbf{z}_j - t_j) > \eta_j) = \Pr(\gamma\mathbf{z}_j - t_j)/\sigma > \theta_j) \tag{2.63}$$

where θ_j is $N(0, 1)$. This is a dichotomous choice model where $(\mathbf{z}, \mathbf{t})$ are the covariates with coefficients $\gamma/\sigma, -1/\sigma$. This is the same model that is estimated for the linear utility function, although the estimated coefficients have different interpretations. Thus the linear willingness to pay function and the linear utility difference function yield identical models and identical estimates of willingness to pay.

Procedure for Estimating a Random Willingness to Pay Model with Linear Willingness to Pay Function

1. *Define the yes/no responses to the contingent valuation question such that yes is coded 1 and no is coded 0.*

2. *Define a data matrix* $\mathbf{X}$ *so that it contains the concatenation of the covariate matrix* $\mathbf{z}$ *and the offered fee vector* $\mathbf{t}$.

3. *Using any standard statistical software, run a probit or logit model with the 1/0 yes/no responses as the dependent variable, and the matrix* X *as the matrix of right hand side variables.*

4. *Recover the reported parameter estimates. The coefficients on the variables in the matrix* $\mathbf{z}$ *represent estimates of* γ/σ. *The coefficient on the offered fee is an estimate of* $-1/\sigma$.

Note that this procedure is identical to the procedure for estimating a random utility model with linear utility function.

Estimating Willingness to Pay With the Linear Willingness to Pay Model

The linear willingness to pay function is once again:

$$WTP(\mathbf{z}_j, \eta_j) = \boldsymbol{\gamma}\mathbf{z}_j + \eta_j. \tag{2.64}$$

Taking the expectation with respect to the unobservable error results in the expression for expected willingness to pay

$$E_\eta(WTP|\mathbf{z}_j, \boldsymbol{\gamma}) = \boldsymbol{\gamma}\mathbf{z}_j. \tag{2.65}$$

However, γ is unknown, and an estimate must be obtained using the estimates of $\boldsymbol{\gamma}/\sigma$ and $-1/\sigma$ from the probit or logit model. A consistent estimate of expected willingness to pay is

$$E_\eta(WTP|\mathbf{z}_j, \boldsymbol{\gamma}) = \frac{\widehat{\left(\frac{\gamma}{\sigma}\right)}}{\widehat{\left(\frac{1}{\sigma}\right)}}\mathbf{z}. \tag{2.66}$$

Since η is assumed to be symmetric around zero, median willingness to pay can be found by setting $\eta = 0$:

$$MD_\eta(WTP|\mathbf{z}_j, \boldsymbol{\gamma}) = \boldsymbol{\gamma}\mathbf{z}_j \tag{2.67}$$

and a consistent estimate of the median can be found by using the estimates of $\boldsymbol{\gamma}/\sigma$ and $-1/\sigma$:

$$MD_\eta(WTP|\mathbf{z}_j, \boldsymbol{\gamma}) = \frac{\widehat{\left(\frac{\gamma}{\sigma}\right)}}{\widehat{\left(\frac{1}{\sigma}\right)}}\mathbf{z}. \tag{2.68}$$

As noted, the linear random willingness to pay model, and the linear random utility model produce identical parameter estimates, and identical welfare estimates. Also note that although the form of the welfare estimates only relies on the mean zero assumption for the error term and not the particular model used to estimate the parameters (probit or logit), the actual estimates of welfare will depend on the model chosen as the estimates are functions of parameter estimates which will vary across assumed distributions.

Just as it is possible to specify and estimate non-linear utility functions, it is also possible to formulate non-linear willingness to pay functions. But the nature of the non-linearity and the motivation for the models differs from the random utility specifications. In the development of non-linear random willingness to pay functions, it is not always evident that the models can be derived from a utility function. Further, these models are often adopted because of the implied distribution of willingness to pay. These models frequently imply a non-negative distribution of willingness to pay. In the following section we discuss an especially popular willingness to pay function, the exponential.

The Exponential Willingness to Pay Function

This model was popularized by Cameron and James. Let willingness to pay be an exponential function of a linear combination of attributes and an additive stochastic preference term:

$$WTP_j = e^{\gamma \mathbf{z}_j + \eta_j} \tag{2.69}$$

where η_j is a stochastic error with mean zero with unknown variance σ^2. The probability of individual j responding 'yes' to an offered bid t_j is equivalent to the probability of the random willingness to pay function being greater than the offered bid:

$$\begin{aligned} \Pr(yes_j) &= \Pr(WTP_j > t_j) \\ &= \Pr(\exp(\gamma \mathbf{z}_j + \eta_j) > t_j) \\ &= \Pr(\eta_j > \ln(t_j) - \gamma \mathbf{z}_j). \end{aligned} \tag{2.70}$$

Normalizing by the unknown standard error, σ, to standardize the stochastic error results in the probability of a yes response

$$\begin{aligned} \Pr(WTP_j &> t_j) = \Pr\left(\frac{\eta_j}{\sigma} > \frac{1}{\sigma}\ln(t_j) - \frac{\gamma}{\sigma}\mathbf{z}_j\right) \\ &= \Pr\left(\theta_j > \beta \ln(t_j) - \gamma^* \mathbf{z}_j\right) \end{aligned} \tag{2.71}$$

where $\theta_j = \frac{\eta_j}{\sigma}, \beta = \frac{1}{\sigma}$ and $\gamma^* = \gamma/\sigma$. The notation for the unknown standard error σ used here is a notation of convenience. It should be made clear that the variance of standard logistic distribution is $\frac{\sigma^2\pi^2}{3}$, which is the normalizing factor for all logit derivations. Drawing on the symmetry of the error term θ_j, we can rewrite this as $\Pr\left(\theta_j < -\beta \ln(t_j) + \gamma^* \mathbf{z}_j\right)$. Since this probability represents a linear combination of functions of covariates $\{\ln(t_j), \mathbf{z}_j\}$, assuming η_j is either normally or logistically distributed results in a model that is estimable with a probit or logit model. Estimation leads to the recovery of $-\frac{1}{\sigma}$, $\frac{\gamma}{\sigma}$.

Procedure for Estimating a Random Willingness to Pay Model with Log-linear Willingness to Pay Function

1. *Define the yes/no responses to the contingent valuation question such that yes is coded 1 and no is coded 0.*

2. *Define a data matrix* $\mathbf{X}$ *so that it contains the concatenation of the covariate matrix* $\mathbf{z}$ *and the natural logarithm of the offered fee vector* $\ln(\mathbf{t})$.

3. *Using any standard statistical software, run a probit or logit model with the 1/0 yes/no responses as the dependent variable, and the matrix* $\mathbf{X}$ *as the matrix of right hand side variables.*

4. *Recover the reported parameter estimates. The coefficients on the variables in the matrix* $\mathbf{z}$ *represent estimates of* γ/σ. *The coefficient on the offered fee is an estimate of* $-1/\sigma$.

Example 6 *Exponential Willingness to Pay Model: The South Platte River Study*

We illustrate the exponential willingness to pay model with the South Platte River study. We choose the same specification as previously adopted, although it is worth noting that it is now possible to introduce income as a separate variable. Table 2.7 gives the estimated models. Although this model looks a good bit different from the linear random utility model, the only effective difference is the inclusion of the log of the bid price, rather than the bid price. Hence the parameter estimates on the other covariates are quite close to the linear model.

Calculating Willingness to Pay for the Exponential Function

The log-linear willingness to pay function is

$$WTP_j = e^{\gamma \mathbf{z}_j + \eta_j}. \tag{2.72}$$

Taking the expectation with respect to the random preference variation η_j, the expected value of WTP is

$$E_\eta(WTP|\mathbf{z}_j, \gamma) = e^{\gamma \mathbf{z}_j} E(e^{\eta_j}). \tag{2.73}$$

For the linear willingness to pay model, expected willingness to pay is independent of the assumed form for the random error as long as the error has zero mean. For the log-linear model, expected willingness to pay will be sensitive to the assumed form of the distribution for η_j.

Probit Formulation

If η_j is distributed normally with mean zero and constant variance σ^2, then e^{η_j} is distributed log-normally with mean $e^{\frac{1}{2}\sigma^2}$ and variance

TABLE 2.7. Estimation of Exponential Willingness to Pay

$\Pr(\theta < (\alpha_0 + \alpha_1\text{unlimwat} + \alpha_2\text{ govtpur}+ \alpha_3\text{environ}+ \alpha_4\text{waterbil}+\alpha_5\text{urban}-\log(t))/\sigma))$		
	θ logistic	θ normal
	Parameter estimate* (Standard error)	Parameter estimate (Standard error)
$-1/\sigma$	−2.27 (0.51)	−1.30 (0.27)
α_0/σ	6.18 (2.18)	3.53 (1.19)
α_1/σ	−1.63 (0.81)	−0.91 (0.44)
α_2/σ	1.67 (0.84)	0.93 (0.48)
α_3/σ	3.18 (1.07)	1.83 (0.58)
α_4/σ	−0.08 (0.04)	−0.04 (0.02)
α_5/σ	1.77 (0.81)	1.03 (0.45)
Log-likelihood	−30.20	−30.30
$-2\ln(L_R/L_U)$	65.49	60.61

*All coefficients different from zero at 95% level of confidence.

$e^{2\sigma^2} - e^{\sigma^2}$. Substituting into the expectation of WTP yields expected willingness to pay from the probit model:

$$E_\eta(WTP|\mathbf{z}_j, \gamma) = e^{\gamma\mathbf{z}_j + \frac{1}{2}\sigma^2}. \tag{2.74}$$

Because η_j is symmetric about zero, median willingness to pay is found by substituting $\eta_j = 0$ into the WTP expressions:

$$MD_\eta(WTP|\mathbf{z}_j, \gamma) = e^{\gamma\mathbf{z}_j}. \tag{2.75}$$

Logit Formulation

If η_j is distributed logistically with mean zero and constant variance $\frac{\sigma^2\pi^2}{3}$, then e^{η_j} is distributed with mean $\frac{\sigma\pi}{\sin(\sigma\pi)}$ and variance $e^{2\sigma^2} - e^{\sigma^2}$, where the unit of measure for $\sin(\sigma\pi)$ is radians (see Appendix B for a derivation of this result). From Appendix B, the distribution of e^{η_j} is only defined for $0 < \sigma < 1$. As σ approaches one from below, the expected value of e^{η_j} approaches infinity. For $\sigma > 1$, the expected value of e^{η_j} does not exist. This implies that the coefficient on the bid in equation 2.71a $\left(\beta = \frac{1}{\sigma}\right)$ must be greater than one for expected willingness to pay to exist (see Appendix B). Substituting into the expectation of WTP yields expected willingness to pay from the logit model

$$E_\eta(WTP|\mathbf{z}_j,\gamma) = \frac{\sigma\pi}{\sin(\sigma\pi)} e^{\mathbf{z}_j\gamma}. \tag{2.76}$$

Median willingness to pay is found by substituting $\eta_j = 0$ into the WTP expressions:

$$MD_\eta(WTP|\mathbf{z}_j,\gamma) = e^{\mathbf{z}_j\gamma}. \tag{2.77}$$

For both the probit and the logit, the difference between median and mean willingness to pay can be considerable when the variance is high. Note that the mean willingness to pay is increasing in the variance of the error. Because the estimators for willingness to pay are so different for the mean and median and for the logit and probit, we calculate them all for the sample mean values of $\mathbf{z}$ found in Table 2.1. As Table 2.8 shows, the observations are very well behaved. The mean increases about 35% over the median for distribution. The medians from the two distributions are quite close, as one would expect. We shall see in applications, where the variance of the random error is much larger, that the mean and median offer quite different estimates.

TABLE 2.8. Mean Willingness to Pay for Exponential Model

	η logistic	η normal
$E_\eta(WTP\|\bar{\mathbf{z}},\gamma)$	19.03	18.15
$MD_\eta(WTP\|\bar{\mathbf{z}},\gamma)$	13.51	13.50

2.3 Conclusion

In this chapter we have reviewed the basic parametric models for model estimation and welfare calculation for dichotomous contingent valuation models. These models have been estimated on a particularly well-behaved data set. We have not explored more complicated random utility models, nor problems of bid choice and welfare calculations. For example, it is clear from the expression for the variance of the parameter estimates that the bid prices influence the parameter variances, because the bids are part of the data. Another issue relates to the uncertainty of parameters that we have ignored in calculating the willingness to pay. We explore these and other issues in the econometrics of dichotomous choice contingent calculation in the following three chapters.

3

Distribution-Free Models for Contingent Valuation

3.1 Introduction

In the progression of contingent valuation models with discrete responses, researchers first developed the kinds of parametric models that were explored in the previous chapter. When the pattern of responses is well behaved, as in the example used throughout the previous chapter, the estimates of willingness to pay will not be especially sensitive to the choice of distribution for the unobserved random component of preferences, or for the functional form of the preference function. However, there are many cases when the distribution or the functional form can have a substantial effect on the estimates of willingness to pay. Several of these cases will be explored in Chapter 4. Because of the sensitivity of willingness to pay for some CV studies, it is useful to develop the least restrictive approach to estimating willingness to pay. This chapter develops measures of central tendency and dispersion of willingness to pay that rely only on the notion that when a respondent answers yes to a contingent valuation question, we have learned that his willingness to pay is not less than the offered bid price.

3.2 The Turnbull Estimator

Responses to discrete choice contingent valuation questions offer the researcher limited information regarding each respondent's true willingness to pay. If the respondent answers yes, then willingness to pay is greater than or equal to the offered price, and if the answer is no, willingness to pay is less than the offered price. All methods for estimating sample and population willingness to pay and covariate effects on willingness to pay estimates start with this basic information. Variation in the characteristics of sampled individuals and variation in the price offered respondents provide the information needed to estimate sample willingness to pay. For each respondent the researcher records the offered price, the yes/no response, and individual specific covariates that can include demographic information from the respondent, such as education, age, income, and responses to other survey questions.

Consider a random sample of T respondents each offered one of M distinct prices, indexed $\{t_j|j = 1, 2, ..., M\}$, for a project. Let WTP_i be individual i's willingness to pay for the proposal. If the individual responds yes to the question 'Are you willing to pay $\$t_j$ for the project?', then we know that $WTP_i \geq t_j$. Otherwise, $WTP_i < t_j$. Since WTP is unobservable to the researcher, it can be thought of as a random variable with a cumulative distribution function $F_W(W)$, the probability that willingness to pay is less than W. The probability of a randomly chosen respondent having willingness to pay less than $\$t_j$ can therefore be written

$$\Pr(WTP_i < \$t_j) = F_W(t_j). \tag{3.1}$$

For simplicity we will denote this probability as F_j such that

$$\Pr(WTP_i < \$t_j) = F_W(t_j) = F_j. \tag{3.2}$$

This is the probability that the respondent will say no to a price of t_j. The two notations, $F_W(t_j)$ and F_j, will be used interchangeably as appropriate. For now, we assume that this probability is the same for different individuals offered the same price. We relax this assumption in section 3.6 to include individual characteristics in the analysis.

The M offered prices now divide the full sample T into a vector of M sub-samples $\mathbf{T} = \{T_1, T_2, ..., T_M\}$ where the number of respondents in each sub-sample (T_j is the number of respondents who get the price t_j) sums to the total sample size: $\sum_{j=1}^{M} T_j = T$. Similarly, the number of yes and no responses can be indexed according to the offered price: $\mathbf{Y} = \{Y_j|j = 1, 2, ..., M\}$, and $\mathbf{N} = \{N_j|j = 1, 2, ..., M\}$, where Y_j is the number of 'yes' responses to bid price t_j and N_j the number of 'no' responses. The summation of the number of yes's across all sub-samples equals the total number of yes responses in the sample, and the summation of the no's across sub-samples equals the total number of no's.

3.2.1 An Unrestricted Distribution-Free Estimator

The sub-samples created by randomly assigning prices to the full sample can be treated as independent and the probability of a no response can be estimated for each sub-sample. When the bids are assigned randomly to the full sample, the M sub-samples can be treated as independent samples from the full population T, each receiving a single bid t_j. To estimate the probability of a yes or no response to the offered bid $\$t_j$, we need information on the true distribution of WTP: $F_W(t_j)$. However, this is exactly the information we do not have. As was the case in Chapter 2, we could choose a distribution for $F_W(t_j)$ and then derive estimable models from the assumed distribution. But in this chapter the focus is on the information that can be drawn from the individual responses to the posed CV questions without imposing unnecessary assumptions. Since the distribution of WTP is unknown, the series of yes/no responses from the sample represents a series of binary outcomes from an unknown data generating process and can be used to formulate an estimate of $F_W(t_j)$.

To derive an estimate of $F_W(t_j)$, define a response variable $I_{ij} = 1$ if individual i responds 'yes' to the offered bid t_j, and $I_{ij} = 0$ if 'no'. Given this limited information, the unknown probability of observing I_{ij} is

$$\Pr(I_{ij}|F_W(t_j)) = F_W(t_j)^{1-I_{ij}}(1 - F_W(t_j))^{I_{ij}}. \tag{3.3}$$

For a given sample of T_j independent and identical individuals each offered the same price t_j, the probability of observing the set of sample yes/no response $\mathbf{I}_j = \{I_{1j}, I_{2j}, ..., I_{T_j j}\}$ is

$$\begin{aligned} \Pr(\mathbf{I}_j|F_W(t_j), T_j) &= \prod_{i=1}^{T_j} F_W(t_j)^{1-I_{ij}}(1 - F_W(t_j))^{I_{ij}} \\ &= F_W(t_j)^{\sum_{i=1}^{T_j}(1-I_{ij})}(1 - F_W(t_j))^{\sum_{i=1}^{T_j} I_{ij}} \end{aligned} \tag{3.4}$$

This probability has an intuitive interpretation for each price-partitioned sub-sample from a discrete choice contingent valuation question. If the sample is chosen randomly and the prices are assigned randomly, then the individual responses to each price can be interpreted as the outcome of individual Bernoulli trials (weighted coin flips) with probability of success equal to $(1 - F_W(t_j))$. Since the individuals are randomly chosen and their responses are independent, the probability of observing a given number of yes's to price j (Y_j) from a sub-sample T_j is the probability of Y_j successes in T_j independent Bernoulli trials with probability of success $1 - F_W(t_j)$. Defining $\sum_{i=1}^{T_j} I_{ij} = Y_j$ as the number of yes responses to $\$t_j$, and $(T_j - Y_j) = N_j$ as the number of no responses, the probability of observing the exact sample of responses to t_j becomes

$$\Pr(Y_j|F_W(t_j), T_j) = \begin{pmatrix} T_j \\ Y_j \end{pmatrix} F_W(t_j)^{N_j}(1 - F_W(t_j))^{Y_j} \tag{3.5}$$

where $\begin{pmatrix} T_j \\ Y_j \end{pmatrix} = \frac{T_j!}{Y_j!(T_j - Y_j)!}$ is the number of combinations of Y_j yes responses that can occur in a random sample of T_j individuals. Because the responses are assumed independent, the sequence of responses does not matter and $\begin{pmatrix} T_j \\ Y_j \end{pmatrix}$ simply counts the number of possible ways Y_j yes responses could occur. Note that (3.5) is the cumulative distribution function of a binomial random variable. The total number of yes responses to any price t_j (Y_j) can be interpreted as a binomial random variable with the probability of observing a single yes response equal to $(1 - F_W(t_j))$.

The problem of estimating the unknown probability $F_W(t_j)$ from the sample of known yes/no responses remains. $F_W(t_j)$ is an unknown distribution, and it is desirable to make minimal assumptions about its form to reduce the risk of bias due to misspecification. One possibility is to interpret $F_W(t_j)$ as an unknown parameter, denoted F_j. Then the probability of observing Y_j yes's from T_j independent respondents becomes a function of F_j. For estimation of the parameters, we choose an estimate of F_j to maximize the likelihood of observing Y_j yes's from T_j respondents. (See Appendix A for a brief treatment of maximum likelihood estimation.) The maximum likelihood estimator for F_j can be found by treating F_j as an unknown parameter, and Y_j, N_j and T_j as known in equation (3.5). The likelihood function for the sub-sample of respondents offered price t_j becomes

$$L(F_j|Y_j, N_j, T_j) = \begin{pmatrix} T_j \\ Y_j \end{pmatrix} F_j^{N_j}(1 - F_j)^{Y_j}.$$

Because the price-partitioned sub-samples are independent (recall prices are assigned randomly), the joint likelihood function for the full sample of T respondents is the product

$$L(F_1, ..., F_M|Y_1, ..., Y_M; N_1, ..., N_M) = \prod_{j=1}^{M} \begin{pmatrix} T_j \\ Y_j \end{pmatrix} F_j^{N_j}(1 - F_j)^{Y_j}.$$

The combinatorial term has no unknown constants to be estimated and so we drop it from the log-likelihood function. The log-likelihood function becomes

$$\ln L = \sum_{j=1}^{M} \left[N_j \ln(F_j) + Y_j \ln(1 - F_j)\right]. \qquad (3.6)$$

Maximizing the log of the likelihood function with respect to F_j for all j yields the system of first order conditions for a maximum

$$\frac{\partial \ln L(F|Y,N)}{\partial F_j} = \frac{N_j}{F_j} - \frac{Y_j}{(1 - F_j)} = 0 \;\; j = 1, M. \qquad (3.7)$$

Because the sub-samples of respondents are independent, the first-order condition for any F_j is independent of all other first-order conditions. Solving the first order conditions for F_j yields the maximum likelihood estimates of F:

$$F_j = N_j/T_j.$$

Recalling that N_j is the number of people responding no to the offered price t_j and T_j is the total number of people offered t_j, F_j is the sample proportion of no responses to the offered price. Intuitively, the maximum likelihood estimate of the probability that a randomly chosen respondent will not be willing to pay $\$t_j$ is equal to the sample proportion of individuals that respond no to $\$t_j$.

Example 7 *Estimating the Distribution-free Estimator*

The estimates of the parameters F_j are illustrated with a contingent valuation study of willingness to pay for water quality. The data are from a 1995 telephone survey conducted by Whitehead, Haab and Huang (1998). The valuation question asked respondents if they would be willing to pay a randomly assigned dollar amount for a program to restore water quality and services of the Albemarle and Pamlico Sounds of North Carolina to their 1980 levels. This is a simple example because there are only four prices, and they are relatively far apart. The results are summarized in Table 3.1.

TABLE 3.1. Turnbull Estimates: Albemarle and Pamlico Sounds

Bid Price (t_j)	Number offered (T_j)	Number of No's (N_j)	$F_j = \frac{N_j}{T_j}$
\$100	190	98	0.516
\$200	144	78	0.542
\$300	166	105	0.632
\$400	154	113	0.734

The example in Table 3.1 suggests the need for a test of the hypothesis that the proportion of no's is statistically different across bids. After all, in column four, the proportions do not differ greatly. We could do pair-wise t-tests, but a likelihood ratio test is more convenient. The pair-wise t-tests will be independent and can be converted into the likelihood ratio test. A likelihood ratio test (see Appendix A) can be constructed as follows. The null hypothesis would be that there is an equal likelihood of saying yes or no, regardless of the price. Using the principle of ignorance, the estimate of the likelihood of saying no would be one-half, so that the null hypothesis would be $F_j = 1/2\ \forall j$. This can be used to calculate $\ln(L_R) = T\ln(0.5)$ by substitution into equation (3.6). The maximum likelihood estimates can be used to calculate the unrestricted log-likelihood function value from equation (3.6) and then the likelihood ratio can be calculated. The restricted likelihood value $\ln(L_R) = -453.3$ and the maximized value is $\ln(L_U) = -429.3$. The quantity $-2\ln(L_R/L_U) = 48.0$. There are four restrictions, because there are four distribution points restricted to be 0.5. Hence $\chi^2_{.99}(4) = 13.3$; since the computed value exceeds the test statistic, we reject the hypothesis of equal proportions.

This is an unusual example, because the F_j are monotonically increasing as the bid price increases (although that is what we would expect, randomness in responses often leads to non-monotonic values of the F_j). Compare it with an example drawn from a study of sewage treatment in Barbados (see McConnell and Ducci). The households were interviewed in person, and asked if they would be willing to pay the given amount in increased water bill for the installation of a sewage system.[1] There are ten bid prices, and an approximately equal number of respondents for each price. The results are given in Table 3.2. The bid prices are given in 1988 \$Barbadian. (In 1988, the exchange rate was about \$Barbadian2 = \$US1.)

The Barbados example differs in several ways. First, there are more bid prices, and hence smaller intervals between bid prices. Further, the total number of interviews completed in the Barbados case is less than in the Albemarle/Pamlico Sound case. In Table 3.1, the number of interviews is 654, while for Barbados, the number is 426. As a consequence, the number of observations per cell is much smaller in Table 3.2, increasing the variance and helping to create the situation in which the portion of 'no' responses decreases as the bid price increases.

From the parameter estimates of the fourth column, we see that the empirical distribution of willingness to pay is not monotonically increasing. It tends to go up, so that a graph of this distribution would look reasonable if it were smoothed. But for five out of the ten bid prices, the probability of no goes down, not up. In retrospect, this results in part from having too many bid prices for the sample size, and too many prices at the upper end of the distribution. We discuss the problem of

[1] While the payment on part of a water bill is a good vehicle in the sense that it is plausible and associates payment with service, it suffers from an uncertain time dimension. The respondent does not know how long the payments will last. A good use of this vehicle would specify clearly the number of periods that the payment would last.

TABLE 3.2. Turnbull Estimates for Sewage Treatment in Barbados

Bid Price (t_j)	Number offered(T_j)	Number of No's (N_j)	$F_j(= N_j/T_j)$
20	44	15	0.341
60	40	31	0.775
80	41	30	0.732
120	47	33	0.702
160	47	43	0.915
200	40	36	0.900
240	42	39	0.929
320	43	39	0.907
440	42	41	0.976
600	40	39	0.975

choosing bids in Chapter 5.

In the following section, we develop the more general case that allows the calculation of these parameters of the empirical distribution of willingness to pay when the proportion of no's is not always increasing with the bid price. This is a form of smoothing pools bids conservatively. We also show how to use the empirical distribution to calculate the mean and variance of the lower bound of sample willingness to pay.

3.2.2 The Turnbull Estimator

When samples are large and as the offered price increases, the proportion of observed no responses to each bid should increase ($F_j \leq F_{j+1}$). In other words, as the bid price increases, we would expect the distribution function to monotonically converge to one for large sample sizes. However, as the previous example shows, in practice nothing guarantees this. Because of random sampling, we often observe non-monotonic empirical distribution functions (proportions of no responses) for some of the offered prices: i.e. $F_j > F_{j+1}$ for some j. In such cases we have two options. We can rely on the asymptotic properties of a distribution-free estimator and accept the small sample monotonicity problems. Or we can impose a monotonicity restriction on the distribution-free estimator. The second approach has come to be known as the Turnbull distribution-free estimator (see Turnbull (1976), Cosslett (1982), or Ayer *et al.*(1955)). It was originally used in contingent valuation by Carson, Hanemann *et al.* (1994) and Haab and McConnell (1997). Variants of it were employed by Duffield, by Kriström (1990) and by McFadden (1994).[2]

The unrestricted distribution-free estimator of the previous section does not guarantee that the probability of a no response will increase with the bid price. If a monotonically increasing distribution function is to be guaranteed, a monotonicity restriction $(F_j \leq F_{j+1}|\forall j)$ must be imposed and the set of $F_j's$ must be estimated simultaneously (the subsamples can no longer be treated as independent). For reference, Table 3.3 summarizes the definitions and parameter relations that will be used in deriving the Turnbull distribution-free estimator.

TABLE 3.3. Definitions and Relations for Turnbull Estimator

Parameter	Definition	Relation
f_j	$\Pr(\$t_{j-1} \leq WTP < \$t_j)$	
F_j	$\Pr(WTP \leq \$t_j)$	$F_j = \sum_{i=1}^{j} f_i$
f_j	$\{f_1, f_2, ..., f_{M+1}\}$	$f_j = F_j - F_{j-1}$
F_{M+1}	CDF at upper bound of WTP Typically $t_{M+1} = \infty$	$F_{M+1} = 1$
F_0	CDF at lower bound on WTP Typically $t_0 = 0$	$F_0 = 0$
M	Number of bids	
Y_j	Number of yes responses to bid t_j	
N_j	Number of no responses to bid t_j	
T_j	Total number offered bid t_j	$T_j = N_j + Y_j$

The log-likelihood function to estimate F_j, $j = 1, 2, ..., M$ subject to the monotonicity restriction $(F_j \leq F_{j+1}|\forall j)$ is

$$\ln L(F_1, F_2, ..., F_M|\mathbf{Y}, \mathbf{N}, T) = \sum_{j=1}^{M} [N_j \ln(F_j) + Y_j \ln(1 - F_j)]. \quad (3.8)$$

Imposing the monotonicity restriction $(F_j \leq F_{j+1})$, the log-likelihood maximization problem becomes

$$\max_{F_1, F_2, ..., F_M} \sum_{j=1}^{M} [N_j \ln(F_j) + Y_j \ln(1 - F_j)]$$

$$\text{subject to } F_j \leq F_{j+1} \forall j \quad (3.9)$$

[2] Carson, Hanemann *et al.* (1994) also developed a double-bounded version of the model, equally conservative in its use of data, that requires iterative ML methods to estimate.

For convenience, this problem can be written in terms of the probability mass points $\{f_1, f_2, ..., f_M, f_{M+1}\}$ rather than the distribution function $\{F_1, F_2, ..., F_M\}$, where $f_j = F_j - F_{j-1}$ is the weight of the distribution falling between price j and the previous price. Intuitively we can think of the f_j as the response to price increases. They should be positive because a higher proportion of respondents should answer no at a higher price. In this form, $F_j = \sum_{i=1}^{j} f_i$, $F_0 = 0$, and $F_{M+1} = 1$. The vector of probabilities $\mathbf{f} = \{f_1, f_2, ..., f_{M+1}\}$ represents a discrete form of the density function. Rewriting the likelihood function in terms of the unknown density parameters rather than the distribution function parameters, the likelihood maximization problem becomes

$$\max_{\mathbf{f}} \ln L(\mathbf{f}|\mathbf{Y}, \mathbf{N}, \mathbf{T}) = \sum_{j=1}^{M}(N_j \ln\left(\sum_{k=1}^{j} f_k\right) + Y_j \ln\left(1 - \sum_{k=1}^{j} f_k\right)) \tag{3.10}$$

subject to $f_j \geq 0$ for all j.

The Kuhn-Tucker first-order conditions for a maximum take the form

$$\begin{aligned} \frac{\partial \ln L}{\partial f_i} &= \sum_{j=i}^{M}\left(\frac{N_j}{\sum_{k=1}^{j} f_k} - \frac{Y_j}{1 - \sum_{k=1}^{j} f_k}\right) \leq 0 \\ f_i &\geq 0 \\ f_i \ln \frac{\partial L}{\partial f_i} &= 0. \end{aligned}$$

To find the solution to the likelihood maximization problem, the set of first order conditions must be solved recursively. By construction, this maximum likelihood problem ensures that $f_1 > 0$ so long as $N_1 \neq 0$. Therefore, the first order condition for f_1 always holds with equality so long as at least one respondent responded no to t_1 (i.e. at least one person has WTP less than the minimum offered price). Assuming this to be the case, solve for f_1 by assuming for the moment that $f_2 \neq 0$. The first two first-order conditions now hold with equality and can be differenced to find

$$\frac{\partial \ln L}{\partial f_1} - \frac{\partial \ln L}{\partial f_2} = \frac{N_1}{f_1} - \frac{Y_1}{1 - f_1} = 0. \tag{3.11}$$

This can be solved directly for f_1,

$$f_1 = \frac{N_1}{N_1 + Y_1}. \tag{3.12}$$

If $f_3 > 0$ we can subtract $\frac{\partial \ln L}{\partial f_3}$ from $\frac{\partial L}{\partial f_2}$ to obtain

$$f_2 = \frac{N_2}{Y_2 + N_2} - f_1.$$

Therefore, f_2 is positive if

$$\frac{N_2}{Y_2 + N_2} > \frac{N_1}{N_1 + Y_1}. \tag{3.13}$$

If the proportion of respondents saying 'no' to t_2 is strictly greater than the proportion saying 'no' to t_1, then the probability that WTP falls in the interval $(t_1, t_2]$ is positive and equal to the difference in the proportions. This pattern continues for the full vector of density estimates $\{f_1, f_2, ..., f_M, f_{M+1}\}$. If the proportion of no responses to each successive offered price monotonically decreases, then the distribution-free maximum likelihood estimate of the density point at price j is the observed proportion of no responses to price j less the sum of the density estimates for all previous prices:

$$f_j = \frac{N_j}{T_j} - \sum_{k=1}^{j-1} f_k.$$

By substitution, we find that the maximum likelihood estimation of the distribution function at each price point is

$$F_j = \sum_{k=1}^{j} f_k = \frac{N_j}{T_j}.$$

After recursive substitution for f_k, the maximum likelihood estimate for an arbitrary f_j simplifies to

$$f_j = \frac{N_j}{T_j} - \frac{N_{j-1}}{T_{j-1}}.$$

These maximum likelihood estimates have an intuitive interpretation. Our best estimate of the probability of a 'no' response to price j is the sample proportion of 'no' responses to that price. The maximum likelihood estimate for the probability that willingness to pay falls between two prices is therefore just the difference in the 'no' proportions between those prices, provided the response no proportions are monotonically increasing.

Recall that this derivation has assumed that the proportion of no responses to t_{j+1} is greater than the proportion of no responses to t_j for all j prices offered. Without loss of generality, suppose $\frac{N_2}{N_2+I_2} < \frac{N_1}{N_1+I_1}$, i.e., the proportion of respondents saying no to t_2 is less than the proportion of respondents saying no to t_1. The unconstrained maximum likelihood estimate of f_2 will be negative, causing a violation of the monotonicity assumption for a valid cumulative distribution function. If we impose the non-negativity constraint, then $f_2 = 0$ and $\frac{\partial L}{\partial f_2}$ becomes irrelevant. Assuming $f_3 \neq 0$, we can now subtract $\frac{\partial L}{\partial f_3}$ from $\frac{\partial L}{\partial f_1}$ with $f_2 = 0$ to obtain the Turnbull first-order conditions

$$\frac{\partial \ln L}{\partial f_1} - \frac{\partial \ln L}{\partial f_3} = \frac{N_1 + N_2}{f_1^*} - \frac{Y_1 + Y_2}{1 - f_1^*} = 0, \tag{3.14}$$

where the $*$ superscript denotes the Turnbull estimate.

Solving for f_1^*:

$$f_1^* = \frac{N_1 + N_2}{N_1 + N_2 + Y_1 + Y_2.} \tag{3.15}$$

Therefore, the Kuhn-Tucker solution to the problem of a breakdown in the monotonicity of the empirical distribution function from t_j to t_{j+1} is to combine the jth and $(j+1)^{th}$ sub-samples into one group and drop the $(j+1)^{th}$ price. Define $N_j^* = N_j + N_{j+1}$, $Y_j^* = Y_j + Y_{j+1}$, and then re-estimate f_j as follows

$$f_j^* = \frac{N_j^*}{Y_j^* + N_j^*} - \sum_{k=1}^{j-2} f_k^*. \tag{3.16}$$

If f_j is still negative, then this process is repeated until a position f_1^* is computed such that $f_1^* > 0$. Then define $F_j^* = \frac{N_j^*}{T_j^*}$.

A Procedure to Calculate the Turnbull Distribution-Free Estimator

1. *For bids indexed* $j = 1, ..., M$, *calculate* $F_j = \frac{N_j}{N_j + Y_j}$ *where* N_j *is the number of no responses to* t_j *and* Y_j *is the number of yes responses to the same bid, and* $T_j = N_j + Y_j$.

2. *Beginning with* $j = 1$, *compare* F_j *and* F_{j+1}.

3. *If* $F_{j+1} > F_j$ *then continue.*

4. *If* $F_{j+1} \leq F_j$ *then pool cells* j *and* $j+1$ *into one cell with boundaries* $(t_j, t_{j+2}]$, *and calculate* $F_j^* = \frac{N_j + N_{j+1}}{T_j + T_{j+1}} = \frac{N_j^*}{T_j^*}$. *That is, eliminate bid* t_{j+1} *and pool responses to bid* t_{j+1} *with responses to bid* t_j.

5. *Continue until cells are pooled sufficiently to allow for a monotonically increasing CDF.*

6. *Set* $F_{M+1}^* = 1$.

7. *Calculate the PDF as the step difference in the final CDF:*

$$f_j^* = F_j^* - F_{j-1}^*.$$

When these steps are taken, we arrive at a set of $f_1^*, ...f_{M^*+1}^*$ and related $F_1^*, ...F_{M^*}^*$ that have the property that the proportion of no responses declines as the bid price increases. We have done a minimal amount of conservative smoothing. In the remainder of the following exposition we assume that either the responses are monotonic from the start or that they have been smoothed as in this procedure.

3.3 Variance-Covariance Matrix

Once the estimates of the distribution function are properly pooled to guarantee monotonicity, the Turnbull estimates of the cumulative distribution function can be treated as unrestricted maximum likelihood estimates of the empirical distribution function. In other words, once the monotonicity violations are removed, the inequality constraints become non-binding and the maximum likelihood problem can be treated as unrestricted:

$$\max_{F_1, F_2, ..., F_M} \ln L(F_1, F_2, ..., F_M | \mathbf{Y}^*, \mathbf{N}^*) \tag{3.17}$$

$$= \sum_{j=1}^{M^*} \left[N_j^* \ln(F_j) + Y_j^* \ln(1 - F_j) \right],$$

and yields maximum likelihood estimates of: $F_j^* = \frac{N_j^*}{T_j^*}$, where the M^* prices now represent the pooled price ranges.

A lower bound on the variance of these estimates can be found by inverting the negative of the matrix of second derivatives of the log-likelihood function. The matrix of second order conditions for a maximum is a diagonal matrix with $\frac{\partial^2 \ln L(F_1, F_2, ..., F_M | Y^*, N^*)}{\partial F_j^2}$ on the diagonal and zeros off the diagonal. The negative of the inverse of the matrix of second derivatives is therefore a diagonal matrix with zeros off the diagonal and $\left[-\frac{\partial^2 \ln L}{\partial F_j^2} \right]^{-1} = \left[\frac{N_j^*}{F_j^{*2}} - \frac{Y_j^*}{(1-F_j^*)^2} \right]^{-1} = \frac{F_j^*(1-F_j^*)}{T_j^*}$, for $j = 1, 2, ..., M^*$, on the diagonal. This implies that covariance$(F_j, F_k) = 0$ for $j \neq k$. The maximum likelihood estimate of the probability of a no response to an arbitrary price j is therefore equal to the sample proportion of no responses to that price, $F_j^* = \frac{N_j^*}{T_j^*}$ with a variance on the estimator of

$$V(F_j^*) = \frac{F_j^*(1 - F_j^*)}{T_j^*}. \tag{3.18}$$

The Turnbull treats the set of responses to price j as a series of independent draws from a binomial distribution with probability of willingness to pay falling below the bid: $F_j^* = \frac{N_j^*}{T_j^*}$, and probability of willingness to pay falling above the price equal to the complement. The variance of the Turnbull estimated cumulative distribution function will be recognized as the variance of (T_j^*) draws from a binomial distribution with probabilities F_j and $(1 - F_j)$. Therefore, within a specific grouping of respondents, the Turnbull treats the yes/no responses as independent draws from a binomial distribution.

The variances of the f_j^*'s are also straightforward. Since F_j^* and F_{j-1}^* have zero covariance

$$V(f_j^*) = V(F_j^*) + V(F_{j-1}^*) = \frac{F_j^*(1 - F_j^*)}{T_j^*} + \frac{F_{j-1}^*(1 - F_{j-1}^*)}{T_{j-1}^*}. \tag{3.19}$$

The covariance (f_i^*, f_j^*) is

$$\begin{aligned} cov(f_i^*, f_j^*) &= cov(F_i^* - F_{i-1}^*, F_j^* - F_{j-1}^*) \\ &= cov(F_i^*, F_j^*) - cov(F_{i-1}^*, F_j^*) \\ &\quad -cov(F_i^*, F_{j-1}^*) + cov(F_{i-1}^*, F_{j-1}^*) \\ &= \left\{ \begin{array}{ll} -V(F_i^*) & j - 1 = i \\ -V(F_j^*) & i - 1 = j \\ 0 & \text{otherwise.} \end{array} \right\} \end{aligned} \tag{3.20}$$

The covariance between any two non-consecutive f_i is zero.

3.4 Lower Bounds for Mean and Median Willingness to Pay

Thus far we have dealt with the estimation of the distribution of willingness to pay. Now we turn to the estimation of measures of central tendency for willingness to pay. Because the Turnbull only uses the information contained in responses to provide estimates of the distribution function, any estimate of mean or median willingness to pay will similarly only use the minimal amount of information.

3.4.1 Median Willingness to Pay

The Turnbull provides an estimate of the range in which median willingness to pay falls. Since the no-response proportions are consistent estimates of the distribution point masses at each price, the price for which the distribution function passes 0.5 is the lower bound on the range of median WTP. The next highest price represents the upper bound on the range of median WTP. For example, if 30% of respondents say no to \$10, and 55% say no to \$15, then median willingness to pay will fall between \$15-\$20. The median represents the price for which the probability of a no response equals 0.5. Since the Turnbull only gives point mass estimates at a discrete number of points, the median can only be defined within a range.

3.4.2 A Lower Bound Estimate for Willingness to Pay

A Single Price Case

For simplicity, consider a case in which all individuals are offered the same price t. In this case, a conservative estimate of expected willingness to pay will be the product of the offered price and the probability of willingness to pay being above the price: $t \cdot (1 - F(t))$. To see why this is a conservative estimate consider the general expression for the expected value of the random variable WTP, assumed to be distributed between 0 and U:

$$E(WTP) = \int_0^U W dF_W(W), \tag{3.21}$$

where U is the upper bound on the range of WTP. By partitioning the range of willingness to pay into two sub-ranges according to the offered price $[0, t)$, and $[t, U]$, the expected value of willingness to pay can be written

$$E(WTP) = \int_0^t W dF_W(W) + \int_t^U W dF_W(W). \tag{3.22}$$

Because $F_W(W)$ is a cumulative distribution function it is increasing. Hence replacing the variable of integration by the lower limit will result in an expression less than or equal to $E(WTP)$, that is, a lower bound on willingness to pay

$$E(WTP) \geq \int_0^t 0 dF_W(W) + \int_t^U t dF_W(W) = t \cdot (1 - F_W(t)). \tag{3.23}$$

The equality holds by assuming that $F_W(U) = 1$. The expression states that expected willingness to pay is at least as great as the offered price multiplied by the probability of a yes response to the offered price. For example, if the offered price is \$10 and the sample probability of a yes response is 0.25, then expected willingness to pay must be at least \$2.50.

We can identify this measure of willingness to pay as $E_{LB}(WTP) = t\cdot(1-F_W(t))$, the lower bound on expected willingness to pay. Substituting in the Turnbull estimate for $F_W(t)$, we obtain a consistent estimate of the lower bound on expected willingness to pay

$$E_{LB}(WTP) = t \cdot \frac{Y}{T}. \tag{3.24}$$

The Multiple Price Case

A similar procedure first employed by Carson, Hanemann *et al.* (1994) can be used to define a lower bound on willingness to pay when M^* distinct prices are randomly assigned to respondents. (Throughout this section we use the notation f_j^* and F_j^*. These refer to the pooled data if the original data are not monotonic. Otherwise they refer to the original data.) Recall the definition of willingness to pay from equation (3.21)

$$E(WTP) = \int_0^U WdF_W(W) \tag{3.25}$$

where U is the upper bound on the range of WTP. The range of willingness to pay can now be divided into M^*+1 subranges: $\{0-t_1, t_1-t_2, ..., t_{M^*}-U\}$. Using these ranges, expected willingness to pay can be written as

$$E(WTP) = \sum_{j=0}^{M^*}\left[\int_{t_j}^{t_{j+1}} WdF_W(W)\right] \tag{3.26}$$

where $t_0 = 0$, and $t_{M^*+1} = U$. Because $F_W(W)$ is an increasing function, we know that $\int_{t_j}^{t_{j+1}} WdF_W(W) \geq \int_{t_j}^{t_{j+1}} t_j dF_W(W)$. Hence we can write

$$E(WTP) \geq \sum_{j=0}^{M^*} t_j \left[F_W(t_{j+1}) - F_W(t_j)\right] \tag{3.27}$$

where we use $\int_{t_j}^{t_{j+1}} t_j dF_W(W) = t_j\left[F_W(t_{j+1}) - F_W(t_j)\right]$. For calculating this sum, one needs the results $F_W(0) = 0$ and $F_W(U) = 1$.

Substituting in the consistent estimator for $F_W(t_j)$, and simplifying notation so $F_W(t_j) = F_j^*$, a consistent estimate of the lower bound on willingness to pay is

$$E_{LB}(WTP) = \sum_{j=0}^{M^*} t_j\left(F_{j+1}^* - F_j^*\right) \tag{3.28}$$

where $F_j^* = \frac{N_j^*}{T_j^*}$, $F_0^* = 0$, and $F_{M^*+1}^* = 1$. This lower bound estimate of willingness to pay has an intuitive interpretation. By multiplying each offered price by the probability that willingness to pay falls between that price and the next highest price, we get a minimum estimate of willingness to pay. The estimated proportion of the sample that has willingness to pay falling between any two prices is assumed to have willingness to pay equal to the lower of those two prices. This estimate is appealing because it offers a conservative lower bound on willingness to pay for all non-negative distributions of WTP, independent of the true underlying distribution. Even though the true distribution of willingness to pay is unknown, $E_{LB}(WTP)$ will always bound expected willingness to pay from below as long as the true distribution of willingness to pay is defined only over the non-negative range. In practice, $E_{LB}(WTP)$ represents the minimum expected willingness to pay for all distributions of WTP defined from zero to infinity.

Using a similar procedure, an upper bound on willingness to pay can be defined as: $E_{UB}(WTP) = \sum_{j=0}^{M^*} t_{j+1}^* \left(F_{j+1}^* - F_j^*\right)$. The problem here, however, lies in the definition of t_{M^*+1}. Since p_{M^*} is the highest offered bid it is necessary to define the upper bound on the range on willingness to pay using an ad hoc method. Income is a possibility, but income can lead to large estimates of the upper bound. Other measures are possible but will be difficult to defend against a charge of being arbitrary.

One advantage of the lower bound estimate of WTP is the distribution of the estimator. Since the f_j^*'s are normal and the t_j are fixed, the $E_{LB}(WTP)$ is also normal. Normality makes its variance worth computing. Rewriting the expected lower bound in terms of the probability mass estimates gives

$$E_{LB}(WTP) = \sum_{j=0}^{M^*} t_j \cdot f_{j+1}^*. \tag{3.29}$$

The variance of the lower bound estimate is

$$V(E_{LB}(WTP)) = \sum_{j=0}^{M^*} t_j^2 V\left(f_{j+1}^*\right) + \sum_{i=1}^{M^*} \sum_{j=1}^{M^*} t_j t_i \underset{i \neq j}{cov} \left(f_{j+1}^*, f_{i+1}^*\right). \tag{3.30}$$

Recalling that $V(f_j^*) = V(F_j^*) + V(F_{j-1}^*)$, and

$$cov(f_i^*, f_j^*) = \left\{ \begin{array}{ll} -V(F_i^*) & j-1=i \\ -V(F_j^*) & i-1=j \\ 0 & \text{otherwise.} \end{array} \right\}$$

The variance of the expected lower bound simplifies to

$$V(E_{LB}(WTP)) = \sum_{j=1}^{M^*} \frac{F_j^*(1-F_j^*)}{T_j^*}(t_j - t_{j-1})^2 \tag{3.31}$$

$$= \sum_{j=1}^{M^*} V\left(F_j^*\right)(t_j - t_{j-1})^2. \tag{3.32}$$

The variance can be used for constructing hypothesis tests and confidence intervals about $E_{LB}(WTP)$. Because $E_{LB}(WTP)$ is a linear function of the asymptotically normal maximum likelihood distribution function estimates f_j^*, $E_{LB}(WTP)$ will be normally distributed with mean defined in equation (3.28) and variance defined in equation (3.31):

$$E_{LB}(WTP) \sim N\left(\sum_{j=0}^{M^*} t_j(F_{j+1}^* - F_j^*), \sum_{j=1}^{M^*} \frac{F_j^*(1-F_j^*)}{T_j^*}(t_j - t_{t-1})^2\right). \tag{3.33}$$

Procedure for Computing Lower Bound Willingness to Pay From a CV Survey with Multiple Prices

1. *Calculate the proportion of no responses to each offered price by dividing the number of no responses by the total number of respondents offered each price. Denote this* F_j^*. *These are derived from pooling if necessary. Recall that* $F_0^* = 0$ *and* $F_{M^*+1}^* = 1$. *These represent consistent estimates of the probability of a no response to each offered price.*

2. *Calculate* $f_{j+1}^* = F_{j+1}^* - F_j^*$ *for each price offered. These represent consistent estimates of the probability that willingness to pay falls between price* j *and price* $j+1$. *To calculate the probability that willingness to pay is between the highest bid* (t_M) *and the upper bound* (t_{M+1}), *we define* $F_{M^*+1} = 1$. *This means that no respondents have willingness to pay greater than the upper bound.*

3. *Multiply each offered price* (t_j) *by the probability that willingness to pay falls between it and the next highest price* (t_{j+1}) *from step 2. We do not need to perform this calculation for the interval* $0 - t_1$ *since it entails multiplying the probability by zero.*

4. *Sum the quantities from step (3) over all prices to get an estimate of the lower bound on willingness to pay:* $E_{LB}(WTP) = \sum_{j=0}^{M} t_j(F_{j+1}^* - F_j^*)$. *In an analogy with consumer surplus, one*

can think of this estimate as the sum of marginal values times quantity adjustments, or the integral over quantity in a demand curve.

5. *Calculate the variance of the lower bound as*

$$V(E_{LB}(WTP)) = \sum_{j=1}^{M^*} \frac{F_j^*(1-F_j^*)}{T_j^*}(t_j - t_{j-1})^2.$$

Example 8 *Willingness to Pay Estimates for the Turnbull*

In a test of real versus hypothetical responses to hypothetical referenda, Cummings *et al.* (1997) perform an experiment in which one random sample is offered a single hypothetical payment (t) of \$10.00 to provide a good, and a second sample is made the same offer except told the payment of \$10.00 is real. Their results are summarized in Table 3.4. Because only a single bid was offered, the Turnbull estimate of

TABLE 3.4. Hypothetical and Real Responses for a Single Price

	Hypothetical	Real	Total
No	102	73	175
Yes	84	27	111
Total	186	100	286

the probability of a no response is simply the proportion of respondents responding no to that bid. The probability of a no response can be estimated as: $F(\$10) = 102/186 = 0.548$ for the hypothetical experiment, and $F(\$10) = 73/100 = 0.730$ for the real experiment. The respective variances are: $V(F(\$10)) = 0.00133$ for the hypothetical responses and $V(F(\$10)) = 0.00197$ for the real responses. The t-statistics for significant difference from zero are 15.03, and 16.45 respectively. The t-statistic for difference in means is 3.17.[3]

A lower bound estimate of willingness to pay is found by multiplying the offered price by the estimate of the probability of a yes $(1 - F(\$10))$. For the hypothetical data, expected willingness to pay is $\$10 \cdot (1 - 0.548) = \$4.52$ with an estimated variance of 0.133. For the real data, the lower bound estimate of expected willingness to pay is $\$10 \cdot (1 - 0.73) =$

[3]The test statistic for difference in means is: $t = \frac{\mu_1 - \mu_2}{\sqrt{\sigma_1^2 + \sigma_2^2}}$ where μ is the relevant mean, σ^2 is the relevant variance.

\$2.70 with an estimated variance of \$0.197. To test the significance of the difference between the two means the standard test for the significance of the difference between two normally distributed variables can be used. The t-statistic is $(\$4.52 - \$2.70)/\sqrt{0.133 + 0.197} = 3.17$. This simple test rejects the hypothesis that willingness to pay in the real and hypothetical experiments is equal.

In a study with several bid prices, Duffield reports the results of a contingent valuation survey to value wolf recovery in Yellowstone National Park. The recorded responses are summarized in the first three columns of Table 3.5.

TABLE 3.5. Turnbull Estimates with Pooling

			Unrestricted	Turnbull	
t_j	N_j	T_j	F_j	F_j^*	f_j^*
5	20	54	0.370	0.343	0.343
10	15	48	0.313	Pooled back	Pooled back
25	46	81	0.568	0.568	0.225
50	55	95	0.579	0.579	0.011
100	106	133	0.797	0.797	0.218
200	82	94	0.872	0.872	0.075
300	72	81	0.889	0.889	0.017
300+	-	-	1	1	0.111

The fourth column represents the unrestricted maximum likelihood estimate of the cumulative distribution function. As can be seen, the responses to the price of \$10 violate the monotonicity assumption for a standard distribution function: $F_{\$10} < F_{\$5}$. Pooling the \$10 and \$5 responses results in the Turnbull distribution and probability mass point estimates reported in the last two columns. Other than the \$10 responses, all other sub-samples satisfy the monotonicity assumption. Using the definition in equation (3.29), we calculate $E_{LB}(WTP)$

$$
\begin{aligned}
&= \sum_{j=0}^{M^*} t_j \cdot f_{j+1}^* = 0 \cdot 0.343 + 5 \cdot 0.225 + 25 \cdot 0.011 + 50 \cdot 0.218 \\
&\quad +100 \cdot 0.075 + 200 \cdot 0.017 + 300 \cdot 0.111 \\
&= \$56.50.
\end{aligned}
$$

The variance is given by $V(E_{LB}(WTP))$

$$\begin{aligned}
&= \sum_{j=1}^{M^*} \frac{F_j^*(1-F_j^*)}{T_j^*}(t_j - t_{j-1})^2 \\
&= \frac{0.343 \cdot 0.657}{102}(5-0)^2 + \frac{0.568 \cdot 0.432}{81}(25-5)^2 + \\
&\quad \frac{0.579 \cdot 0.421}{95}(50-25)^2 + \frac{0.797 \cdot 0.203}{133}(100-50)^2 + \\
&\quad \frac{0.872 \cdot 0.128}{94}(200-100)^2 + \frac{0.889 \cdot 0.111}{81}(300-200)^2 \\
&= \$29.52.
\end{aligned}$$

For this example, the mean lower bound willingness to pay is \$56.50 and with a standard error of 5.50. The 95% confidence interval for lower bound WTP is $56.50 \pm 1.96 \cdot 5.50$ (\$45.71, \$67.28). One of the advantages of the $E_{LB}(WTP)$ is the ease of constructing a confidence interval or performing hypothesis tests, because of the asymptotic normality.

3.5 A Distribution-Free Estimate of WTP

The lower bound estimator assumes that the full mass of the distribution function falls at the lower bound of the range of prices for each mass point. For example, if the probability that willingness to pay falls between t_1 and t_2 is estimated to be 0.25, then for purposes of calculating the lower bound estimate of WTP, the full 25% of the distribution function is assumed to mass at t_1. There are methods for interpolating between price points to describe the distribution between prices. The simplest of such methods is a simple linear interpolation between prices used by Kriström (1990). Instead of assuming a mass point at the lower end of the price range, we can assume that the distribution function is piece-wise linear between price points. Assuming the survivor function is piece-wise linear between prices makes the calculation of the area under the survivor function a matter of geometry. The survivor function between any two prices t_j and t_{j+1} forms a trapezoid with area equal to

$$\begin{aligned}
\int_{t_j}^{t_{j+1}} (1 - F_W(w))dw &= \left(1 - F_{j+1}^*\right)\left(t_{j+1} - t_j\right) \\
&\quad + \frac{[F_{j+1}^* - F_j^*)]}{2}\left(t_{j+1} - t_j\right) \\
&= \left(t_{j+1} - t_j\right)\left(1 - \frac{(F_j^* + F_{j+1}^*)}{2}\right). \qquad (3.34)
\end{aligned}$$

The right hand term in equation (3.34) shows that the piece-wise linear estimator for expected willingness to pay assumes that willingness to pay is distributed uniformly between prices with the probability of a yes equal to the mid-point of the estimated probabilities at the two prices. For example, if 25% respond 'yes' to \$5 and 20% respond 'yes' to \$10 then the probability that WTP is less than any value between \$5 and \$10 is assumed to be 22.5%.

Summing over all offered prices yields the estimate of expected willingness to pay

$$\begin{aligned} E(WTP) &= \sum_{j=0}^{M} \int_{t_j}^{t_{j+1}} [1 - F_W(w)]\, dw \\ &= \sum_{j=0}^{M} (t_{j+1} - t_j) \left(1 - \frac{(F_j^* + F_{j+1}^*)}{2}\right). \end{aligned} \quad (3.35)$$

Two problems occur in calculating expected willingness to pay in this manner: $t_0 = 0$ and $t_{M+1} =$ upper bound on WTP are not offered prices, and as such, the survivor functions at these prices are undefined. If WTP is assumed to be non-negative then the survivor function (distribution function) goes to one (zero) at a price of zero. Unless one has some insight that WTP can be less than zero, it is sensible that the probability of willingness to pay being less than zero is zero. Also, by definition, the survivor function can be defined to go to zero at the upper bound on willingness to pay. However, unless a price is offered such that all respondents say no to the highest price, any assumed upper bound for willingness to pay will be arbitrary. Differentiating equation (3.35) with respect to t^*_{M+1} yields the marginal change in expected willingness to pay for a one unit increase in the upper bound:

$$\frac{\partial E(WTP)}{\partial t^*_{M+1}} = \frac{1 - F^*_M}{2}. \quad (3.36)$$

As the arbitrary upper bound is increased by one dollar, the measure of expected willingness to pay will always increase. On the other hand, the lower bound estimate is independent of the upper bound. A respondent who answers 'yes' to the highest bid is assumed to have WTP equal to the highest bid. Where the piece-wise linear estimate can provide a point estimate of expected WTP, the lower bound estimate provides a more conservative estimate independent of ad hoc assumptions about the upper tail.

3.6 Covariate Effects in the Turnbull Model

The distribution-free models can provide estimates of sample willingness to pay while ignoring variation in willingness to pay due to variation in individual characteristics or variation in the characteristics of the good being valued. For policy purposes, or for purposes of investigating the properties of CV surveys it is often useful to assess changes in WTP due to changes in covariates. The term covariates will be assumed to include individual or scenario-specific characteristics. For example, the NOAA panel protocol states that respondents to CV surveys should be sensitive to the scope of the injury to the good being valued. The larger the injury, the more respondents should be willing to pay for restoration or future avoidance. To test for scope effects, split-sample CV studies are often designed to offer separate sub-samples different sizes of the same good to value. Assuming that all respondents are asked the same question, as is necessitated by the Turnbull estimator, undermines the ability to test for scope effects.

Recall the Turnbull maximum likelihood problem from equation (3.17):

$$\begin{aligned} &\max_{F_1,F_2,\ldots,F_M} \ln L(F_1,F_2,\ldots,F_M|Y^*,N^*) \\ &= \sum_{j=1}^{M^*}\left[N_j^*\ln(F_j)+Y_j^*\ln(1-F_j)\right], \end{aligned} \tag{3.37}$$

where for current purposes it is assumed that the responses satisfy the monotonicity restrictions. Suppose the full sample is sub-divided into K classes indexed $\{k=1,\ldots,K\}$. For each price offered there are now K classes of respondents. The total number of responses from class k to price j is represented by T_{jk}. For example, if one group has high income, and another low income, then $K=2$. Likewise the number of yes responses are indexed Y_{jk}, and the probability of a no response by an individual in class k to price j is F_{jk}. Assuming the classes are independent, an estimate of the probability of a no response to each price for each class can be found by solving the likelihood maximization problem

$$\begin{aligned} &\max_{F_{jk}} \ln L(F_{jk}|Y_{jk},T_{jk}\forall j,k) \\ &= \sum_{k=1}^{K}\sum_{j=1}^{M^*}\left[N_{jk}^*\ln(F_{jk})+Y_{jk}^*\ln(1-F_{jk})\right]. \end{aligned} \tag{3.38}$$

Note however that because the classes are assumed independent, this likelihood maximization problem can be split into K separate likelihood maximization problems: one for each class. In other words, the Turnbull estimator handles covariates by splitting the sample into sub-samples according to the desired characteristics and calculating the Turnbull estimator for each sub-sample independently. Three problems arise:

1. Individuals must be classified into discrete subclasses: Split-sample scope effect tests are straightforward since by design they randomly split the sample. Estimating demographic effects however requires grouping individuals according to their personal characteristics. Some demographic classifications are straightforward, such as categorical income data, or characteristics that can be turned into dummy variables. But, continuous covariates (such as actual income data, or years of experience, or travel distances) require more arbitrary decisions to make them discrete.

2. The variance of the Turnbull distribution function estimates and consequently the variance of the estimated lower bound on WTP is inversely related to the sample size. The smaller the sample size the larger the variance (see equations (3.18) and (3.31)). The more classes to divide the sub-sample, the less information each sub-sample will contain and the less accurate the estimate of WTP.

3. The smaller the sample, the less likely that the resulting distribution function will be monotonic. Hence, there is a limit to the number of splits in the sample.

In practice, testing covariate effects is likely to be limited to one or two discrete covariates.

Example 9 *Contingent Valuation for Sewage Treatment in Barbados*

To illustrate the use of covariates, we employ the CV study of sewage treatment in Barbados that was used to show the possibility of non-monotonic willingness to pay distributions in Table 3.2. Now we investigate the effect of a dichotomous covariate on the distributions.

Prior to the contingent valuation survey, the Barbadian government ran a television program that extolled the virtues of the project that the contingent valuation program was assessing. Did the television program influence the responses in the CV survey sufficiently to affect the estimates of mean WTP? We demonstrate now that the answer is yes by splitting the sample into two groups–one group that saw the television program and another group that did not. In Table 3.6, we provide the two sets of raw data: the number of responses by bid price level and the number and proportion of no's, for the case where the respondent did not see the television program ($CTV = 0$) and for the case where the respondent did see the program ($CTV = 1$).

TABLE 3.6. A Turnbull Model for Sewage Treatment in Barbados

	$CTV = 0$			$CTV = 1$		
$BidPrice(t_j)$	T_j	N_j	$F_j(= N_j/T_j)$	T_j	N_j	$F_j(= N_j/T_j)$
20	29	9	0.310	15	5	0.333
60	31	24	0.774	9	7	0.778
80	26	19	0.731	15	10	0.667
120	32	21	0.656	15	12	0.800
160	34	33	0.971	13	10	0.769
200	30	29	0.967	10	9	0.900
240	31	30	0.968	11	9	0.818
320	24	23	0.958	19	16	0.842
440	30	30	1.000	12	11	0.917
600	29	29	1.000	11	10	0.909

Columns two through four pertain to the $CTV = 0$ data and columns five through seven are for $CTV = 1$. Reading down columns four and seven, one can see that while the general trend is for the probability of no to increase, the increase is not monotonic. Hence both sets of data must be pooled. The pooled results are provided in Table 3.7. For $CTV = 0$, there are four final cells, and for $CTV = 1$, there are five.

TABLE 3.7. Pooled Estimates for Covariate Effects

	$CTV = 0$				$CTV = 1$			
$BidPrice(t_j)$	T_j	N_j	F_j^a	f_j^b	T_j	N_j	F_j^a	f_j^b
20	29	9	0.310	0.310	15	5	0.333	0.333
60	89	64	0.719	0.409	24	17	0.708	0.375
120	—	—	—	—	28	22	0.786	0.078
160	119	115	0.966	0.247	—	—	—	—
200	—	—	—	—	40	34	0.850	0.064
440	59	59	1.000	0.034	23	21	0.913	0.063
>440	—	—	—	—	—	—	1.000	0.087

[a] $F_j = N_j/T_j$
[b] $f_j = F_j - F_{j-1}$

Using the formulas for the means and variances of the lower bounds on willingness to pay, we find that for $CTV = 0$, $E_{LB}WTP = \$28.44$ and for $CTV = 1$, $E_{LB}WTP = \$70.74$. (Note that for $CTV = 0$, $f^*_{M+1} = 0$ and for $CTV = 1$, $f^*_{M+1} = 0.087$.) This is a substantial difference and it appears that the viewing of the television program sponsored by the government in fact had an impact on willingness to pay. We can find out whether the difference in the means is statistically significant by exploiting the normality of the lower bound estimates. For $CTV = 0$, the variance is 9.34 and for $CTV = 1$, the variance is 260.65. The sample means are independent because the sub-samples are separate. Therefore, under the null hypothesis that the difference between the means is zero, the statistic

$$\frac{E_{LB}WTP_0 - E_{LB}WTP_1}{\sqrt{V_0 + V_1}}$$

(where the subscript 1 stands for $CTV = 1$ and 0 for $CTV = 0$) is normal with mean zero, variance 1. The calculated value for this statistic is

$$\frac{70.74 - 28.44}{\sqrt{9.34 + 260.65}} = 2.57.$$

This falls in a 1% critical region for rejecting the null hypothesis. We can therefore conclude that the lower bounds for mean willingness to pay are statistically different when respondents view the government-sponsored program. In fact, it appeared that the government was working to improve the likelihood that the sewage project would be adopted.

3.7 Conclusion

In this chapter we have reviewed simple approaches to the non-parametric treatment of discrete choice contingent valuation methods. The advantage of these approaches lies with their simplicity. Lower bounds of sample mean willingness to pay can be calculated from raw data without assuming any distribution for the unobserved component of preferences. The calculations can be made without resort to computers. Further, the transparency of the estimates gives them an especial cogency. There are, however, many situations where the researcher may need to estimate the effects of independent variables on responses or on willingness to pay. The non-parametric approaches allow only limited exploration of the effect of covariates.

4

The Distribution of Willingness to Pay

4.1 Introduction

In Chapters 2 and 3 we made simplifying assumptions for tractability and ease in estimation in the single-bid dichotomous-choice framework. Functional form and distributional assumptions helped focus on models that can be estimated by hand or in a standard probit or logit framework. Many of these assumptions come at the expense of utility consistency of the underlying decision framework, or more simply consistency with real world observations of behavior. This chapter focuses on models that arise when some of these assumptions are relaxed. We develop models that conform with the economic underpinnings of preferences. These models, while more intuitive, are also more complicated. The additional complications arise in model development, estimation and interpretation. The topics described here and in Chapter 5 are treated as mutually exclusive complications that arise in the estimation of the dichotomous choice models. Obviously, multiple complications can arise at once in practice, adding another layer of complexity.

To use the results of contingent valuation models, researchers use means, medians, or other measures of central tendency of willingness to pay. In the two previous chapters, we have emphasized the two step nature of empirical analysis of contingent valuation: the parameter estimation step and the willingness to pay calculation step. These two steps are sometimes in conflict. In this section, we examine criteria for consistency between the two steps, simple diagnostic tests for suitable distributions of willingness to pay, and a set of simple models that build in consistency between the two steps.

4.2 Central Tendency for Willingness to Pay

In many of the standard models that are estimated, for example, the linear utility function, the implied distribution of willingness to pay will have properties that are not apparent from the utility function. For example, the linear utility function with an additive error implies that willingness to pay will range from minus to plus infinity. Other standard models have different problems. Unsatisfactory results at the calculation stage have led to a variety of 'fixes' for obtaining WTP. However, many of these fixes are often inconsistent with the statistical and economic underpinnings and with the original model of choice. In previous work (Haab and McConnell 1998) we have suggested three criteria for a valid measure of WTP from dichotomous choice contingent valuation studies. Hanemann and Kanninen argue for similar criteria. These criteria are based on the notion that the services, scenarios, public goods, or whatever else the contingent valuation study attempts to value do not provide negative utility. This assumption may sometimes be wrong, but when negative willingness to pay is a possibility, special care in modeling must be taken.

4.2.1 Criteria for a Valid Measure of WTP

It is reasonable to ask the following of measures of willingness to pay:

1. Willingness to pay has a non-negative lower bound and an upper bound not greater than income.

2. Estimation and calculation are accomplished with no arbitrary truncation.

3. There is consistency between randomness for estimation and randomness for calculation.

The rationale for each of the criteria is discussed subsequently. Of the traditional models discussed in Chapters 2 and 3, only the Turnbull estimator satisfies the three criteria. Other models that move towards consistency with these criteria are discussed in later sections. Not all models that fail to satisfy the criteria are misspecified. If the probability that willingness to pay exceeds a bound is small enough, then the problem is minor. Further, when models fail to behave statistically, the problem in most cases is a poorly designed questionnaire, including a set of bids that fails to elicit responses that trace out the probability that an individual will pay a given amount.

Bounds on Willingness to Pay

In the context of valuing public goods with free disposal, WTP will be non-negative. As illuminated by Hanemann and Kanninen, willingness to pay should be bounded above by income and in most cases, bounded below by zero. In the occasional case where the respondent may dislike the CV scenario, regardless of price, then negative willingness to pay (compensation demanded), may be permissible. An example of negative willingness to pay appears in a study of the control of deer as pests in the Washington DC suburbs (see Curtis 1998). If the deer are controlled by hunting, the provision of the service may cause a reduction in well-being for respondents who are strongly sympathetic to animal rights. When individuals can simply ignore public goods, then negative willingness to pay can be ruled out.

Conceptually, the bounds on willingness to pay come most naturally from the expenditure function expression for willingness to pay. In Chapter 2, $m(k,j,u_k)$ is defined as the minimum expenditure function, the least amount of income needed to get respondent j to the utility provided by scenario $k, k=0,1$, given the current utility of $k=0$, represented by u_0. In this case, willingness to pay is defined as

$$WTP_j = m(0,j,u_0) - m(1,j,u_0).$$

Minimum expenditure at the baseline scenario, $m(0,j,u_0)$, equals income, y_j, by definition. Hence

$$WTP_j = y_j - m(1,j,u_0).$$

The most advantageous scenario conceivable would reduce the minimum expenditure to zero: $m(1,j,u_0)=0$, though this is hard to conjure up in practice. In this case, WTP_j equals y_j. When the new scenario offers nothing of value to the respondent, the expenditure function does not change, so that $m(1,j,u_0)=m(0,j,u_0)=y_j$. This gives a theoretical restriction on willingness to pay:

$$0 \leq WTP_j \leq y_j.$$

In practice, it is unlikely that the upper bound will be constraining for most CV studies, with the possible exception of health risk studies of poor people in poor countries. However, it may be feasible to define disposable income or disposable income per family member, yielding a sensible upper bound of willingness to pay. WTP will be negative if the minimum expenditures necessary to achieve the current utility level at the new scenario exceed current income.

For respondent j, willingness to pay will depend on income and the vector of covariates $\mathbf{z}$, $WTP(y_j,\mathbf{z}_j)$. This will be a random variable that reflects random preferences and depends on random parameters. The range of willingness to pay for an individual is zero to income. This leads to the following relevant restrictions.

1. The measure of central tendency of WTP, for example expected value, for an individual will be constrained by zero and income:

$$0 \leq EWTP(y_j, \mathbf{z}_j) \leq y_j.$$

This may hold even when the range of WTP is not restricted, as is the case for reasonable linear utility function models.

2. The sample mean (or sample mean of median) willingness to pay will be likewise constrained:

$$0 \leq \sum_{j=1}^{T} EWTP(y_j, \mathbf{z}_j)/T \leq \overline{y}$$

when $\overline{y}$ is the sample mean income for the sample size T. Similar expressions would hold for the median or other measures of central tendency for the individual.

In concept, WTP should be specified as a non-negative function and the error term should enter in a way that an infinite ranging error term is transformed into a zero to income support for the distribution of WTP. Specifying WTP to be non-negative and less than income ensures that the expectation of willingness to pay will be non-negative for the sample, and conditional expectations of willingness to pay will also be non-negative. If the distribution of willingness to pay is non-negative, then the mean will also be nonnegative. However, the converse is not true. A model which estimates a non-negative mean does not necessarily conform to theoretical restrictions and is not defensible on such grounds.

Estimation and Calculation of WTP without Arbitrary Truncation

Arbitrary truncation of WTP at the calculation step leads to arbitrary estimates of willingness to pay. Examples of truncation at the calculation stage include truncation at the maximum offered bid (Bishop and Heberlein; Sellar, Stoll and Chavas; Bowker and Stoll; Duffield and Patterson), and truncation at an arbitrary probability limit. For example, Brown, Champ, Bishop and McCollum truncate the distribution of WTP at the value of WTP such that $F_{WTP}(Z) = 0.01$. (Boyle and Bishop (1988) adopt a similar procedure). Truncating at zero typically makes the mean increase with the dispersion of WTP. An obvious way to handle the arbitrary truncation is to use the information about the range of WTP in the estimation process. Boyle, Welsh and Bishop, Duffield and Patterson, and Ready and Hu estimate truncated models which account for the truncation at zero in the estimation stage. This creates another problem because models which are truncated at zero tend to have a fat tail, as we discuss below.

Consistency between Randomness for Estimation and Randomness for Calculation

If the model is estimated under the assumption that $E(WTP)$ can extend over the infinite range, then arbitrary truncation raises the awkward question of why this truncation information is used for calculation but not for estimation. But a more troublesome implication from truncating willingness to pay in the calculation stage stems from the inconsistency between the distribution used for estimation and the one used for calculating WTP. If the distribution of WTP is known to have lower and upper bounds which are narrower than implied in the estimation stage, then the initial model is misspecified. In addition, the resulting measures of WTP are not expectations in the statistical sense, because they fail to take the expectation across the range of WTP initially assumed.

4.2.2 Implications of Assuming Standard Forms

Adopting these criteria as reasonable for willingness to pay outlines the difficulties that sometimes arise with some of the standard approaches for modeling dichotomous choice contingent valuation responses. The assumption of functional forms that are equivalent to linear-in-income utility with an additive stochastic component lead to measures of WTP with undesirable economic and statistical properties in some circumstances.

These potential problems are briefly defined and discussed below.

Unbounded Measures of WTP

To see the problem of bounds on WTP note that the derivation of WTP typically depends upon an error term with an infinite support: typically a normally or logistically distributed error. Recall the definitions of WTP (from Chapter 2) for the linear utility function model as it depends on the random error and an M-dimensional vector of covariates, $\mathbf{z}$

$$WTP_j = \mathbf{z}_j\boldsymbol{\alpha}/\beta + \varepsilon_j/\beta$$

the varying parameter model

$$WTP_j = \frac{\alpha_0 + \mathbf{z}_j\gamma + \varepsilon_j^*}{\delta\mathbf{w}_j}$$

and linear willingness to pay model

$$WTP_j = \mathbf{z}_j\gamma + \eta_j. \tag{4.2}$$

In all three cases, the error term (ε or η) is assumed to have a support range of $(-\infty, \infty)$. As such WTP is not bounded from above or below. If the good to be valued is such that WTP is bound from above or below, as is almost always the case, estimation of these standard models is inappropriate.

The log-linear in income random utility model bounds WTP from above by income, but WTP is not bounded from below:

$$WTP_j = y_j - y_j \exp\left(-(\frac{\mathbf{z}_j\boldsymbol{\alpha}}{\beta} + \frac{\varepsilon_j}{\beta})\right).$$

In this model, as $\varepsilon_j \longrightarrow \infty$, $WTP \longrightarrow -\infty$. The exponential willingness to pay model

$$WTP_j = \exp(\mathbf{z}_j\gamma + \eta_j)$$

bounds willingness to pay from below at zero but not from above. Unboundedness of WTP leads to difficulties when the good being valued has free disposal. For example, the standard utility difference model allows a decrease in utility from consumption even if the good is free to consume and free to dispose of. Because of the unrestricted error term, the random utility difference model may predict a utility decrease, and therefore a negative WTP. While there are occasions when utility would decline for some respondents, these are unusual and should be modeled explicitly.

Diagnosing the Distribution of Willingness to Pay

The combined effects of the distribution assumed for the error term and the functional form of the indirect utility function or WTP function can lead to estimates of expected WTP outside the realm of feasible values. We first look at properties of the distribution that lead mean WTP to be negative, and then we examine the fat tail problem that arises when non-negative distributions are assumed.

Simple descriptive diagnostics can help determine whether violation of the upper or lower bound is serious. We look at a linear model, which is more likely to violate the constraints. Consider the model $u_{kj} = \mathbf{z}_j\boldsymbol{\alpha}_k + \beta y + \varepsilon_k$, $k = 0$ for the status quo and $k = 1$ for the improved scenario, where $\varepsilon \equiv \varepsilon_1 - \varepsilon_0 \sim N(0, \sigma^2)$. With this model, the parameter estimates $\boldsymbol{\alpha}/\sigma$, β/σ ($\boldsymbol{\alpha} \equiv \boldsymbol{\alpha}_1 - \boldsymbol{\alpha}_0$) are recovered.

As described in Chapter 2, expected (and median) WTP for respondent j is

$$EWTP_j = \mathbf{z}_j\boldsymbol{\alpha}/\beta$$

where the expectation is taken over the random preference term and the parameters are assumed to be known constants. A reasonable approach for simple diagnostics lies in creating the graph of one minus the cumulative density function of WTP, $1 - F_{WTP}(x)$, which is the probability that WTP exceeds x. For the case of a normal error, the probability that WTP exceeds x is

$$\begin{aligned} \Pr(WTP &\geq x) = 1 - F_{WTP}(x) = \\ \Pr(\mathbf{z}_j\boldsymbol{\alpha}/\beta + \varepsilon_j/\beta &\geq x) = \Phi\left(\frac{\mathbf{z}_j\boldsymbol{\alpha}}{\sigma} - \frac{\beta x}{\sigma}\right) \end{aligned} \tag{4.3}$$

where Φ is the standard normal CDF. This is a convenient form, because parameter estimation delivers the normalized parameter $\boldsymbol{\alpha}/\sigma$, β/σ so that Φ can even be plotted by hand with a few values from a table of normal variates. When there are no covariates, $\mathbf{z}_j\boldsymbol{\alpha}$ is constant, and there is only one graph. Otherwise graphs are conditional on the $\mathbf{z}_j$'s.

The difficulty with the linear model can be seen here. In principle, the probability that willingness to pay is greater than or equal to zero ought to equal one ($1 - F_{WTP}(0) = 1$). However, with the model in (4.3), $1 - F_{WTP}(0) = \Phi\left(\frac{\mathbf{z}_j\boldsymbol{\alpha}}{\sigma}\right)$ for normal error. This probability cannot in general equal one, and can only approach one as $\mathbf{z}_j\boldsymbol{\alpha}/\sigma$ gets very large. For very small variances, the expression approaches zero. To show the influence of the negative range on WTP, write the expected value of WTP as

$$EWTP = \int_0^{\infty}[1 - F_{WTP}(x)]dx - \int_{-\infty}^{0} F_{WTP}(x)dx.$$

The mean of a variate can be calculated as the area under one minus the CDF in the positive range less the area under the CDF in the negative range (see Rohatgi, p. 86). It follows that if WTP is defined as a nonnegative random variable, then

$$EWTP = \int_0^{\infty}[1 - F_{WTP}(x)]dx \tag{4.4}$$

and $1 - F_{WTP}(0) = 1$.

If the distribution is substantially negative, then $EWTP$ may also be negative. In Figure 4.1, if area B is greater than area A, then $EWTP$ will be negative. This occurs when $\Pr(WTP < 0) > 0.5$. All the in-

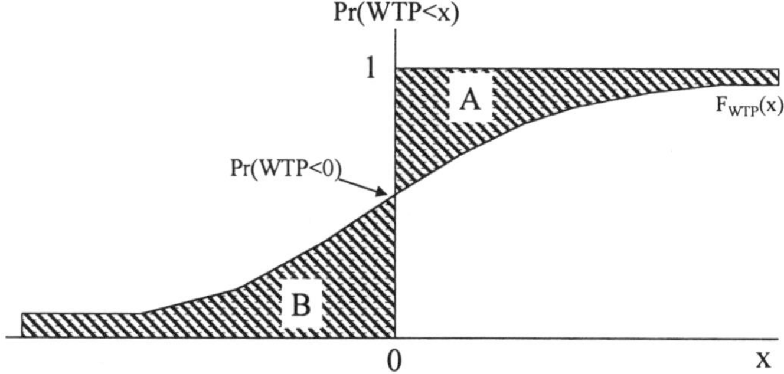

FIGURE 4.1. Expected Willingness to Pay

formation about willingness to pay can be found from this graph. First, it demonstrates the difficulty with the linear model. If households value the improvement described by the CV scenario, then they should have unambiguous improvements in utility when the price is zero, and the probability that WTP is greater than zero ought to equal one. Yet when $t = 0$, $\Pr(WTP > 0) = \Phi(\mathbf{z}_j\boldsymbol{\alpha}/\beta)$, often not close to one.

The right hand tail is less likely to cause problems. For example, the probability that willingness to pay exceeds income, in the normal error case, is

$$\Pr(WTP_j > y_j) = \Phi\left(\frac{\mathbf{z}_j\boldsymbol{\alpha} - \beta y_j}{\sigma}\right).$$

Provided $\beta > 0$ as expected, and y_j large, this value will be comfortably close to zero, or equal to zero for tabled values of $\Phi(\cdot)$.

Combining the left and right hand tail information provides an expression for the probability that WTP lies within the bounds:

$$\Pr(0 \leq WTP_j \leq y_j) = F_{WTP}(y_j) - F_{WTP}(0)$$

which for the normal case becomes[1]

$$\Phi\left(\frac{\mathbf{z}_j\boldsymbol{\alpha} - \beta y_j}{\sigma}\right) - \Phi\left(\frac{\mathbf{z}_j\boldsymbol{\alpha}}{\sigma}\right).$$

If this probability is substantially less than one, and it is likely to be so because $\Phi(\mathbf{z}_j\boldsymbol{\alpha}/\sigma)$ is less than one, then the researchers may be concerned about the range of WTP. In the more general case, the probability that WTP lies in the bounds is given by $F_{WTP}(y_j) - F_{WTP}(0)$.

[1] This suggests the possibility of estimating a truncated model: $\Pr(yes) = \Pr(\alpha - \beta t + \varepsilon > 0 | -\alpha < \varepsilon < \beta y)$.

Consequently, graphing the function $F_{WTP}(x)$ against x is a good way to get a feel for the data.

Example 10 *Misuse of Non-negative Willingness to Pay*

Several studies have misinterpreted equation (4.4) to represent a truncated mean or a method for generating a positive willingness to pay from models estimated on WTP defined over the positive and negative range. This method is often attributed to Hanemann (1984 or 1989). In an attempt to demonstrate the incorrect use of equation (4.4), Hanemann shows that if WTP is distributed as a logistic random variable such that $F_{WTP}(x) = \left(1 + e^{-\alpha-\beta t}\right)$, one could conceivably use equation (4.4) to calculate a positive expression: $EWTP^{\cdot} = \frac{1}{\beta}\ln\left(1 + e^{\alpha}\right).$ However, as Hanemann remarked not once but twice (Hanemann 1984, 1989), $EWTP^{\cdot}$ is not an appropriate measure of welfare, and further, equation (4.4) is wrong if the assumed underlying willingness to pay is not a nonnegative variable. Hanemann (1989) states, "I was careful [in 1984] to add the qualification that WTP be a non-negative random variable, but evidently not careful enough. Several subsequent papers have employed the formula in [our equation (4.4)] without noting the qualification or have applied it to empirical models where WTP was not in fact constrained to be a non-negative random variable." Thus, when underlying WTP is defined over both the positive and negative range, then simply integrating under the positive range of the distribution is incorrect. The expression $EWTP^{\cdot} = \frac{1}{\beta}\ln\left(1 + e^{\alpha}\right)$ will unambiguously overestimate true WTP based on the underlying distribution.

The Problem of Fat Tails

The fat tails problem typically manifests itself in unrealistically large estimates of expected WTP from models that bound WTP from below. The distribution of WTP may be theoretically restricted to lie between zero and income, or some other practical upper bound. Whether this is an effective constraint is an empirical issue. Many problems in regression analysis are subject to theoretical bounds that have no practical impact. For example, a regression with GNP on the left hand side could be modeled as a non-negative variable, but in practice the probability that GNP is negative is extremely close to zero, and so the estimation of a truncated model gives the same parameters as a simple OLS model. To understand the fat tails problem, we first use an example of a CV dataset with a difficult response pattern to demonstrate the consequences. This example provides a demonstration of why fat tails leads to difficult modeling decisions. We then discuss the problem in more detail.

Example 11 *Diagnosing the Fat Tails Problem*

We use a dataset from a contingent valuation survey to estimate WTP for the construction of a waste water disposal system designed to clean up the beaches in Montevideo, Uruguay.[2] Ten randomly assigned bids ranging from \$US5.82 to \$US145.50 were offered to residents of a neighborhood of Montevideo for the waste disposal system. Table 4.1 reports the response totals for each bid.

TABLE 4.1. Response Summary: Montevideo Dataset

Bid	Number Offered	Number No
\$5.82	130	67
14.55	132	78
25.45	128	84
36.36	125	85
54.55	123	85
76.36	122	92
90.91	127	100
109.10	129	100
127.30	130	103
145.50	130	111

Two simple dichotomous choice models are estimated on the 1276 responses: a simple linear WTP function with no covariates:

$$WTP_L = \gamma + \varepsilon$$

and an exponential WTP function with no covariates:

$$WTP_e = e^{\gamma+\varepsilon}.$$

The exponential WTP function restricts WTP to be positive while the linear WTP can take on negative values. The errors are assumed to be normally distributed with mean zero and constant variance (σ^2). Table 8.5 presents the results of probit estimation of the two models. Estimated expected WTP for the linear WTP function model is:

$$E(WTP_L) = \gamma = -\$26.33.$$

[2] See McConnell and Ducci. We call this the Montevideo dataset.

TABLE 4.2. WTP Function Estimates

Variable	Parameter	Model* Linear	Exponential
constant	$\frac{\gamma}{\sigma}$	−0.158	0.499
		(0.064)	(0.144)
Bid	$-\frac{1}{\sigma}$	−0.006	–
		(0.001)	
ln(Bid)	$-\frac{1}{\sigma}$	–	−0.277
			(0.037)
Log-likelihood		−741.7	−740.7
$-2\ln(L_R/L_U)$		55.0	58.4

*Standard errors in parentheses. All coefficients are different from zero at 99% level of confidence.

The corresponding estimate for the exponential model is

$$E\left(WTP_e\right) = \exp(\gamma + \frac{\sigma^2}{2}) = \$4096.49.$$

The linear model allows negative values for WTP despite having no negative bids offered. The symmetry of the normal distribution places an equal mass of the distribution above and below the mean. Since there is a large number of no responses to the low bids in the Montevideo data, the linear model puts a large mass in the negative WTP region. This results in a negative estimate of expected WTP. On the other hand, the exponential WTP function skews the distribution of WTP.

Figure 4.2 illustrates the estimated cumulative distribution functions for the two models. The linear WTP function CDF crosses 0.5 in the negative support of WTP. Over 50% of respondents who were offered the lowest bid in this sample responded no, causing the mean and median to pass through 0.5 at a value lower than \$5.82.[3] The estimated distributional standard error is \$166.67(= 1/0.006), implying that over 68% of the mass of the estimated distribution will be spread over the range (−\$166.67, \$166.67), because 68% of the area of a standard normal lies within plus or minus one standard error of the mean. The exponen-

[3] In a comprehensive survey of the incentive effects of various CV formats, Carson, Groves and Machina argue that when respondents are faced with bids so low that they seem unrealistic, the respondents are likely to replace these bids with 'expected cost'. This would lead to a greater proportion of no's than one would otherwise expect.

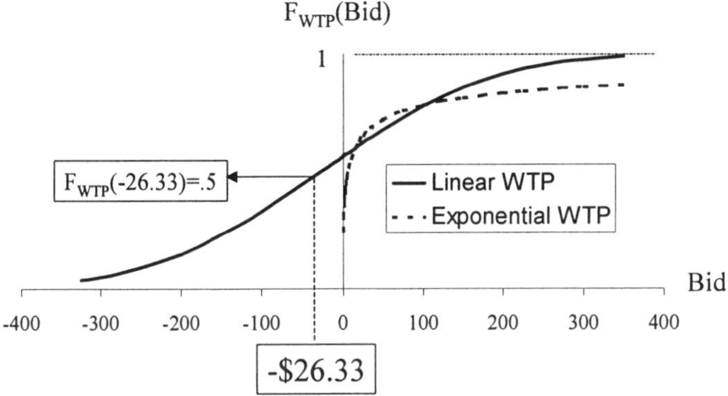

FIGURE 4.2. Estimated CDF's for Montevideo Example

tial WTP function forces a large portion of the mass into the upper tail of the distribution. The significant underestimation of the no responses at the highest bid means that the exponential model is assigning too much weight to WTP values in the upper tail of the distribution when calculating expected WTP. The linear model accurately predicts the percentage of no responses at the highest bid.

Sensitivity of E(WTP) to Distributional Specification

The problems with the tails of the distribution are analogous to the problems of out-of-sample prediction in a regression model. The tails of the distributions are defined well beyond the typical range of offered bids. The assumed distribution outside the range of offered bids can have a large impact on the estimated expected WTP. In the case of symmetric distributions, and infinite range on WTP, the differences between estimated WTP measures across distributional assumptions are typically small. Estimated CDF's tend to do a good job of passing through the range of median WTP as defined by the responses proportions.

Continuing the Montevideo example from above, we estimate two different linear models on the responses: a normal and logistic linear bid model and a normal and logistic log(bid) model. These are models of the form

$$WTP = \gamma + \varepsilon$$

for the linear model and

$$WTP = \exp(\gamma + \varepsilon)$$

for the exponential model. These are estimated as outlined in Chapter 2 by transforming $\Pr(WTP > bid)$, depending on the form of WTP and the distribution of the error. The parameter estimates are in Table 4.3.

TABLE 4.3. Linear and Exponential WTP Functions with Probit and Logit

Variable	Parameter	Model*			
		Linear		Exponential	
		Probit	Logit	Probit	Logit
constant	$\frac{\gamma}{\sigma}$	−0.158	−0.240	0.499	0.827
		(0.064)	(0.100)	(0.144)	(0.23)
Bid	$-\frac{1}{\sigma}$	−0.006	−0.010	–	
		(0.001)	(0.001)		
ln(Bid)	$-\frac{1}{\sigma}$	–		−0.277	−0.460
				(0.037)	(0.060)

*Standard errors in parentheses. All coefficients are different from zero at 99% level of confidence.

Expected $WTP = E(\gamma + \epsilon) = \gamma$ for the normal and logistic linear model; this comes to −\$26.33 for normal linear and −\$24.00 for the logistic linear. For the normal exponential model, expected $WTP = E(\exp(\gamma + \epsilon) = \exp(\gamma + 0.5\sigma^2) =$ \$4096.49. For the logistic exponential model, expected WTP is undefined because $\sigma = 1/0.46 = 2.17 > 1$ (see the Exponential Logistic Distribution section in Appendix B for an explanation). The symmetric linear models produce estimates of expected WTP that are close compared to the exponential models. The exponential model is sensitive to the assumed form of the error distribution.

In the situation where the researcher reasonably believes that WTP is non-negative, but models for unrestricted WTP provide negative $EWTP$, the probable cause is questionnaire design and bid price structure. When respondents answer 'no' too frequently at low bids, the graph of the function, $\Pr(WTP < t)$ will fall too low on the vertical axis, and may lead to negative $EWTP$ estimates. When WTP appears too high, a mechanical explanation is that respondents have not answered 'no' to a sufficient number of high bid price questions. In either case, short of redoing the survey, a reasonable strategy ought to be conservative, such as estimating the lower bound of $EWTP$ from a Turnbull estimator (Chapter 3). The lower bound of $EWTP$, calculated as $EWTP_{LB} = \sum_{j=0}^{M} f_{j+1}^{*} t_j$

from the responses in Table 4.3, equals \$38.23.[4] Since it is a lower bound on all non-negative measures of WTP, it is a reasonable statistical interpretation of the data, given the CV question and interview process.

4.2.3 Bound Probit and Logit Models

Bounds on willingness to pay can be implemented in two ways. One is to estimate an unconstrained linear model and truncate $EWTP$ at zero or income at the calculation stage. This is acceptable as long as $F_{WTP}(y_j) - F_{WTP}(0)$ is close to one, because the inconsistency between estimation and calculation is of small consequence for estimation. Truncating at zero may have a considerable impact on $EWTP$, but typically upper truncations do not. The second approach is to estimate a model that has the correct bounds, and to impose the same bounds in the estimation and calculation stages. Ready and Hu estimate a model which is bound from below and pinched from above (that is, has an estimated upper bound on WTP). In previous research, we have estimated a model based on the beta distribution that has a finite (zero to income) support for WTP (Haab and McConnell 1998). Both models require a complex likelihood function and in both cases convergence is difficult.

A direct way of deriving a model that bounds willingness to pay correctly is to specify the following model:

$$WTP_j = G(\mathbf{z}_j\gamma + \varepsilon_j)y_j$$

where $0 \leq G(\mathbf{z}_j\gamma + \varepsilon_j) \leq 1$ and $G'(\mathbf{z}_j\gamma + \varepsilon_j) \geq 0$. The function $G(\mathbf{z}_j\gamma + \varepsilon_j)$ is willingness to pay as a proportion of income. An especially tractable version of this model is

$$WTP_j = \frac{y_j}{1 + \exp(-\mathbf{z}_j\gamma - \varepsilon)}.$$

The error can be specified as logistic or normal.

If $\varepsilon \sim N(0, \sigma^2)$, then

$$\Pr(yes) = 1 - F_{WTP}(t) = \Phi\left(\frac{\mathbf{z}_j\gamma + \ln\left(\frac{y_j - t}{t}\right)}{\sigma}\right). \tag{4.5}$$

[4] This calculation requires that monotonicity be imposed, because when the price increases from 90.91 to 109.10, the proportion of no responses declines from 0.787 to 0.775. When these cells are merged as described in Chapter 3, the resulting F_j^* are monotonic.

It is readily seen that the numerator on the right hand side of (4.5) is a linear function of $\mathbf{z}_j$ and $\ln\left(\frac{y_j-t}{t}\right)$. The parameters associated with the regressors are $\left\{\gamma/\sigma, \frac{1}{\sigma}\right\}$. Equation (4.5) is therefore a contribution to the likelihood function from a simple probit model.

Similarly, if $\varepsilon \sim logistic(0,\sigma^2)$, then

$$\Pr(yes) = 1 - F_{WTP}(t) = \frac{1}{1+\exp[(-\mathbf{z}_j\gamma - \ln\left(\frac{y_j-t}{t}\right))/\sigma]}. \tag{4.6}$$

Equation (4.6) represents the contribution of a yes response to the logit likelihood function and therefore can be estimated as a simple logit with regressors $\left\{\gamma/\sigma, \frac{1}{\sigma}\right\}$. The procedure for estimating this bound probit or logit model is analogous to the procedure for estimating the probit and logit models of Chapter 2.

Procedure for Estimating the Bound Model

1. *Define the yes/no responses to the contingent valuation question such that yes is coded 1 and no is coded 0.*

2. *Define a data matrix* $\mathbf{X}$ *so that it contains the concatenation of the covariate matrix* $\mathbf{z}$ *and the income/bid term:* $\ln\left(\frac{y_j-t}{t}\right)$.

3. *Using any standard statistical software, run a probit or logit model with the 1/0 yes/no responses as the dependent variable, and the matrix* $\mathbf{X}$ *as the matrix of right hand side variables.*

4. *Recover the reported parameter estimates. The coefficients on the variables in the vector* $\mathbf{z}$ *represent estimates of* γ/σ. *The coefficient on the variable* $\ln\left(\frac{y_j-t}{t}\right)$ *is an estimate of* $1/\sigma$.

Measures of Central Tendency

For the bound probit and logit models, expected WTP does not have a closed solution. Numerical procedures are necessary to integrate under the survival function of WTP. Because both the logistic and normal distributions have median equal to zero, median WTP with respect to the error for the bound probit or logit model is

$$MD(WTP_j) = \frac{y_j}{1+\exp(-\mathbf{z}_j\gamma)}. \tag{4.7}$$

This function is easily calculated from the estimates of the parameters $\left\{\frac{\gamma}{\sigma}, \frac{1}{\sigma}\right\}$.

The marginal effects on median WTP are relatively easy to calculate. Two marginal effects are of interest: a marginal change in a covariate (z_{kj}) and a marginal change in the upper bound (y). For the moment, assume that z is independent of the upper bound. That is, suppose income is not an element of z. The effect of a change in one of an individual's z on median WTP is[5]

$$\frac{\partial MD(WTP_j)}{\partial z_{kj}} = \frac{y_j e^{-\mathbf{z}_j\gamma}}{(1+e^{-\mathbf{z}_j\gamma})^2} \cdot \gamma_k.$$

Dividing the marginal effect by median WTP yields

$$\frac{\partial MD(WTP_j)/MD(WTP_j)}{\partial z_{kj}} = \frac{e^{-\mathbf{z}_j\gamma}}{(1+e^{-\mathbf{z}_j\gamma})} \cdot \gamma_k = (1 - G(\mathbf{z}_j\gamma)) \cdot \gamma_k \tag{4.8}$$

where $G(\mathbf{z}_j\gamma \mid \varepsilon_j)$ at $\varepsilon_j = 0$, is the median proportion of the upper bound. The left hand side of equation (4.8) measures the percent change in median WTP for a marginal change in the covariate. So if median WTP is a small proportion of the upper bound then the parameters can approximately be interpreted as the percent change in median WTP for a unit change in the associated covariate. This is similar to a result for the marginal effects from the exponential model as described in Chapter 2. The two models produce similar results as the upper bound on WTP gets large. They can produce very different results if WTP is a large portion of the upper bound.

Example 12 *The Bound Probit with a Difficult Dataset*

We illustrate the bound probit model with two examples, the first from the misbehaving Montevideo data, and the second from the South Platte River study of Chapter 2. In the Montevideo study, we estimate only one model, the bound probit with an upper bound of income, with no covariates other than the bid. Hence the estimated model is

$$WTP_j = \frac{y_j}{1+\exp(-\gamma - \varepsilon_j)}.$$

The parameter estimates are given in Table 4.4. This dataset provides a good illustration of the effects of bounds. We have previously shown that the mean $WTP's$ for linear probit and logit models are $-\$24.00$ and $-\$26.33$ and $\$4096.49$ for the lognormal. The median for the lognormal

---

[5] If the covariate is y_j and y_j is not an element of z_j, the marginal effect on median WTP is just $G(\mathbf{z}_j\gamma)$. If y_j is an element of z_j, the marginal effect is $y_j G^2 \gamma_y + G$.

TABLE 4.4. Bound Probit for Montevideo Data

Parameter	Variable	Estimate (Standard Error)
Constant	γ/σ	−1.91 (0.14)
$\ln\left(\frac{y_j - bid}{bid}\right)$	$1/\sigma$	0.31 (0.03)
Log-likelihood		−767.4
$-2\ln(L_R/L_U)$		116.7

Parameters different from zero at 99% level of confidence.

was \$6.05. The estimates of willingness to pay are widely dispersed and in two cases, negative.

Using the parameter estimates in Table 4.4, we find the median estimate of WTP, based on equation (4.7) to be

$$MD(WTP_j) = \frac{\bar{y}}{1+\exp(-\gamma)} = \$9.85$$

for mean income, $\bar{y} = \$4410$. The mean, calculated numerically equals \$16.15.[6] These estimates are of course more plausible than the means from the linear models and the exponential willingness to pay models. But one can only regard them as a repair of a difficult dataset rather than well-founded estimates of WTP.

Example 13 *The Bound Probit on Well-Behaved Data*

To illustrate the bound probit in a case where the data is well-behaved, we turn to the South Platte River study. Table 4.5 reports the parameter estimates for two versions of the bound probit model. The first model sets the upper bound equal to household income:

$$WTP_j = \frac{hhinc_j}{1+\exp(-\mathbf{z}_j\gamma - \varepsilon_j)}$$

[6] Numerical approximation of the expected WTP function is carried out by approximating the integrand of: $E(WTP) = \int WTP(\varepsilon)f(\varepsilon)d\varepsilon$ as $\sum_{t=1}^{m} WTP(\varepsilon_t)f(\varepsilon_t)\Delta\varepsilon_t$ for points over the range of ε. For example for $f(\varepsilon)$ normal, set $m = 1000$, let $\varepsilon_1 = -10$ and $\Delta\varepsilon_t = 0.02$

and the second specification sets the upper bound equal to the highest offered bid \$100:

$$WTP_j = \frac{\$100}{1+\exp(-\mathbf{z}_j\gamma - \varepsilon_j)}.$$

The errors are assumed to be normally distributed, so that we estimate probits as described in the procedures above.

TABLE 4.5. Bound Probit Estimates: South Platte River Study

Parameter	Variable	Estimate (Standard Error)	Estimate (Standard Error)
		Upper Bound =hhinc	Upper Bound =\$100
Constant	γ_0/σ	−7.472	−1.848
		(1.635)	(0.819)
unlimwat	γ_1/σ	*−0.620	−0.931
		(0.412)	(0.452)
govtpur	γ_2/σ	0.853	0.973
		(0.421)	(0.464)
environ	γ_3/σ	1.167	1.904
		(0.538)	(0.594)
waterbil	γ_4/σ	−0.034	−0.046
		(0.018)	(0.020)
urban	γ_5/σ	*0.677	1.074
		(0.407)	(0.445)
$\ln\left(\frac{bound-bid}{bid}\right)$	$1/\sigma$	0.951	1.114
		(0.203)	(0.231)
Log-likelihood		−34.4	−30.4
$-2\ln(L_R/L_U)$		54.4	63.8

*All parameters except this different from zero at 95% level of confidence.

For transparency, we calculate the median WTP for the sample average individual as reported in the Table 2.1 of Chapter 2. For the model with household income as the upper bound,

$$MD(WTP) = \$54175/(1+\exp(-\bar{\mathbf{z}}\gamma)) = \$18.73 \qquad (4.9)$$

where $\gamma\bar{\mathbf{z}}$ is the inner product of the means of the covariates from Table 2.1 and the coefficients from Table 4.5:

$$-\bar{\mathbf{z}}\gamma/\sigma = 7.5709.$$

Numerical approximation (see the previous footnote) of the expected WTP functions yields an estimated expected WTP of \$31.55. If the upper bound is assumed to be equal to the highest bid (\$100), then median WTP is estimated to be \$14.22 and expected WTP is \$14.92. The upper bound has a much larger effect on expected WTP than median WTP.

For the income as upper bound model, median WTP is $0.00035 \cdot \bar{y}$. From equation (4.8), the marginal effects of covariates on median WTP are

$$\begin{aligned} \frac{\partial MD(WTP_j)/MD(WTP_j)}{\partial z_{kj}} &= (1 - G(\mathbf{z}_j\gamma)) \cdot \gamma_k \\ &= 0.99965 \cdot \gamma_k. \end{aligned} \tag{4.10}$$

This implies that the parameter estimates can be interpreted as the percentage change in median WTP for a one unit change in the associated covariate. From Table 4.5, a \$1 increase in the monthly water bill will on average decrease median WTP for the South Platte River restoration project by 3.5% $(-0.034/0.95 = 0.035)$.

4.2.4 WTP and the Tails of the Distribution

Bounding WTP between zero and some upper bound tends to decrease the gap between median and expected WTP. Further, decreasing the upper bound on WTP seems to have a larger impact on mean WTP than median WTP. Intuitively, the maximum likelihood estimates of the cumulative distribution function of any WTP function will tend to pass through the empirical distribution function of the responses as defined by the bid-response proportions. The Turnbull distribution-free estimator of Chapter 3 is an extreme example in which the estimated CDF of WTP is the observed empirical distribution function adjusted for monotonicity. In a parametric setting, the continuity of the assumed functional forms and distribution functions will reduce the ability of the estimated CDF to fit the empirical distribution, but the fitted relationship will come as close as possible to fitting the observed relationship subject to the imposed restrictions.

Because the median is the 50th percentile of the distribution, the estimated median WTP will tend to pass closely to the bid range in which the observed median falls. For example, if 45% of a sample responds 'no' to \$10 and 55% of the sample responds 'no' to \$20, then it is reasonable to expect that any estimated median WTP will fall in the \$10-20 range. For this reason it is typically observed that estimated median WTP is much less sensitive to distributional and functional form assumptions than mean WTP. However, if the empirical median (the 50th percentile of the observed distribution) falls above the highest or below the lowest bid then the median will be sensitive to functional form assumptions. The median will not be sensitive to distributional assumptions as long as the assumed error distributions have the same median (as is the case with the normal and logistic distributions).

Expected WTP is much more sensitive to the assumptions made about WTP. Because the expectation of WTP is taken across the full range of WTP (and not just the range of the offered bids), the result will be sensitive to the assumed form of the tails of the distribution. These tails extend well beyond the upper range of the offered bids. Researchers typically define the offered bids based on reasonable expectations about the true WTP. However, if the highest offered bid is such that a large portion of the sample responds 'yes' to the bid, then the resulting estimates of expected WTP will tend to be sensitive to specification assumptions.

Example 14 *The Impact of the Tails*

Consider once again the two examples used in this chapter: the Montevideo dataset and the South Platte River study of Loomis et al (2000). Table 4.6 gives the empirical distribution function of Montevideo data adjusted for monotonicity (see Chapter 3). The original data are given in Table 4.1.

TABLE 4.6. Empirical Distribution: Montevideo Data

Bid	$\Pr(WTP \leq Bid)$
$5.82	0.52
14.55	0.59
25.45	0.66
36.36	0.68
54.55	0.69
76.36	0.75
90.91	Pooled
109.10	0.78
127.30	0.79
145.50	0.85

The empirical median for this sample is less than the lowest bid of $5.82. As stated in the previous section, it is therefore expected that

TABLE 4.7. Central Tendencies of WTP: Montevideo Data

Functional Form	Distribution	$E(WTP)$	$MD(WTP)$
Linear	Normal	−\$26.33	−\$26.33
	Logistic	−\$24.00	−\$24.00
Exponential	Normal	\$4096.49	\$6.06
	Logistic	–	\$6.03

the estimated median will be sensitive to functional form and distributional assumptions. From the previous examples, where the parameters are given in Table 4.3, we calculate the estimated means and medians to demonstrate sensitivity to distribution. The median for each distribution is given by γ for the linear model and $\exp(\gamma)$ for the exponential function. For the exponential function, $EWTP = \frac{\sigma\pi}{\sin(\sigma\pi)}e^{\gamma}$ for the logistic function and $\exp(\gamma + 0.5\sigma^2)$ for the normal. Table 4.7 gives the means and medians for this data.[7] The estimated medians of WTP for the Montevideo study range from −\$26.33 to \$6.06. The means are quite dispersed when they converge. Note that in addition to the 52% of the empirical distribution that falls below the lowest bid, an additional 15% falls above the highest bid. One consequence is the sensitivity of estimated expected WTP to distributional and functional form assumptions: −\$26.33 for the linear probit, infinite (undefined) for the exponential logit, and \$4096.49 for the exponential probit. Because over 67% of the empirical distribution falls outside the relevant range of bids, the results are quite sensitive to the assumed distribution.

Consider now the South Platte River data. Table 4.8 gives the unadjusted and adjusted Turnbull empirical distribution function from Chapter 3.[8]

The tails of the empirical distribution are nailed down in this example. Because of the small sample size and large number of offered bids, a large number of cells had to be pooled to ensure monotonicity of the empirical distribution function. However, the well-defined tails lead to much less sensitive measures of expected and median WTP across functional forms and distributions. Table 4.9 summarizes the estimated mean and median WTP measures. Parameters for the linear and exponential models are in the appropriate table in Chapter 2. The bound model parameters

[7] As noted above, the expected WTP does not converge for the logistic distribution.

[8] Looking at pooled data for the Turnbull in a table can be confusing. A good way of dealing with pools is to realize that when monotonicity doesn't hold the price is thrown out and the observations are put in the cell with the lower price.

TABLE 4.8. Response Summary: South Platte River

Bid	Total Offered	Number No	$\Pr(WTP \leq Bid)$
$1	11	0	0
2	9	0	0
3	10	2	Pooled
5	10	1	0.15
8	10	5	Pooled
10	8	5	Pooled
12	8	3	Pooled
20	8	4	0.50
30	8	8	Pooled
40	6	4	Pooled
50	6	3	0.75
100	1	1	1.00

are found in Table 4.5. The covariate means are found in the first table of Chapter 2. Given the many different models, the range of WTP measures is fairly small. Without imposing bounds, the dispersion is much less than the Montevideo data. Imposing bounds in this case actually stretches out the distribution to make it fit the upper bound of *hhinc*, and as a consequence, increases the mean in that case. Because the measures for the linear and exponential are so close, there is no need to estimate the bound models.

TABLE 4.9. Central Tendencies of WTP: South Platte River

Functional Form	Distribution	$E(WTP)$	$MD(WTP)$
Linear	Normal	$20.40	$20.40
	Logistic	$20.70	$20.70
Exponential	Normal	$18.15	$13.50
	Logistic	$18.64	$13.51
Bound: Upper Bound =hhinc	Normal	$31.55	$18.73
Bound: Upper Bound =$100	Normal	$14.92	$14.22

4.2.5 Summary of Bounding WTP

Bounding willingness to pay is consistent with economic underpinnings and leads to more reliable and plausible estimates of WTP. One practical recommendation emerging from this discussion reflects most difficulties with CV. The problems lie in questionnaire design and bid construction, things that are not easily remedied once the survey has taken place. The set of offered bids should be designed to ensure that the tails of the distribution are well defined. Undefined tails can lead to unreliable measures of central tendency for WTP and raise doubts about estimated marginal effects of covariates on WTP. Sensitivity to distributional and functional form assumptions can be partially eliminated by well placed bids in the survey design. As in most issues of contingent valuation, the careful assessment of central tendency of WTP is best handled at the questionnaire design stage, where the distribution of bids is determined. A conservative approach when there are concerns about the distribution of response data is to calculate the sample mean using the Turnbull lower bound and then estimate an exponential willingness to pay function and calculate its median.

4.3 The Dispersion of Willingness to Pay

Previous sections focused on estimates of central tendency for willingness to pay, in particular, mean and median willingness to pay. Estimates of willingness to pay calculated as functions of estimated parameters are consistent as long as the parameter estimates themselves are derived from consistent estimators. This is a consequence of Slutsky's theorem (see Appendix A.3.1). In the case of maximum likelihood parameter estimates, consistency of the parameter estimates is established if (1) the distribution of WTP is correctly specified; (2) a global maximum to the likelihood function with respect to the parameter vector exists and is identified, and (3) the parameter space is a closed and bounded set. Combining these conditions with Slutsky's theorem, a willingness to pay estimate derived by substituting maximum likelihood parameter estimates into an expression for central tendency will yield a consistent estimate of the true population measure.

It is frequently useful to construct confidence intervals about WTP measures, or to make inferences concerning the measures. One must proceed carefully in constructing tests for WTP. As we have emphasized, there are three sources of randomness or variation in a willingness to pay measure: randomness of preferences, randomness of estimated parameters and variation across individuals in the sample.

In constructing confidence intervals or executing hypothesis tests, one must bear in mind these sources of randomness or variation. For example, there are several different variances that could be calculated. One can calculate a variance with respect to an individual's randomness of preferences, assuming parameters are known constants. Another variance would be the sample variance of the individual expectations of WTP. This variance would result from the effects of covariates across individuals. Further, in most cases, the willingness to pay measure is a non-linear function of parameters, so that when randomness of parameters is investigated, the distribution of the willingness to pay measure will not likely be normal, so that the calculation of a variance will not be sufficient for the construction of confidence intervals.

4.3.1 Uncertainty from Randomness of Preferences

A measure of dispersion of WTP due to preference uncertainty is found by computing the variance of WTP with respect to the assumed unobservable error ε. In general form, we can write an expression for WTP as

$$WTP = w\left(\mathbf{z}|\boldsymbol{\beta},\varepsilon\right)$$

where for the moment we will assume that there is a single individual in our sample and the parameter vector $\boldsymbol{\beta}$ is known with certainty. In this case, the distribution of WTP will depend only on the distribution for the unknown error term ε. This error is assumed to stem from inherent unobservability of preferences on the part of the researcher, and represents a random component of WTP. Expected WTP is found by integrating probability weighted WTP contributions over the support of ε:

$$E_{\varepsilon}\left(WTP\right) = \int_{\varepsilon} w\left(\mathbf{z}|\boldsymbol{\beta},\varepsilon\right) f\left(\varepsilon\right) d\varepsilon - g\left(\mathbf{z}|\boldsymbol{\beta}\right). \qquad (4.11)$$

The assumption of randomness for the error term leads to a variance for WTP of the form:

$$V_{\varepsilon}\left(WTP\right) = \int_{\varepsilon} \left(w\left(\mathbf{z}|\boldsymbol{\beta},\varepsilon\right) - E_{\varepsilon}\left(WTP\right)\right)^{2} f\left(\varepsilon\right) d\varepsilon.$$

The subscript ε indicates that the measure of variance for WTP is with respect to the random preference term. In terms of randomness of preferences, the variance of WTP is established through the assumptions made about the form of the random error term. For example, consider the linear willingness to pay model of the simple form:

$$WTP = \mathbf{z}\boldsymbol{\beta} + \varepsilon.$$

We assume that $\mathbf{z}\boldsymbol{\beta}$ is constant, implying that the variance of WTP is the variance of ε

$$V_{\varepsilon}(WTP) = V(\varepsilon).$$

Depending on the distribution assumed for ε, the form of the variance of WTP with respect to random preferences will vary. As another example, consider the exponential WTP function

$$WTP = e^{\mathbf{z}\boldsymbol{\beta}+\varepsilon}.$$

Once again assuming a known parameter vector for a single individual, an expression for the variances of WTP with respect to ε can be derived. Rewriting WTP as $WTP = e^{\mathbf{z}\boldsymbol{\beta}}e^{\varepsilon}$, the variance of WTP is

$$V_{\varepsilon}(WTP) = \left(e^{\mathbf{z}\boldsymbol{\beta}}\right)^2 V\left(e^{\varepsilon}\right).$$

If ε is assumed to be normally distributed with mean zero and variance σ_{ε}^2, then the variance of WTP will be

$$V_{\varepsilon}(WTP) = \left(e^{\mathbf{z}\boldsymbol{\beta}}\right)^2 e^{\sigma^2}\left(e^{\sigma^2} - 1\right)$$

where $V\left(e^{\varepsilon}\right) = e^{\sigma^2}\left(e^{\sigma^2} - 1\right)$. The randomness due to preferences is assumed by the researcher, and the form of the distribution is also assumed. This form is independent of the data and is to be distinguished from sampling variability and variability due to random parameters. This is simply the distributional variance of WTP for a given individual in the general population. By relying on Slutsky's theorem, we can obtain a consistent estimate of the variance of WTP with respect to preference uncertainty by substituting consistent parameter estimates into the expression for the variance.

Variances can be used for making inferences about willingness to pay, or confidence intervals for willingness to pay, on the assumption that the component $\mathbf{z}\boldsymbol{\beta}$ is known and constant. To investigate the full range of uncertainty, this assumption must be relaxed.

4.3.2 Variation across Individuals in the Sample

Often one wishes to use a sample mean estimate of WTP to expand to a population estimate of central tendency for WTP. Random sampling typically draws heterogeneous users with heterogeneous expected WTP. Calculating the sample variance can help us understand the variation across individuals. Assume again that the population parameters are known, but we observe a representative sample of WTP's from the general population. Consider a general expression for WTP for individual i of the form

$$WTP_i = w\left(\mathbf{z}_i|\boldsymbol{\beta}, \varepsilon_i\right). \tag{4.12}$$

Expression (4.11) shows that expected WTP is generally written as a function of the independent variables $\mathbf{z}_i$ and the known parameter vector. The sample average of the T estimates of WTP represents an estimate of the population average expected WTP:

$$\overline{E_\varepsilon\left(WTP_i\right)} = \frac{\sum_{i=1}^{T} g\left(\mathbf{z}_i|\boldsymbol{\beta}\right)}{T}$$

where $g\left(\mathbf{z}_i|\boldsymbol{\beta}\right) = E_\varepsilon\left(WTP_i\right)$. The interpretation of this quantity is the sample average expected WTP with respect to random preferences. That is, it is the sample average value of the measure of WTP found by taking the expectation of WTP with respect to individual randomness. This quantity is still a function of the parameter vector $\boldsymbol{\beta}$. This sample average measure of expected WTP has associated with it a sample variance. This variance is the variance in the sample average expected WTP caused by sampling from the general population. If another sample of T individuals were drawn from the population, we would obtain another sample average of expected WTP's. The relevant question now becomes, how much can we expect this sample average to vary from one sample to the next. Or another way of phrasing the question is how much does the sample average vary with respect to the true population mean WTP? The sample variance of expected WTP is

$$V_T\left(E_\varepsilon\left(WTP\right)\right) = \frac{\sum_{i=1}^{T}\left(E_\varepsilon\left(WTP_i\right) - \overline{E_\varepsilon\left(WTP_i\right)}\right)^2}{T}$$

where the subscript T denotes the variance of expected willingness to pay with respect to the T sample observations. The sample variance of expected WTP can be used to construct confidence intervals around the sample average to investigate the variability in expected WTP introduced by sampling from a general population. The sample average and sample variance of expected WTP are still a function of the parameters $\boldsymbol{\beta}$. The calculations for the sample mean and variance assume that the parameter vector is known and constant. Consistent estimates of these sample measures can be obtained by substituting consistent estimates of $\boldsymbol{\beta}$ into the appropriate expression. However, when estimates of the parameter vector are used to calculate WTP measures, a third source of randomness is introduced.

4.3.3 Uncertainty from Randomness of Parameters

For ease in exposition, consider again the single individual measure of expected WTP as defined in equation (4.11):

$$E_{\varepsilon}(WTP) = \int_{\varepsilon} w(\mathbf{z}|\beta, \varepsilon) f(\varepsilon) d\varepsilon = g(\mathbf{z}|\boldsymbol{\beta})$$

which depends on the covariate vector $\mathbf{z}$ and the parameter vector $\boldsymbol{\beta}$.

This derivation has assumed that the parameter vector is known. Since the parameters are estimated, they are random variables, and the resulting estimate of expected WTP is still a random variable. The expectation has been taken only with respect to preference uncertainty. We know from Slutsky's theorem that the estimate of expected WTP is a consistent estimate of true WTP. Researchers are often interested in making inferences or constructing confidence intervals about willingness to pay, but realistically wish to incorporate the uncertainty relating to the parameters into the confidence intervals. However, in almost all cases, willingness to pay is a non-linear function of parameter. For example, in the simplest case, where WTP is a linear function of covariates $WTP = \mathbf{z}\boldsymbol{\beta} + \varepsilon$, one estimates $\boldsymbol{\beta}/\sigma$ and $1/\sigma$, and calculates $\beta_k = \beta_k/\sigma \div 1/\sigma$ for each of the parameters, creating a vector of non-normalized parameters. Consequently willingness to pay will be a non-linear function of the parameters. In this case, willingness to pay will not be normally distributed, even when the parameters are. And depending on the algebraic formulation of willingness to pay as a function of parameters, willingness to pay may have a variety of different and unknown distributions. In this case, the best approach is to simulate the confidence interval. This can be done with the Krinsky and Robb procedure.

The Krinsky and Robb Procedure

The Krinsky and Robb procedure for estimating the variance of a function of estimated parameter relies on the asymptotic properties of the maximum likelihood parameter estimates to simulate the asymptotic distribution of the derived willingness to pay function. By repeatedly drawing from the asymptotic distribution of the parameter estimates, we can construct a Monte Carlo simulated distribution of the estimate of WTP. This method was introduced to the economic literature in the context of calculating the variance of estimated elasticities by Krinsky and Robb. Creel and Loomis (1991a,b) and Kling (1991) adapted the method to the non-market valuation context. The method is intuitive, but can be computationally intensive.

In general, consider a vector of maximum likelihood parameter estimates $\widehat{\boldsymbol{\beta}}$. Under certain regularity conditions: (1) the distribution of WTP is correctly specified, (2) a global maximum to the likelihood function with respect to the parameter vector exists and is identified, and (3) the parameter space is a closed and bounded set, the vector of parameter estimates is asymptotically normally distributed with mean $\boldsymbol{\beta}$ (the true parameter vector) and variance-covariance matrix equal to the Rao-Cramer lower bound:

$$V\left(\widehat{\boldsymbol{\beta}}\right) = \left[\frac{-E\partial^2 \ln L(\widehat{\boldsymbol{\beta}})}{\partial\boldsymbol{\beta}\cdot\partial\boldsymbol{\beta}'}\right]^{-1} \tag{4.12}$$

where $L(\widehat{\boldsymbol{\beta}})$ is the appropriate likelihood function (see Appendix A). Most computer packages will provide an estimate of the variance- covariance matrix of the parameter estimates.

The Krinsky-Robb procedure utilizes the asymptotic normal property of the maximum likelihood parameter estimates, and the property of a normal distribution that every K-dimensional normal distribution $N(\boldsymbol{\mu}, \boldsymbol{\Sigma})$ is a linear transformation of K independent $N(0,1)$ normals. Almost any numerical programming software permits random draws from an $N(0,1)$ distribution, and given the information on the asymptotic mean and variance of $\boldsymbol{\beta}$, the $N(0,1)$ variates can be transformed to $N(\widehat{\boldsymbol{\beta}}, \widehat{\mathbf{V}}\left(\widehat{\boldsymbol{\beta}}\right))$. To execute the Krinsky-Robb procedure, draw N observations on the parameter vector $\boldsymbol{\beta}$ from the estimated multivariate normal distribution of the parameters. At each draw, calculate the desired quantity (for example, expected WTP) resulting in N draws from the empirical distribution. The resulting N draws can be used to calculate the sample average value for WTP, the sample variance, or the quantiles of the empirical distribution. By ranking the draws in ascending (or descending) order, a 95% confidence interval around the mean can be found by dropping the top and bottom 2.5% of the observations. The typical confidence interval for willingness to pay constructed this way is not symmetric, which reaffirms the absence of normality for willingness to pay (see Kling 1991, and Creel and Loomis 1991a,b). The primary difficulty in carrying out the Krinsky and Robb procedure is getting the N parameter vector draws from the multivariate normal distribution.

Let $\widehat{\mathbf{V}}\left(\widehat{\boldsymbol{\beta}}\right)$ represent the $K \times K$ estimated variance-covariance matrix for the estimated parameter vector $\widehat{\boldsymbol{\beta}}$ of column dimension K. Let $\mathbf{x}_K$ be a K-dimensional column vector of independent draws from a standard normal density function. Finally let $\mathbf{C}$ be the $K \times K$ lower diagonal matrix square root of $\widehat{\mathbf{V}}\left(\widehat{\boldsymbol{\beta}}\right)$ such that $\mathbf{CC}' = \widehat{\mathbf{V}}\left(\widehat{\boldsymbol{\beta}}\right)$. The matrix $\mathbf{C}$ is sometimes referred to as the Cholesky decomposition matrix. Many software packages that have matrix algebra capabilities have Cholesky decomposition procedures (for example, LIMDEP and GAUSS will both calculate the Cholesky decomposition of a matrix).

A single K-vector draw from the estimated asymptotic distribution of the parameters $\boldsymbol{\beta}_d$ is

$$\boldsymbol{\beta}_d = \widehat{\boldsymbol{\beta}} + \mathbf{C}'\mathbf{x}_K.$$

Repeating this procedure N times produces a simulation of the full distribution of the parameter vector $\widehat{\boldsymbol{\beta}}$ distributed $N(\widehat{\boldsymbol{\beta}}, \widehat{\mathbf{V}}\left(\widehat{\boldsymbol{\beta}}\right))$ under ideal asymptotic conditions. Calculating the measure of WTP of interest at each draw will produce N observations from the asymptotic distribution of the WTP function.

Using the Krinsky and Robb procedure

1. *Estimate the model of interest.*
2. *Obtain the vector of parameter estimates* $\widehat{\boldsymbol{\beta}}$ *and the estimated variance-covariance matrix* $\widehat{\mathbf{V}}\left(\widehat{\boldsymbol{\beta}}\right)$.
3. *Calculate the Cholesky decomposition,* C*, of the variance-covariance matrix such that* $CC' = \widehat{\mathbf{V}}\left(\widehat{\boldsymbol{\beta}}\right)$.
4. *Draw* N *(typically* ≥ 5000*)* K*-dimensional vectors of independent standard normal random variables* x_K.
5. *For each* K*-dimensional vector* x_K*, calculate a new parameter vector from a multivariate normal distribution by calculating:* $\beta_d = \widehat{\beta} + C'x_K$.
6. *For each new parameter vector, calculate the* WTP *function of interest. This will result in* N *simulated values for the function.*
7. *Sort the* N *functional values in ascending order.*
8. *Calculate the empirical statistics (average, median, variance, percentiles) from the sorted values for the* WTP *function.*

Example 15 *South Platte River*

Consider the exponential WTP function from the South Platte River example: $WTP = e^{\mathbf{z}\beta+\varepsilon}$. Table 2.7 provides the parameter estimates for a normally distributed error term. Median WTP for the sample average individual is estimated to be \$13.45 (found by substituting the parameter estimates and mean covariates into the expression for median WTP with respect to the error term: $MD_{\varepsilon}(WTP) = e^{\mathbf{z}\beta}$). Krinsky and Robb estimates for median WTP were calculated using the above procedure for 50000 draws of the estimated parameter vector. At each of the draws median WTP is calculated, providing 50000 draws for median WTP from the empirical distribution. The approximate 95% confidence interval for median WTP is found by taking the 1250 and 48750 observations from the ranked median WTP draws. The Krinsky and Robb 95% confidence interval is [\$10.07, \$18.93]. Note that the Krinsky and Robb confidence interval is not symmetric about the estimated median WTP, as it would be if one were to calculate a confidence interval under the assumption that median WTP is normally distributed.

4.4 Conclusion

Throughout the book we have emphasized the two steps of obtaining welfare measures: the estimation step in which one gets parameter estimates, and the calculation step when the welfare measure is calculated, given the parameters. This chapter essentially covers the second step for WTP measures from contingent valuation. Willingness to pay when derived from contingent valuation studies is random for several reasons. Often it is a function of a random component of preferences, known to the respondent but not to the researcher. And when we compute WTP from a CV survey, we are almost always using parameters that are estimated, infusing another source of randomness. In this chapter we have reviewed the distribution of WTP from various estimators. And most often, researchers wish to estimate a sample mean WTP, because it is a logical step in the expansion of benefits to the population. We have investigated approaches to dealing with uncertainty from preferences and parameters and variation across individuals within the sample.

5

Topics in Discrete Choice Contingent Valuation

5.1 Introduction

Contingent valuation is not a single approach to valuation but a variety of approaches that one might view as a class of methods. We have dealt extensively with the dichotomous choice method because of its popularity but it is by no means the only method. In this chapter we investigate several alternative stated preferences approaches. One area that we give relatively light treatment is the area of stated preferences that has evolved from marketing and transportation literature. The group of methods such as paired comparisons, conjoint analysis, ranking methods often relies on many preference-assessing questions per individual. Chapter 10 discusses these methods briefly.

5.2 Contingent Valuation with Follow-Up Questions

The referendum model, with its apparent incentive-compatible properties, has at least one drawback. Under ideal circumstances it is inefficient relative to open-ended questions such as 'How much would you pay?'. Assuming that the responses are incentive-compatible and unbiased for both mechanisms, it takes many fewer responses to achieve a given variance about the mean or median willingness to pay for the open-ended compared with dichotomous choice questions. The open-ended approach may not be biased for many respondents, but it often leads to extreme responses. Hence researchers have looked for questionnaire design that would retain the incentive properties of discrete choice but would be more efficient. The double-bounded model, first developed by Hanemann, Loomis and Kanninen, was devised with this goal in mind. The greater efficiency of double-bounded models is supported by empirical and theoretical evidence. With a given number of interviews, more information on the distribution of willingness to pay is obtained, and this information lowers the variance of the estimates of mean WTP. The theoretical arguments for efficiency are presented in Hanemann, Loomis and Kanninen, who also provide some empirical evidence. Subsequent researchers have verified the initial findings of Hanemann, Loomis and Kanninen. Numerous other models have been derived as more general forms of the double-bounded model. We will catalogue these models as special cases of the general bivariate model. The bivariate model is a useful point of departure because in its most general form it involves the estimation of two separate models.

The essence of a double-bounded model is as follows. Respondents are presented with initial bid prices. Following their initial responses, they are given new prices, lower if their initial responses were no, higher if the responses were yes. Double-bounded models increase efficiency over single dichotomous choice models in three ways. First, the answer sequences yes-no or no-yes yield clear bounds on WTP. For the no-no pairs and the yes-yes pairs, there are also efficiency gains. These come because additional questions, even when they do not bound WTP completely, further constrain the part of the distribution where the respondent's WTP can lie. Finally, the number of responses is increased, so that a given function is fitted with more observations.[1]

5.2.1 The Bivariate Dichotomous Choice Model

Double-bounded models substantially increase the complexity of the analysis, because now the second question may depend in some way on the first question. There is potential for changes in the incentive-compatibility of the model, or at least some differences in the way respondents treat the first and second questions. It is instructive to look at the double-bounded model in a fairly general form to understand the nature of efficiency gains and the attendant problems. Let t^1 be the first bid price and t^2 be the second. The bounds on WTP are

1. $t^1 \leq WTP < t^2$ for the yes-no responses;
2. $t^1 > WTP \geq t^2$ for the no-yes responses;
3. $WTP \geq t^2$ for the yes-yes responses;
4. $WTP < t^2$ for the no-no responses.

[1] Although statisitically, the number of observations is not doubled as there is correlation between responses from a single individual.

The most general econometric model for the double-bounded data comes from the formulation

$$WTP_{ij} = \mu_i + \varepsilon_{ij}$$

where WTP_{ij} represents the jth respondent's willingness to pay, and $i = 1, 2$ represents the first and second answers. The μ_1 and μ_2 are the means for the first and second responses. We could make the same arguments by having the means depend on individual covariates: $\mu_{ij} = \mathbf{z}_{ij}\boldsymbol{\beta}$. This change in notation would not cause a substantive change in the arguments. This general model incorporates the idea that, for an individual, the first and second responses to the CV questions are different, perhaps motivated by different covariates, perhaps by the same covariates but with different response vectors, and with different random terms. Such a general model is not necessarily consistent with the increases in efficiency that follow intuitively from the Hanemann, Loomis and Kanninen formulation. If respondents consult the same preferences for each question, then this general model would collapse to the original framework, as we demonstrate below. For now, we assume that mean WTP is the same for all individuals, but potentially varies across question.

To construct the likelihood function, we first derive the probability of observing each of the possible two-bid response sequences (yes-yes, yes-no, no-yes, no-no). For illustration, the probability that respondent j answers yes to the first bid and no to the second is given by

$$\begin{aligned} \Pr(yes, no) &= \Pr(WTP_{1j} \geq t^1, WTP_{2j} < t^2) \\ &= \Pr(\mu_1 + \varepsilon_{1j} \geq t^1, \mu_2 + \varepsilon_{2j} < t^2). \end{aligned} \tag{5.1}$$

The other three response sequences can be constructed analogously. The jth contribution to the likelihood function becomes

$$\begin{aligned} L_j(\mu|t) &= \Pr(\mu_1 + \varepsilon_{1j} \geq t^1, \mu_2 + \varepsilon_{2j} < t^2)^{YN} \\ \times \Pr(\mu_1 + \varepsilon_{1j} &> t^1, \mu_2 + \varepsilon_{2j} \geq t^2)^{YY} \\ \times \Pr(\mu_1 + \varepsilon_{1j} &< t^1, \mu_2 + \varepsilon_{2j} < t^2)^{NN} \\ \times \Pr(\mu_1 + \varepsilon_{1j} &< t^1, \mu_2 + \varepsilon_{2j} > t^2)^{NY} \end{aligned} \tag{5.2}$$

where $YY = 1$ for a yes-yes answer, 0 otherwise, $NY = 1$ for a no-yes answer, etc. This formulation is referred to as the bivariate discrete choice model. If the errors are assumed to be normally distributed with means 0 and respective variances of σ_1^2 and σ_2^2 then WTP_{1j} and WTP_{2j} have a bivariate normal distribution with means μ_1 and μ_2, variances σ_1^2 and σ_2^2 and correlation coefficient ρ. By definition, $\rho = \sigma_{12}/\sqrt{\sigma_1^2+\sigma_2^2}$, and σ_{12} is the covariance between the errors for the two WTP functions. Given the dichotomous choice responses to each question, the normally distributed model is referred to as the bivariate probit model. The likelihood function for the bivariate probit model can be derived as follows. The probability that $WTP_{1j} < t^1$ and $WTP_{2j} < t^2$, i.e. the probability of a no-no response, is

$$\Pr(\mu_1 + \varepsilon_{1j} < t^1, \mu_2 + \varepsilon_{2j} < t^2) = \Phi_{\varepsilon_1\varepsilon_2}(\frac{t^1-\mu_1}{\sigma_1}, \frac{t^2-\mu_2}{\sigma_2}, \rho)$$

where $\Phi_{\varepsilon_1\varepsilon_2}(\cdot)$ is the standardized bivariate normal cumulative distribution function with zero means, unit variances and correlation coefficient ρ. Similarly, the probability of a no-yes response is

$$\Pr(\mu_1 + \varepsilon_{1j} < t^1, \mu_2 + \varepsilon_{2j} \geq t^2) = \Phi_{\varepsilon_1\varepsilon_2}(\frac{t^1-\mu_1}{\sigma_1}, -\frac{t^2-\mu_2}{\sigma_2}, -\rho).$$

The probability of a yes-no response is

$$\Pr(\mu_1 + \varepsilon_{1j} \geq t^1, \mu_2 + \varepsilon_{2j} < t^2) = \Phi_{\varepsilon_1\varepsilon_2}(-\frac{t^1-\mu_1}{\sigma_1}, \frac{t^2-\mu_2}{\sigma_2}, -\rho)$$

and the probability of a yes-yes response is

$$\Pr(\mu_1 + \varepsilon_{1j} \geq t^1, \mu_2 + \varepsilon_{2j} \geq t^2) = \Phi_{\varepsilon_1\varepsilon_2}(-\frac{t^1-\mu_1}{\sigma_1}, -\frac{t^2-\mu_2}{\sigma_2}, \rho).$$

Defining $y_{1j} = 1$ if the response to the first question is yes, and 0 otherwise, $y_{2j} = 1$ if the response to the second question is yes, and 0 otherwise, $d_{1j} = 2y_{1j} - 1$, and $d_{2j} = 2y_{2j} - 1$, the jth contribution to the bivariate probit likelihood function becomes

$$L_j(\mu|t) = \Phi_{\varepsilon_1\varepsilon_2}(d_{1j}\left(\frac{t^1-\mu_1}{\sigma_1}\right), d_{2j}\left(\frac{t^2-\mu_2}{\sigma_2}\right), d_{1j}d_{2j}\rho). \qquad (5.3)$$

The bivariate probit model is a general parametric model of two-response surveys. This is the model initially introduced to the contingent valuation literature by Cameron and Quiggin. While the model is quite general, the generality creates a dilemma for CV researchers. If the bivariate probit model is estimated on a dichotomous choice CV question with a follow-up, and the parameter estimates show that either the means, or variances or both differ between the initial bid-price and the follow-up, the researcher must decide which estimates to use to calculate the WTP measure. Also, if the means and variances differ between the initial bid-offer and the follow-up can we be sure that the distributional form itself is not different? It is not clear whether a finding of different means and variances across offered prices is a generalization of the findings in the CV literature, or an indication of an insufficiently sharp maintained hypothesis.

Example 16 *Bivariate Probit: Albemarle/Pamlico Sounds*

The following example comes from a study of WTP for water quality improvements in the Albemarle and Pamlico Sounds in eastern North Carolina. A full description of the data can be found in Huang, Haab and Whitehead. For this telephone survey, respondents were asked a dichotomous choice WTP question with follow-up to value water quality improvements in the Albemarle and Pamlico Sound or the Pamlico Sound only (respondents were offered one or the other scenario). The payment mechanism is annual increases in prices and taxes. Table 5.1 summarizes the bids and responses to the double-bound questions.

TABLE 5.1. Discrete Responses to Doubled-Bounded Questions

		First Question		Second Question	
First Price t^1	Second Price t^2	# of Yes's	# of No's	# of Yes's	# of No's
		Responses to t^1		Responses to t^2	
$100	$50	0	133	23	110
100	200	88	0	24	64
200	100	0	95	29	66
200	400	64	0	19	45
300	150	0	119	23	96
300	600	57	0	16	41
400	200	0	131	25	106
400	800	39	0	6	33

For each initial bid offered (t^1) there are two possible responses. The first row for each initial bid summarizes the no responses to that bid. The second row for each bid summarizes the yes responses. For example, an initial bid of $100 resulted in 88 yes responses and 133 no responses. Of the 133 no responses to $t^1 = \$100$, the follow-up bid ($t^2 = \$50$) resulted in 23 yes responses and 110 no responses. A total of 726 usable responses were obtained for this example. The average income for the 726 responses is $31426; 54% of respondents were offered the Pamlico

Sound only version of the survey. The remainder were asked to value improvements to both the Albemarle and Pamlico Sounds.

Table 5.2 reports the bivariate probit parameter estimates on the two responses. The first four rows are for the first response, the second four rows for the second response. The correlation coefficient is positive

TABLE 5.2. Parameter Estimates for Bivariate Probit

Variable	Estimate	Standard Error
Constant	−0.07	0.15
t^{1*}	−0.002	0.0004
Income/10000	0.34	0.024
Pamlico	−0.11	0.098
Constant*	−0.82	0.17
t^2	−0.0006	0.0005
Income/10000*	0.07	0.02
Pamlico	0.00006	0.11
ρ^*	0.21	0.11
Log-likelihood	−841.46	
$-2\ln(L_R/L_U)$	361.44	

*Different from zero at the 95% level of confidence.

and significantly different from zero, indicating that there is positive correlation between the two responses. However, this correlation is not perfect. The correlation coefficient being less than one indicates that the random component of WTP for the first question is not perfectly correlated with the random component from the follow-up question.

The virtue of the bivariate probit lies in its ability to nest and test other models of two-question responses. The models discussed in the next section represent special cases of the general bivariate probit model in equation (5.3). Each of these models can be tested against the general bivariate model in equation (5.3) using straightforward likelihood ratio tests.

Independent Probits

Suppose there is no covariance between the error terms from the two dichotomous choice responses. In this case, $\sigma_{12} = 0$ or $\rho = 0$. Because a bivariate normal distribution with no correlation is simply the product of two independent univariate normal distributions, the jth contribution to the likelihood function becomes

$$\begin{aligned} L_j(\mu|t) &= \Phi(d_{1j}\left(\frac{\mu_1 - t^1}{\sigma_1}\right), d_{2j}\left(\frac{\mu_2 - t^2}{\sigma_2}\right), 0) \\ &= \Phi_{\varepsilon_1}\left(d_{1j}\left(\frac{\mu_1 - t^1}{\sigma_1}\right)\right)\Phi_{\varepsilon_2}\left(d_{2j}\left(\frac{\mu_2 - t^2}{\sigma_2}\right)\right). \end{aligned} \quad (5.4)$$

The likelihood function for the bivariate probit with zero correlation between responses leads to independent probits on the first and second responses. If there is no correlation between responses, then joint estimation provides no statistical gain relative to two independent probits on the responses, as long as the means differ. A test of independent probits versus a bivariate specification is a significance test on the correlation coefficient. Assuming the correct distributional and functional specifications, if the hypothesis that $\rho = 0$ is rejected then estimation of independent probits on the two responses would result in a loss of efficiency relative to the bivariate probit model. An alternative to the independent probits that assumes the covariance is zero but that exploits the two bids to increase efficiency is to assume that the parameters in the response function are the same: $\mu_1 = \mu_2$, or if $\mu_k = \mathbf{z}\boldsymbol{\beta}_k$ for $k = 1, 2$, then $\boldsymbol{\beta}_1 = \boldsymbol{\beta}_2$.

Composite Error Specification

Consider again the formulation of the bivariate probit model

$$WTP_{ij} = \mu_i + \varepsilon_{ij}$$

but now suppose that the error term can be decomposed into an individual specific (ε_j) and individual/equation specific ($\tilde{\varepsilon}_{ij}$) error such that

$$\varepsilon_{ij} = \varepsilon_j + \tilde{\varepsilon}_{ij}.$$

Assuming $\varepsilon_j \backsim N\left(0, \sigma^2\right)$ and $\tilde{\varepsilon}_{ij} \backsim N\left(0, \sigma_i^2\right)$, the joint distribution of ε_{1j} and ε_{2j} will be a bivariate normal distribution with means zero and correlation coefficient

$$\widetilde{\rho} = \frac{cov\left(\varepsilon_{1j}, \varepsilon_{2j}\right)}{\sqrt{\left(\sigma^2 + \sigma_1^2\right)\left(\sigma^2 + \sigma_2^2\right)}}.$$

The denominator is the product of the standard errors from the marginal distributions for the errors, and the numerator is the covariance between the errors. Substituting in the definition of the covariance, the numerator becomes

$$\begin{aligned} cov\left(\varepsilon_{1j},\varepsilon_{2j}\right) &= E\left(\varepsilon_{1j}\varepsilon_{2j}\right) \\ &= E\left(\varepsilon_j+\tilde{\varepsilon}_{1j}\right)\left(\varepsilon_j+\tilde{\varepsilon}_{2j}\right) \\ &= E\left(\varepsilon_j^2\right)+E\left(\varepsilon_j\tilde{\varepsilon}_{1j}\right)+E\left(\varepsilon_j\tilde{\varepsilon}_{2j}\right)+E\left(\tilde{\varepsilon}_{1j}\tilde{\varepsilon}_{2j}\right) \\ &= \sigma^2. \end{aligned}$$

The first equality holds because the composite errors are mean zero, and the last equality holds because the individual and individual/equation specific errors are assumed independent. The correlation between the WTP responses is then

$$\widetilde{\rho}=\frac{\sigma^2}{\sqrt{\left(\sigma^2+\sigma_1^2\right)\left(\sigma^2+\sigma_2^2\right)}}.$$

Given this formulation, the two WTP responses are distributed bivariate normally with means μ_i, variances $\widetilde{\sigma}_i^2=\sigma^2+\sigma_i^2$, and correlation $\widetilde{\rho}$ as defined above. The composite error formulation is similar to the bivariate probit model in equation (5.3). In fact, estimates of $\widetilde{\sigma}_i^2$ and $\widetilde{\rho}$ from a standard bivariate probit model can be used to recover estimates of the composite error variances through relations

$$\begin{aligned} \sigma^2 &= \widetilde{\rho}\widetilde{\sigma}_1\widetilde{\sigma}_2 \\ \sigma_1^2 &= \widetilde{\sigma}_1^2-\widetilde{\rho}\widetilde{\sigma}_1\widetilde{\sigma}_2 \\ \sigma_2^2 &= \widetilde{\sigma}_2^2-\widetilde{\rho}\widetilde{\sigma}_1\widetilde{\sigma}_2. \end{aligned}$$

However, as the above equations show, non-negativity of the variance parameters σ_1^2 and σ_2^2 requires that

$$\frac{1}{\widetilde{\rho}}\geq\frac{\widetilde{\sigma}_1}{\widetilde{\sigma}_2}\geq\widetilde{\rho}. \tag{5.5}$$

This restriction is not automatically satisfied in the bivariate probit.

For practical purposes, the bivariate probit is a more general specification of the WTP function than the composite error specification. However, if the bivariate probit parameter estimates satisfy the restriction in equation (5.5), the errors can be given a composite error interpretation and the individual and equation specific variances can be derived.

Random Effects Probit

The composite error model is a restricted form of the bivariate probit model, but it allows for a panel data interpretation. There is an error term specific to each response, and an error term that carries across responses from the same individual. This is a general form of a random effects model. Alberini, Kanninen and Carson were among the first to apply a random effects interpretation to a dichotomous choice contingent valuation survey with a follow-up question.

If we restrict the mean of the composite error models to be the same across both responses so that $\mu_1 = \mu_2 = \mu$, and restrict the variances of the marginal distributions to be equal across responses $\sigma_1^2 = \sigma_2^2$, then the jth contribution to the likelihood function (the probability of observing the outcome $[y_{1j}, y_{2j}]$) becomes

$$L_j(\mu|t) = \Phi_{\varepsilon_1\varepsilon_2}(d_{1j}\left(\frac{\mu - t^1}{\widetilde{\sigma}}\right), d_{2j}\left(\frac{\mu - t^2}{\widetilde{\sigma}}\right), d_{1j}d_{2j}\rho). \tag{5.6}$$

Equation (5.6) is a bivariate probit likelihood function (see equation 5.3) with equal means, equal marginal variances ($\widetilde{\sigma} = \sqrt{\sigma^2 + \sigma_1^2} = \sqrt{\sigma^2 + \sigma_2^2}$) and non-perfect correlation between the errors: $\rho = \frac{\sigma^2}{\sigma^2 + \sigma_1^2}$. The random effects probit assumes that the marginal distributions of the responses for the two questions are identical, but the responses are not independent. Instead, the random effects probit accounts for possible individual specific effects that carry across the two responses. Although the random effects probit can be written as a restricted form of the bivariate probit, econometric packages typically have separate routines for the bivariate probit and the random effects probit. Random effects probit routines typically provide estimates of the σ^2 and σ_1^2 rather than $\widetilde{\sigma}$ and ρ. If the correlation coefficient (or equivalently the individual specific variance) is estimated to be indistinguishable from zero, the random effects probit collapses to what is known as the interval data model.

Alberini, Kanninen and Carson estimate another variant of the random effects probit. They incorporate a fixed question effect into the random effects model by allowing the intercept to change across questions. Their formulation is

$$\begin{aligned} WTP_{1j} &= \mu_1 + \varepsilon_{1j} \\ WTP_{2j} &= \mu_2 + \delta + \varepsilon_{2j}. \end{aligned} \tag{5.7}$$

In models with no covariates, they find that the δ is significantly less than zero, implying there is a downward mean shift in WTP between the two responses. To understand this result, it is useful to look at one of the initial models for analyzing two-response CV questions: the interval data model.

Interval Data Model

The interval model is the initial formulation of Hanemann, Loomis and Kanninen. This is the format in which the double-bounded model offers the greatest increase in efficiency, with the least ambiguity about recovered preferences. To understand the initial attraction of the interval data model, consider again the specification of the bivariate dichotomous choice likelihood function in equation (5.3). Now suppose that we impose the restriction that $\mu_1 = \mu_2 = \mu$. In this case, we would expect a gain in efficiency because both answers are used to estimate the parameter μ. Suppose also that the covariance between the two errors is zero. In the normal distribution case, zero covariance implies independence, so we can write the jth contribution to the likelihood function as

$$\begin{aligned} L_j(\mu|\mathbf{t}) &= [\Pr(\mu+\varepsilon_{1j} > t^1)\cdot\Pr(\mu+\varepsilon_{2j} < t^2)]^{YN} \\ \times[\Pr(\mu+\varepsilon_{1j} &> t^1)\cdot\Pr(\mu+\varepsilon_{2j} > t^2)]^{YY} \\ \times[\Pr(\mu+\varepsilon_{1j} &< t^1)\cdot\Pr(\mu+\varepsilon_{2j} < t^2)]^{NN} \\ \times[\Pr(\mu+\varepsilon_{1j} &< t^1)\cdot\Pr(\mu+\varepsilon_{2j} > t^2)]^{NY}. \end{aligned}$$

Here we see that estimation of μ should be more efficient than a single bid model, because we basically double the number of observations. The case originally developed by Hanemann, Loomis and Kanninen assumes that the model in all its parts is the same for each question. That is, for the jth individual

$$WTP_j = \mu + \varepsilon_j,$$

so that the same error applies to each question, as well as the same deterministic part of preferences. Now we write the jth contribution to the likelihood function as

$$\begin{aligned} L_j(\mu|\mathbf{t}) &= \Pr(\mu+\varepsilon_j > t^1, \mu+\varepsilon_j < t^2)^{YN} \\ \times\Pr(\mu+\varepsilon_j &> t^1, \mu+\varepsilon_j > t^2)^{YY} \\ \times\Pr(\mu+\varepsilon_j &< t^1, \mu+\varepsilon_j < t^2)^{NN} \\ \times\Pr(\mu+\varepsilon_j &< t^1, \mu+\varepsilon_j > t^2)^{NY} \end{aligned}$$

Consider the yes-yes sequence. Bayes's rule, $\Pr(a,b) = \Pr(b|a)\Pr(a)$, lets us write $\Pr(WTP > t^1, WTP > t^2) = \Pr(WTP > t^1|WTP > t^2)\cdot\Pr(WTP > t^2) = \Pr(WTP > t^2)$ when $t^2 > t^1$ because in that case the probability that WTP is greater than t^1, given that it is greater than t^2 when $t^2 > t^1$, equals one. Analogous reasoning holds for the no-no sequence. And with the single error, the probability of the yes-no and no-yes pairs is just the probability that willingness to pay falls in the interval. Hence we can rewrite the jth contribution as

$$\begin{aligned} L_j(\mu|\mathbf{t}) &= \Pr(t^2-\mu > \varepsilon_j > t^1-\mu)^{YN} \cdot \Pr(\mu+\varepsilon_j > t^2)^{YY} \\ \times \Pr(\mu+\varepsilon_j &< t^2)^{NN} \cdot \Pr(t^1-\mu > \varepsilon_j > t^2-\mu)^{NY}. \end{aligned} \tag{5.8}$$

Written with the error as normal, this is the likelihood function that Hanemann, Loomis and Kanninen used to estimate their parameters. Under these assumptions, the efficiency gains come from restrictions on the range of the random preferences. As Hanemann, Loomis, and Kanninen's empirical results show, with the corroboration of considerable subsequent research, double-bounded models do provide efficiency gains.

The difficulty with the double-bounded model has been some apparent strategic behavior on the follow-up questions. One rather consistent finding with double-bounded models is that the mean WTP for the sample is smaller when the second question is introduced. This finding was present in the original work by Hanemann, Loomis and Kanninen and has been corroborated in numerous other studies. Systematic analysis of data from double-bounded models suggests that this tendency can be explained by the proclivity of the initial 'yes' respondents to answer 'no' to the second question, regardless of the amount. The consequence is that the aggregate proportion of yes's to a given bid is lower, and the double-bounded responses will yield a smaller mean willingness.

Several explanations for the mixed performance of the double-bounded model have been suggested. For example, the respondent who initially answers 'yes' may feel he is being exploited when asked to pay an even higher amount. Alberini, Kanninen and Carson suggest that a respondent who answers no may feel that the quality of the good may be lowered on the second question. Other interpretations are possible. But the fundamental problem is that the respondent's expectations have been changed after the first question. Initially, assuming no untoward strategic behavior, the respondent has no reason to believe that the first question will be followed by a second question. But when the second question is asked, the respondent may wonder whether another will follow, and adjust his response strategically.

Principally, however, it is the responses that follow an initial 'yes' that appear to cause most of the problems. One means of gaining efficiency from double-bounded questions but avoiding the apparent strategic problems that arise after an initial 'yes' is to adopt a 'one and a half' bid approach, as suggested by Cooper, Hanemann and Signorelli. In this approach, the researcher uses the following responses: initial 'yes', a 'no-yes' combination and a 'no-no' combination. This makes the likelihood function look as follows:

$$\begin{aligned} L_j(\mu|\mathbf{t}) &= [\Pr(\mu+\varepsilon_{1j} > t^1)^Y \\ \times[\Pr(\mu+\varepsilon_{1j} &< t^1)\cdot\Pr(\mu+\varepsilon_{2j} < t^2)]^{NN} \\ \times[\Pr(\mu+\varepsilon_{1j} &< t^1)\cdot\Pr(\mu+\varepsilon_{2j} > t^2)]^{NY} \end{aligned}$$

In this approach, when one assumes that both follow-up questions to the initial 'no' response are the same, a variant of the interval model emerges.

Econometrically, tests of the change in the incentive structure can be carried out in a variety of ways. One approach would be to test whether the parameter vector from the second bid price equals the parameter vector from the first bid price. This can be accomplished in the context of the bivariate probit model. By estimating both the bivariate probit model on both responses and the interval data model, likelihood ratio tests can be used to test the hypothesis that the means and variances are equal across questions. One of the models developed by Alberini, Kanninen and Carson, given in equation (5.7), can be used test for differences. When $\delta < 0$, all else equal the respondent is more likely to answer no on the second question than on the first. Perhaps the most convincing evidence for a change in incentives comes from comparing the proportion of yes responses to a given bid on the first question, and the proportion of yes responses to the same bid on the second question, given that the first answer was yes. Typically one finds that the proportion of yes responses to the same bid is less for those who have already answered yes on a previous question.

5.2.2 *Payment Cards*

In the early years of CV, researchers used a variety of means for determining willingness to pay. One popular approach that can be viewed as a predecessor of discrete choice CV was the payment card approach. In this method, the interviewer describes the scenario to the respondent, explains the need to pay, and then presents a card to the respondent with a list of payments, ranked from highest to lowest or lowest to highest. The respondent is then asked a question of willingness to pay based on the payment card. Four kinds of questions can be asked with a payment card.

1. Pick the amount you are willing to pay.

2. Pick the minimum amount you are willing to pay.

3. Pick the maximum amount you are willing to pay.

4. Pick the range that describes the amount you are willing to pay.

These questions may be asked in different ways. A respondent may be asked to point to the appropriate number, or check it off, or respond orally. But for computing willingness to pay, one must make sense of the response. For the first response, the researcher must assume that the number picked is the respondent's willingness to pay, because the question leaves no room for ambiguity. This might be acceptable if there were a sufficiently large number of payments on the payment card. For example, it would not seem satisfactory to present the respondent with three payments on a payment card, and accept the number picked as the true willingness to pay. The second question, pick the minimum amount you are willing to pay, should not be taken as the true willingness to pay either, if the number of payments is small.

Suppose that there are K payments, $t_1, ..., t_K$, arranged in ascending order so that $t_k > t_{k-1}.$ When a respondent picks payment t_k, the probability that a respondent picks this payment is the probability that willingness to pay lies between t_k and t_{k+1}:

$$\Pr(choose\ t_k) = \Pr(t_k \leq WTP < t_{k+1}).$$

Responses to the payment card can be treated in a parametric model by specifying willingness to pay as $WTP = \mu + \varepsilon$. We assume linearity here for simplicity but results are generalizable to many of the models in Chapters 2-4. If we let $\varepsilon \sim N(0, \sigma^2)$, then

$$\Pr(choose\ t_k) = \frac{1}{\sigma} \int_{(t_k-\mu)/\sigma}^{(t_{k+1}-\mu)/\sigma} \phi(z)dz,$$

which can be rewritten as

$$\Pr(choose\ t_k) = \Phi\left((t_{k+1} - \mu)/\sigma\right) - \Phi\left((t_k - \mu)/\sigma\right)$$

where $\Phi\left((t_{k+1} - \mu)/\sigma\right)$ is the standard normal CDF evaluated at $(t_{k+1} - \mu)/\sigma$. We can then form the log-likelihood function for the responses:

$$\ln L = \sum_{i=1}^{T} \ln(\Phi\left((t_{k+1}(i) - \mu)/\sigma\right) - \Phi\left((t_k(i) - \mu)/\sigma\right)) \qquad (5.9)$$

where individual i picks payment $t_k(i)$. This is a form of an interval model, in which every individual picks some payment. This is similar to part of the interval likelihood function (equation 5.8) and it requires a tailored likelihood. The model estimates $1/\sigma$ as the coefficient on $t_k(i)$ and $t_{k+1}(i)$ and the constant term is μ/σ. One gets $EWTP$ by dividing the estimate of μ/σ by the estimate of $1/\sigma$. If there is a zero payment option, then one would have a discrete response that assigns zero to the WTP function. This would be a form of a spike model, which we explore below.

Questions 3 and 4 also provide a range of WTP. In question 3, we simply change the likelihood function in equation (5.9) so that the interval goes from $t_{k-1}(i)$ to $t_k(i)$. For question 4, we would use the lower and upper bound of the range that is picked for the values of $t_k(i)$ and $t_{k+1}(i)$ in the likelihood function given in equation (5.9). We can estimate the effect of covariates by replacing μ with $\mathbf{z}_i\boldsymbol{\beta}$.

We can also use the Turnbull non-parametric approach of Chapter 3 to analyze the payment card data. Let us interpret the choice of t_k as the respondent's lower bound of his WTP. Then a payment card estimate of the lower bound of $EWTP$ for the sample would be

$$E_{LB,PC}WTP = \sum_{i=1}^{T} t_k(i)/T. \tag{5.10}$$

This turns out to be the same as the Turnbull lower bound estimate from Chapter 3. To see this, we calculate the Turnbull lower bound as

$$E_{LB}WTP = \sum_{k=1}^{M} t_k f_{k+1}$$

where $f_{k+1} = F_{k+1} - F_k$, and F_k is the proportion that will pay less than t_k. To calculate F_k with the payment card approach, define T_k as the number of respondents who pick t_k. Then we define $F_{k+1} = 1 - (T_M + T_{M-1} + ... + T_{k+1})/T$. This implies that $f_{k+1} = F_{k+1} - F_k = T_k/T$. Now we can rewrite equation (5.10) as

$$\begin{aligned}\sum_{i=1}^{T} t_k(i)/T &= \frac{T_1 t_1 + T_2 t_2 + ...T_M t_M}{T} \\ &= \sum_{k=1}^{M} t_k f_{k+1}.\end{aligned}$$

Consequently we can just treat the payment card mechanism in the standard conservative way and we will be getting the Turnbull lower bound mean.

The chief difficulty with the payment card mechanism is that its incentive properties are suspect. This comes in part from the cueing implicit in the list of payments on the payment card. Mitchell and Carson describe payment cards in detail.

5.2.3 Open-Ended Questions

The earliest contingent valuation questions were simply questions that asked the respondents the maximum amount they would pay rather than go without the scenario. There are several difficulties with the incentives of open-ended questions, and they have basically been abandoned as a mechanism. Nothing in the respondents' experience is likely to prepare them for plausible responses to this question. Open-ended questions are also subject to a variety of ambiguous responses. For example, individuals protest by responding with zeros or extremely high values.

The econometric issues with open-ended questions are limited to learning about whether the responses are systematic functions of covariates or sampling splitting or other aspects of the questionnaire or individual. Typically one would have an individual's response as WTP_i, and the sample mean would be $\sum_{i=1}^{T} WTP_i/T$. One might want to estimate a model such as

$$WTP_i = f(\mathbf{z}_i, \varepsilon_i)$$

where $\mathbf{z}_i$ is a vector of individual covariates, including income, and a random element ε_i. This model is estimated as a censored model because $WTP_i \geq 0$. The vector of covariates would be variables of interest to establish the validity of the CV approach. It could also include variables that helped correct for disproportionate sampling to help expand the estimates to the population. Estimation of such models falls under the rubric of continuous dependent variable models and is covered in detail in standard econometrics texts.

5.3 Bid Design Issues

While the focus of this book lies in the estimation of models once data have been collected, the previous section necessitates a discussion of one of the issues surrounding the design of contingent valuation experiments: optimal bid design. The choice of the optimal bid vector is a choice of the number and distribution of bids to offer. Suppose that there are $j = 1, .., m$ bid levels, let t_j be the jth bid level and let T_j be the number of respondents who receive bid t_j. The bid design is completely determined by the $2m$ values of t_j, T_j, $j = 1..., m$. The total number of bids offered, $\sum_{j=1}^{m} T_j$ depends on the budget available for sampling. It is clear that the distribution of bids matters in terms of the efficiency of estimators. The bids are obviously important for efficiency because they are exogenous variables that determine the variance-covariance matrix in the simple dichotomous discrete choice CV where the bid is the only regressor. The optimal bid literature is a useful point of departure, but one should be wary of using an optimal bid design that has not passed severe pragmatic tests. In fact, optimal bid design should be considered part of the construction of the CV instrument. The range of bids may be governed by the respondents' understanding of the question. For example, Carson, Groves and Machina suggest that respondents react to very low bids as unrealistic, and may substitute their guess of a mean instead of the very low bid. This section provides a brief introduction to some of the issues and points the reader to some of the literature on the subject.

The need for bid designs that improve efficiency is exacerbated by the discrete format for CV. Single bid dichotomous choice surveys are inefficient relative to open-ended contingent valuation. A response to a question of the form 'Are you willing to pay $t?' contains considerably less information than a response to a question of the form 'How much are you willing to pay?'. Practitioners, however, are overwhelmingly willing to sacrifice efficiency to forego the unreliability of open-ended responses. This loss of efficiency has been the motivation behind the development of stated preference dichotomous choice surveys in the recent literature. In fact, the multiple choice attribute-based methods may achieve efficiency that rivals open-ended CV questions. These methods are discussed briefly in Chapter 10.

Choosing the offered bid prices can improve the efficiency of dichotomous choice parameter and welfare estimates. The optimal bid design literature chooses bids to maximize efficiency (See Scarpa and Bateman; Kanninen 1993a,b; Alberini 1995a; Nyquist.) An interesting paradox emerges in the context of these optimal bid designs. To design an optimal bid vector, the researcher must have information on the distribution of WTP. In the extreme, the maximum efficiency gain for estimating mean WTP is obtained by offering a single bid equal to the true mean of WTP to all respondents. The paradox arises because if true mean WTP is known, then there is no reason to derive an optimal bid vector (or perform a CV study for that matter). A number of studies have derived optimal bid design mechanisms based on limited amounts of prior information and investigate the properties of the resulting parameter and welfare estimates (e.g. Scarpa and Bateman, Kanninen 1993a,b, Alberini

1995a, Nyquist). However, an overriding theme of each of these studies is that prior information is needed on the distribution of WTP before any optimal design mechanism can be implemented. This leads to the conclusion that iterative contingent valuation surveys can provide efficiency gains relative to dichotomous choice surveys based on randomly assigned bids in a single bid dichotomous choice framework.

This discussion begs the question: what practical advise can be derived from the literature on optimal bid design? The first recommendation is that any information available on the distribution of WTP should be used to help design the vector of offered bids. This information might come from focus groups, or pretests, but as is repeatedly pointed out in the literature, optimal bid designs cannot be derived without some information on the distribution of WTP (even if this is inaccurate or uncertain information). Prior information on the distribution of WTP will serve to identify a preliminary estimate of the central tendency of WTP and also help to identify the location and size of the tails of the distribution. Depending on the goals of estimation, this information is important for identifying the optimal bid placements. For example, if population mean WTP is the measure of interest then more information is gained by offering bids close to the mean than bids in the tails of the distribution. If the variance of WTP is of interest, or marginal effects of covariates are important to estimate then one must identify the distribution of WTP. As is shown in Chapter 4, failure to identify the tails of the distribution can have significant effects on the estimation of parameters. A number of optimal bid design strategies exist for such a situation (C-optimal and D-optimal designs are described in Kanninen 1993a, Alberini 1995a, and Scarpa and Bateman), but in practice, all rely on at least a preliminary guess as to the values of the distributional parameters.

If focus group or pretest information is not available, then the choice of bids is solely at the discretion of the researcher. Practically speaking, it is in the researcher's best interest to allow at least two iterations to the contingent valuation survey. The first iteration provides an ex-ante estimate of the distribution of WTP and this information can be used to improve the design for the second iteration of the survey. Practical approaches to the use of the initial information employ histograms of bid responses and the calculation of the Turnbull lower bound mean and its variance. Kanninen (1993b) discusses iterative CV designs in a formal sense.

5.4 Spikes, Indifference and Uncertainty

In any contingent valuation study, there is some likelihood that survey procedures will encounter respondents who do not care one way or the other about the scenario being described. For example, a survey of householders about their preferences for beach quality may find near universal interest in Barbados, where beaches are prominent. The analogous survey conducted with randomly selected households in the U.S. would be expected to encounter a significant proportion of respondents who have no interest in the outcome.

In the context of utility functions, indifference to the outcome means the respondent receives the same utility whether the good is provided or not, independent of the price charged:

$$u_1(\mathbf{z}_j, y_j) = u_0(\mathbf{z}_j, y_j). \tag{5.11}$$

The subscript 1 denotes provision of the scenario and 0 denotes no provision. Indifference can arise in a survey under two conditions, depending on whether the researcher knows that equation (5.11) holds. When it is known that the respondent is indifferent to the CV proposal, it is also known that the respondent would not be willing to pay for the services proposed. If equation (5.11) can be known with confidence, then the problem with indifferent respondents is resolved. The sample average expected WTP is

$$\begin{aligned} E(WTP) &= 0 \times \Pr(\text{indifferent}) + E(WTP|\text{not indifferent}) \\ &\quad \times \Pr(\text{not indifferent}). \end{aligned}$$

However, it is not always such a simple matter to determine whether the respondent has any interest in the CV scenario. Ideally this question would receive significant attention in questionnaire design. Further, it would be more reliable when asked prior to the main CV question. The danger in sorting out after the yes-no CV question is that respondents may engage in strategic behavior if they perceive that their initial responses are doubted. Further, there are datasets in which the respondents are not asked whether they are indifferent, and so the indifferent respondents cannot be sorted from those who would prefer the scenario at some price. Hence there are three cases.

1. Some respondents are indifferent, and they have been unambiguously identified by the interview process;

2. Some respondents have revealed that they may be indifferent, but there is some uncertainty about their actual indifference;

3. Researchers have good reason to believe that there is indifference, but nothing of potential indifference has been identified by the interview. In this case, the problem can be handled by the model of Haab (1999).

The treatment of nonrespondents may have little impact on the estimate of WTP. Take the simple case in which indifferent respondents will always answer no if they have to pay a price for service that they don't want

$$\Pr(No) = \Pr(u_1(\mathbf{z}_j, y_j - t) < u_0(\mathbf{z}_j, y_j)) = 1 \; if \; u_1(\mathbf{z}_j, y_j) = u_0(\mathbf{z}_j, y_j).$$

The impact of including indifferent respondents on the estimate of WTP can be seen by looking at the effect on the Turnbull lower bound of willingness to pay (see Chapter 3). For simplicity, suppose all individuals in the sample are offered the same bid (t). The estimate of the lower bound of WTP will be bid price $\times$ Proportion of yes. For the case when indifference is ignored

$$E(WTP_{LB}|\text{indifferent misclassified}) = t(T - N - D)/T$$

where N is the number of legitimate negative respondents, D (Don't care) is the number of indifferent responses and T is the total number of responses. The quantity $T - N - D$ represents the total number of yes responses to the bid t, as the D indifferent respondents will respond no. If we look only at the respondents who are not indifferent and drop the indifferent responses, then the total number of yes responses will be $T - N - D$, but now the number of potential responses is only $T - D$. The lower bound on expected WTP for the respondents who care will be

$$E(WTP_{LB}|\text{respondents not indifferent}) = t(T - D - N)/(T - D).$$

We then calculate the full sample willingness to pay (including indifferent respondents) as:

$$\begin{aligned} EWTP_{LB} &= 0 \times \Pr(\text{indifferent}) + E(WTP_{LB}|\text{not indifferent}) \\ &\quad \times \Pr(\text{not indifferent}). \end{aligned}$$

The sample estimate of the probability of indifference is

$$\Pr(\text{indifferent}) = \frac{D}{T}.$$

Substitution yields

$$
\begin{aligned}
EWTP_{LB} &= 0\frac{D}{T} + t\frac{(T-D-N)}{(T-D)}\frac{(T-D)}{T} \\
&= t\frac{(T-D-N)}{T}.
\end{aligned}
$$

This is the same as $EWTP_{LB}$ when the indifferent responses are not dropped. Misclassifying makes no difference. Whether this result holds for parametric models depends on the structure of bid prices. In general though, when indifferent responses are known, they should be dropped. But what is more reassuring is that including the indifferent responses does not have an unambiguous effect on the estimate of WTP. Dropping the indifferent responses raises the conditional estimate of WTP, because sure no's are eliminated. But calculation of the sample mean WTP is lowered when zero WTP is attributed to the indifferent responses.

When there is incomplete information that the respondent is indifferent, several strategies may be reasonable. Respondents may have some positive willingness to pay, and they may also have zero willingness to pay. Here the correct approach depends on whether willingness to pay is non-negative. There are circumstances for some CV scenarios where negative WTP is reasonable.

5.4.1 A General Spike Model

Kriström (1990) provides a general model to allow for indifference in a dichotomous choice CV framework. For the moment, suppose we can distinguish respondents who are indifferent. We allow for both positive and negative WTP. As will be seen, nested within this model are many of the models discussed previously. Following Kriström, but changing notation to remain consistent with previous models, let $F^{-}(W)$ represent the distribution of WTP for those with negative WTP. $F^{-}(W)$ is defined such that as W approaches negative infinity, $F^{-}(W) = 0$. However, as W approaches zero from the negative side, $F^{-}(0^{-}) \to p^{-}$. Similarly, we can define a function to describe those with positive WTP $(F^{+}(W))$ such that $F^{+}(\infty) = 1$ and as $W \to 0$ from the positive range, $F^{+}(0^{+}) \to p^{+}$. The distribution of WTP can be summarized as

$$
F_{WTP}(W) = \left\{ \begin{array}{c} F^{-}(W) \ if\ W < 0 \\ p^{-} \ if\ W \to 0^{-} \\ p^{+} \ if\ W \to 0^{+} \\ F^{+}(W) \ if\ W > 0 \end{array} \right\}.
$$

The Kriström model is an appealing representation of the possible distribution of WTP. It allows individuals to have negative or positive WTP. It allows for a different distribution of WTP between those with positive and those with negative WTP, and it allows for a spike or mass of observations at zero (measured as $p^+ - p^-$). Kriström's model, however, has some drawbacks in application. It is unlikely that a negative bid price will be offered to respondents. As such, there is no information to estimate the form of $F^-(W)$. Unless both benefits and costs of a project are elicited in the survey instrument, the negative portion of WTP will not be estimable in any form other than a point mass at zero.

Consider now an alternative form of the spike model. Define $F(W|$ no indifference) as the conditional distribution function of WTP, given no indifference. The support of WTP is unbounded at this point. Note that it is possible that $WTP = 0$ even with no indifference. This is a counterintuitive result, but becomes clear when it is recalled that for any continuous distribution, the probability of observing any particular outcome is zero. We will consider the case when indifferent respondents can be identified and the case when indifferent respondents can not be identified.

Indifferent Respondents Can Be Identified

Consider the case where the survey has identified those who are not willing to pay anything (i.e., those who are indifferent to the offered good). Define p as the probability of indifference. In this case, the unconditional cumulative distribution function for WTP for $W > 0$ is

$$\begin{aligned} F_W(W) &= p \times F(W|\text{indifference}) + (1-p) \times F(W|\text{no indifference}) \\ &= p + (1-p) \times F(W|\text{no indifference}). \end{aligned} \tag{5.12}$$

This result follows from the realization that $F(W|\text{indifference}) = 1$ if $W > 0$. We will not consider the case of $W \leq 0$ as offered bid prices less than or equal to zero create incentive problems in survey responses. In any case, a question that elicits $WTP < 0$ can always be rephrased to elicit $WTP > 0$ for the complementary good.

Now suppose an individual is offered a single bid $t > 0$. Conditional on no indifference, the probability of a no response is simply:

$$\Pr(no) = \Pr(WTP < t) = F(t|\text{no indifference}). \tag{5.13}$$

Similarly, the probability of a yes response conditional on no indifference is:

$$\Pr(yes) = 1 - \Pr(no) = (1 - F(t|\text{no indifference})). \tag{5.14}$$

Conditional on indifference, the probability of a no response is 1 and the probability of a yes response is zero. The contribution of the jth individual to the likelihood function is:

$$L_j(t) = p^Z \left((1-p) \cdot \Pr(N)\right)^N \cdot \left((1-p) \Pr(Y)\right)^Y \tag{5.15}$$

where $Z = 1$ if the respondent is indifferent and zero otherwise, $N = 1$ if a no response is recorded by a non-indifferent respondent, $Y = 1$ if a yes response is recorded by a non-indifferent respondent, $(1-p)\Pr(N)$ is the unconditional probability of a no response, and $(1-p)\Pr(Y)$ is the unconditional probability of a yes response. Rearranging yields:

$$L_j(t) = p^Z (1-p)^{N+Y} \cdot \Pr(N)^N \cdot \Pr(Y)^Y . \tag{5.16}$$

Noting that $N+Y$ is an indicator of positive WTP, we see that the above model separates into two distinct discrete choice models. The first is a discrete choice model on the indifference decision, and the second is a discrete choice model on the yes/no response. If indifferent respondents can be identified, the probability of indifference can be estimated separately from the yes/no response for those with positive WTP. If one wishes to investigate the effects of covariates on the tendency towards indifference, this can be done in a separate dichotomous choice model (probit or logit for example). If the effects of covariates are not of interest then the maximum likelihood estimate of p will be the proportion of indifferent respondents in the sample.

Note that the appropriate model of yes/no responses includes only those who are not indifferent. It is a direct corollary to this that if indifferent respondents are included in the estimation without directly accounting for them, any parameter estimates of the WTP function will be inconsistent. That is, failure to account for indifference can have undesirable effects on the estimated parameters.

Indifferent Respondents Cannot Be Identified

If indifferent respondents are not identified in the survey, then the model becomes more difficult to estimate. If Z, the indicator of indifference, is unobservable, then the unconditional probability of a no response to an offered bid t becomes:

$$\Pr(N) = \Pr(WTP < t) = p + (1-p) \cdot F(t|\text{no indifference})$$

and the contribution to the likelihood function of a given individual becomes:

$$L_j(t) = \left(p + (1-p)\Pr(N)\right)^{N_T} \cdot \left((1-p)\Pr(Y)\right)^Y$$

where N_T indicates a no response for any reason (indifference or $WTP < t$). This model differs from the previous model in that the estimation of the yes/no response cannot be separated from the estimation of the model of indifference. At this time, standard routines do not exist for estimating this model. A number of recent models have been estimated in the literature that allow for this point mass at zero (see, for example, McFadden 1994, An and Ayala 1996, Werner 1999, and Haab 1999). Typically, the spike model is estimated on positive conditional WTP functions. That is, it is assumed that WTP conditional on no indifference is positive. This gives the spike model a double-hurdle interpretation similar to the Heckman selection model in continuous function models (see Chapter 7). A common result in the existing literature is that the estimate of p (or the parameters of p if it is specified as a function of covariates) is extremely sensitive to the form of the distribution assumed for WTP. Because the estimate of p cannot be separately identified, the estimate is driven solely by the assumed form of $F(W|\text{no indifference})$. (See Haab, 2000 for a derivation.) As such, care must be taken in estimating the spike model when indifferent respondents are not identified.

These models leave us with a significant task for data collection. It is important to identify indifferent respondents in the survey design. If indifferent respondents are not identified, then models that attempt to account for indifference are sensitive to specification error. If indifferent respondents are ignored (either identified or not identified), then the likelihood function is misspecified and parameter estimates will be inconsistent. The logical conclusion is to identify indifferent respondents in the survey process and then estimate the dichotomous choice model on the non-indifferent respondents.

5.5 Conclusion

The topics explored in this chapter by no means exhaust the practical issues that arise in implementing discrete choice contingent valuation. The issues that arise in instrument design are the most significant in all of contingent valuation, and we have touched on these issues only in small ways. These issues are often peculiar to the setting, and involve survey design research rather than the empirical methods of economics.

6

Modeling the Demand for Recreation

6.1 Introduction

In this and the following two chapters, we examine empirical models of the demand for outdoor recreation. Households spend time and money enjoying the natural environment. Government and private actions influence the quantity and quality of recreational sites. Our goal is to show how revealed preference data can be used to estimate welfare effects of various kinds of public actions, from eliminating access to a beach, fishing site or other recreational resource, to changing the quality of the site such as improving fishing or reducing pollution. This requires developing behavioral models, showing how the estimation of these models depends on sampling, and then investigating the calculation of welfare effects from estimated models.

As a method used to value non-market resources, the travel cost method is a good deal older than contingent valuation. It arose in the context of a debate over the use of public lands in western United States. Many of the competing uses for the land–cattle ranching, mining, logging–had marketable outputs. The need for a method that permitted a comparison of the value of market activities with the value of outdoor recreation led to the development of the travel cost method. In a remarkable development, the travel cost model was suggested by Harold Hotelling, in an unpublished letter, who responded to Department of Interior officials requesting a means of evaluating the benefits of public lands. In one of the earliest applications, Clawson computed visitation rates per 100000 population to the major national parks in the US by cost.

When the travel cost method is employed for measuring the benefits and costs of public actions, it can be used in two ways. The original use, and this remains important, was to determine the best use of public land, which might have both commercial potential in the private sector and recreational use in the public sector. But because recreation takes place outdoors, and can be substantially affected by air and water pollution, recreation models are now commonly used to measure the benefits of pollution control or other changes in the policies that influence the quality of sites.

The travel cost model is a model of the demand for the services of a recreational site. The essence of the travel cost model stems from the need to travel to a site to enjoy its service. A participant who chooses to visit a site must incur the cost of overcoming the distance. This characteristic is put succinctly by Burt and Brewer:

> ...the consumer is transported to the commodity for consumption to take place, rather than vice versa. This attribute of outdoor recreation is advantageous for statistical estimation of demand equations because the costs that must be incurred to consume the recreational services provide surrogate prices with more variation in a sample than would usually be generated by market phenomena observed either over time or over space. (p. 813)

All methods that use travel costs rely on the insight that differences in costs cause differences in quantity demanded. Sometimes the differences relate to different costs to different households visiting the same site, and sometimes the cost differences refer to different sites for the same household. Early approaches tended to be zonal–that is, researchers used as the dependent variable the number of visits per capita from a zone in which the distance to the site was approximately equal for all residents who lived in the zone. Because visits per capita equals the product of (visits/users) and (users/population), these models blended participation rate models with models of users' demands.

Travel cost models have developed considerably since their initial use. They can be used to estimate the welfare effects of the elimination of a recreational site or a change in the quality of the site, as outlined in Chapter 1. Smith and Kaoru perform a meta-analysis of benefit estimates from travel cost models, and give a good appreciation of the important issues in estimation. The broader issues of recreational demand modeling are surveyed in Bockstael, McConnell, and Strand (1991). Thousands of applications of the travel cost methods have appeared in economics journals, disciplinary journals and government reports. They have been employed in natural resource injury cases, for example in the Exxon Valdez case by Hausman, Leonard and McFadden to demonstrate monetary damages from the injury. They have been used routinely to evaluate conditions of access in marine recreational fishing in the United States (Hicks, Steinback, Gautam and Thunberg). In one of the earliest studies using the travel cost model to value pollution control, Smith and Desvousges measured the economic benefits of water pollution reduction.

In international work, Strand has used a type of travel cost model to estimate the benefits of coastal zone management in Barbados. Although travel cost models are widely used in the United States, and to a lesser extent internationally, there has been less use of these models in Europe, where there is widespread use of contingent valuation. The scant use of travel cost models in the developing world is to be expected, because there the more pressing environmental problems relate to the health effects of pollution. This is changing in the more developed countries, as researchers use site choice models for analyzing policy measures.

6.2 The Generic Travel Cost Problem

In deciding to visit a recreational site, an individual or a household typically chooses among many alternative recreation sites, and then incurs the cost of travel to visit the chosen site. This decision is often, but not always, made a number of times per season, or per year. Hence individuals make decisions about whether to visit a site as well as the number of times to visit it. In a sample of all households that records visits to a large number of sites over a period of time, such as visits by households to the numerous lakes in Wisconsin during a year, it is typical that many households will not visit any of the sites. If we confine our analysis to users only, then frequently households visit only a few of the many sites available. Thus a common characteristic of recreational datasets is that the observed quantity demanded for most sites is zero. The various approaches of recreational demand models all confront this basic issue.

Estimating models for a typical dataset requires a variety of strategic modeling decisions. The two most critical choices involve the basic structure of the model. One may start with a preference function and then derive the behavioral model, or one may simply start with a behavioral model. The second decision concerns whether one wishes to model the choice among all the sites in the study area, or as few as one site. The demand function approach entails the writing down and estimation of a system of demand functions. The origin of this approach is the work of Burt and Brewer, who estimated demand functions for a small number of reservoirs using aggregate data in the form of visits per capita. Current versions are estimated on individual data, such as the count models by Shonkwiler and by von Haefen. All of these models are direct descendents of the Hotelling travel cost model, in which the individual chooses the number of times to visit a given site. A simple version of this approach is a single site model, which we address in the following chapter.

The alternative to the demand function approach is to begin with a utility function. This approach incorporates the full set of choices, including the choice of whether to participate at each site as well as the number of times to visit each site. The most general version of the utility function approach is the generalized corner solution model, developed by Phaneuf, Herriges and Kling. In this model, the recreationist chooses which sites to visit and how many times to visit each site, in a utility consistent framework. The various versions of the random utility models, including the repeated logit model, are less fully integrated versions of the demand for all sites. Herriges, Kling and Phaneuf (1999) compare the different approaches to modeling the demands. In general, if the number of sites is not large, fully integrated utility-consistent models and demand models are suitable substitutes. However, when the number of alternatives is very large, as it is in many applications, site choice models based on random utility have the advantage of feasibility. In Chapter 8 we investigate the estimation of random utility models.

6.2.1 The Demand for Quality

The goal of the original models of the demand for recreation was to measure the willingness to pay for access to recreation sites. This allowed researchers to compare the recreational value of land with the value of competing uses. But as the awareness of pollution grew, questions broadened to encompass not just the best use of the site but the quality of the site. In a model of trips to a single site, the elementary travel cost model, the researcher usually cannot infer economic values of quality changes because all individuals face the same site quality. Without severe assumptions, the single site model can be used to measure the economic value of access to the site but not the value of changes in the quality of the site.[1]

Improvements in the ability to measure the welfare effects of quality came with the recognition that the quality of recreation sites frequently varies across sites. And often, the consumer chooses sites with different qualities. Each time an individual chooses to visit a given site, he selects

[1] By allowing a single quality measure to interact with an individual-specific covariate, one can coax out the demand for site quality. This allocates all of the welfare leverage to a second order effect, however. If time-series data were available, where the quality variables changed over time, then a single site would provide sufficient information to estimate the effect of quality. Time-series data for recreational demand models has rarely been used.

among a larger set of sites that are differentiated not only by different costs but by different qualities. Using these choices in the various multiple site models such as the random utility model or the generalized corner solution model allows the researcher to estimate the willingness to pay for changes in quality. The random utility model has become the most popular method of approach to modeling the demand for recreation sites, in part because it incorporates the effects of quality on the demand for sites.

Increasingly researchers are combining contingent valuation and behavioral models to measure the effects of quality changes. Essentially one tries to estimate a model that includes a travel cost response and a contingent valuation response for each individual. In single site cross-section data, it would then be feasible to deduce the effects of changes in quality on trips and welfare. For example, Huang, Haab and Whitehead (1997) combine a travel cost model with a contingent valuation question valuing water quality changes in the Albemarle and Pamlico Sounds in North Carolina (also see Cameron (1992), Adamowicz, Louviere and Williams (1994), and Niklitschek and Leon). Other studies have combined revealed travel cost responses with planned future travel plans under varying hypothetical price and quality scenarios (e.g. Englin and Cameron (1996), Whitehead, Haab and Huang (2000)). This topic is addressed again in Chapter 10.

6.2.2 Travel Cost Modeling and Contingent Valuation

In the examples that are estimated in the following sections, the impact of different specifications in the demand for recreation on parameter estimates will be evident. The specification of the contingent valuation models estimated in Chapter 2 received no such depth of analysis. This reflects the great sensitivity of welfare estimates from the travel cost models to the actual specification estimated compared with the welfare estimates from contingent valuation, which tend not to be highly sensitive to specification. Here lies a truly significant difference between contingent valuation and behavioral models. For CV, given the data, the measures of WTP are not grossly sensitive to specification and estimation. But CV can be very sensitive to the collection of data, in particular, to the formulation of scenarios and the central dichotomous willingness to pay questions. And while different methods of gathering travel cost data, including different formulations of questions, can lead to different estimates of WTP, the method is severely sensitive to specification and estimation decisions, given the data. The differing sensitivities of the travel cost model and CV approaches stem from the essence of the models. In the application of discrete choice contingent valuation, bids are chosen independently of other exogenous variables, so that other regressors in a discrete choice CV model are likely to have very low correlation with the bid. Hence the coefficient on the bid will not be sensitive to the set of other covariates included in the model. On the other hand, in travel cost models the travel cost serves as a proxy for price, the basis for welfare measurement. And because travel costs among different sites tend to be highly correlated, welfare measures from different model specifications will be quite different because the travel cost coefficient will be different. This problem is exacerbated by the need to account for the value of time, which also tends to be highly correlated with travel cost, and as we shall see, not so easy to measure.

This interpretation of the relative reliability of CV and travel cost methods of valuing resources contrasts sharply with the historic debate about revealed versus stated preference methods. All methods have their strengths and weaknesses, and it is the care and quality in execution of the particular method rather than the method itself, that determine the reliability of the welfare measures. This conclusion is borne out by the limited empirical evidence comparing welfare measures derived from revealed and stated preference approaches. Studies, including Brookshire et al. (1982) and Carson, Flores et al. (1996) fail to show a systematic difference among the welfare measures from revealed and stated preference models.

All models of the demand for recreation are essentially models of the allocation of time, and as such, must meet the individual's time constraint and income constraint. Thus recreational demand modeling is an application of Becker's model of the allocation of time. Whether the time and income constraints can be collapsed determines the ease with which time can be accounted for properly in the demand for recreation. And while the construction below is carried out for demand functions, the same logical development will hold for random utility models too.

6.3 Construction of Demand Models

We begin with the construction of a demand model derived from an individual's allocation of time and income. This model will yield a generic demand function for a single site. Suppose individual i chooses x_{ij}, the number of trips to site j, for $j = 1, ..., n$ where n is the number of sites. The round-trip travel cost is c_{ij}. The individual also purchases a composite commodity bundle z_i at a price normalized to equal 1, and can spend no more than income, y_i. The budget constraint is therefore

$$\sum_{j=1}^{n} x_{ij}c_{ij} + z_i \leq y_i.$$

Each trip takes t_{ij} units of time, where the units of time must be measured consistently with the rest of the time constraint but otherwise do not matter. Individuals may receive exogenous income, but income is also earned by working. Initially we assume that the hours of work, denoted h, can be chosen. When the individual works h hours per period of time, the time constraint can be written:

$$\sum_{j=1}^{n} x_{ij}t_{ij} + h_i = T_i \tag{6.1}$$

where T is the total time available. The amount of on-site time has been suppressed in this construction. If we assume that the amount of time spent on site is the same for all recreationists, then it does not matter whether t_{ij} measures the total time per trip or the on-site time, because the difference will be the travel time. Hence we can simply use the travel time. But if the on-site time and the value of time vary across individuals, then ignoring on-site time can have an impact on the parameter estimates.

The time constraint in equation (6.1) is the starting point for a standard Becker household model of the allocation of time. Total spendable income is given by

$$y_i = y_i^0 + w_i h_i$$

where w is the after-tax wage rate and y^0 is fixed income. When the time constraint is solved for hours of work (h) and substituted into the income constraint, the budget constraint emerges:

$$\sum_{j=1}^{n} x_{ij}(c_{ij} + w_i t_{ij}) + z_i \leq y_i. \tag{6.2}$$

The preference function for individual i is given by $u(x_{i1}, ...x_{in}, q_1, ...q_n, z_i)$. Each q_j is the exogenous quality for the jth site. The quantity and quality of trips to the various recreational sites yield utility, but other aspects of the trip, such as travel time or inputs used to produce the trip do not provide utility. We represent the quality as one-dimensional here, but there can be several dimensions. For example, in the one dimensional case, q_1 would be a measure of the desirable quality for a site. We assume a weak complementary link between the x's and the q's. If x_{ij} is zero, then the marginal utility of q_j is zero, as outlined in Chapter 1.

From equation (6.2), one sees that the price of a trip for individual i to the jth site is given by

$$p_{ij} = c_{ij} + t_{ij}w_i.$$

The individual prices for the recreational sites are now composed of a time element and a travel cost element. Utility maximization with interior solutions for the quantities leads to the standard demand function outlined in Chapter 1:

$$x_{ij} = f_j(\mathbf{p}_i, \mathbf{q}, y_i^f)$$

where $\mathbf{p}_i = (p_{i1}, ...p_{in})$ is the vector of prices for different recreation sites and $\mathbf{q} = (q_1, ...q_n)$ is the vector of qualities at the different sites. In this setting, we have assumed that each individual faces the same site quality. The appropriate income in this demand equation is full income: $y_i^f = y_i^0 + w_iT_i$. This is the amount of income that could be earned if the person worked all of the available time. The demand for site j is determined by the difference in quality and price for site j versus the other sites. Note that for individual i, the difference between the price for sites j and k is $c_{ij} - c_{ik} + w_i(t_{ij} - t_{ik})$. If time were to include on-site time as well as travel time, say $t_{ij} + \tau$, where τ is the on-site time at all sites, then the price difference would be unchanged.

This is the simplest version of the travel model, where the travel time is converted to cost by the wage rate. While the model is straightforward in concept, the estimation results can be quite sensitive to the measurement of independent variables. With both the cost variables and the quality variables, the question of whether one uses subjective measures or objective measures is a critical one. Randall (1994) has noted that there is a potential discrepancy between observed travel cost and the actual unobservable subjective travel price. Randall argues that measurable travel costs are only ordinal indicators of the actual travel price and as such the travel cost method can only produce ordinal rankings of welfare measures. The need to calculate prices for sites that the recreationists do not visit, as well as the sites visited frequently leads researchers to settle on objectively measured prices, because attempting to measure subjective prices to all unvisited sites, especially for random utility models with many sites, creates a severe interview burden.

The model constructed with the time constraint in equation (6.1) assumes that time is completely fungible, and that time not spent recreating can be spent working, and so converted to income at the wage rate. The demand for individual i for site 1, with the arguments more explicit is

$$x_{i1} = f_1(c_{i1} + t_{i1}w_i, ..., c_{in} + t_{in}w_i, q_1...q_n, y_i^f). \tag{6.3}$$

Note that the travel costs and the time coefficients (c_{ij} and t_{ij}) have individual subscripts as well as site subscripts. Individuals traveling the same distance may have the same cost, but the most general case is that individuals have different costs, because their travel costs vary (for example, because they drive cars of different sizes). Estimating this model is quite demanding, given the constructed correlation among the regressors, and the need for measuring costs and qualities of the substitute sites. The gain from estimating the demand for several sites simultaneously is one of efficiency, but the consequence of a specification of a single site model that excludes the appropriate substitute prices and qualities is biased coefficients. Hence while the complete specification is rarely estimated, researchers should be careful to construct a specification that does not exclude critical variables, especially prices of substitute sites.

6.3.1 The Role of Time

Models of the demand for recreation are essentially models of the allocation of time, and so it is not surprising that they are especially sensitive to assumptions about the value of time. In the basic model outlined above, we assume that all time is fungible–that work time and recreation time can be substituted without limit at the wage rate. This model is frequently estimated, and can be considered the base case. Casual empiricism suggests these assumptions are wrong. Many people work jobs with fixed hours, and so cannot substitute work for leisure. And the after-tax wage rate is in some cases an over-estimate of the opportunity cost of leisure time, because of expenses associated with work and perhaps the marginal disutility of work. Here we present two models that address these two assumptions.

A more general model has the flexibility of allowing individuals to be employed for a fixed time period, or to vary their hours of work and leisure smoothly. A model developed by Bockstael, Strand and Hanemann has the model developed above as a special case. The essence of the Bockstael *et al.* model is that when individuals are at a corner solution in the labor market–that is they work for a fixed salary and cannot vary their hours–then the amount of time per trip becomes a separate argument of the demand function, rather than a component of the cost of the trip. We proceed with several models, assuming that the number of recreation sites is two. For $n = 2$, the base model for site 1 becomes

$$x_{i1} = f_1(c_{i1} + w_i t_{i1}, c_{i2} + w_i t_{i2,}, \mathbf{q}, y_i^f). \tag{6.4}$$

In the corner solution case the demand function for site 1 for individual

i has the form

$$x_{i1} = f_1(c_{i1}, c_{i2}, t_{i1}, t_{i2}, \mathbf{q}, y_i^f). \tag{6.5}$$

The corner solution model implies that recreational time is not fungible with work time, and cannot be converted into a monetary cost. So the demand function depends on separate arguments for travel cost and travel time for each site. Careful attention to the constraints shows that full income in the different models depends on the labor market circumstances. Full income has salary and fixed income but no labor component for the corner solution case: $y_i^f = y_i^0$. In the case where time is fungible, full income has the labor component $y_i^f = y_i^0 + w_i T_i$. The alternative specification for those who are at an interior solution in the labor market is given by equation (6.3). Hence we can write a general expression for the demand for site 1 as

$$x_{i1} = f_1(c_{i1} + \delta_i t_{i1} w_i, c_{2i} + \delta_i t_{i2} w_i, (1 - \delta_i) t_{i1}, (1 - \delta_i) t_{i2}, \mathbf{q}, y_i^f).$$

The indicator variable δ_i equals 0 for individuals who are at a corner solution in the labor market, and 1 for those who are at an interior solution. The question of whether an individual is at a corner or interior solution in the labor market is typically handled through survey questions. For example, a respondent might be asked whether he can work additional hours for additional pay. This information, when combined with some knowledge of occupation can lead to a classification of the respondents according to whether they are in or out of the labor market. This type of demand model can be estimated by defining the appropriate variables with the indicator function.

This type of model comes from the labor supply literature, and while it may be a good specification for dealing with labor supply, where the marginal value of time is endogenous, it has its drawbacks for recreation demand. It is not always so clear that a particular type of job is a fixed salary job or flexible wage job. For example, some administrative jobs may have fixed salaries but working longer hours and doing a better job are a time-honored means of getting salary increases, so that extra time spent working has a monetary value. Further some spouses who work in the home may appear not to have a direct monetary cost. But they may substitute time with a spouse who works at a flexible job, and hence there is a monetary opportunity cost for the spouse not in the formal labor market. In a sense, money can usually compensate for time, and if the amount of time entailed in the particular resource allocation problem is small relative to the consumer's total time and money assets, then it is reasonable to assume that the rate of compensation of money for time is constant.

A simpler but more ad hoc model was proposed by McConnell and Strand. This model ignores the potential for corner solutions in the labor market. Instead it assumes that the opportunity cost of time is a constant proportion of the wage rate. This idea is motivated by the intuition that there may be some disutility from work, as well as empirical evidence from travel literature that the value of time is typically less than the wage rate.[2] It makes additional sense when one recognizes that income or wages are frequently measured as before tax values. The model proposed works effectively only for situations in which the demand for a site does not depend on the price of access to other sites. It assumes that the opportunity cost of time is some proportion, denoted k, of the monetary return to time. We would write the demand for the site (site 1) in a narrowly specified model such as

$$x_{i1} = f_1(c_{i1} + kt_{i1}w_i, \mathbf{q}, y_i^f).$$

Consider a deterministic linear model, where $\boldsymbol{\beta}$ is the parameter vector to be estimated:

$$x_{i1} = \beta_0 + \beta_1(c_{i1} + kt_{i1}w_i) + \beta_2 y_i^f$$

(We drop $\mathbf{q}$ because it does not vary across individuals visiting the same site.) This model is not well specified, because the prices for substitute sites are missing. If k is unknown, but to be estimated, we can rewrite this equation as

$$x_{i1} = \beta_0 + \beta_1 c_{i1} + \beta^* t_{i1} w_i + \beta_2 y_i^f$$

where $\beta^* = \beta_1 k$, so that with an estimate of β^* one can recover an estimate of k, and then calculate the price properly in welfare analysis. This model is useful in a pinch, but rather ad hoc. Smith, Desvousges and McGivney have shown that the model does not always give good estimates of k, which we would assume to lie between 0 and 1.

A more practical approach, but with some intuitive appeal, is to fix the parameter k at some plausible value, such as 0.4 or 0.5. It is certainly reasonable to argue that the opportunity cost of time is less than the wage rate. There are several reasons. Tax rates are positive. Individuals incur expenses for work, so that the wage is gross. With fixed and

[2] Evidence in support of the idea that the opportunity cost of time is less than the wage rate can be found in Calfee and Winston, who use a stated preferences approach to arrive at an estimate of the value of time in the range of 14 to 25% of the wage rate. Other estimates are nearer the 50% range.

exogenously determined k, we would estimate

$$x_{i1} = f_1(c_{i1} + kw_i t_{i1}, c_{i2} + kw_i t_{i2}, y_i^f).$$

The advantage of this over the model that estimates k is that it includes substitute costs. And rather than estimate k directly, one could estimate the model for different values of k and then pick the k that maximizes the likelihood function. In Chapter 7 we encounter an example in which k is fixed.

The importance of careful thinking about the value of time lies in its impact on welfare measures, not for its own sake. For many trips, the time costs are more important than the out of pocket travel costs, and overestimating the opportunity cost of time leads to overestimates of the welfare measures.

The arguments we have made carry over to the random utility model, the subject of Chapter 8. We illustrate briefly here. Suppose that the individual has the time constraints as given in equation (6.1) but now only one of the sites is chosen. Hence when one of the $x_{ij}'s$ is chosen, the others will be zero. The indirect utility function for site j will be $v(y_i^f - p_{ij}, q_j)$. Site j will be chosen when the utility to j is greater than the utility to other sites. When the indirect utility function is linear:

$$v(y_i^f - p_{ij}, q_j) = \lambda(y_i^f - p_{ij}) + \beta q_j$$

as it typically is, then the choice of site is determined by the difference in arguments of the indirect utility function for individual i:

$$v(y_i^f - p_{ij}, q_j) - v(y_i^f - p_{ik}, q_k) = -\lambda(p_{ij} - p_{ik}) + \beta(q_j - q_k)$$

where λ is the marginal utility of income and β the marginal utility of quality. When time and income constraints collapse, the same kind of development as in the demand function holds.

6.3.2 Basic Assumptions of the Travel Cost Model

The basic model as constructed looks like a standard prices-as-parameters demand model. It can be estimated as the equations are laid out. To be confident about welfare calculations, the goal of travel cost models, the circumstances of recreational choice should approximate the conditions assumed in the model. The following conditions ought to hold to allow the calculated surpluses to stand for welfare measures:

1. Travel and time cost is a proxy for the price of a recreational trip. This assumption would be violated if a travel cost item provided

utility for its own sake, such as transport cost on a ferry as part of a trip or the chartering of an especially nice charter boat.

2. Travel time is neutral, providing no utility or disutility. This assumption will be violated when a site is chosen over other sites because traveling to the site provides utility. Of course, traveling always provides some utility or disutility, so one needs to be aware of gross violations of the assumption of neutrality. This issue can be handled empirically by careful model specification.

3. The decision unit is trips of equal length at the site for each household. Substantial variation of trip length across site or household calls for a reconsideration of the model. For example, one would not mix one day and two day trips to a site in the same demand function without further model development. Further, when households choose the amount of time on site–such as how many days to stay at the beach–the model needs reconstruction.[3]

4. The trips are single purpose trips, taken to the recreation site for the purpose of recreation. Multiple purpose trips are difficult to manage, especially when the trips are for multiple days. For example, when a family takes a week's vacation, and someone visits a beach several days during the vacation, the travel cost obviously ought to be computed for the local travel only. More difficult issues arise when the trip is a day trip but the individual takes a round-about route in order to visit several different destinations. Parsons and Wilson provide a systematic way of thinking about multiple purpose trips.

5. The quantity consumed in the basic equation–that is, the x_{ij}–is trips to the same site for all consumers. This assumption rules out models that pool trips from different sites. For example, a model estimated when the x_{ij} are trips to a variety of different freshwater recreational sites within a geographical area, such as a state, in effect compounds coefficients from different site demands. It might look like a demand curve empirically. But this model cannot be used to predict demand or calculate welfare measures at any recreation site unless the demand for each site is identical. For example, if the site of interest is a particular beach on the Chesapeake Bay in Maryland, a travel cost study of total trips to

[3] McConnell (1992) treats the problem of variation in on-site time, including the choice of on-site time.

all Chesapeake beaches will serve little to no purpose in measuring the welfare at the site of interest. However, if the site of interest is the Chesapeake Bay as a whole, then an aggregate study would have some value. In this case it is essential to consider issues of aggregation and substitution.

When these assumptions hold reasonably well, one can make the case for the use of the travel cost model. When any of the assumptions fails, further work on the model is warranted. It is not necessary to drop the travel cost model, because occasionally developing it from first principles will save the model.

6.4 Conclusion

The travel cost model is a model for the demand for the services of recreational sites. It can be used to value the access to sites, or to value the characteristics of sites. There are two broad approaches to estimating the demand for recreation sites. One approach assumes a utility function for site services, and derives the demands. This can be done for the seasonal or annual demands, with the generalized corner solution model, or for a particular choice occasion, with the random utility model. The alternative approach is to estimate the demand functions for sites directly, rather than specifying a utility function. In the following two chapters we explore the estimation of individual demand functions and random utility models, and illustrate each using suitable datasets. a utility function.

7

Single Site Demand Estimation

7.1 Introduction

Models of the demand for recreation currently range from the most complete and complex corner solution models of Phaneuf, Herriges and Kling to much simpler single site models. Multiple site models that are estimated as demand systems, rather than site choice models, are generalizations of single site models. This chapter treats the estimation of single site models. Chapter 8 deals with site choice models.

Estimation of single site demand models begins with an assessment of the data generation process which is governed by the assumed stochastic structure of the demand functions and the sampling procedure. The stochastic structure of demand depends on whether the dependent variable, an individual's trips to a site, is assumed to be distributed continuously or as a count variable. The two most prevalent sampling schemes are a random sample of the population of individuals and an on-site sample of intercepted users. An example of a random sample of the population would be a random phone survey. In this case the population of interest is the total population. A typical on-site survey is an intercept survey, where a sample of recreational users at a site is chosen at random. Other types of surveys are also used that induce sample selection effects. For example, if one were to sample from a list of people with hunting licences, the sample could be considered a representative sample of the population of hunters, but not a representative sample of the population of all people, because hunters have selected themselves onto the list. Whether there is a selection effect depends on the kind of sampling that takes place and the nature of the inferences as well as the use of the analysis. For example, if the inferences relate only to hunters, then the population is the list of licensees, and selection onto the list is not an issue. The goal of estimation is to learn about the behavior of individuals from the relevant population of users. In the hunting example, when we sample from the list of license holders, we gather information about the relevant population of users, which allows us to make inferences about the demand function for the population of hunters.

The nature of sampling is an essential component of the construction of the likelihood function. In the following analysis, we first investigate sampling from lists of population and then on-site sampling.

7.2 Estimation of Censored Models

When sampling from a list or sample frame that includes users as well as non-users of the recreational site, one frequently finds censored data. The observations are censored at zero for people who take no trips. In a statistical sense, the censoring means that the complete distribution of the dependent variable may not be observable and the unobservable portion of the distribution is massed at zero. The sampling list can be large and implicit, as is the case for random digit phone calls, or the list can be explicit and small. An example of this would be estimating a model of angling behavior at a particular site from a sample of anglers drawn from a list of licensed anglers. In either case, the relevant population is contained in the list, but only some of the households sampled from the list will have visited the recreational site. The goal in this kind of analysis is to estimate demand functions and the willingness to pay for individuals drawn from the population of interest, conditional on arguments in the demand functions.

Suppose that the potential demand curve for the site for individual i in the population is given by

$$x_i^* = f(\mathbf{z}_i) + \varepsilon_i \tag{7.1}$$

where $\mathbf{z}_i$ is the row vector of M demand arguments that were derived in Chapter 6:

$$\begin{aligned} \mathbf{z}_i &= (p_{ij},\ j = 1,..,n;\ q_j,\ j = 1,...,n, y_i^f) \\ p_{ij} &= c_{ij} + w_i t_{ij} \end{aligned}$$

and ε_i is a random term that may represent measurement error or specification error. The potential demand function is representative of underlying behavior of the population. It can take on any real value: positive or negative, integer or fractional.

In the models for sampling from lists it is sometimes necessary to allow non-participants–those who are part of the list but have no plans to visit the site–to have different motivations and behavior. For example, when sampling from a list of the population with the goal of estimating the demand for a particular beach, surveyors might interview respondents who have no interest in the beach for reasons such as health and age. These people would not be responsive to prices and hence ought not to be in the sample for demand function estimation. These models are dealt with later in this chapter.

The setup for the sampling from a list model is as follows. We begin with the unobservable demand described in equation (7.1). The data is censored at zero, meaning that we have the dependent variable for all observations, but for some individuals, only zero is recorded. Observable demand (x_i) takes the form

$$\begin{aligned} x_i &= f(\mathbf{z}_i) + \varepsilon_i \text{ for } x_i^* > 0 \\ x_i &= 0 \text{ for } x_i^* \leq 0. \end{aligned} \tag{7.2}$$

This is a model of behavior of the units of the population. The idea is to estimate parameters for the function $f(\mathbf{z}_i)$ and of the distribution of ε_i.

Let $h(\varepsilon_i)$ be the probability density function for ε_i. The density for trips for individuals who take positive trips, which we denote

$$h^*(x_i|x_i^* > 0),$$

is constructed as the conditional probability of observing x_i given a positive number of trips are observed:

$$h^*(x_i|x_i^* > 0) = \frac{h(x_i - f(\mathbf{z}_i))}{\Pr(f(\mathbf{z}_i) + \varepsilon_i > 0)}.$$

The denominator normalizes the density function for positive trips to account for the truncation from not observing zero trips. The probability of observing an individual with zero trips is just $\Pr(f(\mathbf{z}_i) + \varepsilon_i \leq 0)$. We construct the ith contribution to the likelihood function as the product of the probability that trips are zero and the probability that trips are positive times the density of positive trips

$$\Pr(f(\mathbf{z}_i) + \varepsilon_i \leq 0)^{1-I_i} \cdot [\Pr(f(\mathbf{z}_i) + \varepsilon_i > 0) \cdot \frac{h(x_i - f(\mathbf{z}_i))}{\Pr(f(\mathbf{z}_i) + \varepsilon_i > 0)}]^{I_i}$$

where $I_i = 1$ when trips are positive and zero when trips are zero. Consequently the general likelihood for this type of problem is

$$\prod_{i=1}^{T} \Pr(f(\mathbf{z}_i) + \varepsilon_i \leq 0)^{1-I_i} \cdot h(x_i - f(\mathbf{z}_i))^{I_i}. \tag{7.3}$$

To proceed to the estimation stage, we need to make assumptions about the functional form of demand $f(\mathbf{z}_i)$ and the distribution of $\varepsilon_i, h(\varepsilon_i)$.

7.2.1 Estimating Tobit Models of Recreational Demand

The Tobit model is estimated when the specification of the individual demand function is given by

$$f(\mathbf{z}_i) = \mathbf{z}_i\boldsymbol{\beta}$$

where $\boldsymbol{\beta}$ is an $M \times 1$ column vector of parameters to be estimated and ε_i is distributed normally with mean zero, and constant variance: $\varepsilon_i \backsim N(0,\sigma^2)$. We use the general form of the likelihood function equation (7.3) to construct the Tobit likelihood function. Letting $\Phi(\frac{\mathbf{z}_i\boldsymbol{\beta}}{\sigma}) = \int_{-\infty}^{\mathbf{z}_i\boldsymbol{\beta}/\sigma} \phi(t)dt$, ($\phi(t)$ being the density function for an $N(0,1)$ variate) we write

$$L(\boldsymbol{\beta},\sigma|\mathbf{x},\mathbf{z}) = \prod_{i=1}^{T}[1-\Phi\left(\frac{\mathbf{z}_i\boldsymbol{\beta}}{\sigma}\right)]^{1-I_i}\cdot[\frac{1}{\sigma}\phi\left(\frac{x_i-\mathbf{z}_i\boldsymbol{\beta}}{\sigma}\right)]^{I_i} \tag{7.4}$$

since

$$\begin{aligned}\Pr(f(\mathbf{z}_i)+\varepsilon_i &\le 0) = \Pr(\mathbf{z}_i\boldsymbol{\beta}+\varepsilon_i \le 0)\\ &= \Pr(\varepsilon_i \le -\mathbf{z}_i\boldsymbol{\beta})\\ &= 1-\Pr(\frac{\varepsilon_i}{\sigma} \le \frac{\mathbf{z}_i\boldsymbol{\beta}}{\sigma})\\ &= 1-\Phi\left(\frac{\mathbf{z}_i\boldsymbol{\beta}}{\sigma}\right).\end{aligned}$$

The third step follows from the second for distributions that are symmetric about zero (see Appendix B). The second term in the equation (7.4), $\frac{1}{\sigma}\phi\left(\frac{x_i-\mathbf{z}_i\boldsymbol{\beta}}{\sigma}\right)$, follows from the transformation from ε to an $N(0,1)$ variate. That is, suppose that θ has density $\phi(\theta)$ and $\theta = (x-f(\mathbf{z}))/\sigma = g(x)$. Then the density for x is $\phi(g(x))g'(x)$, where $g'(x) = 1/\sigma$.

Olsen has shown that the Tobit likelihood function as defined in equation (7.4) is globally concave in the transformed parameters $\boldsymbol{\beta}/\sigma$ and $\frac{1}{\sigma}$, implying one can get maximum likelihood parameter estimates using standard maximization routines.

The log-likelihood function for the Tobit model is

$$\begin{aligned}\ln(L(\boldsymbol{\beta},\sigma|\mathbf{x},\mathbf{z})) &= \sum\nolimits_{i=1}^{T}(1-I_i)\ln[1-\Phi\left(\frac{\mathbf{z}_i\boldsymbol{\beta}}{\sigma}\right)] \\ &\quad +I_i\{\ln\left[\phi\left(\frac{x_i-\mathbf{z}_i\boldsymbol{\beta}}{\sigma}\right)\right]-\ln(\sigma)\}.\end{aligned} \tag{7.5}$$

The difference between OLS estimation on users only and the Tobit model is seen by noting that the Tobit likelihood functions has an extra term: $\sum_{i=1}^{T}(1-I_i)\ln[1-\Phi(\mathbf{z}_i\boldsymbol{\beta}/\sigma)]$. Maddala shows the maximum likelihood vector of parameter estimates can be written

$$\boldsymbol{\beta}_{ml} = \boldsymbol{\beta}_{ols} - \sigma(\mathbf{Z}_1'\mathbf{Z}_1)^{-1}\mathbf{Z}_0'\gamma_0$$

where $\mathbf{Z}_1$ is the data matrix for the $x_i > 0$ observations, $\mathbf{Z}_0$ is the data matrix for $x = 0$, and $\boldsymbol{\beta}_{ols}$ is the vector of parameter estimates obtained by running OLS on the $x_i > 0$ dataset. The vector γ_0 depends on unknown parameters β but this expression shows that the ordinary least squares estimates fail to capture the full effect of the regressors on the probability of participating.

The Tobit model can be estimated with standard iterative methods for maximum likelihood methods (see Appendix A). The estimation process usually converges quickly, unless there are many regressors and much collinearity.

7.2.2 Marginal Effects in the Tobit

To determine the partial effects of changes in covariates, it is useful to write the prediction of the Tobit. The predicted value of the demand will also be needed in calculating welfare effects. For the censored demand model, the expectation of the quantity of trips demanded for an individual randomly drawn from the population is

$$E(x) = \underbrace{E(x|x^* \leq 0)}_{=0} \cdot \Pr(x^* \leq 0) + E(x|x^* > 0) \cdot \Pr(x^* > 0). \quad (7.6)$$

The first term on the right hand side is zero by definition. In the case of the Tobit when the demand has a linear form and an additive normal error $x^* = \mathbf{z}\boldsymbol{\beta} + \varepsilon$, the expectation of trips, conditional on the trips being positive $E(x|x^* > 0)$, has the form (see Appendix B)

$$\begin{aligned} E(x|x^* > 0) &= E(\mathbf{z}\boldsymbol{\beta} + \varepsilon|\varepsilon > -\mathbf{z}\boldsymbol{\beta}) \quad (7.7) \\ &= \mathbf{z}\boldsymbol{\beta} + \sigma\frac{\phi(-\mathbf{z}\boldsymbol{\beta}/\sigma)}{\Phi(\mathbf{z}\boldsymbol{\beta}/\sigma)} \end{aligned}$$

where Φ is the cumulative density function for the standard normal distribution and ϕ is the probability density function for the standard normal. The term $\phi(-\mathbf{z}\boldsymbol{\beta}/\sigma)/\Phi(\mathbf{z}\boldsymbol{\beta}/\sigma)$ is the inverse Mills ratio. Substituting equation (7.7) into equation (7.6), the expected number of trips for an individual randomly drawn from the population when the demand model is Tobit, is given by

$$E(x) = \Phi(\frac{\mathbf{z}\boldsymbol{\beta}}{\sigma})\mathbf{z}\boldsymbol{\beta} + \sigma\phi(\frac{-\mathbf{z}\boldsymbol{\beta}}{\sigma}). \quad (7.8)$$

The derivative of the latent demand with respect to covariate j is just β_j. When we take the derivative of equation (7.8) with respect to the jth covariate, we get[1]

$$\frac{\partial E\left(x\right)}{\partial z_j}=\Phi(\frac{\mathbf{z}\boldsymbol{\beta}}{\sigma})\beta_j.$$

The covariate effect is just the probability of participation times the slope of the latent demand. The derivative with respect to the conditional demand is more complicated:

$$\frac{\partial E(x|x^*>0)}{\partial z_j}=\beta_j[1-\frac{\mathbf{z}\boldsymbol{\beta}}{\sigma}\frac{\phi(\frac{\mathbf{z}\boldsymbol{\beta}}{\sigma})}{\Phi(\frac{\mathbf{z}\boldsymbol{\beta}}{\sigma})}-(\frac{\phi(\frac{\mathbf{z}\boldsymbol{\beta}}{\sigma})}{\Phi(\frac{\mathbf{z}\boldsymbol{\beta}}{\sigma})})^2].$$

Elasticities are computed by multiplying by $z_j/E\left(x\right)$ or $z_j/E\left(x|x^*>0\right)$.

Example 17 *Estimating a Tobit Model*

To illustrate the workings of a Tobit model, we draw on a dataset used in the study of PCB contamination in New Bedford, Massachusetts.[2] This dataset meets the criterion of being drawn from a sampling list, because it results from a random phone survey of households in the greater New Bedford area. Hence the data and the model pertain to the behavior of representative households. The use of this dataset will illustrate the estimation of demand models and the calculation of welfare measures from the estimated models. The dataset includes household trips to all the saltwater beaches in the New Bedford area for the year 1986. The illustration relates to the demand for trips to the beach at Fort Phoenix, one of approximately a dozen beaches in the area.

The model specification to be used throughout the application is

$$x_i=\beta_0+\beta_1C_{FPi}+\beta_2C_{1i}+\beta_3C_{2i}+\beta_4P_{FPi}+\varepsilon_i.$$

The variables are the costs, including time cost for the beach at Fort Phoenix, the analogous costs for two substitutes, and the variable P_{FPi}, which takes a value of one if the household has a parking pass at Fort Phoenix for the year. Table 7.1 gives the descriptive statistics. The

[1] See Maddala, page 160 and Appendix B for this derivative and the derivative of the conditional demand. This simplified form of the derivative of the unconditional demand stems from the convenient fact that for a standard normal $\partial\Phi(\alpha/\sigma)/\partial\alpha=\sigma^{-1}\phi(\alpha/\sigma)$ and $\partial\phi(\alpha/\sigma)/\partial\alpha=-\alpha\sigma^{-2}\phi(\alpha/\sigma)$.

[2] More details on the study and the data can be found in the report by McConnell (1986) done with the support of Industrial Economics, Inc.

model is estimated using maximum likelihood methods. Many software packages, including SAS and LIMDEP, have routines for estimating Tobit models. This model was estimated in LIMDEP 7.0. The parameter estimates are given in Table 7.2.

TABLE 7.1. Means for New Bedford Beach Trips

Variable	Description	Mean n = 499
x	Trips to Fort Phoenix beach in 1986	3.84
C_{FP}	Round-trip travel costs ($0.084 per mile) plus monetary value of travel time* to Fort Phoenix beach	$3.19
C_1	Round-trip travel costs ($0.084 per mile) plus monetary value of travel time to nearest beach	$2.92
C_2	Round-trip travel costs ($0.084 per mile) plus monetary value of travel time to next nearest beach	$3.92
P_{FP}	1 if household has pass to Fort Phoenix; 0 otherwise	0.026

*The value of time is calculated by finding the wage of the occupational group of the household head in 1985. With the tax rates for Massachusetts and the US, the after-tax wage was calculated. See McConnell (1986) for details.

The parameter estimates are significantly different from zero with the expected signs. The demand curve slopes downward, because the own price effect is negative. The two substitute prices work in the direction one might expect intuitively, with higher costs of substitutes increasing the trip demand. The purchase of a pass also increases the demand for trips. The test for joint significance of all the variables derives from the statistic $-2\ln(L_R/L_U)$ which is distributed as a Chi-squared variable with the number of parameters associated with covariates as the degrees of freedom. L_R is the likelihood function value when all parameters associated with covariates $(\beta_1, .., \beta_4)$ equal zero. L_u is the unrestricted maximized likelihood function value. The tabled value of the $\chi^2_{.99}(4) = 13.3$, so the hypothesis that all of the coefficients are zero can be rejected.

TABLE 7.2. Tobit Model Estimation

$x_i = \beta_0+\beta_1 C_{FPi}+\beta_2 C_{1i}+\beta_3 C_{2i}+\beta_4 P_{FPi}+\varepsilon_i$		
Parameter	Estimate*	Standard Error
β_0	−7.50	3.54
β_1	−5.48	1.25
β_2	2.03	0.95
β_3	2.03	1.13
β_4	16.49	6.21
σ	20.80	1.25
Log-likelihood	−905.72	
-2 $\ln(L_R/L_U)$	30.85	

*All coefficients are different from zero at the 95% level of confidence.

7.3 Welfare Measurement in the Single Site Model

Before dealing with calculation issues, we address the measurement of welfare. Two types of welfare calculations are of interest: the value of access to a recreational site and the value of a change in the quality of a site. In the single site model, the value of access to the site is typically the only plausible welfare calculation that can be extracted from a single study. To understand the difficulty of measuring the welfare effects of a quality change from a single site model, consider the nature of the data gathering enterprise. Recreational data are typically gathered from a survey taken over a period such as a season or a year, or shorter. A deterministic model might look as follows:

$$x_{i1} = f_1(c_{i1} + w_i t_1, c_{i2} + w_i t_2, q_1, q_2, y_i^f)$$

where c_{ij} is the travel cost to site j, w_i is the wage rate, t_j is the time to site j, q_j is the quality at site j, and y_i^f is a measure of full income. This is just the basic travel cost model described in Chapter 6. In the typical data gathering exercise, the different residential locations give rise to the cross-section variation in the c's and t's, which allows the price effects to be calculated. But within a survey period, there is not likely to be sufficient variation in quality to allow the estimation of parameters on these variables. In an econometric sense, this is a simple matter of collinearity between the quality variables and a constant term.

Researchers have tried to overcome this handicap in various ways, which often cause more problems than they solve. One is to use quality variables such as fish catch that appear to vary across the sample, but do so because of random outcomes across individuals, and so could not be reasonably anticipated under normal circumstances. A second way is to use a subjective assessment of quality, where each individual may have different expectations about the quality he or she expects to encounter. There are several difficulties with subjective measures. They are likely to introduce individual-specific error, and they are not subject to control through public policy. All of these approaches rely on unobserved random or systematic variation across individuals. So the most prudent strategy for single site models is to accept the shortcomings of the data, and limit the welfare effects to the value of access to the site.

In Chapter 1 we proposed to calculate the value of access to the site as the willingness to pay rather than do without the site. This is calculated as the area under the utility-constant demand curve for the site. Given the typically low income effects and budget shares of recreational demand models, we can reasonably proceed with the area under the income-constant demand curve as a good estimate of the willingness to pay of household i for access to the site:

$$WTP(access) = \int_{C_i^0}^{C^*} f(p, c_2 + w_i t_2, y_i^f)dp \qquad (7.9)$$

where $C_i^0 = c_1 + w_i t_1$ and C^* is the relevant choke price, that is, the price at which quantity demanded goes to zero.

As with contingent valuation, the empirical process involves two steps: the estimation of parameters of the demand function and the calculation of the welfare measure, given the parameters. In practice, a number of issues arise in the calculation of equation (7.9). The discussion in Chapter 4 of the different sources of randomness in a contingent valuation setting applies also to the travel cost method. In this context, there are two sources of uncertainty: observed trips and estimated parameters. Further, as in the case of contingent valuation, one must decide how to handle the variation in willingness to pay across the sample.

To understand how uncertainty from demand emerges in the calculation of willingness to pay, recall from Chapter 1 that any willingness to pay for access can be written as a function of the quantity demanded or the prices and other exogenous variables. That is, one can write equation (7.9) as

$$WTP(access) = \int_0^{x^0} g(x)dx - x^0 g(x^0) = w(x^0|\boldsymbol{\beta}) \qquad (7.10)$$

where $g(x)$ is the inverse demand function: $p = g(x)$, and x^0 is the equilibrium quantity. Expression (7.10) will be random when the quantity x^0 is random, as it will be when the demand for trips is estimated. Given the other variables in the demand function, we can calculate the area under the demand curve and above the price line as the total value less the total cost, or as in equation (7.9). Hence expression (7.10) can be written as a function of x and parameters only, expressed as $w(x|\boldsymbol{\beta})$. The function $w(x|\boldsymbol{\beta})$ calculates willingness to pay for access, given the parameter estimates. And in practice, this approach is commonly used for single site models. But even in the calculation of welfare according to equation (7.10), there remains the choice of the observed quantity, x, or the predicted quantity. We use the expression

$$E(x_i) = \hat{x}_i$$

to denote the expectation of observation i's trips with respect to the random error of trips. Whether one uses the expectation of trips or observed trips depends on the interpretation of the error. As Bockstael and Strand show, if the error is measurement error, then the trips that are observed are not the true trips taken by the individual. However, if we regard the error as specification error, then in fact we have measured the true quantity of trips, and we are justified in using reported trips. When the error is considered measurement error, it would make sense to take the expectation of trips.

In deciding how to proceed, the ultimate goal of welfare analysis must be kept in mind. A plausible goal is to expand the sample mean willingness to pay to the population. In such a case, it would be reasonable to calculate the welfare for each individual in the sample and then use the sample mean. For a sample size of T, this would be

$$mean\ WTP(access) = \sum_{i=1}^{T} w(x_i|\boldsymbol{\beta})/T \tag{7.11}$$

where the quantity x_i may be either actual or predicted.

Now suppose that two conditions are met: $w(x_i|\boldsymbol{\beta})$ is linear in x_i, i.e., $w(x_i|\boldsymbol{\beta}) = x_i w(\boldsymbol{\beta})$ and the predictions $(\hat{x}_i)$ fit the mean: $\sum_{i=1}^{T} x_i/T = \bar{x} = \sum_{i=1}^{T} \hat{x}_i/T$. Then the sample mean willingness to pay for access will be the same, regardless of whether one uses the observed individual quantities demanded or the predicted quantities demanded. That is $mean\ WTP(access|observed\ trips) = mean\ WTP(access|expected$

trips) because

$$\sum_{i=1}^{T} w(\hat{x}_i|\boldsymbol{\beta})/T = \sum_{i=1}^{T} \hat{x}_i w(\boldsymbol{\beta})/T = \sum_{i=1}^{T} w(x_i|\boldsymbol{\beta})/T = \bar{x}w(\boldsymbol{\beta}).$$

In the applications, we calculate the sample mean willingness to pay, because for most applications, the purpose of demand estimation is benefit calculation that requires aggregate willingness to pay. On occasion, we demonstrate the difference between *mean* $WTP(access)$ when calculated with the actual and observed trips. In cases where the willingness to pay is not linear in the quantity demanded, the difference between WTP calculated with actual and observed trips can be substantial.

7.3.1 Welfare Measurement in the Tobit

The Tobit model is almost always estimated linear in parameters and covariates, and this linear form leads to a measure of willingness to pay that is increasing and quadratic in trips. This causes some difficulty in the calculation stage.

For simplicity, write the latent demand function as $x_i^+ = \beta_{0i}^+ + \beta_1 C_i^0$, where C^0 is the current own-site travel cost and β_{0i}^+ is either a constant or a linear in parameters function of covariate other than own-site travel cost, plus the error term. Let $0 = \beta_0^+ + \beta_1 C^*$ determine the choke price that sets quantity equal to zero such that $C^* = -\beta_0^+/\beta_1$. The individual subscript has been dropped for convenience. Integrating under the demand curve from the current price C^0 to the choke price C^* yields consumer surplus, which equals willingness to pay in this case:

$$\begin{aligned} WTP &= \int_{C^0}^{C^*} (\beta_0^+ + \beta_1 C) dC \\ &= \beta_0^+ C^* + \frac{\beta_1 C^{*2}}{2} - \left[\beta_0^+ C^0 + \frac{\beta_1 \left(C^0\right)^2}{2}\right]. \qquad (7.12) \end{aligned}$$

The following simplification holds for any C:

$$\begin{aligned} \beta_0^+ C + \frac{\beta_1 C^2}{2} &= \frac{2\beta_0^+ \beta_1 C + \beta_1^2 C^2}{2\beta_1} \\ &= \frac{\left(\beta_0^+ + \beta_1 C\right)^2}{2\beta_1} - \frac{\left(\beta_0^+\right)^2}{2\beta_1}. \end{aligned}$$

By definition, $\beta_0^+ + \beta_1 C^* = 0$, and $\beta_0^+ + \beta_1 C^0 = x^+$. Upon evaluation and rearranging, the equation (7.12) becomes

$$WTP = -\frac{(x^+)^2}{2\beta_1}.$$

Using this expression for WTP, we can now investigate the appropriate measure of demand to use in the calculation of welfare.

7.3.2 Welfare with Measurement Error

If the error term is assumed to be measurement error in the dependent variable then Bockstael and Strand show that the expected value of trips is a more appropriate demand measure to use in the calculation of welfare. For the Tobit, this is given by equation (7.8). Note however, that this ignores the uncertainty in parameters, because the expectation has been taken only with respect to the stochastic term in the demand function. A consistent estimate of $E(x)$, denoted $\widehat{E}(x)$, is found by substituting consistent estimates of $\boldsymbol{\beta}$. Tobit maximum likelihood parameter estimates serve this purpose.

With measurement error, a consistent estimate of the value of access from the Tobit model is

$$\widehat{WTP} = -\frac{\left(\widehat{E}(x)\right)^2}{2\widehat{\beta}_1}.$$

7.3.3 Welfare with Specification Error

If, on the other hand, the error term is assumed to represent specification error, then Bockstael and Strand show that the appropriate measure of trip demand is individual observed demand x_i. A consistent estimate of the value of site access with specification error is then:

$$\widetilde{WTP} = -\frac{x^2}{2\widehat{\beta}_1}.$$

The only difference between $\widehat{WTP}$ and $\widetilde{WTP}$ is the measure of trips used in the calculation of the estimate of consumer surplus. Parameter estimates are not affected the assumption about the source of the error. If observed trips are used to calculate welfare, then any individual taking zero trips will have zero consumer surplus: $\widetilde{WTP}(x=0)=0$. However, if the error is due to measurement, and expected trips are used to calculate $\widehat{WTP}$, then all sample individuals will have a positive estimated consumer surplus.

Example 18 *Welfare Measurement in a Tobit*

Recall the previous example from New Bedford, Massachusetts. The basic model specification is:

$$x_i = \beta_0 + \beta_1 C_{FPi} + \beta_2 C_{1i} + \beta_3 C_{2i} + \beta_4 P_{FPi} + \varepsilon_i.$$

The variables are given in Table B.1. The two approaches to calculating welfare can be compared using the prices and quantities for a given observation. Willingness to pay for access is given by

$$WTP = -\frac{x^2}{2\beta_1}$$

where the x can be the observed or expected trips and β_1 is the own-site coefficient on travel cost. For the expected trips, we use the prices and the estimated parameters to calculate expected trips as given in equation (7.8). Otherwise just the observed trip value is used.

The most common goal is to expand the willingness to pay to the population. If the sample is drawn from the sampling list in a representative way, then a reasonable approach is to calculate the sample mean, using either the expected trips approach or the observed trips. That is, the WTP is calculated for each observation in the sample, and then the sample mean is calculated. In this particular case, we find that when we calculate sample mean willingness to pay for the two methods, we get for the expected trips

$$\sum_{i=1}^{T} \frac{\widehat{E}\left(x_i\right)^2 / \left(2 \cdot 5.48\right)}{T} = \$2.16$$

and for the observed trips

$$\sum_{i=1}^{T} \frac{{x_i}^2 / \left(2 \cdot 5.48\right)}{T} = \$10.77.$$

The difference between the two estimates is quite large. It is a consequence of the convex nature of the consumer surplus function for the linear demand curve. In the use of the Tobit, it is perhaps more reasonable to extrapolate to the sample using the first expression above, with expected trips, because the second expression may simply be squaring errors in measurement in trips. But, this is a subjective decision depending on the survey design and confidence in data collection methods. Kling (1992) provides more evidence on the impact of the error measurement.

7.4 Count Models of Recreational Demand

The Tobit model is appealing because it allows for a large mass of observations at zero. But the Tobit has embedded some unsatisfactory assumptions. For example, the derivation of the Tobit is based on the inherent unobservability of an underlying continuous unbounded demand function. This implies that if demand were fully observable, negative trips would be possible. Count data models are intuitively appealing for recreational demand because they deal with non-negative integer valued dependent variables. For recreation, the number of trips is a non-negative integer. The integer characteristic is less important than the non-negative range of the variable. The count model specifies the quantity demanded, trips, as a random non-negative integer, with a mean that is dependent on exogenous regressors. For the Poisson or variants thereof, the functional form for expected demand is typically exponential, though it is easy to estimate a power function. This becomes another advantage of the count model, because it is hard to estimate anything besides a linear model in a Tobit framework. On the other hand, linear expected demands are more difficult to estimate in the count models. In fact, there is little room for flexibility in the functional form of recreational demand models. The class of permissible functions is typically determined by the distribution assumed. We are concerned with single site models in this section. Several researchers have estimated multiple site count models. See, for example, Shonkwiler and von Haefen.

The basic count model is written

$$\Pr(x_i = n) = f(n, \mathbf{z}_i\boldsymbol{\beta}), \ n = 0, 1, 2...$$

In the case of sampling from lists, the demand variable x can take on values from 0 up to a large number. Unless the upper truncation is significant, there is no need to recognize the obviously finite nature of trips with upper truncation or censoring. We will begin with the most common count model, the Poisson.

7.4.1 The Poisson Model

The Poisson probability density function is given by

$$\Pr(x_i = n) = \frac{e^{-\lambda_i}\lambda_i^n}{n!}, n = 0, 1, 2, ... \quad (7.13)$$

The parameter λ_i is both the mean and the variance of the distribution. This particular result has often been found to be violated in recreational data, and will lead to a more general model below. Because it is necessary that $\lambda_i > 0$, it is common to specify it as an exponential function:

$$\lambda_i = \exp(\mathbf{z}_i\boldsymbol{\beta}). \tag{7.14}$$

Given this specification, we can then get the likelihood function in terms of the parameters $\boldsymbol{\beta}$.

The Poisson likelihood function is straightforward. We observe the number of trips each individual takes, and then use equation (7.13) to write the probability of observing that number of trips. The sample likelihood function becomes

$$L(\boldsymbol{\beta}|\mathbf{z},\mathbf{x}) = \prod_{i=1}^{T} \frac{\exp(-\exp(\mathbf{z}_i\boldsymbol{\beta}))\exp((\mathbf{z}_i\boldsymbol{\beta})x_i)}{x_i!}$$

and the log-likelihood function is

$$\ln(L(\boldsymbol{\beta}|\mathbf{z},\mathbf{x})) = \sum\nolimits_{i=1}^{T}[-e^{\mathbf{z}_i\boldsymbol{\beta}} + \mathbf{z}_i\boldsymbol{\beta}x_i - \ln(x_i!)].$$

This log-likelihood function is globally concave in the parameters. Unless there is severe collinearity, maximum likelihood estimation converges quickly.

Marginal Effects in the Poisson

Because the conditional mean of a Poisson is λ, expected trips is given by

$$E(x_i|\mathbf{z}_i\boldsymbol{\beta}) = \lambda_i = \exp(\mathbf{z}_i\boldsymbol{\beta}). \tag{7.15}$$

This gives us a way of understanding the parameters that are estimated from the Poisson. The derivative of expected trips with respect to an independent variable, say z_{ij}, is given by

$$\frac{\partial E(x_i|\mathbf{z}_i\boldsymbol{\beta})}{\partial z_{ij}} = \beta_j \exp(\mathbf{z}_i\boldsymbol{\beta}).$$

The slope of the expected demand function varies with the expected number of trips, going from steep at high levels of expected trips to flat at low levels. The half-elasticity

$$\frac{\partial E(x_i|\mathbf{z}_i\boldsymbol{\beta})}{\partial z_{ij}} \frac{1}{E(x_i|\mathbf{z}_i\boldsymbol{\beta})} = \beta_j$$

gives an alternate interpretation for the parameter estimates. The parameter estimates represent the percentage change in the dependent variable for a unit change in the covariate. This half-elasticity is constant for all values of the associated covariates. The full elasticity can be calculated by multiplying the slope by $z_{ij}/\exp(\mathbf{z}_i\boldsymbol{\beta})$, giving $z_{ij}\beta_j$. The elasticity is a function of the covariate.

Example 19 *Estimating a Poisson Model*

We illustrate the Poisson using the same data and model specification used for estimating the Tobit, described in Table 7.1. The conditional expected trip function is given by

$$E(x_i|\mathbf{z}_i) = \exp(\beta_0 + \beta_1 C_{FPi} + \beta_2 C_{1i} + \beta_3 C_{2i} + \beta_4 P_{FP_i}).$$

The parameters are estimated in LIMDEP 7.0, and are given in Table 7.3. All of the coefficients have the expected sign (negative own-price

TABLE 7.3. Poisson Model Estimation

$E(x_i\|z_i) = \exp(\beta_0+\beta_1 C_{FPi}+\beta_2 C_{1i}+\beta_3 C_{2i}+\beta_4 P_{FPi})$		
Parameter	Estimate*	Standard Error
β_0	1.64	0.07
β_1	−0.47	0.02
β_2	0.12	0.02
β_3	0.17	0.02
β_4	1.07	0.08
Log-likelihood	−3160.60	
$-2\ln(L_R/L_U)$	545.41	

*All estimates different from zero at 99% level of confidence.

effects, and positive cross-price effects) and are different from zero at a high level of confidence. The price coefficient implies that a one dollar increase in the price of a trip to Fort Phoenix results in a 47% decrease in the expected number of trips. This is large, but not surprising in this case given the ease in substitution among local beaches. The likelihood ratio statistic $-2\ln(L_R/L_U)$ under the null hypothesis that all parameters associated with covariates are zero, is large compared to the tabled $\chi^2_{.99}(4)$ of 13.3. The model appears reasonable from a behavioral perspective and statistically acceptable.

Welfare Measurement in the Poisson

The Poisson model can be used to calculate the willingness to pay for access by taking the area under the expected demand function. The observed dependent variable is assumed to be a random draw from a Poisson distribution with mean λ_i. That is, each individual has a distribution of trips from which a single draw is observed. In the Poisson model, all derivations are based on the expected demand function

$$E(x_i) = \lambda_i.$$

The value of access equals the area under the expected demand curve.

For the exponential demand function, the choke price (C^*) is infinite. To see this, consider the simple demand specification: $x = e^{\beta_0+\beta_1 C}$ where C is the travel cost, and β_0 can be a constant or a function covariates other than own-price. For any finite C, $x = e^{\beta_0+\beta_1 C} > 0$. Defining C^0 as the current travel cost, consumer surplus for access is

$$\begin{aligned} WTP(access) &= \int_{C^0}^{\infty} e^{\beta_0+\beta_1 C} dC \\ &= \left[\frac{e^{\beta_0+\beta_1 C}}{\beta_1}\right]_{C=C^0}^{C\to\infty} = -\frac{x}{\beta_1} \end{aligned} \tag{7.16}$$

when $\beta_1 < 0$. There is a significant difference between the WTP(access) for the Poisson and for the Tobit, based on the linear versus exponential demand function form. For the linear model, the WTP is a convex function of trips, while in the exponential, WTP is a linear function of trips. In the Poisson expression for sample mean WTP, one can use the mean of observed trips or mean of the expected trips. because the Poisson model has the property that it is mean fitting. A simple demonstration of this is as follows.

The system of first-order conditions to the log-likelihood maximization problem are $\sum_i (x_i - \lambda_i) z_{ij} = 0, \forall j$. For the first element, $z_{i1} = 1$. This implies that $\sum_i (x_i - \lambda_i) = 0$ and $\sum_i x_i/T = \sum_i \lambda_i/T$. Because WTP is linear in the number of trips, and the Poisson is mean fitting, sample mean consumer surplus based on expected or observed trips will be identical. This is not the case for the Tobit demand models.

Example 20 *Welfare in the Poisson*

To compare the welfare calculations from Poisson and Tobit models, we calculate sample mean consumer surplus. Using the sample mean results in a welfare calculation for the Poisson of $WTP = 3.83/0.47 =$ \$8.15. This would be a reasonable estimate to extrapolate to the population of users.

Example 21 *The Poisson Model with a Power Function*

In the Poisson model, one wants to insure that expected demand is positive, so that the typical choice for functional form is the exponential function of equation (7.14). By taking the logarithms of the strictly positive arguments of demand, we can construct a power function. Let the expected demand be

$$\lambda_i = \exp(\mathbf{z}_i^* \boldsymbol{\beta})$$

where $z_{ik}^* = \log(z_{ik})$ if $z_{ik} > 0$ for all k and $z_{ik}^* = z_{ik}$ if $z_{ik} \leq 0$ for any k. For example, we could replace the price by the log of the price, but leave a dummy variable in its zero-one form. Then the expected demand would be

$$\lambda_i = \prod_{k=1}^{M^+} z_{ik}^{\beta_k} \exp(\sum_{j=M^+ +1}^{M} z_{ij}\beta_j)$$

where the first M^+ variables are transformed and the last $M - M^+$ not transformed. We estimate this model for the dataset of Table 7.1, transforming all the prices but leaving the dummy variable in its natural form. The parameter estimates are in Table 7.4.

TABLE 7.4. Poisson Model with Power Function

$E(x_i \mid z_i) = C_{FPi}^{\beta_1} C_{1i}^{\beta_2} C_{2i}^{\beta_3} \exp(\beta_0 + \beta_4 P_{FPi})$		
Parameter	Estimate*	Standard Error
β_0	1.54	0.08
β_1	−0.96	0.06
β_2	0.36	0.04
β_3	0.26	0.08
β_4	1.14	0.08
Log-likelihood	−3181.9	
$-2\ln(L_R/L_U)$	502.7	

*All estimates different from zero at 99% level of confidence.

The coefficients are all of the expected sign and significant. Welfare is calculated with expected demand. Write the expected demand function as $E(x) = kC^{\beta_1}$ where k is a constant that incorporates the non-own price arguments and C is the own travel cost. Then the welfare measure becomes:

$$\begin{aligned} WTP(access) &= \int_{C^0}^{\infty} kC^{\beta_1}dC \\ &= -\frac{kC^{\beta_1+1}}{1+\beta_1} \; if \; 1+\beta_1 < 0. \end{aligned}$$

If $1 + \beta_1 \geq 0$, the integral[3] does not converge and consumer surplus is not defined. Looking at the coefficients in Table 7.4, we see that $1 + \beta_1 = 0.04$; in effect, demand is inelastic, and consumer surplus is not defined. Given the functional form, it must be inelastic over the whole range of price, an implausible model. We will return to this model in the following section.

7.4.2 The Negative Binomial Model

While the Poisson has some advantages over the Tobit in calculating willingness to pay, it is subject to the potential misspecification of assuming that the conditional mean and variance are equal: $E(x_i|\mathbf{z}_i\boldsymbol{\beta}) = V(x_i|\mathbf{z}_i\boldsymbol{\beta}) = \lambda_i$. For recreational trip data, the variance is often greater than the mean, implying overdispersion in the data. One consequence of overdispersion is that the standard errors estimated in the Poisson model are underestimated, leading too frequently to the rejection of null hypotheses of no association. Greene (1997) reviews several types of tests for overdispersion. Here we look at a specific model, the negative binomial.

Many versions of the negative binomial model exist. Cameron and Trivedi provide a detailed exposition of these models. We focus on a common version of the negative binomial model: a Poisson model with a gamma distributed error term in the mean. Suppose we write the log of the conditional mean from the Poisson model as the sum of $\mathbf{z}_i\boldsymbol{\beta}$ and an unobserved error:

$$\log(E(x_i)) = \mathbf{z}_i\boldsymbol{\beta} + \theta_i$$

where θ_i represents unobserved individual differences (or unobserved heterogeneity). The model provides for systematic and random variation

[3] The integral is evaluated as $\left[\frac{kC^{\beta_1+1}}{\beta_1+1}\right]_{C=C^0}^{C\rightarrow\infty}$. If $\beta_1+1 > 0$, the term is unbounded from above as C increases. If $\beta_1 + 1 = 0$, the term is undefined.

in the mean across individuals. Now we substitute the right hand side into the probability statement for a Poisson random variable to get the distribution of trips, conditional on θ_i:

$$\Pr(x_i|\theta_i) = \frac{\exp(-\exp(\mathbf{z}_i\boldsymbol{\beta} + \theta_i))\exp(\mathbf{z}_i\boldsymbol{\beta} + \theta_i)n}{x_i!}. \tag{7.17}$$

If $exp(\theta_i) = v_i$ has a normalized gamma distribution, with $E(v_i) = 1$, then the density for v_i will be given by[4] $h(v) = \frac{\alpha^\alpha}{\Gamma(\alpha)}\exp(-\alpha v)v^{\alpha-1}$. The unconditional probability function for the number of trips, x_i, is found by integrating out the error v. The resulting probability function is the negative binomial[5]

$$\Pr(x_i) = \frac{\Gamma\left(x_i + \frac{1}{\alpha}\right)}{\Gamma(x_i+1)\Gamma\left(\frac{1}{\alpha}\right)}\left(\frac{\frac{1}{\alpha}}{\frac{1}{\alpha}+\lambda_i}\right)^{\frac{1}{\alpha}}\left(\frac{\lambda_i}{\frac{1}{\alpha}+\lambda_i}\right)^{x_i}$$

where $\lambda_i = \exp(\mathbf{z}_i\boldsymbol{\beta})$. The mean of the negative binomial distribution is $E(x_i) = \lambda_i = \exp(\mathbf{z}_i\boldsymbol{\beta})$. However, now the variance of the dependent variable is $V(x_i) = \lambda_i(1 + \alpha\lambda_i)$. The parameter α can be interpreted as the overdispersion parameter. If $\alpha = 0$, no overdispersion exists and the negative binomial distribution collapses to the Poisson distribution in the limit. To see this, Cameron and Trivedi show that

$$\lim_{\alpha\to 0}\frac{\Gamma\left(x_i + \frac{1}{\alpha}\right)}{\Gamma(x_i+1)\Gamma\left(\frac{1}{\alpha}\right)}\left(\frac{\frac{1}{\alpha}}{\frac{1}{\alpha}+\lambda_i}\right)^{\frac{1}{\alpha}}\left(\frac{\lambda_i}{\frac{1}{\alpha}+\lambda_i}\right)^{x_i} = \frac{e^{-\lambda}\lambda^x}{x!}.$$

For details, see Appendix B. If $\alpha > 0$ then overdispersion exists and the Poisson model is rejected in favor of the negative binomial. In the rare case that $\alpha < 0$, the data are underdispersed. In this case, the Poisson model should still be rejected in favor of the negative binomial. Therefore, a test of $\alpha = 0$ is both a test for overdispersion and a test of the negative binomial model against the null hypothesis of a Poisson.

Example 22 *Estimating a Negative Binomial Model*

To illustrate the negative binomial, we return to the exponential demand function estimated above, with the same specification. Parameter estimates are reported in Table 7.5. The upshot of the estimation

[4] The more general expression for the gamma distribution is $h(v) = \frac{v^{\alpha-1}\exp(-v/\beta)}{\Gamma(\alpha)\beta^\alpha}$. The expectation of v is $\alpha\beta$. By setting $\alpha = 1/\beta$, the distribution is normalized so that the expectation of the variate is one.

[5] See Cameron and Trivedi or Greene (1997) for more details.

TABLE 7.5. Negative Binomial Model Estimation

$E(x_i\|z_i) = \exp(\beta_0+\beta_1 C_{FPi}+\beta_2 C_{1i}+\beta_3 C_{2i}+\beta_4 P_{FPi})$		
Parameter	Estimate*	Standard Error
β_0	1.62	0.42
β_1	−0.53	0.23
β_2	0.18	0.17
β_3	0.18	0.14
β_4	0.86	1.38
α	7.49	0.69
Log-likelihood	−889.3	
$-2\ln(L_R/L_U)$	4542.6	

*Only β_0, β_1 and α are different from zero at the 95% level of confidence.

from the negative binomial is less confidence in the individual parameter estimates, although their magnitude does not change greatly. In particular, the null hypotheses that the substitute prices and the presence of a pass have no impact on the conditional mean can no longer be rejected at any plausible level of significance. The own price coefficient is still negative and significant, but the ratio of the parameter estimate to the standard error falls from 23.5 to 2.3. Nevertheless, if we maintain the hypothesis of the negative binomial, and test the hypothesis that $\beta_1 = \beta_2 = \beta_3 = \beta_4 = 0$, the quantity $-2\ln(L_R/L_U)$ equals 17.8, which exceeds the tabled $\chi^2_{.99}(4)$ of 13.3. Hence the hypothesis that these four parameters are simultaneously zero can be rejected. Note that the quantity $-2\ln(L_R/L_U)$ reported in Table 7.5 refers to the hypothesis that $\beta_1 = \beta_2 = \beta_3 = \beta_4 = \alpha = 0$, not just that the covariate effects are zero, and so the high level of significance implied by the Chi-squared statistic relates not just to the coefficients on the covariates, but includes the coefficient of dispersion, which is highly significant.

This result concerning the test of the Poisson versus the negative binomial is common in models of recreational demand. Recreational demand data are frequently too dispersed to be modeled with a Poisson.

Concerning welfare calculations, we note that the negative binomial still has the property that the sample mean of the predicted value of the trips equals the sample mean of the observed value. Thus the sample mean willingness to pay for access changes only to the extent that the coefficient on the own-travel cost variable changes. Using the new travel cost estimate and the sample mean trips yields the welfare calculation $WTP(access|\bar{x}) = 3.83/0.53 = \$7.22$, compared to the estimate of \$8.15 for the Poisson. Although the more restrictive Poisson model is rejected statistically, the models differ only slightly in their welfare estimates.

Given the individually insignificant estimates of β_2 and β_3 in Table 7.5, we test the hypothesis that they are jointly equal to zero. The restriction that $\beta_2 = \beta_3 = 0$ is tested by comparing the restricted with the unrestricted log likelihood functions. Estimating the same model, leaving out C_1 and C_2 gives a likelihood value of -891.83 (Table 7.6) compared with a value of -889.3 when the variables are included (Table 7.5). The quantity $-2\ln(L_R/L_U) = 5.06$. This is an ambiguous test value. The tabled $\chi^2_{.90}(2)$ and $\chi^2_{.95}(2)$ are 4.61 and 5.99. We cannot reject the hypothesis that these coefficients are both zero at the 95% level, but we can reject at the 90% level. Suppose that we require the significance level to be 95%. Then we would use the model that excludes C_1 and C_2. This model is shown in Table 7.6 resulting in an estimate of β_1 equal to -0.26. Using the mean value of trips of 3.83, we obtain an estimate

TABLE 7.6. Restricted Negative Binomial

$E(x_i\|z_i) = \exp(\beta_0 + \beta_1 C_{FPi} + \beta_4 P_{FPi})$		
Parameter	Estimate	Standard Error
β_0	*2.05	0.36
β_1	*−0.26	0.09
β_4	1.02	1.24
α	*7.65	0.71
Log-likelihood	−891.8	

*Different from zero at the 95% level of confidence.

of mean consumer surplus: $WTP(access|\bar{x}, restricted\ specification) = 3.83/0.26 = \$14.73$. This higher estimate of WTP illustrates a common result from omitting the prices of other recreation sites, which most often work as substitutes. However, the sensible specification is to include the price of substitutes.

Example 23 *The Negative Binomial with a Power Function Demand*

Just as we estimated a power function in the Poisson, we can do the same with the negative binomial. Using the same specification as in Table 7.5, but with the negative binomial distribution rather than

Poisson, we reestimate the model. The parameters are given in Table 7.7.

TABLE 7.7. Negative Binomial with Power Function

$E(x_i \vert z_i) = C_{FPi}^{\beta_1} C_{1i}^{\beta_2} C_{2i}^{\beta_3} \exp(\beta_0 + \beta_4 P_{FPi})$		
Parameter	Estimate	Standard Error
β_0	*1.55	0.08
β_1	*−1.37	0.61
β_2	0.55	0.45
β_3	0.44	0.46
β_4	0.87	1.47
α	*7.53	0.70
Log-likelihood	−889.9	
$-2\ln(L_R/L_U)$	4584.0	

*Different from zero at 95% level of confidence.

Here again we see that the Poisson is deceptive in giving standard errors that are too low. In this version of the count model, only the own price, constant and dispersion parameter are significantly different from zero. Calculating the consumer surplus with the mean value of trips of 3.83, we find $WTP(access|\bar{x}$, power function$) = -3.83/(1+\beta_1) = 3.83/0.37 = \$10.35$. This is considerably higher than the corresponding consumer surplus for the exponential function. Here unfortunately we run into the problem of non-nested hypothesis testing. The exponential and the power function models are not nested, so simple likelihood methods are not available. Intuition sometimes helps, but there is no strong argument for one model or the other in this case. For further discussion of non-nested hypothesis testing see Godfrey (1988).

There are several lessons here. An uncritical acceptance of Poisson results often leads to excessive confidence in parameter estimates. Further, when the substitute prices are omitted from the specification, the estimated demand function will tend to be more inelastic and imply higher consumer surplus for access. But one must also be wary of the effects of collinearity on the precision of estimates in travel cost models. Costs of substitute sites are often highly correlated. This correlation reduces the precision of estimates, making rejection of the null hypothesis of no association more difficult. For example, in the case of Fort Phoenix, in a diagnostic regression of the own travel cost on the substitutes costs, the two substitute travel costs explain 62% of the variance of the own travel cost.[6] This high collinearity explains the low significance of the substitute sites. One may argue for their inclusion, because if they truly belong in the demand function, their exclusion will bias upwards the estimate of consumer surplus.

7.5 Models for On-Site Sampling

We now turn to on-site sampling. This is a frequently adopted sampling method because it ensures that surveys will be conducted with users. In many circumstances on-site sampling is cheaper than a survey of the population, especially when only a small proportion of the population engages in the site activity. If the activity were swimming at a small beach, then it would take a very large phone survey to discover enough users to make precise inferences about users' preferences. The statistical analysis for on-site sampling is carefully analyzed in Shaw. Englin and Shonkwiler apply the analysis.

7.5.1 Truncation

With an on-site sample, we observe only those individuals who take trips–that is only the $x_i > 0$. The demands for the individuals observed will have a truncated error, or truncated demands, because only those individuals with sufficiently small errors will be observed.

Consider a general form of a demand function. For simplicity, suppose that $g(x_i)$ is the probability density function for trips. The probability that an individual will have positive trips is simply $\Pr[x_i > 0]$. The conditional density function for individuals with positive trips, denoted $g\left(x_i|x_i > 0\right)$, becomes

$$g\left(x_i|x_i > 0\right) = \frac{g(x_i)}{\Pr[x_i > 0]} \text{ for } x_i > 0. \tag{7.18}$$

Normalizing by the probability of a positive observation ensures that the density function of the truncated model integrates to one.

---

[6] This comes from a regression of C_{FP} on a constant, C_1, C_2 and P_{FP}, with an R^2 of 0.62.

7.5.2 Endogenous Stratification

In studies of recreational demand, we model the behavior of individuals, and expand the sample results to the population of individuals. Hence we want the sample proportion of individuals of particular types to equal the population proportion. But when the sample is drawn from an on-site survey, individuals who have a high use level are more likely to be drawn. We develop the models that correct for this. The basic analysis is done in Shaw.

Consider a population that uses a recreational site. We divide the population into strata based on the number of trips taken, such that stratum i contains individuals who take i trips. Proportional random sampling occurs when the sampling proportions for a given stratum equal the population proportion. Stratification occurs when the proportion of sampled individuals systematically varies from the population proportion. Endogenous stratification occurs when the systematic variation in the sampling proportion is dependent on the characteristics of the individuals in the sample.

Consider for simplicity a homogeneous population where N_x represents the number in the population taking x trips: $x \in \{0, 1, 2, ...\}$. Let N be the population of users. The population proportion of individuals taking x trips is N_x/N. The on-site sample proportion of individuals taking x trips, $h(x)$,will be

$$h(x) = \frac{xN_x}{\sum_{t=1}^{\infty} tN_t} \tag{7.19}$$

where the numerator is the total trips taken by individuals taking x trips, and the denominator is the total trips taken by the full population. For example, suppose there are two types of users in the population: 25 take 1 trip ($x = 1$) and 75 take 2 trips ($x = 2$). Hence $N_1 = 25$ and $N_2 = 75$. In aggregate there will be 175 trips, 25 by the 25 who take one trip and 150 by those who take two trips. On average, the proportion of type-1 individuals on-site is

$$h(1) = \frac{1 \cdot N_1}{1 \cdot N_1 + 2 \cdot N_2} = \frac{1}{7}.$$

Likewise, the proportion of type-2 individuals on-site is

$$h(2) = \frac{2 \cdot N_1}{1 \cdot N_1 + 2 \cdot N_2} = \frac{6}{7}.$$

If we could pool all the trips, and draw at random, then $h(2)$ would be the probability of drawing an individual with $x = 2$. In fact, sampling takes place on a finite number of days during a recreational year, and we assume that the sampling proportions on those days reflect the proportions that one would achieve if all the recreational trips were pooled.

To see the problem with endogenous stratification, consider the expected number of trips from the population and from the sample. For the population, the expected number of trips from a randomly drawn individual will be

$$E_P(x) = \sum_{x=0}^{\infty} x P_x$$

where P_x is the population proportion of individuals taking x trips. Continuing the example above, the expected number of trips from an individual in the population is

$$\begin{aligned} E_P(x) &= 1 \cdot P_1 + 2 \cdot P_2 \\ &= \frac{25}{100} + 2\frac{75}{100} = 1.75. \end{aligned}$$

For the on-site sample, expected trips is

$$E_S(x) = \sum_{x=0}^{\infty} x h(x)$$

which for the above example is

$$\begin{aligned} E_S(x) &= 1 \cdot h(1) + 2 \cdot h(2) \\ &= \frac{1}{7} + 2\frac{6}{7} = 1.86. \end{aligned}$$

Because the on-site interviewing process is more likely to intercept avid recreators, the sample average number of trips will be higher than the population mean.

For the correct likelihood function, we need to account for the oversampling of avid recreators. Equation (7.19) gives the relationship between the sample observed proportion of individuals taking each quantity of trips $h(x)$ and the population number of individuals taking these trips. Dividing the numerator and denominator by the total number of individuals in the population (N), equation (7.19) becomes

$$h(x) = \frac{x(N_x/N)}{\sum_{t=1}^{\infty} t(N_t/N)} \tag{7.20}$$

$$= \frac{xP_x}{\sum_{t=1}^{\infty} tP_x}. \tag{7.21}$$

Because the population proportions (P_x) of trips are unknown, the number of trips taken by an individual in the population can be thought of as a discrete random variable with probability function:

$$\Pr(trips = x) = g(x) \quad x \in \{0, 1, 2, 3, ...\}$$

P_x can now be represented as

$$P_x = g(x).$$

Substituting into (7.20) gives the sample probability of observing x trips as a function of the population probability

$$h(j) = \frac{jg(j)}{\sum_{t=1}^{\infty} tg(t)}. \tag{7.22}$$

Noting that for a non-negative integer valued random variable (x)

$$\sum_{t=1}^{\infty} tg(t) = \sum_{x=0}^{\infty} tg(t) = E(x),$$

we can write the probability of observing j trips from an individual in an on-site sample as:

$$h(j) = \frac{jg(j)}{E_P(x)}. \tag{7.23}$$

Though not apparent, equation (7.23) accounts for the truncation present in an on-site sample. If we consider only the population of users, then the population probability distribution $g(x)$ is truncated at zero. The probability of observing x by an individual drawn at random from the population is

$$\begin{aligned} \Pr(trips = x | trips > 0) &= g(x|x > 0) \quad x \in \{1, 2, 3, ...\} \\ &= \frac{g(x)}{\Pr(x > 0)} \quad x \in \{1, 2, 3, ...\}. \end{aligned}$$

Substituting into equation (7.22), the probability of observing x trips in an endogenously stratified truncated sample becomes

$$h(j|x > 0) = \frac{j\frac{g(j)}{\Pr(x>0)}}{\sum_{t=1}^{\infty} t\frac{g(t)}{\Pr(x>0)}} \tag{7.24}$$

$$= \frac{jg(j)}{\sum_{t=1}^{\infty} tg(t)} = h(j). \tag{7.25}$$

The normalization constant from the truncation cancels due to the endogenous stratification. Given the endogenous nature of sampling, individual observations must be weighted by the inverse of expected value of trips.

The final consideration is incorporating individual effects into the model. This turns out to be a simple extension of equation (7.23). Let $g(x|\mathbf{z}_i, \theta)$ be the individual-specific distribution of trips for an individual drawn from the population. The individual-specific covariates are represented by the vector $\mathbf{z}_i$ and $\boldsymbol{\beta}$ is a vector of population parameters. The probability of observing a given individual drawn from an on-site sample taking j trips is

$$h(j|\mathbf{z}_i) = \frac{jg(j|\mathbf{z}_i, \theta)}{E_P(x_i)}. \tag{7.26}$$

The Poisson Model

For the Poisson model, $g(x_i) = \frac{e^{-\lambda_i}\lambda_i^{x_i}}{x_i!}$ with $E_P(x_i) = \lambda_i$. Substituting into equation (7.26) yields the truncated and endogenously stratified Poisson probability

$$h(x_i \text{ and interview}|x_i > 0) = \frac{e^{-\lambda_i}\lambda_i^{x_i - 1}}{(x_i - 1)!}. \tag{7.27}$$

Equation (7.27) has a particularly simple form since it can be rewritten as

$$h(x_i \text{ and interview}|x_i > 0) = \frac{e^{-\lambda_i}\lambda_i^{w_i}}{w_i!}$$

where $w_i = x_i - 1$. The right hand side is simply the probability function for a Poisson distribution for the random variable w_i. The endogenous stratified and truncated Poisson can be estimated by running a standard Poisson regression of $x_i - 1$ on the independent variables.

In the case of the normal, equation (7.26) becomes

$$h(x_i|\mathbf{z}_i) = \frac{x_i \frac{1}{\sigma}\phi\left(\frac{x_i - \mathbf{z}_i\boldsymbol{\beta}}{\sigma}\right)}{\Phi(\frac{\mathbf{z}_i\boldsymbol{\beta}}{\sigma})\mathbf{z}_i\boldsymbol{\beta} + \sigma\phi(\frac{-\mathbf{z}_i\boldsymbol{\beta}}{\sigma})}.$$

There is little doubt that the likelihood function constructed from this density would be a great deal harder to maximize than the Poisson version. By simple comparison to the truncated normal model (which is a difficult model to estimate), the on-site normal model is burdensome. The on-site Poisson model, however, is readily estimable.

Example 24 *Estimating an On-Site Count Model*

The on-site count models are illustrated on a dataset involving beach recreation at Lake Erie.[7] This demand function relates to visits to Maumee Bay State Park beach in Ohio. The data were gathered in an on-site survey. We estimate a simple version of the model, where the demand function arguments are income, the own travel cost, and the travel cost to a relevant substitute. The substitute is chosen depending on whether the individual travels from the east or the west. Table 7.8 gives the descriptive statistics. The specification is based on

TABLE 7.8. Means of Variables for Lake Erie Beach Trips

Variable	Description	Mean n = 223
x	Trips to Maumee Bay State Park beach in 1996	5.35
C_{MB}	Round-trip travel costs ($0.33 per mile) plus monetary value of travel time* to Maumee Bay	$27.62
C_1	Round-trip travel costs ($0.33 per mile) plus monetary value of travel time to nearest substitute beach	$37.88
INC	Household income in $10,000	4.74

*The value of travel time is calculated as 30% of the estimated wage rate, which is calculated as household income/2000.

Sohngen *et al.* It is interesting to compare the difference between these covariates and the covariates for the New Bedford example. In the New Bedford case, the travel cost is calculated at $0.084 per mile, compared with $0.33 here, reflecting an increase in the nominal and real price of transportation over 15 years. The details of composing the independent variables can have very large impacts on the welfare measures and are often worth more attention than more sophisticated econometric issues.

The demand function is estimated for the endogenously stratified Poisson model (equation 7.27). For comparison, the results of a truncated Poisson model are also reported. The truncated Poisson ignores the problem of endogenous stratification. The probability density function

[7] We are grateful to Brent Sohngen, who gave us access to this dataset. The data are described in greater detail in Sohngen, Lichtkoppler and Bielen.

for the truncated Poisson, based on equation (7.18), is given by

$$h(x_i|x_i > 0) = \frac{e^{-\lambda_i}\lambda_i^{x_i}}{x_i!(1-\exp(-\lambda_i))}.$$

The results of the endogenously stratified Poisson and the truncated Poisson are both given in Table 7.9. The estimated coefficients imply

TABLE 7.9. Truncated and On-site Poisson Models

$E(x_i\|z_i) = \exp(\beta_0+\beta_1 C_{MBi}+\beta_2 C_{1i}+\beta_3 INC_i)$		
	Truncated Poisson	On-site Poisson
Parameter	Estimate* (S.E.)	Estimate* (S.E.)
β_0	2.020	1.881
	(0.064)	(0.069)
β_1	−0.022	−0.026
	(0.002)	(0.003)
β_2	0.032	0.037
	(0.001)	(0.001)
β_3	−0.003	−0.003
	(0.012)	(0.013)
Log-likelihood	−680.3	−733.2
$-2\ln(L_R/L_U)$	159.1	189.5

*All coefficients except β_3 are different from zero at the 95% level of confidence.

downward sloping demand, and substitute beaches. We calculate the willingness to pay for access to the beach as the sample mean of the consumer surplus using the general expression in (7.16) for the calculation. For the model that accounts for endogenous stratification, the estimate of sample mean WTP is

$$\sum_{i=1}^{223} WTP(E(x)\,|access)/223 = 5.35/0.026 = \$205.77.$$

The truncated model provides a sample mean WTP estimate of \$243.18 $(= 5.35/0.022)$. In this case, failure to account for the on-site nature of the sample results in an 18% overestimate of sample mean WTP.

The Negative Binomial Model

The next natural step is to estimate a negative binomial version of the endogenously stratified count model to test for overdispersion in the process. For the negative binomial model

$$g(x_i) = \frac{\Gamma\left(x_i + \frac{1}{\alpha}\right)}{\Gamma\left(x_i + 1\right)\Gamma\left(\frac{1}{\alpha}\right)} \left(\frac{\frac{1}{\alpha}}{\frac{1}{\alpha} + \lambda_i}\right)^{\frac{1}{\alpha}} \left(\frac{\lambda_i}{\frac{1}{\alpha} + \lambda_i}\right)^{x_i}$$

where $E\left(x_i\right) = \lambda_i$. Substituting into equation (7.26) yields the endogenously stratified truncated negative binomial distribution

$$h\left(x_i \text{and interview} | x_i > 0\right) \tag{7.28}$$

$$= \frac{x_i \Gamma\left(x_i + \frac{1}{\alpha}\right)}{\Gamma\left(x_i + 1\right)\Gamma\left(\frac{1}{\alpha}\right)} \left(\frac{\frac{1}{\alpha}}{\frac{1}{\alpha} + \lambda_i}\right)^{\frac{1}{\alpha}} \left(\frac{1}{\frac{1}{\alpha} + \lambda_i}\right)^{x_i} \lambda_i^{x_i - 1}. \tag{7.29}$$

This expression does not collapse to any recognizable density function, as the Poisson does. Hence the likelihood function implied by equation (7.28) must be programmed into a maximum likelihood routine.

7.6 Zonal Travel Cost Models

In its original form, the travel model was a zonal model. The approach consisted of forming concentric circles around the destination, so that a given zone, the area between two concentric circles, implied a given distance and hence a given travel cost. Differences in visits by distance zone, when corrected by population, would be caused by differences in travel costs. In applications of the zonal travel cost model, distance zones are typically replaced by political jurisdictions, such as counties. The zonal travel cost approach has been supplanted by models of individual behavior for several reasons. Zonal models require aggregate visitation data, often not available. But a more difficult problem is that zonal models assume that behavior of individuals within a zone is identical. Although zonal models aggregate exactly only when individual demands are identical, the approach is occasionally useful.

Suppose that there are J zones that are political jurisdictions or distance zones. The demand by the ith individual in the jth zone is given by x_{ij}. In principle, one wants to estimate a model of the demand for x_{ij} but only aggregate data are available. Hence we use x_j as the demand by a representative individual and model aggregate demand in zone j as given by $X_j \equiv N_j x_j$ where N_j is the number of potential users, often measured simply by population. The model ought to be constructed so that several aspects of recreation demand, the integer nature of trips and the presence of zeros, can be accommodated. As demonstrated by Hellerstein, the Poisson works well in this case. Suppose that individual demand x_j is Poisson. The Poisson has the property that if two random variables a, b are distributed Poisson with parameters λ_i, $i = a, b$ then $a + b$ is distributed Poisson with parameter $\lambda_a + \lambda_b$. So when x_j is distributed Poisson with parameter λ_j, $N_j x_j$ is distributed Poisson with parameter $N_j \lambda_j$. Hence one models the probability function for aggregate trips in zone j as

$$\Pr(X_j) = \exp(N_j \lambda_j)(N_j \lambda_j)^{X_j} / X_j!.$$

The likelihood function for the problem is then the product of the likelihood functions for each zone. Let $\lambda_j = \exp(\mathbf{z}_j \boldsymbol{\beta})$ be the expected demand for the representative individual in zone j where $\mathbf{z}_j$ is the vector of individual characteristics such as the travel and time costs, costs of substitutes, and the other variables that enter the individual demand function. Then the log-likelihood function is

$$\ln L(\boldsymbol{\beta}|\mathbf{z}, \mathbf{X}) = \sum_{j=1}^{J} N_j \exp(\mathbf{z}_j \boldsymbol{\beta}) + X_j(\ln(N_j) + \mathbf{z}_j \boldsymbol{\beta}) - \ln(X_j!).$$

This is not quite the standard log-likelihood function one uses in programs such as LIMDEP. However, it can be converted to such a program by introducing a new covariate $\ln(N_j)$ and constraining the parameter on the new term to equal one. The alternative is to write the likelihood function from scratch. In either case, one needs to observe aggregate visits X_j, the number of users N_j and the covariates $\mathbf{z}_j$ from each zone. The likelihood maximization process recovers the parameters of the individual demand for trips. These parameters can then be used to calculate willingness to pay measures by zone. In this case, expected individual demand in zone j is $\exp(\mathbf{z}_j \boldsymbol{\beta})$ and the willingness to pay for access per individual is given by $-\exp(\mathbf{z}_j \boldsymbol{\beta})/\beta_c$ where β_c is the own travel cost coefficient in the individual demand curve. Aggregation is achieved by multiplying by N_j and summing across distance zones. As in the count model for individual demands, it is possible to estimate the negative binomial.

There are other approaches to modeling in the zonal travel cost model. For example, Cooper and Loomis estimate a logarithmic per capita demand function. The difficulty with this model is that there may be zones with zero trips. The advantage of the Poisson model is that it aggregates well and handles zero trips.

7.7 Differentiating between Participation and the Demand Level

In most recreational behavior, some people choose not to participate at a recreational site, regardless of the price and other traditional demand characteristics. For example, poor health might make households unlikely to visit beaches. Or perhaps the household has a swimming pool at home. In the case of the Tobit, the Poisson and the negative binomial, the researcher assumes that the deterministic and random factors that influence participation are the same as those that influence the number of trips to a site. Researchers have developed a variety of approaches to modeling the participation differently from the quantity choice. We examine several models in this section. These models tend to be harder to estimate and less satisfactory in terms of their parameters than the models that do not try to capture the more complex behavior. When both response functions use some of the same covariates, serious identification problems arise. The simplest model for separating the decisions is the Cragg model, which estimates the two behavioral functions separately. We also illustrate the selection model, and discuss the zero inflated Poisson. The estimated models illustrate the difficulties of the more complex specifications.

7.7.1 The Cragg Model

The Cragg model (Cragg, 1971) is a two stage model that amounts to one hurdle. In the first stage, one estimates a dichotomous choice model that determines whether the individual participates in the activity at the site. In the second stage, a truncated model is estimated, based on the assumption that when the individual decides to participate, the quantity of trips will be positive. The original model was estimated with a probit and a truncated normal, but the idea works for any dichotomous choice model and any truncated model, because the two models are estimated independently. The truncated Poisson is preferable, because the truncated normal is frequently difficult to estimate, being highly non-linear and failing to converge in many cases.

In the recreation demand context, the Cragg model is composed of two decisions. The first decision is whether to participate and the second concerns the level of participation:

$$\begin{aligned} \Pr(x_i &> 0) = F(\mathbf{z}_{i1}) \\ x_i &= f(\mathbf{z}_{i2}, \varepsilon_{i2}) \text{ for } x_i > 0 \end{aligned}$$

where $F(\mathbf{z}_{i1})$ is a cumulative density function and ε_{i2} is a random term for the frequency decision. The Cragg model has been estimated in a variety of settings. Bockstael, Strand *et al.* (1990) find that when the researcher deems it necessary to separate the two decisions, this model seems to work the best.

Example 25 *A Cragg Model Estimated*

The New Bedford beach data from Table 7.1 provide the basis for a simple version of this pair of equations. The model is estimated under the assumption that x_i is distributed as a truncated Poisson and the probability that x_i is greater than zero is a probit. For the probit, let

$$F(\mathbf{z}_i^1)=\Phi[(\beta_{01}+\beta_{11}C_{FPi}+\beta_{21}C_{2i}+\beta_{31}Inc_i+\beta_{41}Age_i)/\sigma]$$

and for the Poisson, assume that

$$\lambda_i=\exp(\beta_{02}+\beta_{12}C_{FPi}+\beta_{22}C_{1i}+\beta_{32}P_{FPi}).$$

The probability of visiting the site contains prices as well as the two socioeconomic variables, age of the respondent and household income. The demand for the number of days, given that the individual participates, depends on prices and the ownership of a pass. For income to influence the number of days, there would have to be a very strong income effect, not likely when travel costs are low.

Parameter estimates for this model are given in Table 7.10. The travel cost coefficients are significant, even for the negative binomial in the simple model. The coefficients of the probit model relate the negative influence of age and income on participation. Higher incomes give households access to more distant beaches and other recreational activities. Age reduces the probability that an individual visits any of the beaches. The own price (travel cost) reduces the participation and visits to the site. The substitute travel costs work less systematically when the model is divided into the level decision and the participation decision.

The welfare calculations are based on the individuals who take positive trips. The sample mean trips, given that trips are positive, is $\sum_{x_i>0} E(x_i|x_i>0)/T_{(x_i>0)}=11.4$, so that the mean willingness to pay for the user group is $11.4/0.11 = \$103$ (where the denominator is the travel cost coefficient from Table 7.10). Given that 34% of the sample are users, this implies a mean willingness to pay for access of \$35 for the sample as a whole, more than ten times the value from a single Poisson

TABLE 7.10. The Cragg Model

$$\Pr(x_i > 0) = \Phi[(\beta_{01} + \beta_{11}C_{FPi} + \beta_{21}C_{2i} + \beta_{31}INC_i + \beta_{41}AGE_i)/\sigma]$$
$$\lambda_i = \exp(\beta_{02} + \beta_{12}C_{FPi} + \beta_{22}C_{1i} + \beta_{32}P_{FPi})$$

Parameter	Estimate	Standard Error
	Probit	
β_{01}	*0.73	0.28
β_{11}	*−0.21	0.06
β_{21}	0.08	0.06
β_{31}	*−0.08	0.02
β_{41}	*−0.01	0.00
	Truncated Poisson	
β_{02}	*2.60	0.06
β_{12}	*−0.11	0.02
β_{22}	−0.01	0.02
β_{32}	*0.44	0.08

	Probit	Poisson
Log-likelihood	−298.5	−1312.7
$-2\ln(L_R/L_U)$	37.2	73.9

*Different from zero at the 95% level of confidence.

model:

$$\begin{aligned} sample\ EWTP &= \sum_{i=1}^{T} WTP(\hat{x}_i|\beta)/T \\ &= \Pr(x=0)\cdot E(WTP|x=0) \\ +\Pr(x &> 0)\cdot E(WTP|x>0) \\ &= 0.66\cdot 0 + 0.34\cdot \$103 = \$35. \end{aligned}$$

This is so much higher than the value estimated in a Poisson that it is worth considering the source of the problem. Increases in the travel cost to Fort Phoenix have two effects: a reduction in trips, given that trips are positive and a reduction in participation. Hence the elasticity of demand for trips, given that they are positive, is quite low, making the surplus estimate high. Much of the demand responsiveness uncovered earlier pertains to the participation decision. This is one of the difficulties of incorrectly accepting the Cragg model. By ignoring the responsiveness that stems from participation decisions, the Cragg model underestimates demand responsiveness, attenuating the coefficient, and hence increasing consumer surplus. Yet another drawback to this specification with the probit and Poisson is that the model is not nested such as a truncated and probit would be.

7.7.2 Sample Selection Models for Recreation Demand

Sample selection issues arise when there are systematic effects from the exclusion of some of the population from the sampling list. To get a feel for selection in the recreation demand context, consider a recreation site in a geographical area with similar sites. If some part of the population does not visit the geographical area, they won't visit the site. In making inferences about the population from the users of the site, it is necessary to explain the process by which people choose to visit the geographical area. On the other hand, inferences about the users of the site can sometimes be made correctly without considering the selection process. So the researcher needs to be aware of the population to which the results are to be expanded. The first applications of selection models in recreation demand are found in Smith (1988).

There are several ways of treating selection effects econometrically. We explain a joint probit-Poisson model that fits the recreational context reasonably well. Suppose that x_2 is observed when $x_1 = 1$. Then consider the following process. Let x_1 be a dichotomous variable equal to one when the individual is selected. Then we can model a variable that indicates the individual visits the site as

$$\begin{aligned} x_{i1} &= 1, \ \mathbf{z}_{i1}\boldsymbol{\beta}_1 + \varepsilon_{i1} > 0 \\ x_{i1} &= 0, \ \mathbf{z}_{i1}\boldsymbol{\beta}_1 + \varepsilon_{i1} \leq 0. \end{aligned}$$

This dichotomous variable can be modeled as a probit with covariates $\mathbf{z}_1$ when the random component is normal with mean zero. The system then becomes

$$\begin{aligned} \Pr(x_{i1} &= 1) = \Phi(\mathbf{z}_{i1}\boldsymbol{\beta}_1/\sigma_1) \\ \Pr(x_{i2} &= n) = \exp(-\lambda_i)\lambda_i^n/n! \\ \lambda_i &= \exp(\mathbf{z}_{i2}\boldsymbol{\beta}_2 + \varepsilon_{i2}), \varepsilon_{i2} \sim N(0, \sigma_2^2). \end{aligned}$$

The error in the expected mean is assumed to be normal, a measure of individual heterogeneity. When ε_1 and ε_2 are correlated, the sample selection model emerges. When the errors are uncorrelated, no selection effect results, and the selection effect and trip quantity are independent. The likelihood function for this model is constructed in Greene (1997), from models developed in Terza.

Example 26 *The Probit-Poisson Selection Model*

The estimation of this model is facilitated by the presence of a routine in LIMDEP version 7.0. The application is to the New Bedford beach data. Consider selection as follows. Households who don't go to the beach at all won't be observed going to the particular beach being analyzed, Fort Phoenix. So probit model analyzes whether the household visits any of the beaches in the New Bedford area, and Poisson models the number of times the household visits Fort Phoenix, given that any beaches are visited. To illustrate the workings of the model, the specifications are parsimonious. For the deterministic part of the Poisson $\lambda_i = \exp(\beta_{02} + \beta_{12}C_{FPi} + \beta_{22}C_{1i})$ where the C's are the travel costs used throughout. For the probit model we estimate

$$\Pr(visit\ beaches) = \Phi[(\beta_{01} + \beta_{11}Res_i + \beta_{21}Inc_i + \beta_{31}Age_i)/\sigma]$$

where *Res* is one when the household resides in the greater New Bedford area, *Inc* is household income in \$10000 units, and *Age* is the age of the respondent. Initially a model that included travel costs was estimated, but the travel cost coefficients were not significant. The results are in Table 7.11. In addition to the coefficients on the covariates, there are two parameters: the variance of the individual error and the correlation between ε_1 and ε_2. All the parameters are estimated in a maximum likelihood routine in LIMDEP.

The parameters of the Poisson, the conditional demand function, are significantly different from zero. Of all the Poisson-like models estimated, this version shows the greatest response to travel costs. The idea of separating the sample into households who use beaches and households who don't gets some support. The probit coefficients are reasonable and significant. However, the correlation coefficient between the two errors is not significant so that one can argue that the two decisions are independent, and that there is no selection bias from analyzing the selected group independently. As a consequence, one can simply discard the respondents who do not go to beaches in the area. Leaving them out of the estimation stage does not affect the parameter estimates because the correlation is zero, and they deserve to be left out of the welfare calculations because if they don't visit the site they have zero willingness to pay for access to the site.

Inflating the Poisson

The last model to be examined is the zero inflated Poisson. This procedure, suggested by Greene (1997), Mullahey, and Haab and McConnell

TABLE 7.11. A Selection Model

$\Pr(visit\ beaches) = \Phi[(\beta_{01} + \beta_{11}Res_i + \beta_{21}Inc_i + \beta_{31}Age_i)/\sigma]$ $\lambda_i = \exp(\beta_{02} + \beta_{12}C_{FPi} + \beta_{22}C_{1i} + \beta_{32}P_{FPi})$		
Parameter	Estimate	Standard Error
	Pr(Visit)	
β_{01}	−0.14	0.72
β_{11}	[b]1.37	0.75
β_{21}	0.08	0.49
β_{31}	[a]−0.01	0.01
	Poisson	
β_{02}	[a]0.85	0.15
β_{12}	[a]−0.45	0.03
β_{22}	[a]0.08	0.03
	Correlation	
ρ	0.40	0.45
Log-likelihood		−831.0
$-2\ln(L_R/L_U)$		2686.4

[a]Different from zero at the 95% level of confidence.
[b]Different from zero at the 90% level of confidence.

(1996), is essentially a mixture model. Indeed Mullahey argues that models with overdispersion will always produce too many zeros. The basic idea is to allow the respondents who have zero trips a different model of behavior, including different regressors, functional form and randomness. The zero inflated Poisson is

$$\Pr(x_i = n) = F(\mathbf{z}_{i1}\boldsymbol{\beta}_1) + (1 - F(\mathbf{z}_{i1}\boldsymbol{\beta}_1))\frac{e^{-\lambda_i}\lambda_i^n}{n!}, n = 0, 1, 2, ..$$

where F is the probability that $x_i = 0$ and $1 - F$ is the probability that the Poisson holds. The probability F will be modeled as a function of covariates in the form of a logit or probit. This is now a double hurdle model, in the sense that for positive trips to emerge, the individual must first overcome the effects of F, and then the covariates in the Poisson need to allow the trips to be positive. The probability of zero trips is given by

$$\Pr(x_i = 0) = F + (1 - F)e^{-\lambda_i}.$$

In terms of covariates, a double hurdle could be health, a covariate in the probability that the Poisson holds, and travel cost, an argument in the Poisson. The model makes sense when the covariates influencing the frequency of trips differ from the arguments that determine the first hurdle, the probability of that the Poisson does not hold. LIMDEP 7.0 provides a built-in version of a likelihood function for this model. However, the estimation process typically has difficulty discriminating between covariates that affect participation and covariates that influence the quantity of trips.

An important implication of the augmented Poisson is the need to understand how individuals make their recreation decisions. To model correctly selection effects and double-hurdles it is important to have knowledge of how individuals choose. Additional information from surveys can go a long way to alleviating the econometric problems caused by sample selection and participation decisions.

7.8 Conclusion

This chapter has introduced the general problem of modeling the demand for recreation and surveyed the various methods of estimating demands for single sites. The general approach shows that estimating recreational demand models is an exercise in the empirics of constructing a Becker model of the allocation of time. The estimation of single site models is an application of econometric models of discrete-continuous variables. The type of model estimated depends on the data generating process, which is the confluence of the sampling method and the stochastic specification of the demand function. Censored models are appropriate for data gathered from surveys administered to samples drawn from lists of the population. One estimates endogenous stratification models when users are sampled on-site.

These general guidelines help in the handling of models, but not in the choice of model. The model one ultimately adopts for welfare analysis depends on the intuitive plausibility of the estimated model. To model selection effects and double-hurdles it is important to have knowledge of how individuals choose. Additional information from surveys can go a long way to alleviating the econometric problems caused by sample selection and participation decisions.

8

Site Choice Models

8.1 Introduction

In Chapters 2 through 5 we dealt extensively with the random utility model of dichotomous choices for contingent valuation. In this chapter we utilize the random utility model as it was originally developed by McFadden and others–to analyze the behavioral choices among mutually exclusive alternatives. The random utility model grew out of efforts to model transportation choices, in which an individual chooses among a set of alternatives, such as car, bus, train or other, as a way of getting to work. The choice of transportation model is amenable to the random utility model for several reasons. The choices are mutually exclusive–the individual chooses only one mode. These mode choices depend on the characteristics of the modes–price, time and convenience and perhaps less strongly on individual characteristics such as income. The choices are repeated many times, but it is unlikely that they are substantially governed by declining marginal values. Recreational decisions, when viewed as the choice over which site to visit, share many of the characteristics of transportation choice. In this chapter we analyze the simplest of random utility models, the site choice model. In this model, the individual chooses which site to visit, given that the individual will visit a site. As we have emphasized in our discussion of recreational modeling, a general model of recreational choice determines choices made over a period of time, such as a season. The most complete model is the generalized corner solution model of Phaneuf, Herriges and Kling. The repeated logit model deals with all of an individual's choices from a set of exogenous choice occasions (Morey, Rowe and Watson).

Multiple site count models generalize single site models by estimating the demands for a set of sites over a period of time. This approach deals with the same issue that generalized corner solution models deal with–the seasonal demand for a group of sites, when some quantities demanded will be positive and others zero. (See Shonkwiler and von Haefen.) This approach appears to be an effective way to model the demands when the number of sites is not very large. It differs from the generalized corner solution models of Phaneuf, Herriges and Kling by starting the modeling process with demand functions rather than utility functions. See von Haefen and Phaneuf for further exposition.

The random utility model differs from both the generalized corner solution model and the count models. It starts with the choice among alternatives, and is capable of modeling the choice among a very large set of alternatives. The random utility model is derived from the demand for characteristics of alternatives. The alternatives themselves are distinct to the degree that their characteristics differ. This aspect of the random utility model enables researchers to measure the effects of introducing new alternatives. In the generalized corner solution model and count demand models, each alternative is distinct, and it is quite difficult to introduce an alternative that is not part of the preference function in the initial model.

8.2 Choices among Alternatives

The random utility model (RUM) was first applied to recreational choices by Bockstael, Hanemann, and Kling. Since then it has become the preferred modeling strategy when the researcher wishes to analyze choices among many alternatives. Morey (1999) develops the various models in detail and Hanemann (1999b) provides the machinery for welfare analysis for the RUM. Parsons has an extensive bibliography of random utility models as used in recreation. Ben-Akiva and Lerman provide a thorough and intuitive development of the appropriate statistical distributions.

The RUM is an appealing modeling strategy for a variety of reasons. On a given choice occasion, it models the choice of one out of many recreational sites, as a function of attributes of the sites. When constructed correctly, the random utility model implies choices that are logical and can answer many kinds of practical welfare questions. The RUM arose from the transportation literature, but in one important sense the application of random utility models to recreation differs from its application to transportation models. In a recreational setting, a taste for variety would seem to be a stronger force than in transportation. Wanting variety, recreationists would alter their choices through a season. To capture this aspect of preferences, one would utilize more general models than the random utility model. Such models would capture the substitution among alternatives that would be induced by the declining marginal utility of visits to a single site.

Random utility models, like single site demand models, deal with choices that individuals have made. For effective use of the data, one must be explicit about the data generating process. Many different kinds of sampling schemes are possible, but it is critical to distinguish two broad types. Exogenous sampling occurs when the researcher chooses sample units with a random or stratified sample of the relevant population. This type of sampling is essentially sampling from a list that is independent of the choices people make. The second type of sampling is choice-based sampling, in which the researcher draws samples that depend on the choices that people have made. For recreational analysis, the most common type of choice-based sample is on-site sampling. Sampling from a list is exogenous but may be proportional or stratified.

Exogenous sampling, from a list, can be achieved in a variety of ways. General population surveys, such as a random digit phone survey or a mail survey (which requires an explicit list), can succeed. But they will often have a high proportion of respondents who do not participate in the recreational activity and hence make no site choices. These sampling strategies can be expensive if the proportion of useful respondents is quite low. For example, in the US, the percent of households that fish or hunt is typically in the 10 to 20 percent range. The percent that visit a specific group of sites would be smaller, making a phone survey expensive. In the empirical example described in this chapter, the data were gathered from a mail survey of the general population.

On-site sampling, a form of choice-based sampling, can cause inconsistencies in parameter estimates if it is not corrected in the estimation process. This is spelled out clearly in Waldman. Essentially the parameter estimates depend on the sample proportions of visits to different sites. For consistent parameter estimates, one needs the predicted probabilities of visits among sites to equal the population proportions. We discuss the issue of on-site sampling in section 8.7 below. Greater depth on the issues of sampling in discrete choice models can be found in Ben-Akiva and Lerman, Chapter 8, and Manski and McFadden, Chapter 1.

Our approach in this chapter goes from the general to the specific. We present the nested logit model and show how that simplifies to the conditional logit model.

The logit model is such a widely used idea, and used in so many different ways, that we give the gist of the model before we give the details. Suppose individual i chooses among $j = 1, ..., J$ mutually exclusive alternatives. Let $\mathbf{X}_{ij}$ be a vector of individual characteristics or attributes for individual i, alternative j and let $\boldsymbol{\beta}_j$ be a conforming vector of parameters. Then for each individual and each alternative, we could calculate $\mathbf{X}_{ij}\boldsymbol{\beta}_j$. An individual characteristic might be the age of respondent i. An attribute of an alternative would be the cost of obtaining alternative j.

8.2.1 Conditional Logit versus Multinomial Logit

The *conditional logit* model, developed by McFadden (1974), gives the probability that individual i chooses alternative j as a function of attributes that vary by alternative and unknown parameters. The site attributes may vary among individuals, but they need not. For example when the attribute is cost of access, individuals with different costs of time will have different access costs. Hence, when we use $\mathbf{X}_{ij}$ as the vector of attributes of site j, individual i, then the probability that individual i chooses alternative j is

$$\Pr{}_i(j) = \frac{e^{\mathbf{X}_{ij}\beta}}{\sum_{k=1}^{J} e^{\mathbf{X}_{ik}\beta}}. \tag{8.1}$$

The goal is to estimate the unknown parameters. Note that the conditional logit depends on differences among alternative characteristics:

$$\frac{e^{\mathbf{X}_{ij}\beta}}{\sum_{k=1}^{J} e^{\mathbf{X}_{ik}\beta}} = \frac{1}{\sum_{k=1}^{J} e^{(\mathbf{X}_{ik}-\mathbf{X}_{ij})\beta}}.$$

As one can see, attributes that do not vary by alternative do not affect probabilities.

The *multinomial logit* model gives the probability that individual i chooses alternative j as a function of individual characteristics and unknown parameters:

$$\Pr{}_i(j) = \frac{e^{\mathbf{X}_i\beta_j}}{\sum_{k=1}^{J} e^{\mathbf{X}_i\beta_k}}.$$

In the multinomial logit, only $J-1$ of the parameters can be recovered:

$$\frac{e^{\mathbf{X}_i\beta_j}}{\sum_{k=1}^{J} e^{\mathbf{X}_i\beta_k}} = \frac{1}{\sum_{k=1}^{J} e^{\mathbf{X}_i(\beta_k-\beta_j)}}.$$

Because we can only estimate differences, one of the parameter vectors is typically normalized to zero. The multinomial logit uses individual characteristics to explain the choice of alternative, and estimates $J-1$ parameter vectors for $J-1$ of the alternatives.

In this chapter we will be concerned exclusively with the conditional logit and its more general version, the nested logit model. These are in essence economic models, because they use the characteristics of alternatives, including prices, to determine choice.

8.3 Some Results for Nested Models

Before venturing into the details of the nested and conditional logit random utility models, we present some results that will be used in understanding the models. First we present the generalized extreme value (GEV) distribution in the context of the random utility model. This will serve as the basic probability statement from which the nested and conditional logit models will be derived. Then we give a property of choice among alternatives that permits the discarding of irrelevant constants. Third we show the expected maximum utility attainable in the GEV framework. This serves as the indirect utility function in the derivation of welfare measures from the multiple choice models.

8.3.1 Notation for Two Level Models

We analyze a nested decision structure and a non-nested structure. In the nested structure, alternatives are arranged into groups of alternatives, or nests. The nests can be viewed as upper level choices; each upper level choice contains a group of lower level choices. We restrict our derivations to a two-level nesting structure. The following results can be extended to the case of more nesting levels, but as will be apparent, the notation becomes burdensome for higher level nesting structures. Greene (1995) gives expressions for four level nested models. Morey (1999) restricts his models to two-level nests and then adds in the possibility of repeating the two-level nest.

Let j and k represent the nesting levels, where j indexes the bottom level choice and k indexes the nest or top level choice. Let K be the number of alternatives or nests in the upper level choice set (indexed k), and $J_1, J_2, ..., J_K$ be the number of alternatives in the lower level for each upper level alternative k. If the individual chooses $k = 1$ at the upper level, then there are J_1 alternatives available to that individual in the lower level (indexed $j = 1, 2, ..., J_1$).

Figure 8.1 shows the general two-level decision structure.

The random utility model is so named because the indirect utility from choosing an alternative is composed of a random part and a deterministic part. In the two level case, utility for the choice combination (j, k) is written

$$u_{jk} = v_{jk} + \varepsilon_{jk}. \tag{8.2}$$

In applications we make the deterministic utility v_{jk} depend on characteristics of the alternatives. Randomness enters through ε_{jk} as the error associated with the alternative combination j, k. This error is

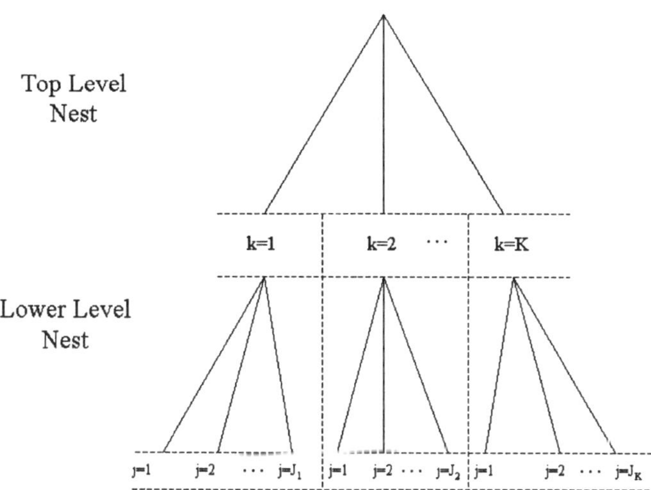

FIGURE 8.1. Structure and Notation for Nested Models

interpreted as part of the preferences known to the individual making but random to the researcher. For a given choice, k, at the upper level, there is a $1 \times J_k$ vector of associated errors defined as $\varepsilon_{\cdot k} = \{\varepsilon_{1k}, \varepsilon_{2k}, ..., \varepsilon_{J_k k}\}$. Combining the K error vectors yields the error vector $\varepsilon = \{\varepsilon_{\cdot 1}, \varepsilon_{\cdot 2}, ..., \varepsilon_{\cdot K}\}$ of dimension $1 \times J$, where $J = \sum_{k=1}^{K} J_k$.

For each choice combination, we define the probability that the researcher will observe the individual choosing a given combination. Let $\Pr(j,k)$ be the unconditional probability of choosing the combination j, k from among all feasible combinations. For reference, Table 8.1 summarizes the notation. The following section is dedicated to the form of $\Pr(j,k)$. It is worth emphasizing that this probability relates to imperfect observation by the researcher. The individual choosing is assumed to have no uncertainty.

8.3.2 The Choice Probability

The choice probability is the researcher's probability of observing the combination (j,k) out of all possible combinations for an individual. As such, $\Pr(j,k)$ is the probability that the indirect utility from choice se-

TABLE 8.1. Notation for GEV Results

Notation	Explanation
j	Lower level index
k	Upper level index
K	# of upper level nests
J_k	# of lower level alternatives for upper level nest k
ε_{jk}	Scalar error associated with the alternative combination j,k
J	$\sum_{k=1}^{K} J_k$ =the total number of alternatives
$\boldsymbol{\varepsilon}_{\cdot k} = \{\varepsilon_{1k}, \varepsilon_{2k}, \ldots, \varepsilon_{J_k k}\}$	Error vector conditional on upper level nest k
$\boldsymbol{\varepsilon} = \{\boldsymbol{\varepsilon}_{\cdot 1}, \boldsymbol{\varepsilon}_{\cdot 2}, \ldots, \boldsymbol{\varepsilon}_{\cdot K}\}$	Full error vector

quence k, j exceeds the indirect utility from any other choice sequence. To derive an expression for $\Pr(j, k)$, we need a distribution of the random terms in the indirect utility function. Kotz, Balakrishnan and Johnson provide a general overview for a class of distributions known as multivariate extreme value distributions. McFadden (1978) utilized a special case of the multivariate extreme value distribution to derive the nested logit model in a site choice context. Ben-Akiva and Lerman give a transparent and intuitive explanation of the GEV.

Generalized Extreme Value Distribution

The generalized extreme value distribution employed by McFadden (1978) is written in the current notation as

$$F(\boldsymbol{\varepsilon}) = \exp\left[-\sum_{k=1}^{K} a_k \left[\sum_{j=1}^{J_k} \exp\left(-\frac{\varepsilon_{jk}}{\theta_k}\right)\right]^{\theta_k}\right] \tag{8.3}$$

where $F(\boldsymbol{\varepsilon})$ is the cumulative distribution function, $a_k > 0$ and $\theta_k \leq 1$ $\forall k$ are parameters of the distribution.

Equation (8.3) represents one specific form of the multivariate extreme value distribution. Other forms exist, but the generalized extreme value distribution has the desirable property of a closed form solution for the expected maximum.

Assume that the individual chooses the alternative that provides the maximum utility. The individual chooses the two-level choice (j,k) if

$$u_{jk} \geq u_{j'k'} \ \forall j', k'. \tag{8.4}$$

When the choice is made according to this rule, the utilities are structured according to equation (8.2), and the stochastic parts are distributed as generalized extreme value in equation (8.3), then we derive the probability that the researcher observes the choice of a given combination.

McFadden's RUM Probability

If ε is distributed as generalized extreme value as in equation (8.3), then the probability of choosing alternative j,k is

$$\Pr(j,k) = \frac{a_k \exp(\frac{v_{jk}}{\theta_k}) \left[\sum_{l=1}^{J_k} \exp(\frac{v_{lk}}{\theta_k}) \right]^{\theta_k - 1}}{\sum_{m=1}^{K} a_m \left[\sum_{l=1}^{J_m} \exp(\frac{v_{lm}}{\theta_m}) \right]^{\theta_m}}. \tag{8.5}$$

Appendix B establishes this proposition. For interpretation, suppose $a_k = e^{\alpha_k}$. With substitution and simplification, equation (8.5) becomes

$$\Pr(j,k) = \frac{\exp(\frac{\alpha_k + v_{jk}}{\theta_k}) \left[\sum_{l=1}^{J_k} \exp(\frac{\alpha_k + v_{lk}}{\theta_k}) \right]^{\theta_k - 1}}{\sum_{m=1}^{K} \left[\sum_{l=1}^{J_m} \exp(\frac{\alpha_m + v_{lm}}{\theta_m}) \right]^{\theta_m}}. \tag{8.6}$$

Because the α_k parameters enter as linear additive constants to v_{jk}, they can be interpreted as upper level nest specific constants. Each nest has a separate constant. In effect, the α_k parameters are location parameters and the θ_k are scale parameters for the different nests. The interpretation of the θ_k will be considered in later sections.

Equation (8.5) describes the probability that the researcher observes the individual choosing the combination (j,k) from all feasible combinations. We assume that the individual is capable of choosing among alternatives by comparing utilities. As researchers we lack complete knowledge of the forces that motivate the individual, so that we can only make probability statements about choice.

Several implications for data organization follow from the structure of the utility function and choice based on maximization. Equation (8.4) provides the basis of choice, and it implies that additive constants independent of alternatives do not affect choice. Suppose that we modify equation (8.2) by adding a constant c to each v_{jk}. Then the maximum based on equation (8.4) does not change:

$$\begin{aligned} u_{jk} &\geq u_{j'k'} \; \forall j', k' \Longrightarrow \\ v_{jk} + c + \varepsilon_{jk} &\geq v_{j'k'} + c + \varepsilon_{j'k'} \; \forall j', k' \Longrightarrow \\ v_{jk} + \varepsilon_{jk} &\geq v_{j'k'} + \varepsilon_{j'k'} \; \forall j', k'. \end{aligned} \tag{8.7}$$

Adding the same constant to the utility of each alternative does not affect the rankings of the alternative. Consequently, components of the utility function that are additive and constant across choices will not be part of the choice probability as given in equation (8.5). Likewise, consider the choice of an alternative, given that the nest is known. That is, suppose we want to predict which site within nest k an individual will choose. Then additive constants that do not vary across the sites within the nest will not affect the probability of choice within the nest. If, given k, alternative j is chosen, then

$$\begin{aligned} u_{jk} &\geq u_{j'k} \; \forall j' \Longrightarrow \\ v_{jk} + c_k + \varepsilon_{jk} &\geq v_{j'k} + c_k + \varepsilon_{j'k} \; \forall j' \Longrightarrow \\ v_{jk} + \varepsilon_{jk} &\geq v_{j'k} + \varepsilon_{j'k} \; \forall j'. \end{aligned} \tag{8.8}$$

Hence an additive constant does not influence the probability of choice within a nest if it does not vary by alternative within the nest. We summarize this result for further use to help organize the data and interpret the probabilities.

1. An additive constant in the utility function does not affect the probability of choice if it does not vary by alternative.

2. An additive constant that varies by nest but not by alternative within a nest does not influence the probability of choice of an alternative, given the nest.

The following section provides the mechanism for welfare calculations.

8.3.3 Expected Maximum Utility

The indirect utility function provides a direct means of calculating willingness to pay. The indirect utility function is the maximized value of the utility function, or in the case of choosing among mutually exclusive alternatives, the maximum of the utilities. If we knew the individual's preferences, we could pick the maximum utility. Being uncertain about preferences, we look instead for the expected maximum utility. Define $\mathbf{u}_{\cdot k} = \{u_{1k}, u_{2k}, ..., u_{J_k k}\}$ as the vector of attainable utilities for upper level choice k. Collect the K utility vectors into a single utility vector across all upper and lower level choices as $\mathbf{u} = \{\mathbf{u}_{\cdot 1}, \mathbf{u}_{\cdot 2}, ..., \mathbf{u}_{\cdot K}\}$. Further, define max($\mathbf{u}$) as the maximum indirect utility attainable (largest element among all possible $u_{jk} = v_{jk} + \varepsilon_{jk}$). Because $\mathbf{u}$ is stochastic from the researcher's perspective, it will be useful to have an expression for the expected maximum utility attainable from a given set of choices.

Expected Maximum Utility for McFadden's RUM

If the error vector ε is distributed as generalized extreme value (GEV) as in equation (8.3), then

$$E\{max(\mathbf{u})\} = \ln\left(\sum_{m=1}^{K} a_m \left[\sum_{l=1}^{J_m} \exp(\frac{v_{lm}}{\theta_m})\right]^{\theta_m}\right) + C \qquad (8.9)$$

where C is a known constant. This is the observer's estimation of the indirect utility function of the individual, when the individual chooses the maximum of $u_{jk} = v_{jk} + \varepsilon_{jk}$ for all j, k and the ε_{jk} are distributed as GEV. The proof of this proposition can be found in detail in Appendix B. Because the additive constant C in the expected maximum indirect utility function has no impact on utility differences, we will drop it in subsequent uses of $E\{max(\mathbf{u})\}$.

8.4 The Basics of Logit Models

The random utility model of site choice assumes that the individual makes a choice among mutually exclusive alternatives based on the attributes of the alternatives. Only the measured attributes of the sites matter to the individual. Two sites that have the same attributes are identical and provide the same deterministic utility to the individual. The choice of sites is determined by utility maximization. Individual characteristics such as age and income can only influence choices when they are interacted with site-specific attributes. We explore approaches for including such variables in subsequent sections.

8.4.1 The Nested Logit Probability

We have constructed the nested logit probability in equation (8.5). This probability and the expected maximum utility are the building blocks for parameter estimation and welfare calculation. We initially assume that J, the total number of alternatives, is the same for all individuals. This restrictive assumption can lead to inconsistent parameter estimates when it is wrong. These issues will be discussed in subsequent sections.

Suppose an individual is observed to choose the choice alternative j, k. Associated with that alternative is conditional indirect utility u_{jk}. Although individuals have complete information about what determines their choice of alternative, the researcher cannot fully observe all of this information. As such the stochastic term captures site-specific omitted variables in the specification of the utility function. We repeat the probability of observing an individual choosing site j, k from among the J possible sites:

$$\Pr(j,k) = \frac{a_k \exp(\frac{v_{jk}}{\theta_k}) \left[\sum_{l=1}^{J_k} \exp(\frac{v_{lk}}{\theta_k})\right]^{\theta_k - 1}}{\sum_{m=1}^{K} a_m \left[\sum_{l=1}^{J_m} \exp(\frac{v_{lm}}{\theta_m})\right]^{\theta_m}} \tag{8.10}$$

where a_m and θ_m $\forall m$ are distributional parameters to be estimated. The expression is homogeneous in the a_m, so that when they are equal, they fall out of the probability expressions. At various points we will find it convenient to use Bayes's rule to write $\Pr(j,k)$ as the product of the conditional probability of choosing site j, given nest k, times the marginal probability of choosing nest k:

$$\Pr(j|k)\Pr(k) = \frac{a_k \exp(\frac{v_{jk}}{\theta_k}) \left[\sum_{l=1}^{J_k} \exp(\frac{v_{lk}}{\theta_k})\right]^{\theta_k}}{\sum_{l=1}^{J_k} \exp(\frac{v_{lk}}{\theta_k}) \sum_{m=1}^{K} a_m \left[\sum_{l=1}^{J_m} \exp(\frac{v_{lm}}{\theta_m})\right]^{\theta_m}}$$

where

$$\Pr(j|k) = \frac{a_k \exp(\frac{v_{jk}}{\theta_k})}{\sum_{l=1}^{J_k} \exp(\frac{v_{lk}}{\theta_k})} \tag{8.11}$$

and

$$\Pr(k) = \frac{\left[\sum_{l=1}^{J_k} \exp(\frac{v_{lk}}{\theta_k})\right]^{\theta_k}}{\sum_{m=1}^{K} a_m \left[\sum_{l=1}^{J_m} \exp(\frac{v_{lm}}{\theta_m})\right]^{\theta_m}}. \tag{8.12}$$

In equation (8.11), we have a conditional logit model for choosing site j among the J_k sites in nest k. In equation (8.12), there is the logit of choosing nest k from among all the nests. These expressions help in estimating occasionally and they help in constructing nests too.

8.4.2 Specifying the Utility Function

We have written the utility function for alternative j,k very generally as u_{jk} and its deterministic component v_{jk} with no explanation of their arguments. We now develop the specification. Hanemann (1999b) offers a full development of the budget-constrained random utility model. The essential idea is that we specify the deterministic part of the preference function to depend on a composite commodity, z, with a price of one, a vector of site-specific attributes denoted $\mathbf{q_{jk}}$ and a vector of nest-specific attributes denoted $\mathbf{s}_k$. Let $v(z, \mathbf{q}_{jk}, \mathbf{s}_k)$ be the deterministic function. Now suppose that the full cost of travel to site j,k is given by c_{jk}. This cost includes time and travel costs. When time and income are not fungible, the utility function will include an additional argument for time. The budget constraint for individual i will be $y^i = z^i + c_{jk}$ where y is the individual's full income. (To avoid notation clutter we will suppress the observation index throughout most of the chapter. But it is likely that many attributes of sites will vary across individuals. And through interaction with dummy variables or site attributes, individual attributes can be made to vary across sites.) The deterministic utility enjoyed by an individual who chooses site m,n is $v(y - c_{mn}, \mathbf{q}_{mn}, \mathbf{s}_n)$.

To make the RUM model operational, a specific form must be assumed for the indirect utility function. The most convenient and common form is linear in parameters and variables, although for ease of estimation only linearity in parameters is necessary. A typical specification would be

$$v(y - c_{jk}, \mathbf{q}_{jk}, \mathbf{s}_k) = \beta_y(y - c_{jk}) + \mathbf{q}_{jk}\boldsymbol{\beta} + \mathbf{s}_k\gamma \tag{8.13}$$

where $\boldsymbol{\beta}$ and γ are column vectors conformable with $\mathbf{q}_{jk}$ and $\mathbf{s}_k$. It is intuitive to think of β_y as the marginal utility of income. Because this utility function can be written $\beta_y y - \beta_y c_{jk} + \mathbf{q}_{jk}\boldsymbol{\beta} + \mathbf{s}_k\gamma$ we see that the term $\beta_y y$ is an additive constant and according to equation (8.7) will not affect the probability of choice, so it can be dropped. Instead we will analyze choices based on equation (8.14)

$$v(y - c_{jk}, \mathbf{q}_{jk}, \mathbf{s}_k) = -\beta_y c_{jk} + \mathbf{q}_{jk}\boldsymbol{\beta} + \mathbf{s}_k\gamma. \tag{8.14}$$

Up to a limit imposed by feasibility, we can allow the coefficients on site-specific variables to change by nest:

$$v(y - c_{jk}, \mathbf{q}_{jk}, \mathbf{s}_k) = -\beta_y c_{jk} + \mathbf{q}_{jk}\boldsymbol{\beta}_k + \mathbf{s}_k\gamma.$$

This is done in the same way as in a linear regression model: for each element of $\mathbf{q}_{jk}$, say q_{jk}^1, create an additional variable equal to q_{jk}^1 for nest k and zero for other nests. In practice, this can lead to a dimensionality problem with a large number of upper level choices. Substituting equation (8.14) into (8.10) gives

$$\Pr(j,k) = \frac{a_k \exp(\frac{-\beta_y c_{jk}+\mathbf{q}_{jk}\boldsymbol{\beta}+\mathbf{s}_k\boldsymbol{\gamma}}{\theta_k})\left[\sum_{l=1}^{J_k}\exp(\frac{-\beta_y c_{lk}+\mathbf{q}_{lk}\boldsymbol{\beta}+\mathbf{s}_k\boldsymbol{\gamma}}{\theta_k})\right]^{\theta_k-1}}{\sum_{m=1}^{K} a_m\left[\sum_{l=1}^{J_m}\exp(\frac{-\beta_y c_{lm}+\mathbf{q}_{lm}\boldsymbol{\beta}+\mathbf{s}_m\boldsymbol{\gamma}}{\theta_m})\right]^{\theta_m}}. \tag{8.15}$$

Using equations (8.11) and (8.12) we can write the probability of choosing alternative j, conditional on choosing upper level nest k:

$$\Pr(j|k) = \frac{\exp(\frac{-\beta_y c_{jk}+\mathbf{q}_{jk}\boldsymbol{\beta}}{\theta_k})}{\sum_{l=1}^{J_k}\exp(\frac{-\beta_y c_{lk}+\mathbf{q}_{lk}\boldsymbol{\beta}}{\theta_k})}. \tag{8.16}$$

(Compare with equation 8.1.) According to equation (8.8), this probability is independent of additive parts of the utility function that do not change within the nest, so that $\mathbf{s}_k\boldsymbol{\gamma}$ falls out.

We also use equation (8.12) to write

$$\Pr(k) = \frac{a_k\left[\sum_{l=1}^{J_k}\exp(\frac{-\beta_y c_{lk}+\mathbf{q}_{lk}\boldsymbol{\beta}+\mathbf{s}_k\boldsymbol{\gamma}}{\theta_k})\right]^{\theta_k}}{\sum_{m=1}^{K} a_m\left[\sum_{l=1}^{J_m}\exp(\frac{-\beta_y c_{lk}+\mathbf{q}_{lm}\boldsymbol{\beta}+\mathbf{s}_m\boldsymbol{\gamma}}{\theta_m})\right]^{\theta_m}}. \tag{8.17}$$

Rearranging yields a common expression for this probability:

$$\Pr(k) = \frac{a_k\exp(\mathbf{s}_k\boldsymbol{\gamma}+\theta_k I_k)}{\sum_{m=1}^{K} a_m\exp(\mathbf{s}_m\boldsymbol{\gamma}+\theta_m I_m)}. \tag{8.18}$$

The variable

$$I_m = \ln\left(\sum_{l=1}^{J_m}\exp(\frac{-\beta_y c_{lm}+\mathbf{q}_{lm}\boldsymbol{\beta}}{\theta_m})\right) \tag{8.19}$$

is known as the inclusive value for nest m, and θ_m is the inclusive value parameter. Note the similarity between the inclusive value and the indirect utility function as given in expected maximum utility in equation

(8.9). Combining results, the nested logit probability of choosing alternative j, k is

$$\Pr(j,k) = \frac{e^{\frac{-\beta_y c_{jk} + \mathbf{q}_{jk}\boldsymbol{\beta}}{\theta_k}}}{\sum_{l=1}^{J_k} e^{\frac{-\beta_y c_{lk} + \mathbf{q}_{lk}\boldsymbol{\beta}}{\theta_k}}} \times \frac{a_k e^{\mathbf{s}_k \boldsymbol{\gamma} + \theta_k I_k}}{\sum_{m=1}^{K} a_m e^{\mathbf{s}_m \boldsymbol{\gamma} + \theta_m I_m}}. \tag{8.20}$$

In practice, several simplifications are often made. For example, it is common to allow some nests to have the same θ or even to impose $\theta_k = \theta$ for all k. Further, many models assume that most $a_k = a$. But the greatest simplifications lead to the conditional logit model.

8.4.3 The Conditional Logit Model

Consider the nested logit model as defined in equation (8.20). Suppose as a special case, that $\theta_k = 1$ and $a_k = a \; \forall k$. The probability of observing the choice j, k becomes

$$\Pr(j,k) = \frac{e^{-\beta_y c_{jk} + \mathbf{q}_{jk}\boldsymbol{\beta}}}{\sum_{l=1}^{J_k} e^{-\beta_y c_{lk} + \mathbf{q}_{lk}\boldsymbol{\beta}}} \times \frac{e^{\mathbf{s}_k \boldsymbol{\gamma} + I_k}}{\sum_{m=1}^{K} e^{\mathbf{s}_m \boldsymbol{\gamma} + I_m}}. \tag{8.21}$$

which upon substitution of the expression for the inclusive value in equation (8.19) becomes

$$\begin{aligned} \Pr(j,k) &= \frac{e^{-\beta_y c_{jk} + \mathbf{q}_{jk}\boldsymbol{\beta}}}{\sum_{l=1}^{J_k} e^{-\beta_y c_{lk} + \mathbf{q}_{lk}\boldsymbol{\beta}}} \times \frac{e^{\mathbf{s}_k \boldsymbol{\gamma}} \sum_{l=1}^{J_k} e^{-\beta_y c_{lk} + \mathbf{q}_{lk}\boldsymbol{\beta}}}{\sum_{m=1}^{K} e^{\mathbf{s}_m \boldsymbol{\gamma}} \sum_{l=1}^{J_m} e^{-\beta_y c_{lk} + \mathbf{q}_{lm}\boldsymbol{\beta}}} \\ &= \frac{e^{-\beta_y c_{jk} + \mathbf{q}_{jk}\boldsymbol{\beta} + \mathbf{s}_k \boldsymbol{\gamma}}}{\sum_{m=1}^{K} \sum_{l=1}^{J_m} e^{-\beta_y c_{lm} + \mathbf{q}_{lm}\boldsymbol{\beta} + \mathbf{s}_m \boldsymbol{\gamma}}} = \frac{e^{v_{jk}}}{\sum_{m=1}^{K} \sum_{l=1}^{J_m} e^{\mathbf{v}_{lm}}} \end{aligned}$$

where $v_{jk} = -\beta_y c_{jk} + \mathbf{q}_{jk}\boldsymbol{\beta} + \mathbf{s}_k \boldsymbol{\gamma}$. Since the upper nest serves no purpose now, we create a single index n for each unique (j,k) and write the conditional logit probability of choosing alternative m as

$$\Pr(m) = \frac{e^{v_m}}{\sum_{n=1}^{J} e^{\mathbf{v}_n}}. \tag{8.22}$$

Equation (8.22) represents the conditional logit probability of choosing alternative m $(m = 1, ..., J)$ from among all $J = \sum_{m=1}^{K} J_m$ alternatives. Compare this with equation (8.1). McFadden (1974) derived this model by assuming that the errors of the indirect utility function were independently and identically distributed across alternatives following a Type-I extreme value distribution (see Appendix B for a description).

8.5 Independence of Irrelevant Alternatives

Although the conditional logit model is a special case of the nested logit, it was developed first. The conditional logit grew out of efforts to explain the choice among an array of alternatives. The nested logit emerged partly as a response to the problem with the conditional logit that has come to be known as the independence of irrelevant alternatives (IIA).

The IIA principle can be stated as follows: the relative probability of choosing between any two alternatives is independent of all other alternatives. More specifically, define S_R as a set of alternatives available to the individual, and S_{R+I} as a broader set of alternatives $(S_R \subset S_{R+I})$. The IIA principle states

$$\frac{\Pr(l|S_R)}{\Pr(m|S_R)} = \frac{\Pr(l|S_{R+I})}{\Pr(m|S_{R+I})}$$

where $\Pr(l|S_R)$ indicates the probability that alternative l is chosen from among the set S_R.

Clearly, the IIA property holds for the conditional logit model. From equation (8.22), the relative probability of choosing site m to choosing site p is:

$$\frac{\Pr(m)}{\Pr(p)} = \frac{e^{v_m}}{\sum_{n=1}^{J} e^{\mathrm{v}_n}} \div \frac{e^{v_p}}{\sum_{n=1}^{J} e^{\mathrm{v}_n}} = \frac{e^{v_m}}{e^{v_p}} \tag{8.23}$$

which is independent of introducing an irrelevant alternative.

For the conditional logit, the IIA property implies that the relative probability of choosing between sites will remain constant even if a perfect substitute is introduced. To see why this is a problem, suppose there are two sites available (A and B). For simplicity, let the probability of choosing each site be 0.5. The relative probability of choosing A to B is 1 (or odds of 1:1). Now introduce a third alternative C that is identical to site B (a perfect substitute). We would expect that the individual would still choose A with probability 0.5 and then split the remaining 0.5 between B and C (so that $\Pr(B) = \Pr(C) = 0.25$). If such were the case, the relative probability of choosing A to B would become 2. However, because of the IIA property, a conditional logit model would maintain the odds ratio at 1:1 for alternatives A and B, clearly an undesirable result. The relative probability of choosing A to (B or C) should be 1. If a viable substitute to an alternative is introduced, the conditional logit model would still predict that the relative probability of choosing site j,k to site p,r would stay the same, as if the new site didn't exist.

The nested logit RUM relaxes the restrictive IIA assumption to some degree. Consider the nested logit probability as defined in equation (8.5). The relative probability of choosing alternative j,k to alternative p,r is now

$$\begin{aligned}\frac{\Pr(j,k)}{\Pr(p,r)} &= \frac{a_k e^{\frac{v_{jk}}{\theta_k}}\left[\sum_{l=1}^{J_k} e^{\frac{v_{lk}}{\theta_k}}\right]^{\theta_k-1}}{\sum_{m=1}^{K} a_m\left[\sum_{l=1}^{J_m} e^{\frac{v_{lm}}{\theta_m}}\right]^{\theta_m}} \div \frac{a_r e^{\frac{v_{pr}}{\theta_r}}\left[\sum_{l=1}^{J_r} e^{\frac{v_{lr}}{\theta_r}}\right]^{\theta_r-1}}{\sum_{m=1}^{K} a_m\left[\sum_{l=1}^{J_m} e^{\frac{v_{lm}}{\theta_m}}\right]^{\theta_m}} \\ &= \frac{a_k e^{\frac{v_{jk}}{\theta_k}}\left[\sum_{l=1}^{J_k} e^{\frac{v_{lk}}{\theta_k}}\right]^{\theta_k-1}}{a_r e^{\frac{v_{pr}}{\theta_r}}\left[\sum_{l=1}^{J_r} e^{\frac{v_{lr}}{\theta_r}}\right]^{\theta_r-1}}. \end{aligned} \tag{8.24}$$

IIA no longer holds for changes within nests k and r, but changes outside these two nests are still irrelevant. Consider the case when $r = k$; i.e., alternatives j and p are in the same nest. The relative probabilities are

$$\Pr(j,r)/\Pr(p,r) = \frac{e^{\frac{v_{jr}}{\theta_r}}}{e^{\frac{v_{pr}}{\theta_r}}} = e^{(v_{jr}-v_{pr})/\theta_r}.$$

which is independent of all other alternatives in nest r as well as all other nests. The IIA assumption holds within a given nest for the nested logit model. However, if $r \neq k$ then equation (8.24) shows that the changes in nest k (other than site j) will change the relative probability of choosing site j to site p. Similarly, adding or subtracting a site from nest r will change the relative probability of choosing site j to site p. The nested logit model relaxes the IIA assumption across nests, but maintains the assumption within nests. Continuing the A,B,C example from above (recall that B and C are perfect substitutes), grouping B and C together in a nest allows the relative probability to other sites to change with the addition of alternatives.

We have illustrated the characteristic of IIA with the conditional logit model. This is a property of the conditional logit, but also of any distribution for which the errors are uncorrelated. In chapter 10 we survey mixed logit models, which provides a means of eliminating the IIA property of logit models.

Returning to the parametrization of the indirect utility function, we have still to decide on the appropriate functional form for the remaining portion of the indirect utility function v_{jk} (maintaining the linear in income specification). Standard econometric packages (such as SAS and LIMDEP) require the estimated function to be linear in the set of estimated parameters. In general, this means that for estimation, the indirect utility function typically takes the form: $v_{jk}\left(\mathbf{q}_{jk},\mathbf{s}_k\right)=\mathbf{X}_{jk}\boldsymbol{\beta}^*$, where $\mathbf{X}_{jk}\equiv\{c_{jk},\mathbf{q}_{jk},\mathbf{s}_k\}$ and $\boldsymbol{\beta}^*\equiv\left\{-\beta_y,\boldsymbol{\beta},\boldsymbol{\gamma}\right\}$. Note that in this formulation, the estimated parameter associated with the price of a trip is the negative of the marginal utility of income. As such, we would expect this parameter to be negative.

8.6 Estimating the Models

In this section we deal with the estimation of random utility models from population surveys where the sampling is exogenous. That is, we sample individuals from a relevant population group, and learn from these individuals the choices they made in selecting alternatives. In this sample the probability that an individual is selected is independent of the probability that an individual chooses a given site. Further, we assume that the relative sample weights are the same for different individuals so that the likelihood function is the simple product of the individual contributions. Hence the sample probabilities of site choice are consistent estimates of population site choice, and the sampling does not influence parameter estimates. In section 7 we will explore the consequences of on-site sampling, in which the sample proportions of visits depend on the sampling. For a general discussion of sampling in random utility model estimation, see Manski and McFadden (1981). In general, the sampling scheme is critical to estimation, and sampling with endogenous weights will tend to yield inconsistent parameter estimates unless properly managed.

Two methods have been used for estimating the nested logit RUM. The first is a limited information maximum likelihood (LIML) approach that relies on two-stage estimation of the choice probability in equation

(8.20). The second is the full information maximum likelihood approach (FIML) which jointly estimates all parameters of the likelihood function. Let $\delta_{jk} = 1$ when the individual chooses site (j, k) and 0 otherwise. Then the individual contribution to the likelihood function for the nested logit RUM is

$$L(\boldsymbol{\beta}, \boldsymbol{\gamma}, a_1, ..., a_K, \theta_1, ...\theta_K | \mathbf{q}_{jk}, \mathbf{s}_k)$$

$$= \prod_{k=1}^{K} \prod_{j=1}^{J_k} \Pr(j, k)^{\delta_{jk}}$$

$$= \prod_{k=1}^{K} \prod_{j=1}^{J_k} \left[\frac{e^{\frac{-\beta_y c_{jk} + \mathbf{q}_{jk}\boldsymbol{\beta}}{\theta_k}}}{\sum_{l=1}^{J_k} e^{\frac{-\beta_y c_{lk} + \mathbf{q}_{lk}\boldsymbol{\beta}}{\theta_k}}} \times \frac{a_k e^{\mathbf{s}_k \boldsymbol{\gamma} + \theta_k I_k}}{\sum_{m=1}^{K} a_m e^{\mathbf{s}_m \boldsymbol{\gamma} + \theta_m I_m}} \right]^{\delta_{jk}}.$$

The log-likelihood contribution for a given individual is

$$\ln L(\boldsymbol{\beta}, \boldsymbol{\gamma}, a_1, ..., a_K, \theta_1, ...\theta_K | \mathbf{q}_{jk}, \mathbf{s}_k)$$

$$= \sum_{k=1}^{K} \sum_{j=1}^{J_k} \delta_{jk} \ln \left[\frac{e^{\frac{-\beta_y c_{jk} + \mathbf{q}_{jk}\boldsymbol{\beta}}{\theta_k}}}{\sum_{l=1}^{J_k} e^{\frac{-\beta_y c_{lk} + \mathbf{q}_{lk}\boldsymbol{\beta}}{\theta_k}}} \times \frac{a_k e^{\mathbf{s}_k \boldsymbol{\gamma} + \theta_k I_k}}{\sum_{m=1}^{K} a_m e^{\mathbf{s}_m \boldsymbol{\gamma} + \theta_m I_m}} \right]$$

which can be rewritten as:

$$= \sum_{k=1}^{K} \sum_{j=1}^{J_k} \delta_{jk} \ln [\Pr(j|k)] + \sum_{k=1}^{K} \sum_{j=1}^{J_k} \delta_{jk} \ln [\Pr(k)] \qquad (8.26)$$

where $\Pr(j|k)$ and $\Pr(k)$ are defined in equations (8.16) and (8.17). The first term is the sum of the log-likelihood contributions from a conditional logit model based on the lower level decisions. That is, the lower level probability of choosing j, k is the probability of choosing j from among the J_k alternatives in nest k. Similarly, the second double-summation term is the log-likelihood contribution from a conditional logit among the K upper level alternatives, i.e., the probability of choosing k from among the K alternatives at the upper level. Computing capacity has expanded so that the FIML is programmed in most software, and is the preferred approach. Nevertheless, as an aid to understanding the process we outline the LIML.

8.6.1 Procedure for two-stage (LIML) estimation

1. The number of models estimated at the lower stage equals the number of distinct θ_k's. Each θ_k is a scale parameter that normalizes the $\boldsymbol{\beta}$ vector. Suppose one wants only one θ_k. Then estimate the lower level model

$$\Pr(j|k) = \frac{\exp(-\beta_y c_{jk} + \mathbf{q}_{jk}\boldsymbol{\beta})/\theta}{\sum_{m=1}^{J_k} \exp(-\beta_y c_{mk} + \mathbf{q}_{mk}\boldsymbol{\beta})/\theta}.$$

Covariates should include only those variables that vary by lower level nests $(c_{jk}, \mathbf{q}_{jk})$. This model yields the parameter vector $(-\beta_y, \boldsymbol{\beta})/\theta$.

2. Calculate the inclusive value

$$I_k = \ln\left(\sum_{m=1}^{J_k} \exp(-\beta_y c_{mk} + \mathbf{q}_{mk}\boldsymbol{\beta})/\theta\right)$$

for all k for each individual.

3. Estimate a conditional logit for the upper level choice.

$$\Pr(k) = \frac{\exp(\gamma \mathbf{s}_k + \theta I_k + \alpha_k D_k)}{\sum_{n=1}^{K} \exp(\gamma \mathbf{s}_n + \theta I_n + \alpha_n D_n)}.$$

The D_k are dummy variables = 1 for nest k, 0 otherwise. Only $K-1$ dummy variables can be created if the model includes a constant. Covariates should include variables that vary by upper level choice $(\mathbf{s}_k)$, and the calculated inclusive value as regressors and D_k.

Parameters from the two-step procedure are consistent but not efficient. The standard errors are too small relative to their probability limits. Increased computing power has made the two-stage estimation method somewhat obsolete. In the next section we describe the full-information maximum likelihood (FIML) estimation approach. Brownstone and Small explore the empirical evidence on FIML and LIML estimators for nested logit models.

8.6.2 FIML Estimation

Full information maximum likelihood methods estimates the full model using maximum likelihood. Equation (8.26) defines the log-likelihood function to be maximized with respect to the parameter vector:

$$\{\boldsymbol{\beta}, \gamma, a_1, ..., a_K, \theta_1, ...\theta_K\}.$$

Example 27 *Beach Choice*

To illustrate the estimation of the random utility model we use an example of beach day trip choice by Delaware residents.[1] The data come from a random mail survey of 1000 households in the fall of 1997. The dataset from which the models are estimated pertains to the 400 households who took day trips. In the survey, individuals chose from a set of 62 beaches in New Jersey, Delaware, Maryland and Virginia.

Choosing a nesting structure for the nested logit model is a strategic modeling decision that often has considerable impact on welfare measures. In most cases, one constructs the nests based on an understanding of the choice setting. We explore the problems of choosing a nesting structure in the following sections. In this problem, the Delaware Bay acts as a natural boundary between coastal beaches in Virginia, Maryland and Delaware (South beaches), and those in New Jersey (North beaches). This natural boundary provides a simple nesting structure for beach choice decisions. First, individuals choose between visiting a South beach or a North beach, and then conditional on this choice, individuals choose the actual beach to visit. The questionnaire asked individuals the number of day, overnight and extended stay trips they had made to each of the 62 beaches in the past year. For our purposes we utilize only the single day trips reported by the individual. Each respondent reports the number of day trips to each beach over the course of the year. In total, the sample of 400 households took 9,330 day trips to the 62 study beaches. Respondents took 620 trips to North beaches and 8710 trips to South beaches. For illustration of the nested logit model, we treat each trip as an independent observation without explicitly recognizing the potential correlation across trips for an individual. In general, treating each trip as an independent observation probably produces more efficiency than is warranted because it seems likely that there is correlation across different trips for the same individual. Treating trips this way gives for each individual *number of trips* $\times$ *number of alternatives* cases, each of which is treated as an observation. For a discussion of independence across choice occasions in the context of recreation models see Herriges, Kling and Phaneuf (1999) or Haab (2001).

---

[1] We thank George Parsons for generously giving us access to this dataset. For a full description of the data see Parsons, Massey and Tomasi.

Individual covariates do not vary across trips and are assumed constant across the year. Models that account for linkages between site choice and the number of trips taken are discussed in subsequent sections.

Table 8.2 describes the variables used in the beach choice estimation models. The indirect utility function for all models is assumed to be

TABLE 8.2. Variable Definitions and Means

Variable Name	Description	Mean N=9330
c*	Trip cost + time cost	\$122
LG	Length of beach in miles	0.62
BW	Boardwalk present=1	0.40
AM	Amusement park near beach =1	0.13
PR	Private or limited access beach=1	0.26
PK	State, Federal Park or wildlife refuge=1	0.10
W	Wide beach (=1 if width > 200 feet)	0.26
NW	Narrow beach (=1 if width ≤ 75 feet)	0.15
CT	Atlantic City=1	0.02
SF	Good surfing location=1	0.35
HR	Presence of high rises=1	0.24
PW	Part of the beach is a park area=1	0.15
FC	Restroom facilities available=1	0.39
PG	Parking available at beach=1	0.45

*Travel costs are calculated at \$0.35 per mile, and time costs are calculated as annual income/2040, or income per hour.

linear-in-income and all other covariates as in equation (8.13):

$$
\begin{aligned}
v_{jk}=&\beta_y(y-c_{jk})+\beta_1 LG_{jk}+\beta_2 BW_{jk}+\beta_3 AM_{jk}\\
&+\beta_4 PR_{jk}+\beta_5 PK_{jk}+\beta_6 W_{jk}+\beta_7 NW_{jk}+\beta_8 CT_{jk}\\
&+\beta_9 SF_{jk}+\beta_{10} HR_{jk}+\beta_{11} PW_{jk}+\beta_{12} FC_{jk}+\beta_{13} PG_{jk}.
\end{aligned}
$$

All the covariates vary by site. *I.e.*, there are no nest-specific variables. Table 8.3 presents the estimation results from a conditional logit model based on equation (8.22) on all 62 beaches (no nesting). All coefficients are significant and the signs are plausible. An increase in the length of the beach increases the probability of choosing that beach as does the presence of a boardwalk or amusement rides. Privatizing a beach decreases the probability of visitation, and very wide or very narrow beaches have lower probabilities of visitations than beaches between 75

TABLE 8.3. Parameters of Conditional Logit

Parameter	Estimate[a]	Standard Error
β_y	0.06	0.001
β_1	0.06	0.03
β_2	0.60	0.11
β_3	1.26	0.05
β_4	−0.36	0.05
β_5	0.23	0.12
β_6	−0.74	0.05
β_7	−0.32	0.07
β_8	0.82	0.10
β_9	0.89	0.04
β_{10}	0.51	0.06
β_{11}	0.93	0.08
β_{12}	−0.15	0.08
β_{13}	0.49	0.13
Log-likelihood	−23374.47	
$-2\ln(L_R/L_U)^b$	30263.38	

[a]All coefficients different from zero at 95% level of confidence.
[b]The restrictions are $\beta_j = 0\ \forall j$.

and 200 feet wide. The restroom facility result is unexpected. There is no obvious reason why the presence of restroom facilities decreases the probability of a day trip to a beach. Also, the presence of high-rises at the beach decreases the probability of visitation.

The nested logit model is based on a particularly simple structure:

$$\theta_{North} = \theta_{South} = \theta.$$

That is, only one value of θ is estimated. Further, we have assumed that the alternative-specific constants are equal:

$$a = a_{North} = a_{South}.$$

When the nest-specific constants are equal, they will fall out of the estimation, as can be seen by looking at equation (8.5).

Table 8.4 gives the parameter estimates for the nested logit model on the same data (see equation 8.26). The beaches are split into North and South nests at the upper level as it is expected that the substitution patterns among New Jersey beaches by Delaware residents are similar, but as a group, the substitution patterns may differ from the pattern among beaches in Delaware, Maryland and Virginia. The signs and sig-

TABLE 8.4. Nested Logit

Parameter	Estimate	Standard Error
β_y	0.08	0.002
β_1	0.25	0.03
β_2	0.82	0.13
β_3	1.02	0.05
β_4	−0.35	0.06
β_5	[a]0.12	0.13
β_6	−0.70	0.05
β_7	−0.41	0.08
β_8	0.74	0.11
β_9	0.85	0.05
β_{10}	−0.60	0.06
β_{11}	0.53	0.09
β_{12}	[a]−0.11	0.09
β_{13}	0.27	0.14
θ	0.50	0.01
Log-likelihood	−23110.47	
$-2\ln(L_R/L_U)$[b]	19760.14	

[a]All coefficients except these different from zero at 95% level of confidence.
[b]The restrictions are $\beta_j = 0\ \forall j$ and $\theta = 1$.

nificance of the nested logit coefficients correspond to those from the conditional logit, with the exception of the restroom facility and state park coefficients. Both of these have the same sign as the conditional logit but the null hypothesis that they are equal to zero can not be rejected at any reasonable confidence level. The inclusive value coefficient θ is significantly different from zero and one, indicating that there is correlation in patterns of substitution across North and South beaches, but this correlation is not perfect as is assumed in the conditional logit. By rejecting the null hypothesis that $\theta = 1$, we reject the conditional logit in favor of the two-level nesting structure. We also reject the complete IIA of the conditional logit in favor of IIA in the two branches. More tests for nesting structure are discussed in section 8.10 below.

8.7 Estimation with On-site Sampling

In many circumstances, it is much cheaper to gather samples on-site than to contact people by phone, mail, or in person. As in the case of the single site model, the cost advantage in a multiple site model is particularly great when the proportion of population participating in the activity is quite low. However, a problem arises in estimating the population probability of choosing an alternative from an on-site sample: the probability estimates will be determined by the sampling scheme. That is, given an on-site sample, all inferences about population parameters are based on the fact that individual i was interviewed at site j. To see the problem with on-site samples (often referred to as choice-based samples), consider a simple case. Let the total sample size be N, and let N_j be the sample number of individuals interviewed at site j, where $j = 1, ..., K$. Further, let P_j represent the population proportion of trips to site j such that $\sum_{j=1}^{K} P_j = 1$. Given independence across individuals, trips and sites, the joint probability of observing N_1 individuals at site 1, N_2 individuals at site 2, and so on, is the multinomial probability

$$\Pr(N_1, N_2, ..., N_K|\mathbf{P}) = \frac{N!}{\prod\limits_{k=1}^{K} N_k!} \prod_{j=1}^{K} P_j^{N_j} \tag{8.27}$$

where $\mathbf{P} \equiv \{P_1, ..., P_K\}$. Treating the population proportions as unknown and the sample number of interviews as known, equation (8.27) can be interpreted as a likelihood function. The log-likelihood function is

$$\ln L(\mathbf{P}|N_1, N_2, ..., N_K) = \ln(C) + \sum_{j=1}^{K} N_j \ln(P_j)$$

where $C = N!/\prod\limits_{k=1}^{K} N_k!$ is constant with respect to the unknown parameter vector $\mathbf{P}$. By imposing the constraint $\sum_{j=1}^{K} P_j = 1$, we can show that the maximum likelihood estimates for the population proportions P_j are equal to the sample proportions:

$$\widehat{P_j} = \frac{N_j}{\sum\limits_{k=1}^{K} N_k}.$$

This is an intuitive result. With no additional information, the best guess for the population proportion of individuals taking a trip to a given site will be equal to the sampled proportion of individuals taking a trip.

The problem of an on-site sample arises because the sampling scheme is often independent of the population proportions taking trips. As an extreme, consider a sampling scheme in which an equal number of individuals is intercepted and interviewed at each site. In this case, the maximum likelihood estimates of the population proportions will be equal across all sites even if the true population proportions are not. In the typical case, failure to account for the sampling plan will result in parameter estimates that combine sampling plans and individual behavior, when what we really want is just the behavior.

Example 28 *The Effects of On-Site Sampling*

To show the effect of on-site sampling, we use a simple example motivated by Waldman. Suppose that there are just two choices and the true model is $u_j = x_j\beta + \varepsilon_j$, where $j = 1, 2$, and x_1 and x_2 are alternative specific scalars. The log-likelihood function for this model becomes

$$L(\beta|x) = N_1 \ln[\frac{\exp(x_1\beta)}{\exp(x_1\beta) + \exp(x_2\beta)}] + N_2 \ln[\frac{\exp(x_2\beta)}{\exp(x_1\beta) + \exp(x_2\beta)}]$$

Maximizing the expression with respect to β yields the following closed form solution:

$$\beta = \log(n_1/n_2) \div (x_1 - x_2).$$

Hence the parameter estimate depends on the *samples taken at each site*, as well as the differences in the values of the attributes. But if the samples are distributed evenly at each site, then $\beta = 0$, regardless of the values of the attributes. This is an extreme case, but it illustrates the basic point: the parameter estimates are determined by the sampling proportions. If these proportions are different from the population proportions then inconsistent parameter estimates will result.

8.7.1 A Solution to On-Site Sampling

To formulate a solution for the problem of on-site sampling, we write the probability of an individual taking a trip to a particular site based on the information we have in the sample. For a given individual intercepted on-site, we know simply that the individual was interviewed at that site. The probability of interviewing a given individual at a particular site will be a function of the number of trips the individual takes to each site, and the number of individuals interviewed at each site. In particular, the probability of observing individual i being interviewed at site j will be

$$P_{ij} = \frac{N_j p_{ij}}{\sum_{k=1}^{K} N_k p_{ik}} \tag{8.28}$$

where N_j is the number of individuals sampled at site j, and p_{ij} is i's proportion of all trips by all individuals to site j. The numerator represents the expected number of interviews at site j for individual i over the course of the season. That is, if 100 individuals are interviewed at site j, and individual i takes 10% of all trips taken to site j, then it would be expected that individual i would be interviewed 10 times. This implies that individuals are interviewed with replacement at a given site. In general, this is not a concern as long as an individual's trips are a negligible proportion of the total. Nevertheless, the results below hold only when the on-site sampling scheme mimics sampling with replacement. The denominator in equation (8.28) represents the expected number of interviews for individual i across all sites. Thus, P_{ij} represents the expected proportion of interviews for individual i at site j.

Denoting the number of trips taken by individual i to site j as x_{ij}, and the total number of trips taken by all individuals to site j as $x_{\cdot j}$, such that $x_{\cdot j} = \sum_i x_{ij}$, we write the proportion of total trips to j taken by i as

$$p_{ij} = x_{ij}/x_{\cdot j}.$$

Substituting into equation (8.28), we see that the probability of individual i being interviewed at site j is

$$P_{ij} = N_j \frac{x_{ij}}{x_{j\cdot}} / \sum_{k=1}^{K} N_k \frac{x_{ik}}{x_{\cdot k}}. \tag{8.29}$$

Denoting the total number of interviews at all sites as N, the total number of trips taken by individual i to all sites as $x_{i\cdot}$, and the total number of trips taken by the population as x, we can write P_{ij} as

$$\begin{aligned} P_{ij} &= \frac{N_j/N}{x_{\cdot j}/x} \frac{x_{ij}}{x_{i\cdot}} / \sum_{k=1}^{K} \frac{N_k/N}{x_{\cdot k}/x} \frac{x_{ik}}{x_{i\cdot}} \\ &= \frac{\frac{\rho_j}{W_j} \Pr_i(j)}{\sum_{k=1}^{K} \frac{\rho_k}{W_k} \Pr_i(k)} \end{aligned}$$

where $\rho_j = N_j/N$ is the sample proportion of interviews at site j, $W_j = x_{\cdot j}/x$ is the population proportion of total trips taken to site j and

$\Pr_i(j) = \frac{x_{ij}}{x_{i\cdot}}$ is the unknown probability of observing individual i take a trip to site j.

In random samples, the probability of observing a given individual choosing alternative j is conditioned on the site characteristics ($\mathbf{X}_{ij} \equiv \{c_{ij}, \mathbf{q}_{ij}\}$). Let $\Pr_i(j) = \Pr(j|\mathbf{X}_{ij})$, the population probability that individual i with site characteristics $\mathbf{X}_{ij}$ will choose site j. Consider the probability statement that we interview an individual at site j given by

$$P_{ij} = \frac{\frac{\rho_j}{W_j} \Pr(j|\mathbf{X}_{ij})}{\sum_{k=1}^{K} \frac{\rho_k}{W_k} \Pr(k|\mathbf{X}_{ik})} \tag{8.30}$$

where $\Pr(j|\mathbf{X}_{ij})$ simply denotes the conditioning of the population probability on individual-site specific covariates. Equation (8.30) represents the on-site sample 'corrected' probability that individual i takes a trip to site j. Equation (8.30) illustrates a fundamental result regarding on-site sampling and the conditional logit model: *Simple weighting of the unknown population probability by the ratio of the sampled proportion of site visitors* (ρ_j) *to the population proportion* (W_j) *will not solve the problems caused by on-site sampling.*

To understand this result, consider the contribution to the on-site sample likelihood function by individual i

$$L_i(\beta|\mathbf{X}_{i1}, ..., \mathbf{X}_{iJ}) = \prod_{j=1}^{K} P_{ij}^{\delta_{ij}}$$

where δ_{ij} is an indicator variable that is equal to one if the individual is interviewed at site j, and zero otherwise. Substituting the expression for the on-site choice probability in equation (8.30) and rewriting the likelihood function in log form, the ith contribution to the log-likelihood function becomes

$$\begin{aligned}\ln L(\beta|\mathbf{X}_{i1}, ..., \mathbf{X}_{iJ}) &= \sum_{j=1}^{K}\left[\begin{array}{c}\delta_{ij}\ln\left(\frac{\rho_j}{W_j}\Pr(j|\mathbf{X}_{ij})\right) - \\ \delta_{ij}\ln\left(\sum_{k=1}^{K}\frac{\rho_k}{W_k}\Pr(k|\mathbf{X}_{ik})\right)\end{array}\right] \\ &= \sum_{j=1}^{K}\left[\delta_{ij}\ln\left(\frac{\rho_j}{W_j}\Pr(j|\mathbf{X}_{ij})\right)\right] - \\ &\quad \ln\left(\sum_{k=1}^{K}\frac{\rho_k}{W_k}\Pr(k|\mathbf{X}_{ik})\right).\end{aligned}$$

The first summation term on the right hand site is the log of the on-site weighted probability, where the weight is the sample proportion to population proportion. That is, the probability of taking a trip to site j ($\Pr(j|\mathbf{X}_{ij})$) is weighted by the relative proportions of sampled trips to population trips to site j $\left(\frac{\rho_j}{W_j}\right)$. However, there is additional weighting in the second term on the right hand side. Failure to account for this term will result in inconsistent parameter estimates. The correction for the problem of on-site sampling requires a tailored likelihood function, and programming into an econometrics package. Below, we discuss solutions to the problem of on-site sampling that can be implemented using standard econometric packages.

8.7.2 The On-site Conditional Logit

If $\Pr(j|\mathbf{X}_{ij})$ is conditional logit, and there are no site-specific constants in $\mathbf{X}_{ij}$, then the choice-based sampling problem can be solved by including a set of site-specific constants in the model. Consider the conditional logit probability:

$$\Pr(j|\mathbf{X}_{ij}) = \frac{e^{\mathbf{X}_{ij}\beta^*}}{\sum_h e^{\mathbf{X}_{ih}\beta^*}}.$$

Substituting into equation (8.30) gives

$$\begin{aligned} P_{ij} &= \frac{\frac{\rho_j}{W_j}\frac{e^{\mathbf{X}_{ij}\beta^*}}{\sum_h e^{\mathbf{X}_{ih}\beta^*}}}{\sum_k \frac{\rho_k}{W_k}\frac{e^{\mathbf{X}_{ik}\beta^*}}{\sum_h e^{\mathbf{X}_{ih}\beta^*}}} \\ &= \frac{\frac{\rho_j}{W_j}e^{\mathbf{X}_{ij}\beta^*}}{\sum_k \frac{\rho_k}{W_k}e^{\mathbf{X}_{ik}\beta^*}} \end{aligned} \tag{8.31}$$

which can be rewritten

$$P_{ij} = \frac{e^{\mathbf{X}_{ij}\beta^*+\gamma_j}}{\sum_k e^{\mathbf{X}_{ik}\beta^*+\gamma_k}} \tag{8.32}$$

where $\gamma_j = \ln\left(\frac{\rho_j}{W_j}\right)$ and the sum is over all sites. Equation (8.32) is the equivalent of a conditional logit model with a full set of site-specific constants. Because a full set of site-specific constants cannot be estimated (because of the dummy variable trap), it is necessary to normalize on one of the constants. Without loss of generality, we normalize on alternative

1 such that equation (8.32) becomes

$$P_{ij} = \frac{e^{\mathbf{X}_j\beta+\nu_j^*}}{\sum_k e^{\mathbf{X}_k\beta+\nu_k^*}} \tag{8.33}$$

where $\nu_j^* = \ln\left(\frac{\rho_j}{W_j}\frac{W_1}{\rho_1}\right)$ and $\nu_1^* = 0$.

When uncorrected, choice-based sampling provides results that simply reflect the sampling, rather than the choices that individuals have made. For consistent estimates of parameters, the sample mean probabilities of site choice need to approach the population proportions. When sampling is on-site, estimation without correction will provide consistent estimators only accidentally.

8.7.3 Consequences and Solutions in Practice

To investigate further the consequences of and the possible solutions to choice-based sampling, we consider four possible cases:

Case 1: Population proportions are known, and X contains site-specific constants.

If the population weights are known, then the problem of choice-based sampling becomes a problem of properly adjusting the site-specific constants. Suppose $\mathbf{X}_{ij}\beta = \alpha_j + \mathbf{X}_{ij}^*\beta^*$, where α_j is a constant associated with site j. Then equation (8.33) becomes:

$$P_{ij} = \frac{e^{\mathbf{X}_{ij}^*\beta^*+\alpha_j^*}}{\sum_k e^{\mathbf{X}_{ik}^*\beta^*+\alpha_k^*}} \tag{8.34}$$

where $\alpha_j^* = \alpha_j + \gamma_j^*$. Because γ_j^* is known if the population weights are known, we can estimate a conditional logit with a full set of site-specific constants and then adjust the constants by the appropriate weights. That is, a conditional logit with alternative-specific constants will return estimates of $\boldsymbol{\beta}^*$ and α_j^*. Estimates of α_j can be found by subtracting γ_j^* from α_j^*. Cosslett (1981) shows that this procedure yields consistent and efficient (maximum likelihood) estimates of α_j and $\boldsymbol{\beta}^*$.

Case 2: Population weights are known, and X does not contain site-specific constants.

If $\mathbf{X}_j\boldsymbol{\beta}$ does not contain a constant then the population weights must be directly incorporated into the likelihood function. This is difficult, and a better procedure might be to proceed according to case 1. Site-specific constants may be appropriate in a RUM. If we proceed according to case 1, and estimate the model assuming site-specific alternatives, we can simply adjust the resulting constant estimates by the known population weights. Under ideal circumstances (perfect specification), the set of site-specific constants will be insignificantly different from γ_j^*. This procedure will provide consistent estimates of β^*. However, there is a loss of efficiency relative to incorporating the weights directly into the likelihood function.

Case 3: Population weights are unknown, and X contains site-specific constants.

In the case where the population weights are unknown, the problem of choice-based sampling is difficult to solve. Consistent estimates of $\boldsymbol{\beta}^*$ can be obtained, but estimates of α_j cannot be identified. This is straightforward because estimates provided by a conditional logit with a full set of site-specific alternatives will yield estimates of $\boldsymbol{\beta}^*$ and α_j^* (as in case 1 above). The problem, however, is that γ_j^* is unknown and its estimate is embedded in the estimate of α_j^* along with the estimates of α_j. Separate identification of the weight factors and the constants is not possible. Ignoring the weights and estimating a model with site-specific alternatives results in consistent estimates of $\boldsymbol{\beta}^*$ (see Cosslett 1981). The problem is the inability to identify α_j. Failure to identify estimates of α_j means we cannot calculate estimates of the population probability estimate $\Pr(j|\mathbf{X}_{ij}) = \frac{e^{\mathbf{X}_{ij}\beta}}{\sum_h e^{\mathbf{X}_{ih}\beta}}$. This probability is fundamental to welfare calculations from the RUM (as seen below).

Case 4: Population weights are unknown, and X does not contain site-specific constants.

A possible (but not happy) solution to the problem in case 3 is to assume that the true population model does not have site-specific constants, and to estimate a model that does have a set of constants. In this case, it is necessary to assume that the estimates of the site-specific constants are direct estimates of the weight factors γ_j^*. Under this assumption, the estimates of $\boldsymbol{\beta}^*$ will be consistent, but less efficient than the case where the weights are known (case 2) as information from the sample is used to estimate the weight factor. This method requires one to maintain the assumption that site-specific constants are not needed in the population models and as a result estimates of the site-specific constants simply represent the choice-based sampling weights.

Cases 3 and 4 highlight the conundrum of choice-based sampling in RUM's. If choice-based sampling is ignored and no site-specific constants are included in the model, estimates of $\boldsymbol{\beta}$ will be inconsistent and inferences based on those parameter estimates (including welfare measures) will be invalid. If a set of site-specific alternatives is included, the estimates of the constants must be taken on faith to be direct estimates of the weight factors γ_j^*. Otherwise, it is not possible to calculate the population probabilities $\Pr(j|\mathbf{X}_j) = \exp(\mathbf{X}_j\boldsymbol{\beta})/\sum_h e^{\mathbf{X}_h\boldsymbol{\beta}}$, and welfare measures are once again invalid.

The obvious conclusion to this discussion is that case 1 represents the most satisfactory model for addressing choice-based sampling. This means that information is needed on the population proportions of visitors to correct the non-random choice-based sample. Ideally, these proportions would be known quantities and not estimates, but this is unrealistic. Using estimated population proportions results in a decrease in efficiency relative to known proportions, but this is an unavoidable consequence. The alternative is to ignore choice-based sampling and have inconsistent parameter estimates and invalid welfare estimates.

8.8 Welfare Calculations

Just as in the other models we have reviewed, welfare measurement in random utility models is a two step process: estimation of parameters and calculation of welfare effects. The standard welfare measure used in random utility modeling are often attributed to Small and Rosen and Hanemann (1982, 1999b). We use the indirect utility function in equation (8.9) as a basis of welfare calculation. Writing it as a function of the arguments of the utility function gives: $V(\mathbf{c},\mathbf{q},\mathbf{s},y) =$

$$\ln\left(\sum_{m=1}^{K} a_m\left[\sum_{l=1}^{J_m}\exp(\frac{v_{lm}}{\theta_m})\right]^{\theta_m}\right)$$

$$= \ln\left(\sum_{m=1}^{K} a_m\left[\sum_{l=1}^{J_m}\exp(\frac{v(y-c_{lm},\mathbf{q}_{lm},\mathbf{s}_m)}{\theta_m})\right]^{\theta_m}\right). \quad (8.35)$$

Here we have assigned arguments to the site utility function: $v_{lm} = v(y-c_{lm},\mathbf{q}_{lm},\mathbf{s}_m)$ but we have not assigned a functional form to the utility function. We define WTP implicitly with the indirect utility function, as explained in chapter 1. WTP will be computed as the willingness to pay to achieve conditions $(\mathbf{c}^*,\mathbf{q}^*,\mathbf{s}^*)$ when the current conditions are $(\mathbf{c},\mathbf{q},\mathbf{s})$. This change can incorporate changes in travel costs, removal of sites or changes in the quality of sites or characteristics of nests. (The elimination of a site can be simulated by letting the cost go to infinity.) WTP is defined implicitly as

$$V(\mathbf{c},\mathbf{q},\mathbf{s},y) = V(\mathbf{c}^*,\mathbf{q}^*,\mathbf{s}^*,y-WTP). \quad (8.36)$$

When $V(\mathbf{c}^*, \mathbf{q}^*, \mathbf{s}^*, y) > V(\mathbf{c}, \mathbf{q}, \mathbf{s}, y), WTP > 0$ and has the standard interpretation. When $V(\mathbf{c}^*, \mathbf{q}^*, \mathbf{s}^*, y) < V(\mathbf{c}, \mathbf{q}, \mathbf{s}, y)$, $WTP < 0$, and one may think of this as the amount of income that compensates the individual for the reduction in the attribute vectors. It is perhaps easiest to think of WTP as a benefit measure–positive for improvements in the circumstances and negative for deteriorations. For example, when sites are removed, WTP will be negative, and when the quality of sites improves, WTP will be positive.

It is clear from the expression for the indirect utility in equation (8.35) that the welfare measure depends on the functional form of the utility functions. Suppose the utility function is additive and linear in income:

$$v_{jk} = \beta_y y + \tilde{v}_{jk}$$

where $\tilde{v}_{jk}$ is the non-income component of utility. The arguments of $\tilde{v}_{jk}$ are $\mathbf{q}_{jk}, \mathbf{s}_k$, and c_k. Then willingness to pay can be written as an explicit function of the difference between expected maximum utilities before and after the change. That is, suppose that the deterministic utilities for the alternatives change to $\tilde{v}^*_{jk}$. Then the willingness to pay[2]

---

[2] A brief recapitulation: $\ln\left(\sum_{m=1}^{K} a_m \left[\sum_{l=1}^{J_m} e^{\frac{\tilde{v}_{lm}+\beta_y y}{\theta_m}}\right]^{\theta_m}\right) =$

$$\begin{aligned}
&= \ln\left(\sum_{m=1}^{K} a_m \left[\sum_{l=1}^{J_m} e^{\frac{\tilde{v}^*_{lm}+\beta_y(y-WTP)}{\theta_m}}\right]^{\theta_m}\right) \\
&= \ln\left(\sum_{m=1}^{K} a_m \left[e^{\beta_y(y-WTP)/\theta_m}\sum_{l=1}^{J_m} e^{\frac{\tilde{v}^*_{lm}}{\theta_m}}\right]^{\theta_m}\right) \\
&= \ln\left(\sum_{m=1}^{K} a_m e^{\frac{\beta_y(y-WTP)}{\theta_m}\theta_m} \left[\sum_{l=1}^{J_m} e^{\frac{\tilde{v}^*_{lm}}{\theta_m}}\right]^{\theta_m}\right) \\
&= \ln\left(e^{\beta_y(y-WTP)}\right) \\
&\quad + \ln\left(\sum_{m=1}^{K} a_m \left[\sum_{l=1}^{J_m} e^{\frac{\tilde{v}^*_{lm}}{\theta}}\right]^{\theta_m}\right)
\end{aligned}$$

Of course $\ln\left(e^{\beta_y(y-WTP)}\right) = \beta_y(y - WTP)$; substitute this, and then extract $\beta_y y$ from the left hand side in the same way. Clearing the terms leaves the expression in the text.

will be

$$WTP = [\ln\left(\sum_{m=1}^{K} a_m \left[\sum_{l=1}^{J_m} \exp(\frac{\tilde{v}_{lm}^*}{\theta_m})\right]^{\theta_m}\right)$$
$$- \ln\left(\sum_{m=1}^{K} a_m \left[\sum_{l=1}^{J_m} \exp(\frac{\tilde{v}_{lm}}{\theta_m})\right]^{\theta_m}\right)] \cdot \beta_y^{-1}. \quad (8.37)$$

This is the indirect utility in the original state less the indirect utility after the change, normalized by the marginal utility of income. The term $\tilde{v}_{jk}$ will depend on the site-specific characteristics such as costs and time and quality characteristics, as well as the nest characteristics. We have omitted the individual's index, but some of the arguments of $\tilde{v}_{jk}$ vary across individuals. For example, in a model of fishing choice, costs of travel might vary depending on whether the angler is trailering a boat. In practice, researchers calculate welfare measures for two kinds of changes: in the attributes of the sites or nests, and in the availability of sites. The latter measure constitutes the value of access to sites.

8.8.1 Welfare Measures for Quality Changes

The characteristics of sites can change in a variety of ways. Beaches can be wider, catch rates at fishing sites can be higher, water pollution can increase. These changes can occur at a single site or at all sites. One of the advantages of the RUM is its ability to describe in a realistic way the kinds of changes that households might experience. To write out the calculations of welfare changes, it is necessary to write out explicit forms of the utility functions. These forms are usually linear in parameters, and quite frequently linear in variables. We start with the linear utility function given in equation (8.13)

$$v(y - c_{jk}, \mathbf{q}_{jk}, \mathbf{s}_k) = \beta_y(y - c_{jk}) + \mathbf{q}_{jk}\boldsymbol{\beta} + \mathbf{s}_k\boldsymbol{\gamma}.$$

Now suppose that $\mathbf{q}, \mathbf{s}$ change to $\mathbf{q}^*, \mathbf{s}^*$. Using the basic welfare measure for the constant marginal utility of income gives the following expression for WTP

$$WTP = \left[\begin{array}{c} \ln\left(\sum_{m=1}^{K} a_m \left[\sum_{l=1}^{J_m} \exp(\frac{-\beta_y c_{lm} + \mathbf{q}_{lm}^*\beta + \mathbf{s}_m^*\gamma}{\theta_m})\right]^{\theta_m}\right) \\ - \ln\left(\sum_{m=1}^{K} a_m \left[\sum_{l=1}^{J_m} \exp(\frac{-\beta_y c_{lm} + \mathbf{q}_{lm}\beta + \mathbf{s}_m\gamma}{\theta_m})\right]^{\theta_m}\right) \end{array}\right] \beta_y^{-1}. \quad (8.38)$$

With a linear utility function, this is the basic expression for calculating the welfare effects of quality changes at different sites. Essentially one computes the indirect utility with and without the change, and then normalizes by the marginal utility of income. This measure of willingness to pay is intuitively appealing because it reflects all of the changes that occur, not just at the sites that the individual actually visits. In fact, what the individual is observed to do influences only the parameter estimates, not the welfare calculations.

Incremental Quality Changes

Suppose that the change in quality takes the following simple form:

$$\mathbf{q}_{jk}^{*} = \mathbf{q}_{jk} + \Delta\mathbf{q}$$

where $\Delta\mathbf{q}$ is a vector of incremental changes in site attributes that are the same across sites. For example, suppose we want to value the addition of 10 parking places at all beaches, or we want to calculate the value of an additional mile of recreation trails at all state parks. To simplify matters a bit, we use the following notation: $\mathbf{X}_{jk} = \{c_{jk}, \mathbf{q}_{jk}, \mathbf{s}_k\}$ and $\boldsymbol{\beta}^{*} = \{-\beta_y, \boldsymbol{\beta}, \gamma\}$. The new set of site characteristics will be $\{c_{jk}, \mathbf{q}_{jk} + \Delta\mathbf{q}, \mathbf{s}_k\}$. Substituting into the expression for WTP for quality change in equation (8.38) yields

$$WTP = \beta_y^{-1} \left[\begin{array}{c} \ln\left(\sum_{m=1}^{K} a_m \left[\sum_{l=1}^{J_m} \exp\left(\frac{\mathbf{X}_{lm}\beta^{*} + \Delta\mathbf{q}\beta}{\theta_m}\right) \right]^{\theta_m} \right) \\ -\ln\left(\sum_{m=1}^{K} a_m \left[\sum_{l=1}^{J_m} \exp\left(\frac{\mathbf{X}_{lm}\beta^{*}}{\theta_m}\right) \right]^{\theta_m} \right) \end{array} \right] \tag{8.39}$$

where $\boldsymbol{\beta}$ is the vector of parameters associated with the changed quality attributes. Because the term does not change by nest or site, it can be factored, just as income or WTP has been factored earlier. Upon simplification, the value of the quality change becomes:

$$\begin{aligned} WTP &= \Delta\mathbf{q}\boldsymbol{\beta}/\beta_y + \ln\left(\frac{\sum_{m=1}^{K} a_m \left[\sum_{l=1}^{J_m} \exp\left(\frac{\mathbf{X}_{lm}\beta^{*}}{\theta_m}\right) \right]^{\theta_m}}{\sum_{m=1}^{K} a_m \left[\sum_{l=1}^{J_m} \exp\left(\frac{\mathbf{X}_{lm}\beta^{*}}{\theta_m}\right) \right]^{\theta_m}} \right) \\ &= \frac{\Delta\mathbf{q}\boldsymbol{\beta}}{\beta_y}. \end{aligned} \tag{8.40}$$

The log sums are equal, so the logarithm of the ratio is zero. In this special case, the value of a quality change across all sites can be found by taking the sum of the quality changes multiplied by the associated parameters and dividing by the marginal utility of income. It should be emphasized that this only holds for the special case in which there is a $\Delta\mathbf{q}$ change in a site attribute across all sites. This derivation, however, gives a simple interpretation to the parameters of the linear random utility model. The parameter estimates normalized by the marginal utility of income measure the value of a one unit change in the corresponding covariate across all sites. For a utility enhancing quality change, $\Delta\mathbf{q}\boldsymbol{\beta} \geq 0$ and $WTP \geq 0$ represents the willingness to pay for the quality improvement. Similarly, for a utility degrading quality change, $\Delta\mathbf{q}\boldsymbol{\beta} \leq 0$ and $WTP \leq 0$ represents the increment in income that will compensate the individual for foregoing the change.

The Conditional Logit RUM

To this point, the derivations have assumed a general form for the error distribution: the generalized extreme value error. As shown previously, if $\theta_m = 1$ and $a_m = a$ for all m, then the nested logit random utility model collapses to the conditional logit random utility model. Suppose that the site utility function is linear in income and attributes, as in equation (8.13). In this case, the value of a change in site attributes from $\mathbf{q}$, $\mathbf{s}$ to $\mathbf{q}^*, \mathbf{s}^*$ is found from equation (8.37):

$$WTP = \beta_y^{-1} \cdot \left[\begin{array}{c} \ln\left(\sum\limits_{m=1}^{K} a_m \left[\sum\limits_{l=1}^{J_m} \exp(\frac{\tilde{v}_{lm}^*}{\theta_m}) \right]^{\theta_m} \right) \\ - \ln\left(\sum\limits_{m=1}^{K} a_m \left[\sum\limits_{l=1}^{J_m} \exp(\frac{\tilde{v}_{lm}}{\theta_m}) \right]^{\theta_m} \right) \end{array} \right]. \tag{8.41}$$

Substituting $\theta_m = 1$ and $a_m = a$ for all m and $v(y - c_{jk}, \mathbf{q}_{jk}, \mathbf{s}_k) = \beta_y(y - c_{jk}) + \mathbf{q}_{jk}\boldsymbol{\beta} + \mathbf{s}_k\gamma$, the value of these changes becomes

$$WTP = \beta_y^{-1} \cdot \left[\begin{array}{c} \ln\left(\sum\limits_{k=1}^{K} \sum\limits_{j=1}^{J_m} \exp(-\beta_y c_{jk} + \mathbf{q}_{jk}^*\boldsymbol{\beta} + \mathbf{s}_k^*\gamma) \right) \\ - \ln\left(\sum\limits_{k=1}^{K} \sum\limits_{j=1}^{J_m} \exp(-\beta_y c_{jk} + \mathbf{q}_{jk}\boldsymbol{\beta} + \mathbf{s}_k\gamma) \right) \end{array} \right].$$

This can be rewritten as a single summation by creating a new index $n, n = 1, ..., J$, each n for a j, k combination:

$$WTP = \beta_y^{-1} \cdot \left[\begin{array}{c} \ln\left(\sum\limits_{n=1}^{J} \exp(-\beta_y c_n + \mathbf{q}_n^*\boldsymbol{\beta} + \mathbf{s}_n^*\gamma) \right) \\ - \ln\left(\sum\limits_{n=1}^{J} \exp(-\beta_y c_n + \mathbf{q}_n\boldsymbol{\beta} + \mathbf{s}_n\gamma) \right) \end{array} \right]. \tag{8.42}$$

Example 29 *The Value of Lengthening Beaches*

For a simple demonstration of estimating the welfare of changing a characteristic of all sites by some increment, consider the beach model of Parsons, Massey and Tomasi estimated in Tables 8.4 and 8.3. The only continuous variables included in the example are the travel cost of a trip, and the length of the beach in miles. Suppose we wanted to know the value of an additional mile of beach at all beaches. That is, what is the willingness to pay by each individual per trip to have the option of an additional mile of beach at each beach. From equation (8.40), the WTP for an additional mile at each beach is simply the ratio of the parameter estimate on the length of the beach divided by the marginal utility of income. For the nested logit model, this value is: $WTP = \Delta q\beta_1/\beta_y = 0.251/0.083 = \$3.02$ per trip. For the conditional logit model, this estimate is $WTP = 0.064/0.055 = \$1.16$.

The Non-Linear in Income Case

The balanced budget random utility model is a model of a choice occasion. It is hard to be definitive about the nature of the budget for a choice occasion. Hence linearity in income is an attractive feature because income then disappears from probability statements and welfare calculations. The elimination of income is also advantageous because income is most likely measured with a good deal of error. It is frequently interpolated from ranges and may mix before and after tax income. Nevertheless, some formulations of the site utility function include income in a non-linear way.

Suppose the site utility function is given by $v(y - c_{jk}, \mathbf{q}_{jk}, \mathbf{s}_k)$, and the random part of preferences is distributed GEV, so that we have a nested model. Then WTP is implicitly defined by

$$\sum_{m=1}^{K} a_m \left[\sum_{l=1}^{J_m} \exp(\frac{v(y - c_{lm}, \mathbf{q}_{lm}, \mathbf{s}_m)}{\theta_m})\right]^{\theta_m}$$
$$= \sum_{m=1}^{K} a_m \left[\sum_{l=1}^{J_m} \exp(\frac{v(y - c_{lm} - WTP, \mathbf{q}^*_{lm}, \mathbf{s}^*_m)}{\theta_m})\right]^{\theta_m}. \quad (8.43)$$

For a non-linear-in-income indirect utility function, there will typically be no closed form solution for WTP. When this is the case, the researcher must resort to approximations to the WTP or numerical methods for finding a solution to equation (8.43). The approximation creates linearity with a first order Taylor's series. It can also be solved by simulation, for which there is an evolving literature. (For example, see Herriges and Kling.)

Despite the increasing ability to compute non-linear income effects, it is unclear whether this is a worthwhile enterprise. The non-linear income effect has a variety of problems. It is not obvious what budget is being balanced on a single choice occasion, nor what income ought to be included in a RUM model. Income effects in a random utility model are as apt to measure the differential impacts of socioeconomic status as the effect of budget constraints. The heart of the conceptual issue is whether the marginal utility of income is constant. It is not unreasonable to argue that the marginal utility of income varies by income levels and hence across respondents. It is more implausible to maintain that the marginal utility of income changes because of different costs at different sites.

One means of modeling different income effects is simply to use a system of dummy variables for different levels of income. For example, let the income term be

$$\beta_{y1}\delta_1(y - c_{jk}) + \beta_{y2}\delta_2(y - c_{jk})$$

where $\delta_1 = 1$ when $y \leq y^*, 0$ otherwise, and $\delta_2 = 1 - \delta_1$. For a given individual, the income drops out of the probability statement. The income term becomes

$$-\beta_{y1}\delta_1 c_{jk} - \beta_{y2}\delta_2 c_{jk}.$$

This allows the marginal utility to vary by household but leaves it constant for a household with respect to the typical changes that occur in a RUM model so that the welfare calculations for linear-in-income utility functions work.

8.8.2 The Loss of Sites

Nested Logit

The RUM is frequently used to value the loss of access to a subset of sites. For example, suppose an oil spill results in the closure of a subset of beaches along the east coast of the United States. The RUM can be used to measure the welfare effects of this closure. The researcher knows only part of the individual's preferences, and must use the expected indirect utility function to measure the welfare effects of the loss of a site. The value of lost access is based on the change in expected maximum utility after the site is eliminated. Assume a constant marginal utility of income indirect utility function of the form: $v_{jk} = \tilde{v}_{jk} + \beta_y y$. Then we can utilize the basic WTP statement in equation (8.37). The loss of access is modeled by simply dropping the sites that are eliminated when computing the $\tilde{v}^*_{jk}$. Without loss of generality, suppose the site that is closed is site 1, 1 (that is, the first site in the first nest). Then utilizing equation (8.37) gives

$$\begin{aligned} WTP_{11} &= \beta_y^{-1} \cdot [\ln(a_1 \left[\sum_{l=2}^{J_1} \exp(\frac{\tilde{v}_{l1}}{\theta_1})\right]^{\theta_1} + \sum_{m=2}^{K} a_m \left[\sum_{l=1}^{J_m} \exp(\frac{\tilde{v}_{lm}}{\theta_m})\right]^{\theta_m}) \\ & \quad - \ln(\sum_{m=1}^{K} a_m \left[\sum_{l=1}^{J_m} \exp(\frac{\tilde{v}_{lm}}{\theta_m})\right]^{\theta_m})]. \end{aligned} \quad (8.44)$$

This WTP will be negative because the site is lost. This is the basic expression one would program for the welfare calculation. The extension to more sites or other sites involves omitting them from the sums in the first term on the right. The computations do not strain computer capacity but, since many sites are involved, the results of the computation are not always obvious. Bearing in mind that the correct way to calculate welfare measures entails the use of equation (8.44), we can rewrite it as an expression that is more grounded in observation:

$$WTP_{11} = \ln\left(\frac{a_1 C^{\theta_1} + D}{a_1 \left[C + e^{\frac{\tilde{v}_{11}}{\theta_1}}\right]^{\theta_1} + D}\right) \cdot \beta_y^{-1}$$

$$C = \sum_{l=2}^{J_1} \exp(\frac{\tilde{v}_{l1}}{\theta_1})$$

and

$$D = \sum_{m=2}^{K} a_m \left[\sum_{l=1}^{J_m} \exp(\frac{v_{lm}}{\theta_m})\right]^{\theta_m}.$$

From the equations for the conditional probability of selecting a site, given the nest (equation 8.16) and the marginal probability of choosing a nest (equation 8.17) we can see that $D/(a_1 \left[C + e^{\frac{\tilde{v}_{11}}{\theta_1}}\right]^{\theta_1} + D) = 1 - \Pr(1)$. The remaining terms can be rewritten so that

$$\begin{aligned} & a_1 C^{\theta_1}/(a_1 \left[C + e^{\frac{\tilde{v}_{11}}{\theta_1}}\right]^{\theta_1} + D) \\ = \; & (1 - \Pr(1|1))^{\theta_1} \Pr(1). \end{aligned}$$

Hence the expression for willingness to pay can be written

$$WTP_{11} = \ln[(1 - \Pr(1|1))^{\theta_1} \Pr(1) + (1 - \Pr(1))] \cdot \beta_y^{-1}. \qquad (8.45)$$

The argument of the logarithm is less than one, so that the WTP is less than zero, because a site is being removed. In the context of the nested logit, the term $\Pr(1)$ is the probability of choosing the first nest. The expression makes intuitive sense. As the probability of choosing the first site, $\Pr(1|1)$, goes to zero, WTP goes to zero. When $\Pr(1|1)$ goes to one WTP goes to $\ln(1 - \Pr(1))$. As the probability of choosing the first nest goes to one, WTP becomes $\theta_1 \ln(1 - \Pr(1))$.

This formula can be used to assess the sample mean WTP. A consistent estimate of WTP_{11} is found by substituting consistent estimates of $\Pr(1)$, $\Pr(1|1)$, θ_1, and β_y in equation (8.45). Consistent estimates of $\Pr(1)$, and $\Pr(1|1)$ can be found by observing the sample proportion of individuals choosing nest 1, and choosing site 1 conditional on choosing nest 1. Consistent estimates of the parameters θ_1 and β_y are found from maximum likelihood estimation of the nested logit model. The formula can also be used to calculate an individual's willingness to pay, by computing the probabilities with the individual's covariates. Calculating the probabilities helps assess the welfare measures intuitively but provides no computational advantage.

Example 30 *Value of Loss of Access: Nested Logit*

Continuing the beach example from Parsons, Massey and Tomasi, we find the two beaches with the largest proportion of visits were Cape Henlopen State Park (denoted CH) ($\Pr(CH) = 0.262$) and Rehobeth Beach (denoted R) ($\Pr(R) = 0.127$). Both beaches are located in the South nest, and the conditional proportion of trips taken (conditional on each trip being to a South beach) is 0.281 for Cape Henlopen ($\Pr(CH|S)$) and 0.136 for Rehobeth ($\Pr(R|S)$). Of the trips taken, 0.933 ($\Pr(S)$) are to South beaches. From equation (8.45), the willingness to pay for loss of access to Cape Henlopen and Rehobeth independently from the nested logit model estimated in Table 8.4 are

$$\begin{aligned} WTP_{CH} &= \ln[(1 - \Pr(CH|S))^{\theta_1} \Pr(S) + (1 - \Pr(S))] \cdot \beta_y^{-1} \\ &= \ln\left[(1 - 0.281)^{0.50} (0.933) + (1 - 0.933)\right] / 0.083 \\ &= -\$1.84 \end{aligned}$$

and

$$
\begin{aligned}
WTP_R &= \ln[(1-\Pr(R|S))^{\theta_1}\Pr(S)+(1-\Pr(S))]\cdot\beta_y^{-1} \\
&= \ln\left[(1-0.136)^{0.50}(0.933)+(1-0.933)\right]/0.083 \\
&= -\$0.82.
\end{aligned}
$$

These calculations are the same as one would make using expression (8.37) but they can be checked more intuitively with the probabilities. Note that we have used the probabilities calculated at the mean vector of covariates. We address variation across individuals and randomness below.

Conditional Logit

If we assume the conditional logit ($\theta_m = 1$ and $a_m = a$ for all m), the willingness to pay for access to site 1 comes from the general expression

$$WTP_1 = \beta_y^{-1}\cdot\ln(\sum_{j=2}^{J} e^{\tilde{v}_j}/\sum_{j=1}^{J} e^{\tilde{v}_j}) \tag{8.46}$$

where we have substituted a single index in the absence of nests. The probability of selecting site h is $e^{\tilde{v}_h}/\sum_{j=1}^{J} e^{\tilde{v}_j}$. Using this result we simplify the WTP to avoid the loss of site 1:

$$WTP_{11} = \ln(1-\Pr(1))/\beta_y. \tag{8.47}$$

This expression makes intuitive sense, just as the nested logit analogue. If the probability goes to zero, the willingness to pay goes to zero. These measures of the economic losses from the elimination of a site as a function of probabilities are useful in assessing in a quick way what the logit and nested logit models tell us about welfare calculations.

For very small $\Pr(1,1)$, $\ln(1-\Pr(1,1)) \approx -\Pr(1,1)$, implying

$$WTP_{11} \approx -\Pr(1,1)/\beta_y. \tag{8.48}$$

Taking the average across all N individuals in the sample, the sample average WTP to prevent loss of access becomes:

$$\overline{WTP}_{11} \approx -\frac{\sum \Pr(1,1)}{N\beta_y} = -\frac{\overline{\Pr(1,1)}}{\beta_y} \tag{8.49}$$

where $\overline{\Pr(1,1)}$ is the sample mean probability of visiting site 1. In the sampling is exogenous, a consistent estimate of this probability is found by observing the sample portion of individuals visiting site 1. Therefore, a quick approximation to the value of lost access to a site in the conditional logit framework is the sample proportion of visitors to that site divided by the negative of the marginal utility of income. The accuracy of this approximation will diminish quickly as the probability of visitation to the eliminated site increases. For example if $\Pr(h) = 0.01$, $\ln(1 - \Pr(h)) = -0.01005$, less than a 1% difference. But if $\Pr(h) = 0.1$, $\ln(1 - \Pr(h)) = -0.105$, a 5% error. The expressions for WTP based on probabilities are sometimes convenient for quick calculations of WTP, but don't substitute for the correct calculations of individual WTP.

Example 31 *Value of Loss of Access: Conditional Logit*

In the beach example, the unconditional proportions of individuals choosing the two most popular beaches: Cape Henlopen (CH) and Rehobeth (R) beaches are 0.262 and 0.127. Substituting these probabilities and the conditional logit estimate of the marginal utility of income from Table 8.3 into equation (8.47) gives the value of loss of access to these two beaches per trip as

$$\begin{aligned} WTP_{CH} &= \ln(1 - \Pr(CH))/\beta_y \\ &= \ln(1 - 0.262)/0.0545 \\ &= -\$5.57 \end{aligned}$$

and

$$\begin{aligned} WTP_{R} &= \ln(1 - \Pr(R))/\beta_y \\ &= \ln(1 - 0.127)/0.0545 \\ &= -\$2.49. \end{aligned}$$

Using the approximation in equation (8.49), we find the values of lost access to these two beaches are \$4.81 and \$2.33 per trip. The approximation for Cape Henlopen is off by almost 14% while the approximation for Rehobeth is off by 6%. These are the most visited beaches in the sample. For a beach with very small proportion of visitors (for example, a number of beaches have only one trip out of 9330 for the sample) the approximation is much better.

Loss of Access to Multiple Sites

The same measure can be used to value the loss of any subset of sites. However, because logit models and their nested versions require that one alternative be chosen, the WTP to prevent lost access to all alternatives simultaneously is not well defined. This can be seen from equation (8.46) by noting that if all sites are eliminated, the numerator goes to zero, leading to an undefined operation. This is sensible, because the models we have analyzed relate to site choice, and the decision not to visit any site is not part of the analysis.

Welfare measures in the random utility model depend on substitution among sites. The value of the loss of two sites independently is less than the value of those same two sites simultaneously. Consider the case of eliminating two sites (sites 1 and 2) to a single individual. Take the simple case of a decision structure with no nests, and sites indexed $j = 1, ..., J$. Equation (8.47) defines the value of lost access to site 1 as

$$WTP_j = -\ln(1 - \Pr(j))/\beta_y$$

where $\Pr(j)$ is the probability the individual will visit site j. This would be calculated using equation (8.46). The elimination of site one assumes that sites 2 through J are viable substitutes for site 1, so a portion of the probability of visiting site 1 will be shifted to the viable substitutes. The value of lost access in equation (8.47) generalizes to the case of eliminating a subset of sites J_S as

$$WTP_{J_S} = -\ln\left(1 - \sum_{h \in J_S} \Pr(h)\right)/\beta_y$$

where the sum is across the set of sites to which access is eliminated. For the elimination of sites 1 and 2, this measure becomes:

$$WTP_{12} = -\ln(1 - \Pr(1) - \Pr(2))/\beta_y. \qquad (8.50)$$

As more sites are eliminated, the substitutes for the remaining sites are reduced. The WTP to avoid loss of access goes up as the number of substitutes declines. To see that the sum of the values of independent losses of sites 1 and 2 is less than the value of the losses of sites 1 and 2 simultaneously, sum WTP_1 and WTP_2:

$$WTP_1 + WTP_2 = -\ln[(1 - \Pr(1)) \cdot (1 - \Pr(2))]/\beta_y.$$

$WTP_1 + WTP_2$ will be less than WTP_{12} in absolute value because $(1 - \Pr(1))(1 - \Pr(2)) > 1 - \Pr(1) - \Pr(2)$ which holds for all $\Pr(j) > 0$.

Example 32 *Value of Loss of Access to Multiple Sites*

In the beach example from the previous section, we calculate the conditional logit estimate of the sample mean value of lost access to Cape

Henlopen (CH) as \$5.58 per trip, and the sample mean value of lost access to Rehobeth as \$2.48 per trip. The sum of these, \$8.06, is an underestimate of the simultaneous loss of both sites. The correct estimate of the value of lost access per trip to both sites is:

$$\begin{aligned} WTP_{CH,R} &= -\ln\left(1 - \Pr(CH) - \Pr(R)\right)/\beta_y \\ &= -\ln(1 - 0.262 - 0.127)/0.0545 \\ &= \$9.03. \end{aligned} \tag{8.51}$$

Ignoring the loss of substitutability between the two sites underestimates the value of lost access by 11% (\$0.97) per trip. When the number of eliminated sites grows, the discrepancy grows.

8.8.3 Summary: Welfare Measures

We repeat the results for measuring welfare with the nested and conditional logit models in the following table. We assume that the utility function is given by

$$v_{jk} = \beta_y y + \tilde{v}_{jk}$$

for the nested logit version and by

$$v_n = \beta_y y + \tilde{v}_n$$

for the conditional logit, so that we have a general form for the utility function except that utility is linear in income. These welfare measures are written down for convenience. Our discussion has focused on the loss of sites, because that is the most frequent use of RUM models. But nothing about the discussion or Table 8.5 prevents the calculation of welfare measures for adding sites. One needs to observe the attribute vector for the new sites, and then let the new site indexes reflect the addition of sites. Valuing a new service is an advantage that a random utility model does not share with other approaches such as the generalized corner solution model or the generalized count model. It is a consequence of the specifying utility as a function of attributes, rather than idiosyncratic commodity demands.

8.8.4 Statistical Properties of WTP

The random utility model requires more effort in the estimation and calculation stages than the single site modes or most contingent valuation models. As a consequence, there is relatively less exploration of the properties of estimates of WTP. Part of the uncertainty in WTP

TABLE 8.5. WTP for Logit Models

	Conditional Logit	Nested Logit
Loss of Sites	$\frac{1}{\beta_y}\ln(\frac{\sum_{n\in J^*}\exp(\tilde{v}_n)}{\sum_{n=1}^{J}\exp(\tilde{v}_n)})$	$\frac{1}{\beta_y}\ln\frac{\sum_{m\in K^*} a_m\left[\sum_{l\in J_m^*}\exp(\frac{\tilde{v}_{lm}}{\theta_m})\right]^{\theta_m}}{\sum_{m=1}^{K} a_m\left[\sum_{l=1}^{J_m}\exp(\frac{\tilde{v}_{lm}}{\theta_m})\right]^{\theta_m}}$
Change in Site Attrib.	$\frac{1}{\beta_y}\ln(\frac{\sum_{n=1}^{J}\exp(\tilde{v}_n^*)}{\sum_{n=1}^{J}\exp(\tilde{v}_n)})$	$\frac{1}{\beta_y}\ln\frac{\sum_{m=1}^{K} a_m\left[\sum_{l=1}^{J_m}\exp(\frac{\tilde{v}_{lm}^*}{\theta_m})\right]^{\theta_m}}{\sum_{m=1}^{K} a_m\left[\sum_{l=1}^{J_m}\exp(\frac{\tilde{v}_{lm}}{\theta_m})\right]^{\theta_m}}$

Notes: The deterministic utility is $\beta_y y + \tilde{v}_{jk}$. In the loss of sites case, for the conditional logit, there are J alternatives in the base case and J*in the new scenario. For the nested logit, there are K nests and J_k sites per nest in the base case, and K* nests and J_k^* sites per nest in the new scenario. In the change of attribute case, $\tilde{v}_{jk}^*$ is the new site utility.

estimates is already expected out in order to get the indirect utility function. Equation (8.9) in effect eliminates the randomness in preferences that confounds estimates of WTP in CV models and other recreational demand models. With the randomness in preferences having been expected out, one is left only with uncertainty in parameters. A quick look at Table 8.5 illustrates the substantial nonlinearity of WTP as a function of random parameters. This uncertainty is not necessarily small. Random utility models often have large numbers of parameters. The only effective way to grasp the randomness of individual WTP estimates is to execute the Krinsky-Robb procedure, inducing the distribution of the WTP estimate by taking draws from the normal distribution given by the parameter estimates.

One must also be cognizant of the difference between the WTP estimate for an individual, calculated from Table 8.5 with an individual's covariates, and the sample mean, which would be the mean of individual estimates of WTP. Since WTP is a non-linear function of covariates, the sample mean of WTP will not equal the WTP calculated at the mean of the covariates.

8.9 Linking the Site Choice with the Quantity of Trips

The random utility model is feasible and flexible, but is not fully consistent with a utility-theoretic choice of the number of days within a period of time, such as a year or a recreational season. We have discussed before some of the various ways one can model the number of days consistently. The conceptually most attractive approach is the generalized corner solution of Phaneuf, Herriges and Kling. The corner solution approach incorporates the choice of whether to visit a site with the number of times to visit the site in a way that is consistent with demand theory. This model presents an especial challenge when there are large numbers of alternatives. A second alternative is the repeated logit model, in which the recreationist is assumed to have a fixed number of choice occasions, and for each occasion chooses whether to recreate and then, conditional on choosing to recreate, picks the site. The repeated logit requires the assumption that the choices are independent across choice occasions. See Morey, Rowe and Watson for more on the repeated logit model. A practical and popular approach to incorporating the number of days involves first estimating the site choice model and then connecting it with a quantity-determining equation. Since the original paper by Bockstael, Hanemann and Kling, researchers have used this approach, which has come to be known as a linked model. It allows the researcher to measure both the site effects and the quantity effects of changes in the site attributes. Herriges, Kling and Phaneuf deal extensively with the linked model.

To understand the need for a connection between site attributes and the number of days recreationists spend on an activity, imagine an extreme circumstance. Suppose that one is modeling the site choice of recreational fishing over a period of time, say a year. And suppose for biological reasons, the catch rate for a major species is dramatically reduced. When the catch rate is an important attribute, this could have a substantial effect on the deterministic utility at each site, reducing the expected maximum utility. It would be quite reasonable to expect the total number of days the angler spends fishing to change as well. Indeed, for large changes that are equal at all sites, there may be no site reallocation but there may well be large changes in the number of trips. Recall that for a conditional logit, the addition of a constant to each alternative's utility does not alter the choice probabilities. The linked model is a way to handle this issue.

In the linked model, one calculates the indirect utility according to equation (8.9). This depends on the costs and attributes of all the alternatives in the individual's choice set. It can accommodate different choice sets for different individuals if that approach has been used in the estimation of the site choice model. A crude approach to welfare can now be constructed. Note that the indirect utility will change when the attribute vector, prices, or access to sites changes. Conditional on choosing a site, the indirect utility divided by marginal utility of income is the WTP for a trip. The drawback of this measure is that individuals are required to choose a site–that is, they do not have the option in the site choice model of not choosing a site. Denote the change in the value per day as

$$P = [V(\mathbf{c}, \mathbf{q}, \mathbf{s}, y) - V(\mathbf{c}^*, \mathbf{q}^*, \mathbf{s}^*, y)]\beta_y^{-1}$$

where the indirect utility function $V(\mathbf{c}, \mathbf{q}, \mathbf{s}, y)$ is the expected maximum utility, and should be computed according to equation (8.35). (See Morey 1994 for more details on this inequality.) Then the following inequality holds:

$$x^0 P \leq \text{true welfare effect} \leq x^* P.$$

The superscript 0 indicates the initial value of days and the asterisk indicates the subsequent level of days. When $P < 0$, then the true welfare effect is negative, but multiplying by the initial number of days will give damages that are too large in absolute value but negative, and hence too small (too negative). Multiplying by the final value of the days gives a damage estimate that is too small in absolute value, but because $P < 0$, too big. When $P > 0$, trips will increase, and the initial quantity of trips times P will not account for the increased demand.

Of course, knowing the level of trips after the change is not so easy. A practical but utility-inconsistent approach is to predict the change in trips. Consider the demand function for individual i:

$$x_i^0 = f(V^i, \mathbf{z}^i, \eta^i)$$

where V^i is the individual's calculated expected maximum utility, $\mathbf{z}^i$ is a vector of socioeconomic variables and η^i is a random element. One can estimate this equation, recognizing that the quantity demand is censored, so that a Tobit or Poisson is appropriate. Then following the change in the attribute vector, a new value of V^i is calculated. This can be used to predict the new level of trips, x_i^*. Then one can use various combinations of x^0 and x^* to approximate welfare. Using this equation we calculate the welfare measure from the linked model as

$$WTP = \hat{x}^* \cdot [V(\mathbf{c}, \mathbf{q}, \mathbf{s}, y) - V(\mathbf{c}^*, \mathbf{q}^*, \mathbf{s}^*, y)]\beta_y^{-1}$$

where the $\hat{x}^*$ is a prediction of the new level of trips based on a new value for V. Naturally this would be calculated for individual i, and the covariates would reflect the opportunities that the ith individual faces. This would be an overestimate of the true WTP for the change.

There are several difficulties with the linked approach. Hausman, Leonard and McFadden develop a variant of the model, with the claim that it is utility-consistent. However, as Herriges, Kling and Phaneuf report, the utility-consistent claim is quite limited. There is econometric difficulty with the estimation of the function $f(V^i, z^i, \eta^i)$ because the argument V is a function of estimated parameters, and hence the parameter estimates are inconsistent. Murphy and Topel explain this problem and provide an approach for correction.

8.10 Estimation Issues

8.10.1 Nesting Structures

A significant literature has emerged investigating methods for testing the nesting specification in nested logit models. The structure of nests is a strategic modeling decision, based on an understanding of choices that individuals make and a sense of how to structure plausible preferences. This is a case where there may be conflict between the behavioral implications of an assumed decision process and the fit of the model as implied by statistical tests. In many cases, the sequence of choices implies a clear nesting structure that can be imposed. For example, in the choice between geographic regions (North and South) and then the recreation beach conditional on the region, the nesting structure is clear: first the individual chooses between North and South and then the individual chooses which beach to visit. Reversing the decision process is nonsensical. The individual cannot first choose the site and then choose the geographic region as the choice of site implies the choice of region. Other nests are feasible. For example, one might consider counties as upper level nests. It would not be nearly as natural as the North-South nest, however.

This discussion assumes that the source of the appropriate nesting structure comes from individual behavior. But, as Kling and Thomson note, 'while sequential decision making may be an intuitively appealing way to interpret [inclusive value] parameters, such [nesting structures] can be due to any similarities among alternatives that are unobserved to the researcher' (p. 104). This implies that while behavior might be a primary determinant in designing the appropriate nesting structure, lack of information on the part of the researcher must also be considered in designing the nests. Nevertheless the appropriate set of nests is a strategic research choice that should be made with a full understanding of the recreationists' motivation and behavior.

Likelihood Dominance

In any of these cases, there are methods for testing between two nesting structures based on competing but plausible models of behavior. Because there are so many different nests that can be constructed, it makes little sense to test among nests that are not somehow plausible models of behavior. Kling and Thomson advocate the use of a likelihood dominance criterion introduced by Pollak and Wales. When comparing between two nested logit models (called A and B) estimated on the same data, but with different nesting structures, the likelihood dominance criterion chooses the model with the larger log-likelihood function value as long as the difference between the log-likelihood functions satisfies

$$\chi^2_{d_B-d_A+1} - \chi^2_1 > 2(\ln(L_B) - \ln(L_A)) > \chi^2_{d_B+1} - \chi^2_{d_A+1}.$$

Here d_A is the number of estimated parameters in model A, d_B is the number of estimated parameters in model B and χ^2_d is the critical value from a Chi-squared distribution with d degrees of freedom and a given critical level. (For the test to be valid, the models are assigned the A and B labels so that $d_B \geq d_A$.) Note that this test has a similar form and interpretation to the likelihood ratio test. If the difference between the log-likelihood functions $\ln(L_B) - \ln(L_A)$ is large and positive, then the likelihood dominance criterion favors nesting structure B. If the difference is large and negative then the likelihood dominance criterion favors model A. If the difference is small, the test is inconclusive.

Testing IIA

Related to the issue of testing the nesting structure is testing the validity of the independence of irrelevant alternatives assumption. Recall the nested logit model described in equation (8.26)

$$\ln L^i(\boldsymbol{\beta}, \gamma, a_1, ..., a_K, \theta_1, ...\theta_K | \mathbf{q}_{jk}, \mathbf{s}_k)$$

$$= \sum_{k=1}^{K}\sum_{j=1}^{J_K} \delta_{jk} \ln \left[\frac{e^{\frac{-\beta_y c_{jk} + \mathbf{q}_{jk}\boldsymbol{\beta}}{\theta_k}}}{\sum_{l=1}^{J_k} e^{\frac{-\beta_y c_{lk} + \mathbf{q}_{lk}\boldsymbol{\beta}}{\theta_k}}} \times \frac{a_k e^{\mathbf{s}_k\gamma + \theta_k I_k}}{\sum_{m=1}^{K} a_m e^{\mathbf{s}_m\gamma + \theta_m I_m}} \right] \quad (8.52)$$

The IIA assumption holds within a given upper level nest, but does not hold across upper level nests. The IIA assumption holds across all sites if $\theta_k = 1$ for all k, and $a_k = a_m$ for all k,m. These are the same conditions that must hold for the nested logit model to collapse to the conditional logit model. A simple test for the violation of the IIA assumption in a conditional logit model is a likelihood ratio test between the nested logit model (the unrestricted model) and the conditional logit model (the restricted model). The degrees of freedom for the test will be equal to the number of inclusive value parameters plus the number of alternative specific constants in the nested logit model. In the beach example, only one parameter, θ, separates the nested logit model from the conditional logit model. The likelihood ratio test is equivalent to a t-test on the parameter. Testing for IIA can also be done with the procedure developed by Hausman and McFadden.

8.10.2 Choice Sets

In many recreational settings, the sampled individuals choose from rather different choice sets. Consider a model of recreational fishing in which one of the nests is fishing from a private boat. This nest will not be available to individuals who do not own or have easy access to a private boat. The set of alternative sites assumed to be available to an individual has a significant impact on the estimated economic value of a recreational trip. The impact is felt in two ways. First, having the incorrect set of choices can result in inconsistent parameter estimates. Second, welfare calculations will be incorrect if done with the wrong choice set. For example, if too many sites are included, then the WTP to prevent the loss of a site within the choice set will be underestimated. In determining the choice set, we face the trade-off between tractability of data and integrity of the behavioral model.

Consider the standard formulation of the recreation site choice model in which an individual is assumed to choose the recreation alternative that yields the highest level of utility from among a set of alternatives $S = \{1, ..., J\}$. The universal set S includes all of the alternatives. In the individual's contribution to the log-likelihood function (equation 8.26), the choice set is all of the alternatives. More reliable parameter estimates come from choice sets that conform with the choices individuals actually consider. Individual-specific choice sets can be incorporated into the framework by assuming that the ith individual chooses the utility maximizing alternative from a subset (S^i) of the universal choice set S. Individual i will therefore choose alternative j if the indirect utility of choosing site j exceeds the indirect utility of visiting all other sites that are contained with that individual's choice set. For the ith individual we now include superscripts to denote individual-specific covariates:

$$\Pr\left(v\left(y^i - c^i_j, \mathbf{q}^i_j, \mathbf{s}^i_k\right) + \varepsilon^i_j \geq v\left(y^i - c^i_m, \mathbf{q}^i_m, \mathbf{s}^i_m\right) + \varepsilon^i_m \ \ \forall\, m \in S^i\right). \tag{8.53}$$

From the researcher's perspective, the probability that individual i chooses alternative j can now be written

$$\Pr{}_i(j) = \frac{e^{v^i_j}}{\sum\limits_{m \in S^i} e^{v^i_m}}. \tag{8.54}$$

Note that the denominator is summed over the sites in the individual's choice set.

Some Recent Choice Set Studies

Haab and Hicks (1999) survey the recent literature on choice set issues in recreation demand modeling. Several studies have attempted to narrow choice sets in recreation site choice models by ruling out sites based on individual or site specific characteristics. Parsons and Hauber use distance to rule out sites. They find that distance based choice sets can be successful in reducing the dimension of the site choice problem provided valid substitute or complementary sites are not mistakenly excluded. Parsons, Plantinga and Boyle define five different choice set selection mechanisms for analysis of lake choice in Maine and find that welfare estimates vary considerably across choice set and aggregation treatments. Similarly, Jones and Lupi investigate the effect of changing the set of substitute activities on welfare measurement in this context and conclude that the degree of bias introduced by an ill-defined substitution set is an empirical question that will vary on a case-by-case basis.

Peters, Adamowicz and Boxall allow survey respondents to determine the sites they 'considered' before choosing the actual site visited, thereby allowing the respondent to define the choice set. Hicks and Strand use a similar approach, but rely on the survey respondent's familiarity with sites instead of the sites they considered. Parsons, Massey and Tomasi combine data on actual site choices made by individuals and stated information about sites considered or familiar to individuals. They find that conventional discrete site choice models may understate recreational values if the choice set is ill-defined. Their found relatively little difference between models that eliminate unfamiliar sites from the choice set (as in Hicks and Strand and Peters *et al.*) and models that included unfamiliar sites, but allowed the utility function to vary by familiarity level.

Haab and Hicks (1997) extend models proposed by Manski, and Swait and Ben-Akiva (1987a,b) which allow the choice set to be estimated as a function of individual and site specific characteristics. They find that the endogenous choice set model can perform significantly better than more traditional site choice models.

8.10.3 Sampling Alternatives

The conditional logit random utility model can be computationally burdensome as the number of available alternatives becomes large (although as computing power increases, this becomes less of an issue). It is not uncommon for studies in some recreational applications to contain hundreds of alternatives available to the individual. Random sampling of alternatives can reduce the computational problem substantially. Random sampling involves estimating a standard conditional logit model on the alternative chosen by the individual plus a randomly selected subset of the remaining alternatives in the individuals choice set. Parsons and Kealy (1992) have shown in application to recreation demand studies, random draws of alternatives can provide surprisingly consistent results by reducing the set of alternatives from hundreds to less than 10. Thus one can reduce the computational burden dramatically with little loss in the efficiency of estimates.

To understand why random sampling of alternatives will provide consistent estimates of the parameters from a full conditional logit model, we rely on the discussion by Ben-Akiva and Lerman. Consider drawing a random sample of size M from the ith individual's full set of alternatives S^i. Denote this subset S^i_M. It is understood that the subset of alternatives S^i_M contains the actual alternative chosen by the individual plus $M-1$ other alternatives chosen according to some sampling scheme. The conditional probability of observing individual i choosing subset S^i_M, given the choice of alternative k, will be denoted $\Pr\left(S^i_M|k\right)$. By definition, the probability of individual i choosing alternative k, and the sampling subset S^i_M is

$$\Pr\left(S^i_M, k\right) = \Pr(S^i_M|k) \cdot \Pr{}_i(k). \tag{8.55}$$

where $\Pr_i(k)$ is as defined in equation (8.54). The probability of interest however is the probability of individual i choosing site k, given the randomly chosen subset S^i_M. With Bayes rule, this probability can be written

$$\Pr(k|S^i_M) = \frac{\Pr\left(S^i_M, k\right)}{\Pr(S^i_M)}. \tag{8.56}$$

The numerator is defined in equation (8.55). The denominator can be rewritten

$$\Pr(S_M^i) = \sum_{m \in S_M^i} \Pr\left(S_M^i | m\right) \Pr{}_i(m). \tag{8.57}$$

Upon substitution, the conditional probability of choosing site k given S_M^i becomes

$$\Pr(k|S_M^i) = \frac{\Pr(S_M^i|k) \cdot \Pr(k)}{\sum_{m \in S_M^i} \Pr\left(S_M^i|m\right) \Pr(m)}. \tag{8.58}$$

The numerator is the product of choosing sample set of size M for individual i (S_M^i) and the ith individual's probability of choosing site k. (We suppress the individual subscript i on all variables but the choice set.) The denominator is the sum of such products across the sites in the choice set M. McFadden (1978) shows that this conditional probability exists if $\Pr(S_M^i|k) > 0$ for all k. In other words, if the sampling scheme is such that the probability of choosing any particular subset is positive given the actual choice of alternatives, then the conditional probability of choosing any particular site exists and can be used to estimate parameters of the indirect utility function consistently. This is known as the *positive conditioning property.* The model that results when the positive conditioning property holds is not a conditional logit model. Substituting the exact forms of $\Pr{}_i(k)$and $\Pr{}_i(m)$ into equation (8.58) and rearranging yields the probability expression

$$\begin{aligned} \Pr\left(k|S_M^i\right) &= \frac{\Pr\left(S_M^i|k\right) \cdot e^{v_k} / \sum_{j \in S_M^i} e^{v_j}}{\sum_{m \in S_M^i} \Pr\left(S_M^i|m\right) e^{v_m} / \sum_{j \in S_M^i} e^{v_j}} \\ &= e^{v_k + \ln\left(\Pr(S_M^i|k)\right)} \sum_{m \in S_M^i} e^{v_m + \ln\left(\Pr(S_M^i|m)\right)}. \end{aligned} \tag{8.59}$$

This expression is similar to the conditional logit probability of choosing site k from among the sampled subset of alternatives S_M^i with the addition of the terms $\ln\left(\Pr(S_M^i|k)\right)$. These additional terms correct for using only a subset of the full set of alternatives. As such, standard conditional logit estimating techniques based on choosing among the sampled subset of alternatives will not in general provide consistent estimates of the parameters of the indirect utility function. However, a common special case allows standard conditional logit estimation among the sampled subset of alternatives. Suppose $\Pr(S_M^i|j) = \Pr(S_M^i|k) = \Pr(S_M^i)$ for all

$j, k \in S_M^i$. That is, suppose the conditional probability of choosing a particular subset of alternatives is the same for all sites contained in the sampled subset. This is referred to as the *uniform conditioning property.* Substituting the uniform conditioning property into equation (??), the conditional probabilities cancel and the resulting probability

$$\Pr\left(k|S_M^i\right) = \frac{e^{v_k}}{\sum\limits_{m \in S_M^i} e^{v_m}} \tag{8.60}$$

is the conditional logit probability of choosing site k from among the M sampled alternatives. This means that if the alternative sampling scheme is such that the uniform conditioning property holds, consistent estimates of the parameters of the indirect utility function can be found by estimating a conditional logit model on the chosen alternative from among the sampled subset.

Ben-Akiva and Lerman give two examples of sampling schemes that satisfy the uniform conditioning property. The first is to sample randomly M alternatives without replacement from all of the J possible alternatives. If the chosen alternative is among the sample, then the subsample has M elements. If the chosen alternative is not an element of the subsample then the chosen alternative is added to the subsample to create a sample with $M + 1$ elements. The second alternative is to choose randomly $M - 1$ alternatives from among the $J - 1$ non-chosen alternative (without replacement) and then simply add the chosen alternative to create a subsample of size M. To demonstrate that the uniform conditioning property holds for this scheme, note that the conditional probability of randomly choosing any M dimensional subset is

$$\Pr\left(k|S_M^i\right) = \frac{1}{\frac{(J-1)!}{(M-1)!(J-M)!}}. \tag{8.61}$$

The uniform conditioning property states that this probability must be the same regardless of the conditioning alternative (k). Because this probability simply counts the number of ways $M - 1$ alternatives can be chosen from $J - 1$ choices, it is independent of the conditioning alternative. Note that in this expression, one could include an individual-specific subscript on the universal choice set J to account for the fact that one might have tailored each choice set for the individual *before* sampling. Further, nothing about sampling among alternatives carries over to calculating welfare measures. There one must deal with the full of alternatives.

8.10.4 Aggregation of Sites

In some settings, researchers employ geographic areas or governmental subdivisions as alternatives. These larger areas are aggregates of what Ben-Akiva and Lerman call elemental sites. An elemental site is the ultimate destination of the individual. For example, for a recreational angler launching a boat, a boat ramp would be an elemental site. If the researcher analyzes the county in which the individual launches his boat, the county should be viewed as an aggregate site. Aggregate sites are used in random utility modeling rather than the elemental sites for a variety of reasons; the researcher may only know the aggregate sites as a destination or there may be too many elemental sites to include in the analysis.

Ignoring the effects of aggregation can give misleading results. Consider two aggregate sites that have elemental sites that are similar in attractiveness but that aggregate site A has many more elemental sites than aggregate site B. If we looked strictly at the results of estimating a model with attributes as analyzed previously in this chapter, we would find that all of the influence of the larger number of elemental sites would be attributed to the characteristics of the larger sites.

The complete analysis for correcting aggregation is presented by Ben-Akiva and Lerman. We give the conclusion. The analysis is quite similar to the nested logit model because the aggregate site may be thought of as a nest of elemental sites. Suppose that the utility of an elemental site is given by

$$u_{jk} = v_{jk} + \epsilon_{jk}$$

where j is the elemental site and k is the aggregated site and there are M_k elemental sites. The utility of the aggregate site will simply be the maximum of the utility of the elemental sites. If the elemental utilities are IID, then the utility of the aggregate will approximate extreme value. Then Ben-Akiva and Lerman show that we can write the systematic utility of the aggregate sites as

$$v_k = \bar{v}_k + \theta \ln M_k + \theta \ln B_k$$

where $\bar{v}_k$ is the mean utility of the elemental sites, M_k is the number of elemental sites and B_k is the variance of the elemental sites for aggregate site k. To get $\bar{v}_k$ we use the mean attribute vector for the aggregate site and the parameter vector: $\bar{v}_k = \bar{\mathbf{X}}\boldsymbol{\beta}$; M_k is a count of the elemental sites, and B_k is the variance of the u_{jk}. The coefficient θ is the parameter of the distribution of type I extreme value, assumed to be equal to one. It can either be constrained to be equal to one or estimated. If one assumes that variability is equal across aggregate sites, then the B_k

term disappears. And it may be hard to find good proxies for B_k. Nevertheless, this specification accounts for aggregating over sites.

8.10.5 Socioeconomic Variables

There are occasions when a researcher may want to use individual characteristics to influence choices. As we discussed in several places, individual attributes that do not vary across alternatives will drop from logit probabilities. For example, we have shown how income will drop from a linear income less cost term. Suppose that we want to show the influence of individual characteristic z_i on the choice among alternatives. A first order approximation of the deterministic part of the utility function would be

$$v_i(j) = \boldsymbol{\beta}\mathbf{x}_{ij} + \alpha_j z_i$$

for $j = 1, ...K$. The difference in utility for alternatives j and m will be $v_i(j) - v_i(m) = \boldsymbol{\beta}(\mathbf{x}_{ij} - \mathbf{x}_{im}) + (\alpha_j - \alpha_m)z_i$ which will be feasible for a random utility model. In a random utility context, this model can be estimated by constructing a system of $K - 1$ variables $z^*_{ij} = z_j\delta_{jm}$ where $\delta_{jm} = 1$ for $j = m$, 0 for $j \neq m$. We can only have $K - 1$ of these variables; a full set of K dummy variables creates a singular matrix of regressors. This simply means that we choose the value of one parameter, say α_1 without loss of generality, to be zero. This approach essentially constructs a mixture of a conditional logit model, in which choices depend on the characteristics of alternatives, and a multinomial model, in which choices depend on individual characteristics. Note that we could have only individual characteristics, without the $\boldsymbol{\beta}\mathbf{x}_{ij}$ term, and we would have simply a multinomial logit model.

8.11 Conclusions

In this chapter we have given an exposition of the random utility model that will help users in the modeling and estimation process. We have limited our discussion to the elemental models–conditional and nested logits. When site choices are made among just a handful of sites, the generalized corner solution models and the generalized count models may perform equally well. But when the number of sites is quite large, nested logit and conditional logit models are especially desirable.

9

Hedonic Price Equations

9.1 Introduction

In this chapter we address the problem of estimating hedonic price equations. Hedonic prices result when quality differentiated goods are sold in competitive markets. This is the only topic in the book in which we deal with market outcomes. Hedonic models fall under the rubric of non-market valuation because goods and services occasionally have qualities that are not provided by the market. Most of the environmental applications relate to house prices, although hedonic wage equations have been used to model the willingness to pay to avoid risk. Houses are just bundles of attributes. Some of the qualities, such as floor space, are obviously market-induced. Others, such as exposure to air pollution, are non-market. The essence of hedonic modeling is to use the systematic variation in price of goods that can be attributed to the characteristics of goods to impute the willingness to pay for the characteristics.

There is a vast literature on hedonic models. Good overviews include the chapters by Bartik and Smith, and Palmquist (1991). A recent review of more advanced topics can be found in Palmquist (forthcoming). Evidence of the workings of hedonic models for air quality has received substantial documentation in the meta-analysis by Smith and Huang (1993, 1995). These papers review the hedonic studies of air pollution that were completed by the late 1980s. While the meta-analysis lends support for the idea that property values reflect air pollution, it also demonstrates the sensitivity of estimates of marginal willingness to pay to strategic modeling and research decisions. This is of course true of all non-market valuation methods but the evidence appears more prominent when one sees a meta-analysis of the method.

Hedonic models have been widely used to value environmental amenities, especially air quality. The variety of applications of hedonic models rivals the contingent valuation method. For example, hedonic prices equations have been estimated for agricultural commodities, automobiles, wines and labor services. The earliest applications of hedonics to the housing market involved efforts to document the effect of air pollution on housing prices by Ridker and Henning and by Nourse in 1967. These early models used census tract data that gave mean or median housing prices. Current research uses the transactions prices of individual dwellings. Smith and Huang (1993) provide evidence of the effect of air quality on housing prices with a meta-analysis of the relevant housing price studies covering 25 years. The thrust of their research supports the idea that air pollution affects housing prices. Estimating the effect of air quality on housing values is somewhat more straightforward than water quality, because there is more cross-section variation in air quality than in water quality. Air quality can vary spatially across a large metropolitan area because of meteorological conditions. This variation can be employed in hedonic models if there are sufficient air quality monitors to reflect the variation. There are fewer studies of the effect of water pollution on housing prices, principally because of the difficulties of disentangling the water quality effect from the effects of other variables that are part of the 'location on the water front' effect. This effect includes the improved view, access to water recreation, and perhaps disamenities such as congestion from boat traffic. Identifying the effect of water quality requires more variation in the water quality variable. One means of obtaining that variation involves the use of observations of the housing market over time (for example Mendelsohn, Hellerstein *et al.*) Research by Leggett and Bockstael demonstrates that including a single variable to account for water pollution may overestimate the price effects of water pollution if the variable also proxies for other undesirable characteristics from the source of the pollution. Careful accounting for the sources of water pollution, including all the attributes of the polluting source, may reduce the estimates of damage from water pollution per se. Hedonic models are also used to value a variety of other environmental variables, including locating near a hazardous waste site and noise pollution.

To form an intuitive feel for hedonic prices, imagine a competitive housing market, and consider two houses that are identical in attributes and location except that one house has three bedrooms and the other has two bedrooms. The difference in the market prices of the two houses will necessarily reflect the value of the extra bedroom. If the price difference is less than the willingness to pay for the extra bedroom, buyers will bid up the price of the three bedroom house until the price reflects the difference. A price difference in excess of the willingness to pay for the extra room cannot be sustained because buyers will bid up the price of the two bedroom house relative to the three bedroom house. There is no reason to expect that the same market mechanism will not account for the differences in non-market attributes of houses although with greater error. The differences in prices of houses with different non-market attributes, holding all other attributes constant, will reflect the willingness to pay for the differences in the non-market attributes.

The practice of hedonic modeling began with Waugh's study of price differences in fresh vegetables in 1926. While applications were common, it was not until Rosen fully rationalized hedonic models that the complete workings of hedonic models were understood. Rosen's model begins with a distribution of utility maximizing buyers and a distribution of profit maximizing sellers. Equilibrium is achieved when variations in the price of the good reflect variations in its quality in such a way that buyers and sellers cannot do better by making other deals. Formally, the hedonic price equation arises when sellers maximize the profits from selling goods with characteristic bundle $\mathbf{z} = \{z_1, ...z_C\}$, where z_c is characteristic c for the good, C being the number of characteristics. Buyers maximize utility, allocating income among the quality-differentiated goods and the other goods. There is no uncertainty or hidden information. Buyers and sellers know the characteristics and agree on the quantity. The equilibrium hedonic price function is given by

$$p = h(\mathbf{z}, \boldsymbol{\alpha}) \tag{9.1}$$

where p is the price of the good–for example, the price of a house–$\mathbf{z}$ is the vector of attributes and $\boldsymbol{\alpha}$ is a vector of parameters describing the shape of the hedonic function. The shape depends on the number of buyers and sellers and their characteristics. The representation of equation (9.1) is considered approximate. For simplicity, we will denote the hedonic price function as $p = h(\mathbf{z})$. The equilibrium conditions that give rise to the hedonic price equation may not give an exact solution. Rosen solves the equilibrium conditions for one hedonic price equation, but this assumed smooth distributions of producers and consumers, and a single characteristic. In general, the functional form of the hedonic price equation is unknown, and uncertainty about this functional form causes part of the random error.

In the housing market, the hedonic price equation emerges from competitive bidding among home owners and buyers when buyers purchase only one home. The equilibrium will persist when buyers have maximized their utility subject to a budget constraint. Suppose households have the preference function $u(x, \mathbf{z}; \boldsymbol{\beta})$, where x is a composite bundle of commodities, $\mathbf{z}$ is the vector of attributes of a house, and $\boldsymbol{\beta}$ is a vector of parameters of the household preference function. The budget constraint is given by $y = h(\mathbf{z}) + x$, where x is a composite bundle. This constraint implicitly assumes that the buyer takes only one unit of the hedonic good. Maximizing utility subject to the budget constraint implies optimal conditions for each attribute:

$$\frac{\partial u(x, \mathbf{z}; \boldsymbol{\beta})}{\partial z_c} = \lambda \frac{\partial h(\mathbf{z})}{\partial z_c}, \; c = 1, ..., C \tag{9.2}$$

where λ is the marginal utility of income. Of course, hedonic attributes are not purchased individually. Rather, there is an equilibrating process that allocates houses among households. But when the equilibrium is satisfied, then equation (9.2) holds and provides a connection between the hedonic price and marginal willingness to pay, which is $\lambda^{-1}\frac{\partial u(x,\mathbf{z};\beta)}{\partial z_c}$.

In practice, because buyers choose among a fixed set of houses, rather than optimizing at the margin, one might argue that the housing market would not be in equilibrium as described in equation (9.2). And if the equilibrium conditions do not hold, then the welfare conclusions do not follow. However, the sorting mechanism by which households purchase houses appears to induce an equilibrium with the marginal conditions described in equation (9.2). Simulation work by Cropper *et al.* provides evidence that when housing stock is allocated among buyers by maximum bid or by the solution of an assignment problem, the equilibrium conditions given in equation (9.2) are satisfied.

The choice of functional form is an important strategic research decision. When households are heterogeneous, the functional form of the hedonic price equation is only mildly restricted. It will slope upward for utility-bearing characteristics and it probably will not be linear. The hedonic price function should be increasing in desirable attributes–a lower price associated with a higher desirable attribute level would induce movement in the housing market, as buyers competed for the lower price-high attribute bundles. When the good can be unbundled, so that the buyer can purchase different sets of attributes from different sources, the hedonic price function becomes linear. But linear hedonic price functions are also an accident of the data, so that one may find linearity without implying unbundling. Flexible functional forms have been adopted but the cross-product terms tend to increase the already significant collinearity of attributes, and reduce the precision of estimates. Indeed part of the empirical challenge of hedonic models is to deal with the trade-off between a complete functional form and collinearity. We focus on this issue in the following sections.

9.2 Welfare Measurement in Hedonic Models

It is not surprising that in a more complicated model of equilibrium, the welfare analysis is also more complicated. The hedonic equation is an outcome of a market equilibrium. In the housing market, it represents the sorting process that allocates households to houses. Even if it were possible to estimate a demand for attributes equation, welfare measurement in the hedonic model would not be straightforward. But as we shall discuss briefly, the demand for hedonic attributes, in the standard model of quantity as a function of prices and income, does not typically exist. And even if it were to exist in principle, it is unlikely that its parameters could be identified in the typical hedonic setting.

It is therefore fortunate that in measuring welfare effects in hedonic models, the need for the preference function rather than the hedonic price function is rare. The preference function is useful in the case when the research is focused on the question of the generic value of an attribute. That is, if we wanted to compare the willingness to pay for changes in air quality in different cities, without consideration for the housing market, the cleanest approach would be to use the preference function, which would give a measure of willingness to pay independent of local housing conditions. But when the question concerns the value of the changes in the local housing market, then the hedonic price function itself will usually suffice, or at least be useful for bounds.

Two types of changes need to be considered for welfare measurement for a change in the vector of housing characteristics, depending on the size and extent of the change in characteristic vector. One corresponds to what Palmquist (1992) calls a local change, in which the change in the characteristic vector is not big enough or extensive enough to cause a new hedonic function to be formed. For example, there is a reduction in air pollution but not big enough to induce the significant movement of households that would lead to a new hedonic schedule. The second case occurs when the changes in the attribute vector are sufficient to bring about a new hedonic price equation.

Consider the case where there is a change in attributes so small enough to maintain the given hedonic price equation. To make the welfare effects clearer, suppose that there are two groups–renters and owners. Since the change in attribute vector is small, it is reasonable to assume that the utility level of renters will not change. If air quality improves, the houses affected will simply be resorted along the given hedonic price function. Houses with better air quality will move up the hedonic function. If the increase in hedonic price induced by the improvement is greater than moving costs, then renters will relocate to houses with air quality that they enjoyed before the air quality improvements. If the moving costs exceed the price difference caused by changes in air quality, but the hedonic price rises anyway, then renters will stay in their original houses, and pay the higher rent predicted by the hedonic price equation with the new air quality. The gain to the homeowners from the new air quality, and the welfare increase for an affected house is

$$WTP = h(\mathbf{z}^*) - h(\mathbf{z})$$

where $\mathbf{z}^*$ is the new vector of attributes, including better air quality, and $\mathbf{z}$ is the original vector. This calculation of course needs only the hedonic price function.

If moving costs are sufficiently high so that no households change their housing, then there will be no resorting of renters and houses. The renters will gain from the improvement in air quality. The amount they will gain is given by the willingness to pay that is implicitly defined as

$$u(y - h(\mathbf{z}) - WTP, \mathbf{z}^*; \boldsymbol{\beta}) = u(y - h(\mathbf{z}), \mathbf{z}; \boldsymbol{\beta})$$

where $\mathbf{z}^*$ is a new and improved vector of attributes, and $\mathbf{z}$ is the original vector. Here WTP is the maximum amount of income that the household will give up to obtain the new vector, with the understanding that the hedonic function does not change, and the household remains in the house. This is an easy calculation to make when the parameters of the preference function, $\boldsymbol{\beta}$, are known. This however requires that the hedonic identification problem be solved.

When vectors of housing characteristics change sufficiently to cause households to relocate and also cause a new hedonic price function to form, the welfare measure is much more complicated. The most reasonable approach for this situation is the general equilibrium approach developed by Sieg, Smith, Banzhaf and Walsh, who model jointly the equilibrium in the choice among communities and the housing market equilibrium. Bartik (1982) provides bounds for this case.

It is often remarked that the hedonic price function reveals the marginal value of attributes. This is true because equation (9.4) shows that the marginal cost as given by the hedonic function equals the marginal value. This property of the hedonic price equation can be useful in interpreting the equation but it offers little help in calculating welfare effects unless it is known with some confidence that marginal values are approximately constant.

9.3 The Identification Problem

When estimating willingness to pay from a preference function rather than the hedonic function, one wants to use the parameters of preferences. The difficulty is that these parameters cannot be identified from the equilibrium conditions, and they cannot be extracted from the hedonic price equation. Much of the discussion of the hedonic equilibrium is carried out using the bid function. This is the solution to the condition

$$u(y - B(y, \mathbf{z}; \boldsymbol{\beta}), \mathbf{z}; \boldsymbol{\beta}) = u^0 \tag{9.3}$$

where $B(y, \mathbf{z}; \boldsymbol{\beta})$ is the amount that the household with preferences $\boldsymbol{\beta}$ will pay for the bundle $\mathbf{z}$ when their alternative choices allow them utility level u^0. Of course, written this way, this is also the willingness to pay function, but to be consistent with the hedonic literature we maintain the terminology 'bid function'. The difficulty in identifying the parameters of the preference function can seen by rewriting the equilibrium conditions in equation (9.2) in terms of the marginal bid function (which is also equal to the marginal willingness to pay function):

$$B_c(x, \mathbf{z}; \boldsymbol{\beta}) = \frac{\partial h(\mathbf{z})}{\partial z_c} \tag{9.4}$$

where the left hand side is the marginal value or marginal bid function:

$$\frac{\partial u(x, \mathbf{z}; \boldsymbol{\beta})}{\partial z_c} / \lambda \equiv B_c(x, \mathbf{z}; \boldsymbol{\beta})$$

and the right hand side of (9.4) is the marginal cost function. The interpretation of the marginal bid function comes from implicit differentiation of equation (9.3). One may think of this set of equations as a simultaneous system. The endogenous variables in this system are the attributes, and the household's chosen attributes. They enter both the marginal cost and marginal benefit functions. The researcher must solve the identification problem for the parameters of the preference function, $\boldsymbol{\beta}$. This is not, however, a garden variety identification problem. There are no simple exclusion rules for identification. Exogenous variables that influence marginal values also influence the marginal costs. Various approaches have been suggested for recovering parameters. Epple provides a complete statement of identification in hedonic models. With a few exceptions, researchers have abandoned any attempts to recover preferences, and work instead with the hedonic price function.

9.4 Estimating Hedonic Price Equations

The estimation of hedonic price equations is a regular event, and the econometric issues that arise are well documented. While initial work on hedonic models exploited US Census tract data on housing prices, which were aggregated, the typical study now uses individual housing data. The data generation process is quite direct. In current practice, records of actual transactions form the bulk of datasets. Sales are recorded and characteristics of houses collected. Frequently all sales within a period of time are used, so that there is no selection process. And while the price of houses cannot be negative, the variance is typically small enough to render the statistical likelihood of a non-positive price quite low. One can safely treat the data without worrying about truncation or censoring. Hence the estimation process itself is straightforward, being principally ordinary least squares or a variant of least squares with heteroscedastic errors.

When estimating a hedonic price function, one faces a series of decisions and some well-known econometric problems. Typically one has a dataset that includes transaction price and the relevant housing attributes. The strategic choices concern the extent of the market, the functional form of the hedonic price equation, and the set of included variables. The set of covariates typically includes two types of variables: the most critical are the attributes of the house such as number of bedrooms, number of bathrooms, the presence of air conditioning, and other variables descriptive of the house; the other attributes describe the neighborhood, location and environment of the house, such as crime rates, school test scores, median income, distances from important destinations, and environmental measures such air quality readings from monitors. The nature of the equilibrium for attributes within a house and for the spatial distribution of houses in an area typically induces a good deal of collinearity among the attributes.[1] Larger houses tend to have more of everything–more bathrooms go with more bedrooms and other amenities. And the market allocates housing to land such that the larger houses typically have better environmental quality. Hence attributes of houses tend to be correlated. And distances tend to be inherently correlated.

Collinearity makes parameter estimates imprecise and intuitively makes inferences on the effects of some attributes difficult to disentangle. Consider, for example, efforts to measure the separate hedonic effects of air pollution and location near the Pacific Ocean in the Los Angeles housing market. Location near the ocean is clearly a valuable attribute and air pollution is undesirable. Because the prevailing winds come from the

[1]Early evidence of the collinearity is provided by Harrison and Rubinfeld. This paper became famous because of its illustration of collinearity.

west, and temperatures are higher further inland, air pollution builds up monotonically with distance from the ocean. Hence as one considers houses further from the ocean, air pollution, an undesirable attribute, will be higher, as will distance from the ocean. Both have a negative effect on housing prices, and sorting them out takes more and different kinds of variation in housing prices, distance from the ocean, and air pollution.

The question of functional form arises because the nature of the equilibrium conditions in the housing market permits a wide variety of solutions. When choosing functional form and the set of included variables, the researcher must bear in mind the almost inevitable conflict with collinearity. High collinearity makes the choice of a very flexible functional form less attractive, because the interactive terms of a flexible functional form cause even greater collinearity.

Local real estate markets may be segmented when the stocks of housing differ or when groups of buyers in one market have different preference functions from buyers in another area. The segmentation will persist if buyers do not search among different markets, or if there are informational barriers among markets. Persistent market segmentation causes the hedonic price equation to differ among markets. Segmented markets are revealed when the hedonic price functions for the different market differ in functional form and covariates. Were a very general functional form available, then it would accommodate different forms for different segments of the housing market. Combining market segments with different hedonic price functions can result in a larger random error, which means less precise parameter estimates. A model estimated from two distinct housing markets would yield a weighted average of two different hedonic functions, with uncertain implications. Michaels and Smith studied the issue empirically, consulting with realtors, and found evidence that real estate markets in Boston were segmented. What this means in practice relates to the collection and use of data. In the US, one can frequently collect housing prices for transactions within a county. However, for the residential housing market, a county or a city may contain a number of real estate markets. On the other hand, if the market were agricultural land, then a single market might encompass a number of counties. For the actual choice of the extent of the market, there is no substitute for local knowledge of the real estate market.

Other econometric problems may also arise. Leggett and Bockstael probe the specification bias that can arise when one includes a single attribute of a polluting facility, but excludes other attributes of the facility. They find that by including the relevant attributes, the hedonic effects of water pollution on housing values become less pronounced.

9.4.1 The Box-Cox Function

A very general functional form was proposed by Halvorsen and Pollakowski. In parametric form the hedonic price function for the ith house is

$$p_i(\mu) = \sum_{c=1}^{C} \alpha_c z_{ic}(\lambda) + 0.5 \sum_{c=1}^{C} \sum_{g=1}^{C} \beta_{cg} z_{ic}(\theta) z_{ig}(\theta) + \varepsilon_i \qquad (9.5)$$

where ε_i is typically a normally distributed error with a constant variance, the α's and β's are linear parameters on the transformed variables, and the transformation of any variable x is the typical form for Box-Cox models:

$$\begin{aligned} x(\lambda) &= (x^\lambda - 1)/\lambda \text{ for } \lambda \neq 0 \\ &= \ln(x) \text{ for } \lambda = 0. \end{aligned}$$

Only variables that are positive can be transformed. Dummy variables or other variables that take on zero or negative values cannot be raised to a non-integer power. The same form of transformation holds for all of the variables, including, in the most general case, the hedonic price, although the parameters of the transformation, μ, λ, θ, may differ. For different values of the exponents (μ, λ, θ), this functional form has the quadratic, the translog, simple linear models and a variety of other functional forms as special cases. For example, if $\mu = 0, \lambda = 1,\ \beta_{cg} = 0$, for all c, the semi-log hedonic price function emerges.

More generality increases one's ability to explain variation in the hedonic prices. A model with quadratic terms cannot predict the hedonic price worse than a model without the terms. But more complicated functional forms, especially quadratic forms, make it harder to distinguish the effects of individual regressors because of the induced collinearity and might easily do worse in predicting marginal prices. In a study of functional form using a simulated dataset, Cropper *et al.* found that the linear function $(\mu = 1, \lambda = 1,\ \beta_c = 0)$ and a linear-quadratic function $(\mu = 1, \lambda = 1,\ \theta = 1)$ give the smallest mean square error of the true marginal value of the attribute. But when some of the regressors are measured with error, the linear Box-Cox model $(\mu = 1,\ \beta_c = 0)$ gives the smallest mean squared error of the marginal value of attributes. If one cannot estimate the marginal values of attributes accurately, despite the good fit of the overall model, then the specification loses its appeal. Consequently, it has become common practice to estimate functional forms for hedonic models that are simpler than the general form in equation (9.5).

9.4.2 Estimating Box-Cox Models

Some computer packages have Box-Cox routines built into the estimation routines. In other cases, one needs to locate the optimal values of the transformation parameters in a grid search. We show the likelihood for the case where the quadratic terms are omitted. The generalization needed to include the quadratic terms is obvious, but it seems unlikely that one would want to transform these variables too. To write the likelihood function when the errors are independently distributed normals, we note that the density function for the random error of the ith observation is given by

$$f(\varepsilon_i) = \frac{1}{\sqrt{2\pi\sigma^2}} \exp(-\frac{\varepsilon_i^2}{2\sigma^2}).$$

From equation (9.5) (and dropping the quadratic terms), we note that $\varepsilon_i = p_i(\mu) - \sum_{c=1}^{C} \alpha_c z_{ic}(\lambda)$, and

$$f[p_i(\mu) - \sum_{c=1}^{C} \alpha_c z_{ic}(\lambda)] = \frac{1}{\sqrt{2\pi\sigma^2}} \exp(\frac{[p_i(\mu) - \sum_{c=1}^{C} \alpha_c z_{ic}(\lambda)]^2}{2\sigma^2}).$$

Transforming random variables from ε_i to p_i, the probability density function for p_i becomes

$$pdf(p_i) = p_i^{\mu-1} f(p_i(\mu) - \sum_{c=1}^{C} \alpha_c z_{ic}(\lambda)).$$

To see this, let $f(\epsilon)$ be the density of ϵ, and let $\epsilon = g(p)$. Then the density of p is $f(g(p))g'(p)$. In this case $g(p) = p_i(\mu) - \sum_{c=1}^{C} \alpha_c z_{ic}(\lambda)$ and $g'(p) = p^{\mu-1}$. The log-likelihood function for T observations is

$$\sum_{i=1}^{T} (\mu - 1) \ln(p_i) - T \ln(\sigma) - \sum_{i=1}^{T} \{[p_i(\mu) - \sum_{c=1}^{C} \alpha_c z_{ic}(\lambda)]^2 / 2\sigma^2\}.$$

One can maximize this likelihood function analytically to estimate parameters, or one can use a grid search. A grid search is relatively easy to implement because, given the value of μ, the optimizing values of α_c and λ are least squares estimates.

In practice, welfare measures are made with estimated hedonic price equations. For the general Box-Cox hedonic price function in equation (9.5), the marginal effect of a change in characteristic c for housing unit i is given by

$$\frac{\partial p_i}{\partial z_{ic}} = p_i^{1-\mu}(\alpha_c z_{ic}^{\lambda-1} + z_{ic}^{\theta-1} \sum_{g=1}^{C} \beta_{cg} z_{ig}(\theta)).$$

This equation is just the parametric version of equation (9.4). It simplifies to all the familiar models under benchmark values of μ, λ and θ.

When calculating marginal values or even predicted price changes for finite welfare effects, it is customary to use the coefficients of the hedonic price equation as if they were the true values. No effort is made to disentangle preferences from other effects on the hedonic price function, nor to interpret the error in the hedonic price function. In the expression for $\partial p_i/\partial z_{ic}$, the price will be an argument unless $\mu = 1$. If the price is known for certain, this causes no additional randomness. In the typical case, however, the price has a random term. This is the case when the hedonic price function is specified as the logarithm of price as a linear function of characteristics, $\partial p_i/\partial z_{ic} = p_i\alpha_c$, which includes the error from the hedonic price. The error in the hedonic price equation is not part of welfare measurement if $\mu = 1$.

Example 33 *Estimating a Hedonic Price Function*

We illustrate the estimation and interpretation of a hedonic price function using a dataset on waterfront housing transactions between 1993 and 1997 in Anne Arundel County, Maryland.[2] This dataset, originally assembled by the Maryland Office of Planning, is a subset of the dataset used in the published work on water quality on the Chesapeake Bay by Leggett and Bockstael. For the study of hedonic models, the dataset is unique in several ways. First, it focuses on water quality, rather than the more common environmental characteristic, air quality. Second, it includes what Leggett and Bockstael call 'emitter effects'. These are characteristics of the sources of water pollution, such as waste water treatment plants. The inclusion of emitter effects helps discriminate among other attributes of the emitters, such as odor, from the water quality effects per se. And finally, the dataset uses assessed value of the structure, rather than characteristics of the house such as square footage, number of bedrooms, presence of a garage, pool or air-conditioning. In effect, estimating a hedonic price model with assessed value of the structure rather than the individual characteristics of the house reduces collinearity by eliminating a set of highly correlated characteristics. The cost is that the assessed value of the structure may be measured with error if the assessment is wrong. That will not only attenuate the parameter

[2] We thank Nancy Bockstael and Chris Leggett for allowing us to use the dataset and for helping with the details of the data. The original data are from the Maryland Office of Planning. A more fully developed study of these housing transactions can be found in the paper by Leggett and Bockstael.

on assessed value of the structure, but will contaminate other parameters as well. In practice, it is far better to include the housing-specific attributes rather than the assessed value of the structure. The suspicious role of the assessed value led Leggett and Bockstael to estimate models with the assessed value subtracted from the housing price. In a later section we estimate a hedonic model with attributes of the house as covariates rather than the assessed value of the structure.

In illustrating the hedonic model, we follow approximately, but not exactly, the Leggett-Bockstael specification.[3] Table 9.1 describes the characteristics and gives the means.

TABLE 9.1. Hedonic Price Function Variables

Variable	Description	Mean n=741
PRICE ($1000)	Sales price adjusted to constant dollars	335.91
VSTRU ($1000)	Assessed value of structure	125.84
ACRES	Acres per house	0.90
ACSQ	Acres squared	2.42
DISBA	Distance to Baltimore	26.40
DISAN	Distance to Annapolis	13.30
ANBA	Distance to Baltimore ×distance to Annapolis	352.50
BDUM	Distance to Baltimore ×percent who commute	8.04
PLOD	Percent of land with 3/4 miles developed at very low density	0.18
PWAT	Percent of land with 3/4 miles that is wetlands or water	0.32
DBAD	Minimum distance to an industrial or municipal source of waste	3.18
F.COL	Mean fecal coliform concentration	109.70

Source: Maryland Office of Planning,
Anne Arundel County Department of Health

The covariates warrant some discussion. The VSTRU is a proxy for

[3] The reader should also note that the dataset that we use has 741 observations while the original Leggett-Bockstael dataset contains 1183 observations. The empirical results of this chapter are not comparable to the Leggett-Bockstael models because the set of observations is quite different.

all of the house-specific characteristics such as the number of bedrooms, bathrooms, and the like but excluding the land. The ACRES variable captures the effect of the amount of land, and the squared terms allow for the likely declining value of more land per house. The assorted distance variables capture the amenities and commuting attractions of Annapolis and Baltimore. The land use variables represent landscape and environmental effects. The variables PLOD and PWAT are landscape variables. They should capture the attraction of water on the price of the house. In this version of the hedonic price equation, DBAD captures the effects of some of the larger sources of water pollution by measuring the minimum distance to such facilities. The price of the house should increase with distance from such a source.

The variable of particular interest in the original research, F.COL, is the weighted mean of the fecal coliform count for the three nearest monitoring stations. Coliforms can cause gastroenteritis and emit odors at high levels. Excessive coliform levels impair water contact sports. In any hedonic model, the attributes associated with the house, such as lot size, or with the structure itself, such as number of bedrooms, are typically fairly easily chosen. But the environmental variable must be picked with care. Whether one is assessing the hedonic effects of air quality or water quality or other environmental characteristics, the question of subjective perceptions of the environment versus objective measures of environmental quality must be confronted. The problem, which arises when behavioral methods are used, is that the researcher does not know what cues or measures influence behavior. In many water quality studies, and especially studies of hazardous waste sites, it has been the practice to use the distance to the offending facility as a measure of its intensity. Gayer, Hamilton and Viscusi construct more precise measures of risk, and use them in addition to distance measures as a way of assessing the damages of hazardous waste sites. For the waterfront houses in the Leggett-Bockstael study, information about fecal coliform was regularly publicized by the Anne Arundel County Department of Health. While one may use objective measures of an environmental variable, there is little assurance that the people who are assumed to respond to the pollution measure are aware of the measure or know what it means. In this case, the publicity surrounding the water quality measure assures some harmony between objective measures and subjective perceptions.

We estimate four functional forms: the linear model, Box-Cox transformation of the dependent variable, the semi-log dependent variable model (a special case of dependent variable transformation), and a full model where both dependent and independent variables are transformed. All models are estimated with the Box-Cox routine in LIMDEP version

7.0. The most general specification is

$$p_i(\mu) = \sum_{c=1}^{C} \alpha_c z_{ic}(\lambda) + \varepsilon_i$$

where the z_{ic}'s are given in Table 9.1. Although we have emphasized the empirical evidence that supports the notion of simple hedonic price functions, we will show the estimation of more complicated forms for the sake of illustrating the approach. The variables PLOD and PWAT are not transformed because they can take the value of zero.

The estimated coefficients for the four models are given in Table 9.2. The house and land variables are all significant with the right signs in different functional forms. The coefficients on the variables VSTRU, ACRES, ACSQ and PWAT do not change across functional forms. However, the location and environmental variables are more fragile. In particular, F.COL is not significant for the semi-log and the general Box-Cox (columns three and five).

The models in Table 9.2 are nested versions of the last column, in that each is derived with a restriction on the parameters μ or λ. We can use the log-likelihood values in the last row to test the restrictions on the parameters. The test of the linear model versus the general Box-Cox involves two restrictions. The quantity $-2\ln(L_U/L_R)$ is distributed as $\chi^2(2)$. In this case, $-2\ln(L_U/L_R) = 1279.4$, which exceeds the tabled value for $\chi^2_{.99}(2)$ of 9.2. We can also compare the first two columns with the third column for testing, which entails one restriction. (The tabled value of the statistic for one restriction at the 99% level of confidence: $\chi^2_{.99}(1) = 6.6$.)

For example, conditioned on $\lambda = 1$ (the right hand side is not transformed), we can reject the linear left hand side ($-2\ln(L_U/L_R) = 1063.8$) and we can reject the log transformation of the price (the semi-log model) compared with a more general transformation ($-2\ln(L_U/L_R) = 112.2$). We can also reject the transformation of the left hand side only by comparing the fourth and fifth column likelihood values. In this case $-2\ln(L_U/L_R) = 215.6$. The transformations change the interaction among characteristics. The linear case is the only additively separable hedonic function. Consequently the effects of covariates become harder to disentangle as the complexity of the functional form increases. And it is important to bear in mind that maximizing the likelihood function models the most likely behavior underlying the hedonic price function, but it does not necessarily minimize the errors associated with the marginal bids. Adding interactions increases explanatory power but compounds marginal values.

TABLE 9.2. Estimation for Selected Functions

Characteristic	Parameter Estimates (Standard errors in parentheses)			
	$\mu = 1$ $\lambda = 1$	$\mu = 0$ $\lambda = 1$	$\mu = 0.43^c$ $\lambda = 1$	$\mu = 0.16^c$ $\lambda = 0.33^c$
VSTRU	^{a}1.37	^{a}0.0028	^{a}0.037	^{a}0.25
	(0.040)	(0.0008)	(0.009)	(0.05)
ACRES	^{a}116.9	^{a}0.31	^{a}3.72	^{a}1.79
	(7.62)	(0.06)	(0.87)	(0.32)
ACSQ	^{a}−7.33	^{a}−0.023	^{a}−0.26	^{a}−0.49
	(0.79)	(0.005)	(0.06)	(0.09)
DISBA	^{a}−3.96	−0.01	^{a}0.13	^{a}-1.00
	(1.74)	(0.007)	(0.06)	(0.35)
DISAN	^{a}−11.80	^{a}−0.047	^{a}−0.49	^{a}−1.43
	(2.50)	(0.014)	(0.13)	(0.43)
ANBA	^{a}0.36	0.001	^{a}0.013	^{a}0.45
	(0.09)	(0.0005)	(0.004)	(0.17)
DBAD	2.78	^{a}0.042	^{a}0.32	0.07^a
	(2.50)	(0.009)	(0.10)	(0.03)
F.COL	^{a}−0.052	−0.00012	^{b}−0.0015	−0.011
	(0.025)	(0.00010)	(0.0009)	(0.008)
The following variables are not transformed.				
BDUM	^{a}−10.2	^{a}−0.03	^{a}−0.36	^{a}−0.05
	(1.89)	(0.008)	(0.10)	(0.02)
PLOD	^{b}71.69	^{a}0.27	^{a}2.88	0.32
	(37.27)	(0.13)	(1.37)	(0.26)
PWAT	^{a}119.97	^{a}0.35	^{a}4.20	^{a}0.74
	(25.89)	(0.11)	(1.26)	(0.23)
Const.	^{a}238.69	^{a}5.77	^{a}22.38	^{a}10.83
	(47.44)	(0.60)	(3.55)	(1.62)
Log-like.	−4882.7	−4406.9	−4350.8	−4243.0
$-2\ln\left(\frac{L_R}{L_U}\right)$	1250.4	1402.0	1524.2	1729.8

^{a}Different from zero at the 95% level of confidence.

^{b}Different from zero at the 90% level of confidence.

^{c}These are the optimal transformation parameters.

Example 34 *Calculating Welfare Effects*

To illustrate the use of the hedonic function, and to anticipate some of the difficulties one is likely to encounter, we calculate the marginal value of F.COL, and the estimate of the WTP for a finite change in this characteristic. Because an undesirable attribute is increasing, we measure the WTP to avoid the increase. The marginal value is given by expression (9.4). For computational ease, we calculate the welfare effects at the mean price. The basic expression is

$$WTP = h(\mathbf{z}^*) - h(\mathbf{z})$$

but we can make it simpler by writing

$$p = (\mu\mathbf{z}(\lambda)\boldsymbol{\alpha} + 1)^{1/\mu} = h(\mathbf{z}).$$

Then we use $h(\mathbf{z}) = \bar{p}$, and $\mathbf{z}(\lambda)\boldsymbol{\alpha} = (p^{\mu} - 1)/\mu$ so

$$h(\mathbf{z}^*) = (\bar{p}^{\mu} + (\mu z_c^*(\lambda) - z_c(\lambda))\alpha_c)^{1/\mu}. \tag{9.6}$$

Hence we use only the transformation parameters, the coefficient on F.COL, the mean price and the initial and final value of F.COL in the welfare calculation. Recall from Table 9.2, the coefficient on F.COL is not significantly different from zero for the semi-log and the general Box-Cox, so that welfare measures of the second and fourth row of Table 9.3 would not be significantly different from zero. In practice one would not calculate welfare measures with insignificant coefficients.

TABLE 9.3. Welfare Measures for a Change in F.COL

Functional Form	Estimated Coefficient: α_c	Marginal Value[a]	Discrete Change[b]
$\mu = \lambda = 1$	-0.052	-0.052	-2.60
$\mu = 0, \lambda = 1$	-0.00012[c]	-0.040	-2.01
$\mu = 0.43, \lambda = 1$	-0.0015	-0.041	-2.06
$\mu = 0.16, \lambda = 0.33$	-0.011[c]	-0.063	-2.74

[a]Marginal value $= \partial h/\partial z_c = p^{1-\mu} z_c^{\lambda-1}\alpha_c$;
assuming $z_c = 109$, $p = 335.91$.
[b]In \$1000's; using equation (9.6).
[c]For illustration; coefficient not significantly different from zero.

In the selected sample of observations, the marginal values are all quite close, considering the different functional forms. For a discrete change in the characteristic F.COL, we assume that it begins at the mean value of the sample, 109, and increases to 159, a substantial increase but still below the state standard of 200 for this biological pollutant. The estimates suggest that a household in a house with the mean vector of attributes, at the mean price, would pay between $2000 and $3000 to avoid an increase in F.COL of 50. Even the estimates of willingness to pay to avoid the discrete changes in the characteristic are relatively close. Note that a first order approximation using the marginal values: $\widehat{WTP} = \Delta z_c \frac{\partial h(z)}{\partial z_c}$ is close to the estimates of the discrete change. The discrepancy is greatest for the generalized Box-Cox of the last row, where $\Delta z_c \frac{\partial h(z)}{\partial z_c} = 50 \times -0.063 = -3.15$, compared with the discrete change of -2.74. This is natural because for this function, the departure from linearity is greatest. Also the parameter has less relative precision than in the other functional forms.

For the sample of observations that we are utilizing, the estimates of willingness to pay for a change in an environmental characteristic are similar in concept but fairly different in application from other types of valuation. A number of issues cloud the use of hedonics. The estimates of WTP are present discounted values, because the house itself is an asset. Tax deductions for interest payments create a wedge between a change in the price of housing and willingness to pay. The change in the environmental attribute may vary substantially among households because the distribution of the environmental characteristic varies among houses. Calculating aggregate WTP for a policy that affects the distribution of the environmental characteristic requires some efforts in understanding the spatial distribution of the characteristic.[4]

Example 35 *A Hedonic Model with Housing Attributes*

To emphasize the importance of including the housing attributes rather than the assessed value of the structure, we estimate another hedonic model for illustration. The environmental disamenity in this case is the nitrogen reading in well water. The houses are part of the suburban housing market of Baltimore, Maryland. When a house with well water (as opposed to publicly provided water) is sold, the water must be tested. The test includes measurement of nitrate levels in the water. High levels of nitrates typically stem from excess agricultural nutrients and are

[4]The Leggett-Bockstael paper evaluates a strategy of water quality improvements to a subset of the houses that is based on a knowledge of the distribution of water quality in the housing market and provides a realistic scenario for valuing changes in water quality.

undesirable for medical reasons.[5] The standard for nitrates is 10 ppm. Levels higher than that must be treated, although rather inexpensive filters work well.

We provide this illustration to emphasize the importance of housing attributes, as well as to reinforce the workings of the hedonic model. The variables are given in Table 9.4. This model has the attributes of the house, plus the additional neighborhood covariates, the scores of third grade students on achievement tests and location variables. The sales price is the actual selling price, and the transactions occurred during the period 1985 to 1991.

TABLE 9.4. Hedonic Price Function Variables

Variable	Description	Mean n=1853
PRICE	Sales price	202719.00
TIMETREND	Monthly time trend, running from 1 to 84 over the months of sales	69.23
NUMBED	Number of bedrooms	3.59
FULLBATH	Number of full baths	1.98
LIVAREA	Square feet of living area	1070.80
LOTSIZE	Lot size in acres	24.10
DIST	Distance to Baltimore	4.04
SCORE	Neighborhood elementary school test score	0.18
NITRATE	Nitrates in well in ppm	4.05
PUBSEW*	House on public sewer	0.25
HALFBATH	Number of half baths	0.66
POOLIN*	Inground pool	0.06
HEATPUMP*	Heatpump	0.49
CARROLL*	House in Carroll County	0.35
HOWARD*	House in Howard County	0.13
BALTO*	House in Baltimore County	0.28

*Indicator variables taking a value of one if the condition holds.

We estimate only two of the four models that were estimated for the waterfront data in the previous section: the linear and the semi-log (in

[5] More details about the effects of nitrates and the implications of a suite of models for the value of nitrate can be found in the dissertation by McCormick. We thank Charles McCormick for giving us access to the data.

which the dependent variable is the logarithm of price). This is perhaps more typical of hedonic practice, though it is still good procedure to test the basic formulations for variations, especially when gauging the effects of an environmental variable. One of the results of the Cropper *et al.* simulations demonstrates that less prominent attributes are more likely to show instability with respect to specification or measurement error than the critical variables, such as the number of bedrooms. Table 9.5 provides parameter estimates for the two OLS models.

TABLE 9.5. Hedonic Model with Housing Attributes

	Transformation			
	$\mu = 1$ $\lambda = 1$		$\mu = 0$ $\lambda = 1$	
Characteristic	Estimate	S.E.	Estimate	S.E.
TIMETREND	[b]−254.0	137.9	−0.00014	0.0006
NUMBED	[a]15206	1856	[a]0.082	0.008
FULLBATH	[a]22772	2140	[a]0.127	0.009
LIVAREA	[a]129.4	5.45	[a]0.00055	0.00002
LOTSIZE	[a]4085.2	291	[a]0.018	0.0012
DIST	[a]−2042.1	244	[a]−0.0077	0.001
SCORE	[a]9123.3	3672	[a]0.037	0.016
NITRATES	[a]−1151.5	384	−0.0036	0.0017
HALFBATH	[a]16805	1969	[a]0.105	0.009
POOLIN	[a]8762.4	4296	[a]0.062	0.018
HEATPUMP	[a]35270	2325	[a]0.173	0.01
PUBSEW	138.0	2436	−0.0002	0.01
CARROLL	[a]11752	2979	[a]0.053	0.013
HOWARD	[a]59708	4010	[a]0.254	0.017
BALTO	[a]22798	3728	[a]0.103	0.016
Constant	[a]−57425	20188	[a]10.78	0.87
Log-likelihood	−22467.00		421.50	
$-2ln(L_R/L_U)$	2506.00		2706.00	
Adjusted R^2	0.74		0.76	

[a]Different from zero at the 95% level of confidence.
[b]Different from zero at the 90% level of confidence.

The specification includes the indicator variables for the counties, as well housing attributes. The county indicators should also be considered location variables, although one might test for whether the housing markets really are the same.[6] For this model, we give the adjusted R^2, a measure of goodness of fit for ordinary least squares models. The advantage of including attributes can best be assessed with the linear model. The housing attributes with which most people are familiar, such as bedrooms and bathrooms, are valued directly with the linear model. So we can see directly that the marginal value of an extra bedroom is about \$15000 and the value of an additional full bath about \$22000. The semi-log function gives approximate percent changes in housing prices from a change in the attribute level. So, for example, an extra bedroom would imply an increment in price of about \$16500 for a house worth \$200000.

The results of the estimation can be used to value changes in the environmental disamenity, nitrates in the well water. Consider an increase in nitrates from 10 to 15 parts per million. The linear model predicts the willingness to pay to avoid an increase in NITRATES: $\widehat{WTP} = \Delta z_c \frac{\partial h(z)}{\partial z_c} = 5 \times 1151 = \$5755$. We can calculate a 95% confidence interval with the standard error on the coefficient of NITRATES, which is 384; the 95% confidence interval is $5755 \pm 5 \times 1.96 \times 384$ which gives the interval \$1992 to \$9518. For the semi-log, when the house is valued at \$200000, $\frac{\partial h(z)}{\partial z_c} = 200000 \times -0.0036 = -\$720$. This is a fair amount less than the linear model gives, and the WTP to avoid the increase in NITRATES is $5 \times 720 = \$3600$. Assuming the price is not a random variable, we calculate the 95% confidence interval as $200000 \times (0.0036 \pm 1.96 \times 0.0017) \times 5$, where the standard error of the coefficient on nitrates equals 0.0017. This confidence interval is \$268 to \$6932. As a consequence of predicting the percent change in the housing price, the coefficient has a larger variance on WTP, despite similar t-statistics. In both cases, the confidence intervals for finite changes in attributes are large, even when the coefficients are significant, even when the hedonic price is assumed constant. This suggests the need to look into random willingness to pay in greater depth.

9.4.3 Randomness of Willingness to Pay Estimates in Hedonic Models

In the development of contingent valuation models and the assorted travel cost models, we have emphasized the two steps involved in obtaining estimates of willingness to pay: estimation of parameters and

[6] A simple test for similar housing markets would be to test whether the vector of coefficients is the same for all four counties.

calculation of welfare measures. In the hedonic model, the two steps are present, but the estimation step receives much greater attention than the calculation stage. Despite the lesser prominence of the calculation step in hedonic models, it is worth considering the role of uncertainty in WTP estimates.

The typical estimate for the WTP of an owner of a housing unit is

$$WTP = h(\mathbf{z}^*) - h(\mathbf{z})$$

where $h(\mathbf{z})$ is the deterministic part of the hedonic price function. We can get some insight into the role of randomness by using the linear Box-Cox model. Solving for the price in the Box-Cox model gives

$$p = (\mu\mathbf{z}(\lambda)\boldsymbol{\alpha} + 1 + \varepsilon)^{1/\mu} = h(\mathbf{z}). \qquad (9.7)$$

In the linear case, $\mu = 1$ and the calculation is

$$WTP = [\mathbf{z}^*(\hat{\lambda}) - \mathbf{z}(\hat{\lambda})]\hat{\boldsymbol{\alpha}}$$

where the hats indicate that the parameters are estimates. When only characteristic c changes, the calculation is $WTP = [z_c^*(\hat{\lambda}) - z_c(\hat{\lambda})]\hat{\alpha}_c$. Now only the parameters contribute to randomness. If the model is completely linear, i.e., $\lambda = 1$, then the only randomness is in the coefficient $\hat{\alpha}_c$, which is asymptotically normally distributed $N(\alpha_c, \sigma_c^2)$. Consequently, in the linear case, WTP is normally distributed with $EWTP = \alpha_c(z_c^* - z_c)$ and variance $\sigma_c^2 \cdot (z^* - z)^2$. In the linear case we find randomness without resorting to an interpretation of the randomness of the hedonic function. If $\lambda \neq 1$ then the estimate of WTP is no longer normally distributed. The distribution can be simulated by getting the joint distribution of μ, λ and the relevant α_c's, and following the Krinsky-Robb procedure (see Chapter 4) of taking a large number of random draws from the joint distribution of parameters, calculating the WTP, and then forming the $(1 - x)100\%$ confidence interval by removing the $x/2$ proportion of largest and smallest values of simulated WTP.

Suppose that we have estimated the general Box-Cox model. The estimate of WTP is

$$\begin{aligned} WTP &= (\mu\mathbf{z}^*(\lambda)\boldsymbol{\alpha} + 1 + \varepsilon)^{1/\mu} - (\mu\mathbf{z}(\lambda)\boldsymbol{\alpha} + 1 + \varepsilon)^{1/\mu} \quad \mu \neq 0 \\ &= \exp(\mathbf{z}^*(\lambda)\boldsymbol{\alpha} + \varepsilon) - \exp(\mathbf{z}(\lambda)\boldsymbol{\alpha} + \varepsilon) \quad \mu = 0. \end{aligned} \qquad (9.8)$$

In these cases, WTP is not distributed normally. One can simply invoke consistency, and calculate the WTP at the probability limit of the random variables. It can also be handled with the Krinsky-Robb procedure. The estimation results give the variance-covariance matrix of all the parameters, and one can take a large number of draws from this distribution to simulate the distribution of WTP.

Consider an alternative approach that economizes on covariate information. Using expression (9.7), we can write

$$\mu\mathbf{z}(\lambda)\boldsymbol{\alpha}+1+\varepsilon=p^{\mu}.$$

Now denote the vector of covariates that change as $\bar{\mathbf{z}}$ so that $\mathbf{z}^{*}(\lambda)=\mathbf{z}(\lambda)+\boldsymbol{\Delta}\bar{\mathbf{z}}(\lambda)$. Then we can write WTP as

$$WTP=\left(p^{\mu}+\mu\boldsymbol{\Delta}\bar{\mathbf{z}}(\lambda)\boldsymbol{\alpha}\right)^{1/\mu}-p.$$

This expression is easier to calculate than the expression in equation (9.8). It won't be normally distributed unless $\mu=\lambda=1$. Randomness is here in terms of the parameters and the error in the hedonic price. One can accept the consistency result and substitute in the probability limits. Alternatively, one can utilize the Krinsky-Robb procedure outlined earlier, recognizing the sources of uncertainty.

9.5 Conclusion

This chapter has explored the econometrics of hedonic price modeling. Our treatment has been elementary, attempting to give a sense of the empirical approaches that one takes in hedonic modeling, without great detail. We have omitted some emerging issues. There seems good likelihood of heteroscedasticity, which can be addressed in a straightforward way. A more difficult but potentially more important problem is spatial autocorrelation, which also leads to heteroscedasticity. Leggett and Bockstael correct several of their models for heteroscedasticity, and they also explore the presence of spatial autocorrelation. The availability of housing price data is growing substantially in the US, due to electronic storage and retrieval. Datasets that include repeat sales are becoming more common. These datasets allow inferences about price changes over time, and hence allow one to assess empirically the change in environmental quality not just spatially but temporally.

10

New Directions in Non-market Valuation

In the concluding chapter we give a brief synopsis of several developments in non-market valuation that are increasingly present in the literature but have not been addressed in the previous chapters of the book. This treatment is brief. We give the flavor of the approaches, their advantages and refer to the more important papers or books on the topics.

10.1 Stated Preferences for Multiple Attributes

Until recently, the preferred approach to contingent valuation was to describe a given scenario and then to design a single question that required the respondent to choose between a desirable scenario with a monetary payment and some type of less desirable scenario, with no payment. Over the past decade, many economists working on valuing environmental amenities and public goods have turned to methods that are variously known as stated preferences, conjoint analysis, and attribute-based methods. These approaches evolved from evaluation methods for marketing and transportation. The methods present the respondent with a set of alternatives, each fully characterized by levels of attributes and a cost. Depending on the approach adopted, the respondent may rank the scenarios, choose the preferred scenario, or even rate the scenario on a cardinal scale. The framework for analysis of these questions has frequently been the random utility framework.

The essence of stated choice methods lies in the presentation to the respondent with numerous decisions over alternatives with multiple attributes. This characteristic turns stated choice methods into hedonic models, in the sense that the methods are able to provide measures of willingness to pay for discrete changes in a variety of attributes that are part of the choice. But they differ from the dichotomous choice contingent valuation in other ways too. Typically the problem is stated in the context of a private choice, rather than a public choice, even though the vehicle, such as a tax, may be the same. There are several advantages of this approach. It allows the researcher to combine revealed and stated preferences in a fairly detailed manner that deals with attributes. For example, one may combine behavioral data typically used for random utility models with similar data from stated preference experiments that would let researchers obtain parameter estimates that might not be available from either method alone. Further, because the stated preference methods value multiple attributes, results from these models can be used to manage the independent valuation and summation problem of Hoehn and Randall (1989). Consider two projects that pass a benefit-cost test simultaneously but independently. When these projects provide amenities that are substitutes, then when considered in isolation, the second one will provide less benefits than independent valuation would predict. This can be corrected when one accounts for the amenities that are inherent in a project. Using attribute-based stated preferences methods can help in this regard.

The literature on the multiple attribute stated preference methods has grown extensively. The recent book by Louviere, Hensher and Swait provides a complete reference on the topic. Holmes and Adamowicz give a good overview with intuitive treatment of the experimental design of questions. Hanemann and Kanninen build the basic statistical models for the estimation of preferences from these questions, depending on whether the respondents rank the alternatives, rate them cardinally or choose the preferred alternative.

Stated preference studies require extensive work on questionnaire development, just as dichotomous choice contingent valuation, but the experimental design literature plays a much more critical role in the development of scenarios. This can be understood from the basic setup of a multiple attribute stated preferences study. The preference elicitation part of a survey instrument has the following components:

- The number of attributes for a given alternative;
- The number of alternatives per choice occasion;
- The number of replications of choice occasions.

A given alternative is constructed with measurable attributes, even if discrete. Suppose there are attributes $q_1, ..., q_A, p$, where A is the number of attributes and p is the cost of the scenario. Although the researcher is free to choose as many attributes as desired, the larger the number of attributes, the more difficult the choice for the respondent. Further, increases in the number of attributes raise the effective sample size required to obtain a given level of precision on parameter estimates.

Mostly for reasons of ensuring coherent answers from respondents, researchers tend to limit A, the number of attributes, to three or four. For example, Mazzotta, Opaluch, and Grigalunas study the preservation of wetlands and shellfish areas on Long Island, in New York state. They offer respondents a choice between the status quo, at zero price, and two other priced options, with varying levels of wetlands and shellfish areas. By observing the choice among alternatives, they could estimate preferences for the attributes that comprised each alternative. In this case the attributes were various forms of land use.

Given the selection of the attributes to be valued and the range over which the attributes are to be varied, the researcher can determine the alternatives to be presented to respondents. The number of choice occasions is the size of the choice set. Let S^1 be an alternative that is fully described by $q_1^1, ...q_A^1, p^1 = \mathbf{q}^1, p^1$. A choice or ranking is made when the respondent is presented with alternative $S^1, ..., S^N$, where N is the number of alternatives offered. An essential property of the choices is that they are mutually exclusive. Then under appropriate separability restrictions on a respondent's preference function, one can write the utility for a given alternative. If a respondent chooses S^1 then he could not also choose S^2 (or any other S).

The alternatives need to be constructed so that the respondent is forced to make trade-offs. That is, if one scenario dominates the rest in the choice occasion in the sense that it has more of all good attributes and less of all the bad attributes, then little would be learned in the choice. Although increasing the number of scenarios or alternatives (N) per choice occasion is a way of increasing the precision of parameter estimates, forcing the respondent to choose among too many alternatives may make the outcomes less meaningful. Depending on the choice setting, the number of alternatives or scenarios per choice occasion is typically not much larger than a handful, but it of course depends on how familiar the respondent is with the attributes of the alternatives.

Finally, the researcher may provide multiple choice occasions by repeating the experiments for a given respondent, but varying the alternatives from one replication to the next. If respondents don't grow weary from additional choice occasions, and they answer consistently across occasions, then adding another choice occasion is like obtaining a bigger sample but of course with considerably less cost. Hence there is a temptation to offer many choice occasions. Here too the researcher must be cognizant of the potential excess burden imposed on the cognitive ability of respondents. They may handle a few choices well but adopt a simpler choice method when the number of replications becomes excessive. For example, a recent study of sportsfishing by the National

Marine Fisheries Service gave the respondent four choice occasions. For each choice occasions, the respondent would choose among three alternatives: two trips and the alternative of not taking a trip. And each alternative contained four attributes and a cost per trip.

The combinations of attributes, alternatives and replications that are feasible is a subject of substantial research in the stated preference literature. In a study of the implications of more attributes, larger choice sets, and more alternatives, Swait and Adamowicz analyzed six stated preference studies in which the number of attributes ranged from five to 15, the alternatives ranged from three to six, and the number of replications ranged from eight to 16. They found that the variance of tastes increased when the alternatives were similar and when the number attributes increased. They did not analyze the effects of increased replications.

Discrete choice contingent valuation and multiple attribute stated preferences share many common traits, and typically attempt to assess the same part of a respondent's preferences. For both approaches, great care is needed in devising questions that induce the responses that reveal preferences suitably. One of the biggest difference between discrete choice CV methods and attribute-based methods is the need for experimental design in the construction of alternatives and replications in attribute-based stated preferences methods. Experimental design is absolutely essential for a credible and defensible stated preference study.

The need for experimental design stems from the complete control that the researcher exercises over the values of exogenous variables. In the experimental design literature, the independent variables or attributes are known as factors, and the values they take on are factor levels. A full factorial design for a survey creates an alternative for each possible combination of all factors or attributes. For example, suppose that the attribute-price set is q_1, q_2, p and the attributes and prices can take on $(3, 4, 5)$ values (q_1 takes on three values, q_2 four values, etc.). Then there are $3 \cdot 4 \cdot 5 = 60$ possible combinations in a full factorial design. When some portion of the full factorial design is included it is a fractional factorial design.

The key design issues stem from selecting the appropriate fractional design. To illustrate, consider an illustrative case of two attributes–water quality and price. Suppose that water quality takes on low, medium and high values, and the price is \$10, \$20, and \$30. The full factorial design is given in the following Table 10.1. If low water quality is always offered with \$10, medium with \$20, and high with \$30, then there will be perfect collinearity and one will not be able to disentangle the two effects. On the other hand, if high, \$10 is compared with low, \$20, there's no trade-

TABLE 10.1. An Elementary Design Matrix

Low, $10	Low, $20	Low, $30
Medium, $10	Medium,$20	Medium, $30
High, $10	High,$20	High, $30

off for the respondents and hence nothing to be learned. Numerous other difficulties can arise without careful preparation of the exogenous variables. The chapter by Holmes and Adamowicz and the book by Louviere, Hensher and Swait provide excellent coverage of the design problems.

The estimation and welfare calculations that are applied with multiple attribute stated preference experiments are much the same as applied to random utility models of Chapter 8. Given the mutually exclusive assumption about the scenarios, one can then write the utility from a particular alternative, say j, as

$$U^*(S^j, y - p_j) = U(\mathbf{q}^j, y - p_j).$$

By choosing among the scenarios or ranking the scenarios respondents implicitly reveal preferences for the attributes $q_1^j, ..., q_A^j$. If $U(\mathbf{q}, y - p_j)$ has an additive random term that is distributed extreme value, then the choice or ranking decisions will allow the estimation of conditional logit models, using stated choices rather than revealed choices as in Chapter 8. In practice, the preference function $U(\mathbf{q}, y - P_j)$ is expressed as a linear function of the q's and sometimes of their interactions, including quadratic terms. The ability to estimate interaction and quadratic terms is enhanced by the experimental control of the attributes. And the estimation of these non-linear terms gives the stated preference methods the ability to determine substitutes and complements, as well as declining marginal values. Ranking and choice result in similar econometrics, because choice simply means ranking the best scenario.

The stated preference approaches for multiple attributes provide more information than dichotomous choice CV because they involve respondents in more choices. By inducing more choices per respondent, one gets more information about preferences, and better precision on preference parameter estimates. Further, when one of the scenarios (or alternatives) is the status quo, the calculation of WTP relative to the status quo is easily done.

Multiple attribute approaches are not complete substitutes for dichotomous choice CV. Extensive information must be conveyed to respondents, making the method unlikely to succeed on the phone or in any setting where the interview is conducted orally.

10.2 Mixed Logit Models

In an econometric sense, the stated preference models are closer to site choice models than might appear. In effect, each site choice model has a number of 'experiments' for each respondent. In a site choice model, an individual chooses a particular site, but the sites that are not chosen are also part of the analysis, and influence the parameter estimates and standard errors. An econometrics program does not know the difference between more alternatives per individual and additional individuals, despite the fact that individuals may differ greatly. The random parameter or mixed logit model is one approach for dealing with randomness that is individual-specific. The initial applications of this model to recreational demand are due to Train (1998, 1999), though the model has a much longer history. Additional applications include Breffle and Morey. The mixed logit model assumes that the parameters of the logit model have errors that are specific to the individual. A simple mixed logit model would follow from the utility for alternative j for individual i with C attributes:

$$u_j^i = \sum_{c=1}^{C} z_{jc}\tilde{\beta}_{ci} + \varepsilon_j.$$

For this model, the parameters are taken to be random but distributed independently of the utility errors. Typically the parameters have the following form:

$$\tilde{\beta}_{ci} = \beta_c + \eta_{ci}$$

where the η_{ci} may be $N(0, \sigma_c^2)$. Utility for individual i can then be written

$$u_j^i = \sum_{c=1}^{C}(z_{jc}\beta_c + z_{jc}\eta_{ci}) + \varepsilon_j.$$

When the ε_j have the type I extreme value distribution, independently distributed across individuals and sites, the probability that individual i chooses site j out of J alternatives becomes

$$\Pr{}_i(j) = \int_S \frac{\exp(\sum_{c=1}^{C}(z_{jc}\beta_c + z_{jc}\eta_{ci}))}{\sum_{k=1}^{J}\exp(\sum_{c=1}^{C}(z_{kc}\beta_c + z_{kc}\eta_{ci}))} f(\eta)d\eta$$

where $f(\eta)$ is the joint density of the parameter errors. Because the randomness makes the potential behavior much richer, the mixed logit model can approximate any form of probability. Note that IIA does not hold, because the ratio of probabilities for sites j and k becomes

$$\begin{aligned}\frac{\Pr_i(j)}{\Pr_i(k)} &= \int_S \frac{\exp(\sum_{c=1}^{C}(z_{jc}\beta_c + z_{jc}\eta_{ci}))}{\sum_{k=1}^{J}\exp(\sum_{c=1}^{C}(z_{kc}\beta_c + z_{kc}\eta_{ci}))} f(\boldsymbol{\eta})d\boldsymbol{\eta} \div \\ &\quad \int_S \frac{\exp(\sum_{c=1}^{C}(z_{jc}\beta_c + z_{jc}\eta_{ci}))}{\sum_{k=1}^{J}\exp(\sum_{c=1}^{C}(z_{kc}\beta_c + z_{kc}\eta_{ci}))} f(\boldsymbol{\eta})d\boldsymbol{\eta}.\end{aligned}$$

This does not factor the way the logit model does, so that the ratio of probabilities depends on the attributes of all of the alternatives. For almost all versions of the density function, closed forms for this probability are not available. Instead estimation by simulation is used, in which the parameters functions of the distributions of both errors. The mixed logit model also requires numerical integration to calculate welfare effects. Train (forthcoming) gives a thorough analysis of the method and guidance for implementing the mixed logit.

The intuitive advantage of the mixed logit model comes from covariance among the errors, consistent with the panel-like structure of the data. Suppose that the η_{ci} are distributed independently with variance $V(.)$. The covariance between two utilities for individual i for alternatives j and k is

$$\begin{aligned}cov(u_j^i, u_k^h) &= \sum_{c=1}^{C} z_{kc}^2 V(\eta_{ci}) + V(\varepsilon_j)\ i = h\,, j = k \\ &= \sum_{c=1}^{C} z_{kc} z_{jc} V(\eta_{ci})\ i = h\,, j \neq k \\ &= 0\ i \neq h.\end{aligned}$$

This error structure exposes the panel-like data that make up a dataset for a random utility model. Additional choices in a dataset are correlated within an individual's cases. As in the standard RUM, the correlation between any two alternatives for different individuals is zero. The mixed logit model captures the nature of randomness better than the simple logit model, but it comes at the cost of more complex estimation and more strategic estimation decisions. With the mixed logit model one also needs to choose the distribution for the random part of parameters. These choices include which parameters to make random, whether to make parameters correlated, and what distributions the parameters will have. Packaged programs such as LIMDEP now estimate mixed logit models. But the number of strategic decisions the researcher must make with a mixed logit model is expanded, and the latitude for different results from different strategic models grows.

The more common way of forming panel data is to combine time-series and cross-sections of observations. Forming a panel when the individual makes decisions at different times can help remove some individual-specific errors with unknown but perhaps unattractive properties. These properties, being unknown, are assumed away in cross-sectional analysis. And even when the models estimated are like the mixed logit models, there may be choice-specific errors that do not disappear. True observations of individual choices at different points in time can provide additional support for valuation models that current models are unable to provide.

10.3 Combining Stated and Revealed Preferences

Researchers have begun combining stated and revealed preference models in an attempt to cross-validate results from each. Initially the motivation behind such models was to use behavioral observation from individuals to ground the hypothetical responses from a stated preference survey in observable behavior. The idea that was more or less openly accepted was that the revealed preferences somehow were closer to the truth than stated preferences. This interpretation has been called into question for a number of reasons. Revealed preferences are typically based on observations from market outcomes. However, the institutional setting of the markets can influence the market outcomes. There are as many cues in a market transaction as there are in CV questions. Further, while behavior may be observed, behavior and values are connected by strategic research decisions and substantial randomness in non-linear functions. So-called revealed values are difficult to validate because real values are typically not observable. As such, assuming revealed behavior represents the benchmark for validating stated responses calls into question the test itself. Randall (1998) gives a succinct summary of the problems and benefits of combining revealed and stated preferences:

> In a number of research contexts, the consistency of the two kinds of data has been established, typically after applying some kind of endogenous scaling method (e.g., Cameron, 1992; Adamowicz, Louviere and Williams, 1994). Given our culture as economists, there is always a tendency to treat one of the datasets (typically an observed choice data set) as a benchmark against which to scale data generated by the other(s)... I would caution that we have less reason than we think for maintaining the premise of differential validity; it

> makes more sense to learn everything that can be learned by combining these kinds of data sets without imposing preconceived notions of their validity.

The combination of stated and revealed preference responses can come in a number of forms. Through proper scaling, revealed and stated choices of combinations of product attributes can be pooled (stacked) to estimate jointly parameters of attributes. The methodology has been applied to value non-market goods (e.g., Adamowicz, Louviere *et al.*, 1994; Adamowicz, Swait *et al.*, 1997). An important issue is whether the two types of discrete choices can be pooled together under a single preference structure. Swait and Louviere (1993) develop a procedure to test for compatibility of revealed and stated choices and to estimate the relative variances in these two types of data. The compatibility of revealed and stated choices is often supported by these studies. For example, Whitehead, Haab and Huang (2000) use reported recreation trips to the Albemarle and Pamlico Sounds in North Carolina as the baseline revealed behavior. Then they hypothetically change the water quality in the Sounds and ask respondents for their stated future number of trips under the hypothetical change. Because water quality does not vary significantly in the Sounds over a given short time period, it is difficult to identify WTP for quality changes using revealed behavior in a single site framework (see Chapter 6). Loomis (1993) has shown that stated preferences for recreation trips under hypothetical quality changes can in fact be reliable and valid approximations to actual trips. Including stated responses to hypothetical changes in water quality allows for the identification of parameters associated with water quality that otherwise would be unidentified. Englin and Cameron, and Layman, Boyce and Criddle also combine revealed trips with stated trip intentions to improve the efficiency of estimates of WTP for water quality improvements.

In other examples of combining revealed and stated preferences researchers have combined recreation trips with dichotomous choice contingent valuation responses to elicit WTP for site amenities (see for example, Cameron, 1992, Englin and Cameron, 1996; Huang, Haab, and Whitehead; McConnell, Weninger and Strand; Niklitscek and Leon; and Loomis (1997)). By deriving the WTP function and recreation demand function from the same preference structure it is possible to test the consistency of preferences across revealed and stated responses. Huang, Haab and Whitehead urge caution in using this approach as it is important to ensure that the baseline reference level of site amenities are the same across the revealed and stated preference responses. For example, if past trips are used as the revealed preference measures, but the

WTP question is asked in terms of a future quality change, the reference level of site amenities may differ and the preference structures may be inconsistent across the revealed and stated responses. the reference level of site amenities may differ and the preference structures may be inconsistent across the revealed and stated responses.

10.4 Preview

Throughout the book, we have discussed the construction, specification, and estimation of models for behavioral and stated preference data. In the empirical analysis, the models have been estimated from cross-sectional data exclusively. These cross-sectional analyses have been useful for understanding models and for developing techniques. A danger of continuing to rely on cross-section data comes from the potential for omitted variables. This difficulty can be alleviated in part with panel data. A further advantage of panel data on individual behavior lies in its ability to model temporal substitution. Such data requires multi-period surveys, and carries all the problems attendant with collecting panel data. But for serious corroboration of non-market values, such as one finds in Chay and Greenstone, such data is essential.

References

Adamowicz, W., J. Louviere and M. Williams (1994), 'Combining Revealed and Stated Preference Methods for Valuing Environmental Amenities', *Journal of Environmental Economics and Management,* **26**, 271-92.

Adamowicz, W., J. Swait, P. Boxall, J. Louviere and M. Williams (1997), 'Perceptions versus Objective Measures of Environmental Quality in Combined Revealed and Stated Preference Models of Environmental Valuation', *Journal of Environmental Economics and Management,* **32**, 65-84.

Alberini, A. (1995a), 'Optimal Designs for Discrete Choice Contingent Valuation Surveys', *Journal of Environmental Economics and Management,* **28**, 287-306.

— (1995b), 'Efficiency vs Bias of Willingness-to-Pay Estimates: Bivariate and Interval-Data Models', *Journal of Environmental Economics and Management,* **29**, 169-80.

Alberini, A., B. Kanninen and R. Carson (1997), 'Modeling Response Incentive Effects in Dichotomous Choice Contingent Valuation', *Land Economics,* **73**, 309-24.

An, M. and R. Ayala (1996), 'A Mixture Model of Willingness to Pay', Department of Economics Working Paper, Duke University.

Arrow, K., R. Solow, P.R. Portney, E.E. Leamer, R. Radner and H. Schuman (1993), 'Report of the NOAA Panel on Contingent Valuation', *Federal Register*, **58**, 4601-14.

Ayer, M., H.D. Brunk, G.M. Ewing, W.T. Reid and E. Silverman (1955), 'An Empirical Distribution Function for Sampling with Incomplete Information', *Annals of Mathematical Statistics,* **26**, 641-7.

Bartik, T.J. (1982), 'Measuring the Benefits of Amenity Improvements in Hedonic Price Models', *Land Economics*, **64**, 172-83.

Bartik, T.J. and V.K. Smith (1987), 'Urban Amenities and Public Policy', in E.S. Mills, ed., *Handbook on Urban Economics,* Amsterdam: North Holland Publishers.

Becker, G.S. (1965), 'A Theory of the Allocation of Time', *Economic Journal,* **75**, 493-517.

Ben-Akiva, M., and S.R. Lerman (1985), *Discrete Choice Analysis: Theory and Application to Travel Demand,* Boston, MA: MIT Press.

Bishop, R.C. and T.A. Heberlein (1979), 'Measuring Values of Extra-market Goods: Are Indirect Measures Biased?', *American Journal of Agricultural Economics,* **61**, 926-30.

Bockstael, N.E., W.M. Hanemann and C. Kling (1987), 'Modeling Recreational Demand in a Multiple Site Framework', *Water Resources Research,* **23**, 951-60.

Bockstael, N.E., M. Hanemann and I.E. Strand (1986), 'Measuring the Benefits of Water Quality Improvement Using Recreation Demand Models', Environmental Protection Agency, Cooperative Agreement CR-81143-01-1.

Bockstael, N.E. and K.E. McConnell (1993), 'Public Goods as Characteristics of Non-Market Commodities', *Economic Journal,* **103**, 1244-57.

Bockstael, N.E., K.E. McConnell, and I. E. Strand (1991), 'Recreation Benefits', in J. Braden and C. Kolstad, eds., *Measuring the Demand for Environmental Quality,* Amsterdam: North Holland Press, 227-70.

Bockstael, N.E. and I.E. Strand (1987), 'The Effect of Common Sources of Regression Error on Benefit Estimation', *Land Economics,* **63**, 11-18.

Bockstael, N.E., I.E. Strand and W.M. Hanemann, (1987), 'Time and the Recreation Demand Model', *American Journal of Agricultural Economics* **69**, 293-302.

Bockstael, N.E., I.E. Strand, K.E. McConnell and F. Arsanjani (1990), 'Sample Selection Bias in the Estimation of Recreation Demand Functions', *Land Economics,* **66**, 40-49.

Bowker, J.M. and J.R. Stoll (1988), 'Use of Dichotomous Nonmarket Methods to Value the Whooping Crane Resource', *American Journal of Agricultural Economics,* **70**, 372-81.

Boyle, K.J. and R.C. Bishop (1988), 'Welfare Measurement Using Contingent Valuation: A Comparison of Techniques', *American Journal of Agricultural Economics,* **70**, 20-28.

Boyle, K.J., M.P. Welsh and R.C. Bishop (1988), 'Validation of Empirical Measures of Welfare Change: Comment', *Land Economics,* **64**, 94-98.

Boyle, K.J., M.P. Welsh and R.C. Bishop (1993), 'The Role of Question Order and Respondent Experience in Contingent-Valuation Studies', *Journal of Environmental Economics and Management,* **25**, S80-S99.

Breffle, W.S. and E.R. Morey (2000),'Investigating Preference Heterogeneity in a Repeated Discrete-Choice Recreation Demand Model of Atlantic Salmon Fishing', *Marine Resource Economics,* **15**, 1-20.

Brookshire, D.S., M.A. Thayer, W.D. Schulze and R.C. d'Arge (1982), 'Valuing Public Goods: A Comparison of Survey and Hedonic Approaches', *American Economic Review,* **72**, 165-77.

Brookshire, D.S., M.A. Thayer, J. Tschirhart and W. D. Schulze (1985), 'A Test of the Expected Utility Model: Evidence from Earthquake Risks', *Journal of Political Economy,* **93**, 369-89.

Brown, T.C., P.A. Champ, R.C. Bishop and D.W. McCollum (1996), 'Which Response Format Reveals the Truth about Donations to a Public Good?', *Land Economics,* **72**, 152-66.

Brownstone, D. and K.A. Small (1989), 'Efficient Estimation of Nested Logit Models', *Journal of Business and Economic Statistics,* 7, 67-74.

Burt, O.R. and D. Brewer (1971), 'Estimation of Net Social Benefits from Outdoor Recreation', *Econometrica,* **39**, 813-27.

Calfee, J. and C. Winston (1998), 'The Value of Automobile Travel Time: Implications for Congestion Policy', *Journal of Public Economics,* **69**, 83-102.

Cameron, A.C. and P.K. Trivedi (1986), 'Econometric Models Based on Count Data: Comparisons and Applications of Some Estimators and Tests', *Journal of Applied Econometrics,* **1**, 29-53.

Cameron, T. (1987), 'A New Paradigm for Valuing Non-Market Goods Using Referendum Data: Maximum Likelihood Estimation by Censored Logit Regression', *Journal of Environmental Economics and Management,* **15**, 355-79.

— (1991), 'Interval Estimates of Non-Market Resource Values from Referendum Contingent Valuation Surveys', *Land Economics,* **67**, 413-21.

— (1992), 'Combining Contingent Valuation and Travel Cost Data for the Valuation of Nonmarket Goods', *Land Economics,* **68**, 302-17.

Cameron, T.A. and M.D. James (1987), 'Efficient Estimation Methods for Use with "Closed-Ended" Contingent Valuation Survey Data', *Review of Economics and Statistics,* **69**, 269-76.

Cameron, T.A. and J. Quiggin (1994), 'Estimation Using Contingent Valuation Data from a "Dichotomous Choice with Follow-Up" Questionnaire', *Journal of Environmental Economics and Management,* **27**, 218-34.

Cameron, T.A., W.D. Shaw, S.E. Ragland, J. Mac Callaway and S. Keefe (1996), 'Using Actual and Contingent Behavior Data with Differing Levels of Time Aggregation to Model Recreation Demand', *Journal of Agricultural and Resource Economics,* **21**, 130-49.

Carson, Richard T. (2000), 'Contingent Valuation: A User's Guide', *Environmental Science & Technology,* **34**, 1413-18.

— (forthcoming, 2002) *Contingent Valuation: A Comprehensive Bibliography and History,* Northampton, MA: Edward Elgar.

Carson, R.T., N.E. Flores, K.M. Martin, and J.L. Wright (1996), 'Contingent Valuation and Revealed Preference Methodologies: Comparing the Estimates for Quasi-Public Goods', *Land Economics,* **72**, 113-28.

Carson, R.T, Groves, T. and M. Machina (2000), 'Incentive and Informational Properties of Preference Questions', University of California, San Diego Working Paper.

Carson, R.T., W.M. Hanemann, R.Kopp, J.A. Krosnick, R.C. Mitchell, S. Presser, P.A. Ruud and V.K. Smith (1994), 'Prospective Interim Lost Use Value Due to DDT and PCB Contamination in the Southern California Bight', NOAA Contract No. 50-DGNC-1-00007.

Carson, R.T., W.M. Hanemann, R.Kopp, J.A. Krosnick, R.C. Mitchell, S. Presser, P.A. Ruud, V.K. Smith, M. Conaway and K. Martin (1998), 'Referendum Design and Contingent Valuation: The NOAA Panel's No-Vote Recommendation', *The Review of Economics and Statistics,* **80**, 484-7.

Carson, R.T. and R.C. Mitchell (1993), 'The Value of Clean Water: The Public's Willingness to Pay for Boatable, Fishable, and Swimmable Quality Water', *Water Resources Research,* **29**, 2445-54.

Carson, R., R. Mitchell, W.M. Hanemann, R. Kopp, S. Presser and P. Ruud (1992), 'A Contingent Valuation Study of Lost Passive Use Value from the Exxon Valdez Oil Spill', Report to the Attorney General of Alaska, reprinted by Natural Resource Damage Assessment, Inc.

Chay, K.Y. and M. Greenstone (2000), 'Does Air Quality Matter? Evidence from the Housing Market', University of Chicago Department of Economics Working Paper.

Chen, H. and A. Randall (1997), 'Semi-nonparametric Estimation of Binary Response Models with an Application to Natural Resource Valuation', *Journal of Econometrics*, **76**, 323-40.

Clawson, Marion (1959), 'Methods of Measuring the Demand for and the Value of Outdoor Recreation', Reprint No. 10, Resources for the Future.

Cooper, J., W.M. Hanemann and G. Signorelli (forthcoming), 'One and One-half Bids for Contingent Valuation', *The Review of Economics and Statistics.*

Cooper, J. and J. Loomis (1992), 'Sensitivity of Willingness-to-Pay Estimates to Bid Design in Dichotomous Choice Contingent Valuation Models', *Land Economics,* **68**, 211-24.

Cosslett, S.R. (1981), 'Efficient Estimation of Discrete-Choice Models' in C. Manski and D. McFadden, eds., *Structural Analysis of Discrete Data with Econometric Applications,* Cambridge, MA: MIT Press.

— (1982), 'Distribution-Free Maximum Likelihood Estimator of the Binary Choice Model', *Econometrica,* **51**, 765-82.

Cragg, J.G. (1971), 'Some Statistical Models for Limited Dependent Variables with Applications to the Demand for Durable Goods', *Econometrica,* **39**, 829-44.

Creel, M. and J. Loomis (1990), 'Theoretical and Empirical Advantages of Truncated Count Data Estimators for Analysis of Deer Hunting in California', *American Journal of Agricultural Economics,* **72**, 434-41.

— (1991a), 'Confidence Intervals for Welfare Measures with Application to a Problem of Truncated Counts', *The Review of Economics and Statistics*, **73**, 370-73.

— (1991b), 'Confidence Intervals for Evaluating Benefits Estimates from Dichotomous Choice Contingent Valuation Studies', *Land Economics*, **67**, 64-73.

Cropper, M.L., L.B. Deck and K.E. McConnell (1988), 'On the Choice of Functional Form for Hedonic Price Equations', *The Review of Economics and Statistics,* **70**, 668-75.

Cummings, R.G., S. Elliott, G.W. Harrison and J. Murphy (1997), 'Are Hypothetical Referenda Incentive Compatible?', *Journal of Political Economy,* **105**, 609-21.

Curtis, John A. (1998), 'Valuing Preferences for Deer Management in Maryland' Unpublished Ph.D. Dissertation, University of Maryland Department of Agricultural and Resource Economics.

Domencich, T. and D. McFadden (1975), *Urban Travel Demand-A Behavioral Analysis*, Amsterdam: North Holland Publishers.

Duffield, J.W. (1991), 'Existence and Nonconsumptive Values for Wildlife: Application to Wolf Recovery in Yellowstone National Park', Western Regional Research Project W-133, Benefits and Costs in Natural Resources Planning, Fourth Interim Report.

Duffield, J.W. and D.A. Patterson (1991), 'Inference and Optimal Design for a Welfare Measure in Dichotomous Choice Contingent Valuation', *Land Economics,* **67**, 225-39.

Englin, J. and T.A. Cameron (1996), 'Augmenting Travel Cost Models with Contingent Behavior Data: Poisson Regression Analyses with Individual Panel Data', *Environmental and Resource Economics,* **7**, 133-47.

Englin, J. and J.S. Shonkwiler (1995), 'Estimating Social Welfare Using Count Data Models: An Application to Long-Run Recreation Demand under Conditions of Endogenous Stratification and Truncation', *The Review of Economics and Statistics,* **77,** 104-12.

Epple, D. (1987), 'Hedonic Prices and Implicit Markets: Estimating Demand and Supply Functions for Differentiated Markets', *Journal of Political Economy,* **95**, 59-80.

Freeman III, A.M. (1993), *The Measurement of Environmental and Resource Values: Theory and Methods*, Resources for the Future, Washington D.C.

Gayer, T., J.T. Hamilton and K.Viscusi (2000), 'Private Values of Risk Trade-offs at Superfund Sites: Housing Market Evidence on Learning about Risk', *The Review of Economics and Statistics,* **82**, 439-51.

Godfrey, L.G. (1988), *Misspecification Tests in Econometrics: The Lagrange Multiplier Principle and Other Approaches*, Cambridge, MA: Cambridge University Press.

Greene, W.H. (1995), *LIMDEP Version 7.0: User's Manual*, Bellport, NY: Econometric Software.

— (1997), *Econometric Analysis*, 3rd edition, New Jersey: Prentice-Hall, Inc.

Hausman, J. and D. McFadden (1984), 'Specification Tests for Multinomial Logit Models', *Journal of Econometrics,* **52,** 1219-40.

Haab, T.C. (1999), 'Nonparticipation or Misspecification? The Impacts of Nonparticipantion on Dichotomous Choice Contingent Valuation', *Environmental and Resource Economics,* **14,** 443-61.

— (forthcoming), 'Temporal Correlation in Models of Recreation Demand with Limited Data', *Journal of Environmental Economics and Management.*

Haab, T.C. and R. Hicks (1997), 'Accounting for Choice Set Endogeneity in Random Utility Models for Recreational Demand', *Journal of Environmental Economics and Management,* **34**, 127-47.

— (1999), 'Choice Set Considerations in Models of Recreation Demand: History and Current State of the Art', *Marine Resource Economics,* **14,** 255-70.

Haab, T.C., J.C. Huang and J.C. Whitehead (1999), 'Are Hypothetical Referenda Incentive Compatible? A Comment', *Journal of Political Economy*, **107**, 186-196.

Haab, T.C. and K.E. McConnell (1996), 'Count Data Models and the Problem of Zeros in Recreation Demand Analysis', *American Journal of Agricultural Economics,* **78**, 89-102.

— (1997), 'Referendum Models and Negative Willingness to Pay: Alternative Solutions', *Journal of Environmental Economics and Management,* **32**, 251-70.

— (1998), 'Referendum Models and Economic Values: Theoretical, Intuitive, and Practical Bounds on Willingness to Pay', *Land Economics,* **74**, 216-29.

Halvorsen, R. and H.O. Pollaskowski (1981), 'Choice of Functional Form for Hedonic Price Equations', *Journal of Urban Economics,* **10**, 37-49.

Hammack, Judd and Gardner M. Brown (1974), *Waterfowl and Wetlands: Towards Bioeconomic Analysis,* Johns Hopkins Press, Baltimore.

Hanemann, W.M. (1980), 'Measuring the Worth of Natural Resource Facilities: Comment', *Land Economics*, **56**, 482-90.

— (1982), 'Applied Welfare Analysis with Qualitative Response Models', Department of Agricultural and Resource Economics Working Paper No. 241, University of California at Berkeley.

— (1984), 'Welfare Evaluations in Contingent Valuation Experiments with Discrete Responses', *American Journal of Agricultural Economics,* **66**, 332-41.

— (1989), 'Welfare Evaluations in Contingent Valuation Experiments with Discrete Response Data: Reply', *American Journal of Agricultural Economics,* **71**, 1057-61.

— (1991), 'Willingness to Pay and Willingness to Accept: How Much Can They Differ?', *American Economic Review*, **81**, 635-47.

— (1999a), 'The Economic Theory of WTP and WTA' in Ian J. Bateman and Ken C. Willis eds., *Valuing Environmental Preferences: Theory and Practice of the Contingent Valuation Method in the US, EC, and Developing Countries*, Oxford: Oxford University Press.

— (1999b), 'Welfare Analysis with Discrete Choice Models', in Joseph Herriges and Catherine Kling, eds., *Valuing Recreation and the Environment*, Cheltenham, UK and Northampton, MA: Edward Elgar.

Hanemann, W.M. and B. Kanninen (1999), 'The Statistical Analysis of Discrete-Response CV Data', in Ian J. Bateman and Ken C. Willis, eds., *Valuing Environmental Preferences: Theory and Practice of the Contingent Valuation Method in the US, EC, and Developing Countries*, Oxford: Oxford University Press.

Hanemann, W.M. and B. Kriström (1995), 'Preference Uncertainty, Optimal Designs and Spikes' in P. Johansson, B. Kriström and K. Mäler, *Current Issues in Environmental Economics*, Manchester, UK: Manchester University Press, 58-77.

Hanemann, W., J. Loomis and B. Kanninen (1991), 'Statistical Efficiency of Double-Bounded Dichotomous Choice Contingent Valuation', *American Journal of Agricultural Economics,* **73**, 1255-63.

Harrison, D., Jr. and D.L. Rubinfeld (1978), 'Hedonic Housing Prices and the Demand for Clean Air', *Journal of Environmental Economics and Management,* **5**, 81-102.

Harrison, G. and B. Kriström (1995), 'On the Interpretation of Responses to Contingent Valuation Surveys', in P.O. Johansson, B. Kriström and K.G. Mäler, eds., *Current Issues in Environmental Economics*, Manchester, UK: Manchester University Press.

Hausman, J.A. (1981), 'Exact Consumer's Surplus and Deadweight Loss', *American Economic Review,* **71**, 662-76.

— (ed.), (1993), *Contingent Valuation, A Critical Assessment*, New York: North-Holland Publishers.

Hausman, J.A., G.K. Leonard and D. McFadden (1995), 'A Utility-Consistent, Combined Discrete Choice and Count Data Model: Assessing Use Losses Due to Natural Resource Damage', *Journal of Public Economics,* **56**, 1-30.

Heckman, J. (1979), 'Sample Selection Bias as a Specification Error', *Econometrica,* **47**, 153-61.

Hellerstein, D. (1991), 'Using Count Data Models in Travel Cost Analysis with Aggregate Data', *American Journal of Agricultural Economics,* **73**, 860-866.

Hellerstein, D. and R. Mendelsohn (1993), 'A Theoretical Foundation for Count Data Models', *American Journal of Agricultural Economics,* **75**, 604-11.

Herriges, J. and C. Kling (1999), 'Nonlinear Income Effects in Random Utility Models', *The Review of Economics and Statistics*, **81**, 62-73.

Herriges, J.A., C.L. Kling and D.J. Phaneuf (1999), 'Corner Solution Models of Recreation Demand: A Comparison of Competing Frameworks', in J.A. Herriges and C.L. Kling, eds., *Valuing Recreation and the Environment*, Cheltenham, UK and Northampton, MA: Edward Elgar.

Herriges, J.A. and D.J. Phaneuf (1999), 'Controlling Correlation across Choice Occasions and Sites in a Repeated Mixed Logit Model of Recreation Demand', Iowa State University Department of Economics Working Paper.

Hicks, R., S. Steinback, A. Gautam and E. Thunberg (1999), 'Volume II: The Economic Value of New England and Mid-Atlantic Sportfishing in 1994', Silver Spring, MD: NMFS Office of Science and Technology, NOAA Technical Memorandum.

Hicks, R. and I. E. Strand (2000), 'The Extent of Information: Its Relevance for Random Utility Models', *Land Economics*, **76**, 374-85.

Hoehn, John and Alan Randall (1989), 'Too Many Proposals Pass the Benefit-Cost Test' *American Economic Review,* **79**, 544-51.

Holmes, T. and W.L. Adamowicz (forthcoming), 'Attribute-Based Methods' chapter 5 in P. Champ, K. Boyle and T. Brown eds., *A Primer on Nonmarket Valuation,* Kluwer Academic Publishers, Dordrecht, The Netherlands.

Horowitz, J. and J. Louviere (1995), 'What Is the Role of Consideration Sets in Choice Modeling?' *International Journal of Research in Marketing,* **12**, 39-54.

Horowitz, J.K. and K.E. McConnell (forthcoming), 'A Review of WTA and WTP Studies', *Journal of Environmental Economics and Management.*

Huang, J., T.C. Haab and J.C. Whitehead (1997), 'Willingness to Pay for Quality Improvements: Should Revealed and Stated Preference Data Be Combined?', *Journal of Environmental Economics and Management,* **34**, 240-55.

Johanssen, P.O., B. Kriström and K.G. Mäler (1989), 'Welfare Evaluations in Contingent Valuation Experiments with Discrete Response Data: Comment', *American Journal of Agricultural Economics,* **71**, 1054-56.

Johnson, N. and S. Kotz (1970), *Continuous Univariate Distributions-2*, New York: John Wiley.

Johnson, N.L., S. Kotz and A.W. Kemp (1992), *Univariate Discrete Distributions*, 2nd edition, New York: John Wiley and Sons.

Jones, C. and F. Lupi (2000), 'The Effect of Modeling Substitute Activities on Recreational Benefit Estimates: Is More Better?', *Marine Resource Economics,* **14**, 357-74.

Just, R.E., D.L. Hueth and A. Schmitz (1982), *Applied Welfare Economics and Public Policy*, Englewood Cliffs, N.J.: Prentice-Hall.

Kanninen, B. (1993a), 'Optimal Design for Double-Bounded Dichotomous Choice Contingent Valuation', *Land Economics*, **69**, 138-46.

— (1993b), 'Design of Sequential Experiments for Contingent Valuation Studies', *Journal of Environmental Economics and Management,* **25**, S1-S11.

— (1995), 'Bias in Discrete Response Contingent Valuation', *Journal of Environmental Economics and Management,* **28**, 114-25.

Kling, C.L. (1989), 'The Importance of Functional Form in the Estimation of Welfare', *Western Journal of Agricultural Economics*, **14**, 161-8.

— (1991), 'Estimating the Precision of Welfare Measures', *Journal of Environmental Economics and Management*, **21**, 244-59.

— (1992), 'Some Results on the Variance of Welfare Estimates from Recreation Demand Models', *Land Economics*, **68**, 318-28.

Kling, C.L. and C.J. Thomson (1996), 'The Implications of Model Specification for Welfare Estimation in Nested Logit Models', *American Journal of Agricultural Economics,* **78**, 103-14.

Kotz, S., N. Balakrishnan and N. Johnson (2000), *Continuous Multivariate Distributions Volume 1: Models and Applications,* 2nd edition, New York: John Wiley and Sons, Inc.

Krinsky, I. and A. Robb (1986), 'On Approximating the Statistical Properties of Elasticities', *The Review of Economics and Statistics,* **86**, 715-19.

Kriström, B. (1990), 'A Non-Parametric Approach to the Estimation of Welfare Measures in Discrete Response Valuation Studies', *Land Economics,* **66**, 135-39.

— (1997), 'Spike Models in Contingent Valuation', *American Journal of Agricultural Economics,* **79**, 1013-23.

LaFrance, J. (1990), 'Incomplete Demand Systems and Semilogarithmic Demand Models', *Australian Journal of Agricultural Economics,* **34**, 118-31.

Layman, R.C., J.R. Boyce and K.R. Criddle (1996), 'Economic Valuation of the Chinook Salmon Sport Fishery of the Gulkana River, Alaska, under Current and Alternative Management Plans', *Land Economics,* **72**, 113-28.

Leggett, C. and N.E. Bockstael (2000), 'Evidence of the Effects of Water Quality on Residential Land Prices', *Journal of Environmental Economics and Management,* **39**, 131-144.

List, J.A. (2001), 'The Effect of Market Experience on the WTA/WTP Disparity', University of Maryland Department of Agricultural and Resource Economics Working Paper.

Loomis, J.B. (1993), 'An Investigation into the Reliability of Intended Visitation Behavior', *Environmental and Resource Economics,* **3**, 183-91.

— (1997), 'Panel Estimators to Combine Revealed and Stated Preference Dichotomous Choice Data', *Journal of Agricultural and Resource Economics,* **22**, 233-45.

Loomis, J.B. and J.C. Cooper (1993), 'Testing Whether Waterfowl Hunting Benefits Increase with Greater Water Deliveries to Wetlands', *Environmental and Resource Economics*, **6**, 545-61.

Loomis, J.B., M. Creel and T. Park (1991), 'Comparing Benefit Estimates from Travel Cost and Contingent Valuation Using Confidence Intervals for Hicksian Welfare Measures', *Applied Economics,* **23**, 1725-31.

Loomis, J., P. Kent, L. Strange, K. Fausch and A. Covich (2000), 'Measuring the Total Economic Value of Restoring Ecosystem Services in an Impaired River Basin', *Ecological Economics,* **33**, 103-17.

Louviere, J.J. (1988), 'Conjoint Analysis Modelling of Stated Preferences', *Journal of Transport Economics and Policy*; **22**.

Louviere, J., D. Hensher and J. Swait (2000), *Stated Choice Methods-Analysis and Application.* Cambridge: Cambridge University Press.

Maddala, G.S. (1983), *Limited-dependent and Qualitative Variables in Econometrics*, New York: Cambridge University Press.

Manski, C. (1977), 'The Structure of Random Utility Models', *Theory and Decision,* **8**, 229-54.

Manski, C. and D. McFadden (1981), 'Alternative Estimators and Sample Designs for Discrete Choice Estimators' in C. Manski and D. McFadden, eds., *Structural Analysis of Discrete Data with Econometric Applications,* Cambridge, MA: MIT Press.

Mazzotta, M., J. Opaluch and T. Grigalunas (1997), 'Valuing Estuarine Resources: A Contingent Choice Study of the Peconic Estuary System', Working Paper, Department of Resource Economics, University of Rhode Island.

McConnell, K.E. (1986), 'The Damages to Recreation Activities from PCB's in New Bedford Harbor', Report for Ocean Assessment Division, Rockville, MD: National Oceanic and Atmospheric Administration.

— (1992), 'On-site Time in the Demand for Recreation' *American Journal of Agricultural Economics,* **74**, 918-25.

McConnell, K.E. and J.H. Ducci (1989), 'Valuing Environmental Quality in Developing Countries: Two Case Studies', Paper presented at the ASSA annual meetings, Atlanta, GA.

McConnell, K. E. and I. E. Strand (1981), 'Measuring the Cost of Time in the Demand for Recreation', *American Journal of Agricultural Economics*, **63**, 153-56.

McConnell, K., Q. Weninger and I. Strand (1999), 'Testing the Validity of Contingent Valuation by Combining Referendum Responses with Observed Behavior', in J. Herriges and C. Kling, eds., *Valuing Recreation and the Environment*, Cheltenham, UK and Northhampton, MA: Edward Elgar, 199-216.

McCormick, C.A. (1997), 'Groundwater Contamination and Property Values: A Hedonic Price Approach', Unpublished Ph.D. Dissertation, Department of Economics, University of Maryland, College Park.

McFadden, D. (1974), 'Conditional Logit Analysis of Qualitative Choice Behavior', in P. Zarembka, ed., *Frontiers in Econometrics*, New York: Academic Press, 105-142.

— (1978), 'Modeling the Choice of Residential Location', in A. Karlqvist, L. Lundqvist, F. Snickars and J.W. Weibull, eds., *Spatial Interaction Theory and Planning Models*, Amsterdam: North-Holland, 75-96.

— (1994), 'Contingent Valuation and Social Choice', *American Journal of Agricultural Economics,* **76**, 689-708.

Mendelsohn, R., D. Hellerstein, M. Huguenin, R. Unsworth and R. Brazee (1992), 'Measuring Hazardous Waste Damages with Panel Models', *Journal of Environmental Economics and Management,* **22**, 259-71.

Michaels, R.G. and V.K. Smith (1990), 'Market Segmentation and Valuing Amenities with Hedonic Models: The Case of Hazardous Waste Sites', *Journal of Urban Economics,* **28**, 223-42.

Mitchell, R. and R. Carson (1989), *Using Surveys to Value Public Goods,* Resources for the Future, Washington, D.C.

Morey E. (1999), 'Two RUM's Uncloaked: Nested Logit Models of Site Choice and Nested Logit Models of Participation and Site Choice', in J. Herriges and C. Kling, eds., *Valuing Recreation and the Environment*, Cheltenham, UK and Northhampton, MA: Edward Elgar, 65-116.

Morey, E.R., R. Rowe and M. Watson (1993), 'A Repeated Nested Logit Model of Atlantic Salmon Fishing', *American Journal of Agricultural Economics,* **75**, 578-92.

Mullahey, J., (1986), 'Specification and Testing of Some Modified Count Data Models', *Journal of Econometrics*, **33**, 341-65.

Murphy, K.M. and R.H. Topel (1985), 'Estimation and Inference in Two-Step Econometric Models', *Journal of Business and Economic Statistics*, **3**, 370-79.

Neill, H.R., R.G. Cummings, P.T. Ganderton, G.W. Harrison and T. McGuckin (1994), 'Hypothetical Surveys, and Real Economic Commitments', *Land Economics,* **70**, 145-54.

Niklitschek, M. and J. Leon (1996), 'Combining Intended Demand and Yes/No Responses in the Estimation of Contingent Valuation Models', *Journal of Environmental Economics and Management,* **31**, 387-402.

Nourse, H. (1967), 'The Effect of Air Pollution on House Values', *Land Economics,* **43**, 181-89.

Nyquist, H. (1992), 'Optimal Design of Discrete Response Experiments in Contingent Valuation Studies', *The Review of Economics and Statistics*, **74**, 559-63.

Olsen, R.J. 1978, 'Note on the Uniqueness of the Maximum Likelihood Estimator for the Tobit Model', *Econometrica*, **46**, 1211-15.

Palmquist, R.B. (1984), 'Estimating the Demand for the Characteristics of Housing', *The Review of Economics and Statistics,* **66**, 394-404.

— (1991), 'Hedonic Methods', in J.B. Braden and C.D. Kolstad (eds.), *Measuring the Demand for Environmental Quality*, Amsterdam: North Holland Publishers, 77-120.

— (1992), 'Valuing Localized Externalities', *Journal of Urban Economics,* **31**, 59-68.

— (forthcoming), 'Property Value Models', in K.-G. Mäler and J. Vincent, eds., *Handbook of Environmental Economics,* Amsterdam: North Holland Publishers.

Parsons, G. (2001), 'A Bibliography of Revealed Preference Random Utility Models in Recreation Demand', University of Delaware Department of Economics, Working Paper.

Parsons, G. and A. Hauber (1998), 'Spatial Boundaries and Choice Set Definition in a Random Utility Model of Recreation Demand', *Land Economics,* **74**, 32-48.

Parsons, G.R. and M.J. Kealy (1992), 'Randomly Drawn Opportunity Sets in a Random Utility Model of Lake Recreation', *Land Economics,* **68**, 93-106.

Parsons, G.R., M. Massey and T. Tomasi (1999), 'Familiar and Favorite Sites in Random Utility Models of Recreation Demand', *Marine Resource Economics,* **14**, 299-315.

Parsons, G.R., A.J. Plantinga and K.J. Boyle (2000), 'Narrow Choice Sets in Random Utility Models of Recreation Demand', *Land Economics,* **76**, 86-99.

Parsons, G.R. and A.J. Wilson (1997), 'Incidental and Joint Consumption in Recreation Demand', *Agricultural and Resource Economics Review,* **26**, 1-6.

Peters, T., W. Adamowicz and P. Boxall (1995), 'The Influence of Choice Set Consideration in Modeling the Benefits of Improved Water Quality', *Water Resources Research,* **613**, 1781-7.

Phaneuf, D.J., J.A. Herriges and C.L. Kling (2000), 'Estimation and Welfare Calculations in a Generalized Corner Solution Model with an Application to Recreation Demand', *The Review of Economics and Statistics,* **82**, 83-92.

Pollak, R. and T. Wales (1991), 'The Likelihood Dominance Criterion', *Journal of Econometrics,* **47**, 227-42.

Randall, A. (1994), 'A Difficulty with the Travel Cost Method', *Land Economics*, **70**, 88-96.

— (1998), 'Beyond the Crucial Experiment: Mapping the Performance Characteristics of Contingent Valuation', *Resource and Energy Economics,* **20**, 197-206.

Ready, R. and D. Hu (1995), 'Statistical Approaches to the Fat Tail Problem for Dichotomous Choice Contingent Valuation', *Land Economics,* **71**, 491-99.

Ridker, R.G. and J.A. Henning (1967), 'The Determinants of Residential Property Values with Special Reference to Air Pollution', *The Review of Economics and Statistics*, **49**, 246-57.

Rohatgi, V.K. (1976), *An Introduction to Probability Theory and Mathematical Statistics,* New York: John Wiley and Sons.

Rosen, S. (1974), 'Hedonic Prices and Implicit Markets: Product Differentiation in Price Competition', *Journal of Political Economy,* **82**, 34-55.

Ruud, P.A. (2000), *An Introduction to Classical Econometric Theory,* New York: Oxford University Press.

Scarpa, R. and I. Bateman (2000), 'Efficiency Gains Afforded by Improved Bid Design versus Follow-up Valuation Questions', *Land Economics*, **76**, 299-311.

Sellar, C., J.R. Stoll and J.P. Chavas (1985), 'Validation of Empirical Measures of Welfare Changes: A Comparison of Nonmarket Techniques', *Land Economics,* **61**, 156-75.

Shaw, D. (1988), 'On-Site Samples' Regression: Problems of Non negative Integers, Truncation, and Endogenous Stratification', *Journal of Econometrics,* **37**, 211-23.

Shonkwiler, J.S. (1999), 'Recreation Demand Systems for Multiple Site Count Data Travel Cost Models' in Joseph Herriges and Catherine Kling, eds., *Valuing Recreation and the Environment*, Cheltenham, UK and Northampton, MA: Edward Elgar.

Sieg, H., V.K. Smith, H.S. Banzhaf and R. Walsh (2001), 'Estimating the General Equilibrium Benefits of Large Changes in Spatially Delineated Goods', North Carolina State University Working Paper.

Small, K.A. and H.S. Rosen (1981), 'Applied Welfare Economics with Discrete Choice Models', *Econometrica*, **49**, 105-30.

Smith, V.K. (1988), 'Selection and Recreation Demand', *American Journal of Agricultural Economics*, **70**, 29-36.

— (1996), 'Can Contingent Valuation Distinguish Economic Values for Different Public Goods?', *Land Economics*, **72**, 139-51.

— (1999), 'Of Birds and Books: More on Hypothetical Referenda', *Journal of Political Economy,* **107**, 197-201.

Smith, V.K. and H.S. Banzhaf (2001), 'A Diagrammatic Exposition of Weak Complementarity and the Willig Condition', North Carolina State University Department of Agricultural and Resource Economics Working Paper.

Smith, V.K. and W.H. Desvousges (1985), 'The Generalized Travel Cost Model and Water Quality Benefits: A Reconsideration', *Southern Economic Journal,* **52**, 371-81.

Smith, V.K., W.H. Desvousges and M.P. McGivney (1983), 'The Opportunity Cost of Travel Time in Recreation Demand Models', *Land Economics,* **59**, 259-77.

Smith, V. K. and J.C. Huang (1993), 'Hedonic Models and Air Pollution: Twenty-Five Years and Counting', *Environmental and Resource Economics,* **3**, 381-94.

— (1995), 'Can Markets Value Air Quality? A Meta-Analysis of Hedonic Property Value Models', *Journal of Political Economy,* **103**, 209-27.

Smith, V. K. and Y. Kaoru (1990), 'Signals or Noise? Explaining the Variation in Recreation Benefit Estimates', *American Journal of Agricultural Economics,* **72**, 419-33.

Smith, V.K. and G. van Houtven (2001), 'Non Market Valuation and the Household', North Carolina State University Department of Economics Working Paper.

Sohngen, B., F. Lichtkoppler and M. Bielen (1999), 'The Value of Day Trips to Lake Erie Beaches', Technical Bulletin TB-039, Columbus, OH: Ohio Sea Grant Extension.

Strand, I. (2000), 'Modeling Demand for and Economic Value of Beaches and Their Characteristics: Residential Use in Barbados', Report to the Organization of American States.

Swait, J. and M. Ben-Akiva (1987a), 'Empirical Test of a Constrained Choice Discrete Choice Model: Mode Choice in Sao Paulo, Brazil', *Transportation Research,* **21B**, 91-102.

— (1987b), 'Incorporating Random Constraints in Discrete Choice Models of Choice Set Generation', *Transportation Research,* **21B**, 91-102.

Swait, J. and J. Louviere (1993), 'The Role of the Scale Parameter in the Estimation and Comparison of Multinomial Logit Models', *Journal of Marketing Research,* **30**, 305-14.

Terza, J. (1998), 'Estimating Count Data Models with Endogenous Switching: Sample Selection and Endogenous Treatment Effects', *Journal of Econometrics,* **84**, 129-54.

Thill, J. (1992), 'Choice Set Formation for Destination Choice Modeling', *Progress in Human Geography*, **16**, 361-82.

Train, K.E. (1998), 'Recreation Demand Models with Taste Difference over People', *Land Economics,* **74**, 230-39.

— (1999), 'Mixed Logit Models for Recreation Demand', in J.A. Herriges and C.L. Kling, eds., *Valuing Recreation and the Environment: Revealed Preference Methods in Theory and Practice*, Cheltenham, UK and Northampton, MA: Edward Elgar, 121-40.

—(forthcoming), *Discrete Choice Methods with Simulation*, Cambridge: Cambridge University Press.

Turnbull, B. (1976), 'The Empirical Distribution Function with Arbitrarily Grouped, Censored, and Truncated Data', *Journal of the Royal Statistical Society*, **38B**, 290-95.

Vartia, Y.O. (1983), 'Efficient Methods of Measuring Welfare Change and Compensated Income in Terms of Ordinary Demand Functions', *Econometrica*, **51**, 79-98.

von Haefen, R. (2000), 'A Complete Characterization of the Implication of Slutsky Symmetry for the Linear, Log-Linear, and Semi-Log Incomplete Demand System Models', U.S. Bureau of Labor Statistics Working Paper.

von Haefen, R. and D. Phaneuf (2001), 'Estimating Preferences for Outdoor Recreation: A Comparison of Continuous and Count Data Demand Systems', Department of Agricultural and Resource Economics, North Carolina State University, Working Paper.

Waldman, D.M. (2000), 'Estimation in Discrete Choice Models With Choice-Based Samples', *The American Statistician*, **54**, 303-306.

Waugh, F. (1928), 'Quality Factors Influencing Vegetable Prices', *Journal of Farm Economics,* **10**, 185-96.

Werner, M. (1994), 'Allowing for Indifference in Dichotomous Choice Contingent Valuation Models', in *Public Choice Issues in Environmental Economics,* Unpublished Ph.D. Dissertation, University of California San Diego Department of Economics.

— (1999), 'Allowing for Zeros in Dichotomous-Choice Contingent Valuation Models', *Journal of Business and Economic Statistics,* **17**, 479-86.

Whitehead, J.C (1993), 'Total Economic Values for Coastal and Marine Wildlife: Specification, Validity, and Valuation Issues', *Marine Resource Economics,* **8**, 119-32.

— (1995), 'Willingness to Pay for Quality Improvements: Comparative Statics and Interpretation of Contingent Valuation Results', *Land Economics,* **71**, 207-15.

Whitehead, J. and T. Haab (2000), 'SE MRFSS: Distance and Catch Based Choice Sets', *Marine Resource Economics,* **14**, 283-98.

Whitehead, J.C., T.C. Haab and J.-C Huang (1998), 'Part-Whole Bias in Contingent Valuation', *Southern Economic Journal,* **65**, 160-68.

— (2000), 'Measuring Recreation Benefits of Quality Improvements with Revealed and Stated Behavior Data', *Resource and Energy Economics*, **22**, 339-54.

Willig, R.D. (1976), 'Consumer Surplus without Apology', *American Economic Review*, **66**, 589-97.

— (1978), 'Incremental Consumer's Surplus and Hedonic Price Adjustment', *Journal of Economic Theory*, **17**, 227-53.

Appendix A

Maximum Likelihood Estimation

Here we give a cursory description of maximum likelihood methods. We provide no proof for the properties of the ML estimators, nor the properties that support such proofs. For more details and greater rigor, see Ruud (2000) or Greene (1997).

Maximum likelihood techniques represent a general technique for obtaining estimates of parameters from an unknown population distribution. The technique relies on the information contained in a sample of observations drawn from the population distribution to identify the estimates of the population parameters. Maximum likelihood estimation is a direct extension of standard statistical inference from a sample drawn from an unknown population distribution. We start with a simple example of the technique of maximum likelihood estimation and then discuss in more detail the properties of the resulting estimator.

Consider a simple example. Suppose we know that a given measure (for simplicity we'll call this age) in a population is distributed across the population according to a normal distribution with mean, μ, and variance, σ^2. The distributional parameters μ and σ^2 are unknown. In this simple case, it is not necessary to assume a form for the population distribution, but for illustrative purposes we have assumed normality for the distribution of age in the population. We also assume that the ages of individuals within the population are independently and identically distributed. We would like to gain information on the population mean and variance from a sample of observations. Suppose we draw a sample of 20 individuals randomly from the general population and record their ages as: $\mathbf{A} = \{a_1, ..., a_{20}\}$. For a given observation in the sample, the probability of observing the outcome a_i is:

$$f\left(a_i|\mu,\sigma^2\right) = \frac{1}{\sqrt{2\pi\sigma^2}} e^{-\frac{(a_i-\mu)^2}{2\sigma^2}}.$$

Because the sample draws are independent, the probability of observing the full sample of outcomes given the population parameters μ and σ^2 is

$$\Pr\left(\mathbf{A}|\mu,\sigma^2\right) = \prod_{i=1}^{20} f\left(a_i|\mu,\sigma^2\right). \tag{A.1}$$

This probability statement is typically interpreted as a function of the random sample **A** given values for μ and σ^2. Because in actuality, **A** is observable and μ and σ^2 are unknown, this interpretation can be reversed. Rewriting equation (A.1) as

$$L\left(\mu, \sigma^2 | \mathbf{A}\right) = \prod_{i=1}^{20} f\left(a_i | \mu, \sigma^2\right) \tag{A.2}$$

we can interpret the probability of observing the sample **A** given a particular value of μ and σ^2 as the likelihood of observing that sample for *any* value of μ and σ^2. Equation (A.2) is known as the likelihood function. It should be emphasized that the likelihood function is a probability statement. Choosing the values of μ and σ^2 to maximize the likelihood function results in the maximum likelihood estimates for μ and σ^2.

When the probabilities are independent, it is often easier to maximize the natural logarithm of the likelihood function rather than the likelihood function itself because the logarithm operator converts the product of terms into the sum of terms

$$\ln\left(L\left(\mu, \sigma^2 | \mathbf{A}\right)\right) = \sum_{i=1}^{20} \ln\left(f\left(a_i | \mu, \sigma^2\right)\right).$$

In this case, the log-likelihood function becomes

$$\ln\left(L\left(\mu, \sigma^2 | \mathbf{A}\right)\right) = \sum_{i=1}^{20} \left(-\frac{1}{2}\ln(2\pi) - \frac{1}{2}\ln\left(\sigma^2\right) - \frac{\left(a_i - \mu\right)^2}{2\sigma^2}\right).$$

We maximize this function with respect to the unknown parameters because we want to determine the parameter values that would maximize the likelihood of the observation. Assuming that the log-likelihood function is concave, we differentiate with respect to μ and σ^2 to find the first-order conditions for a maximum

$$\begin{aligned}
\frac{\partial \ln\left(L\left(\mu, \sigma^2 | \mathbf{A}\right)\right)}{\partial \mu} &= -\sum_{i=1}^{20} \frac{a_i - \mu}{\sigma^2} = 0 \\
\frac{\partial \ln\left(L\left(\mu, \sigma^2 | \mathbf{A}\right)\right)}{\partial \sigma^2} &= \sum_{i=1}^{20} \left(-\frac{1}{2\sigma^2} + \frac{\left(a_i - \mu\right)^2}{2\sigma^4}\right) = 0.
\end{aligned}$$

Solving for μ and σ^2 gives the maximum likelihood estimates

$$\begin{aligned}
\mu &= \frac{\sum_{i=1}^{20} a_i}{20} \\
\sigma^2 &= \frac{\sum_{i=1}^{20} \left(a_i - \mu\right)^2}{20}.
\end{aligned}$$

For this simple example, the maximum likelihood estimate of the population mean age is simply the sample average, and the estimate of the variance is the sample variance about the average. In general, the first-order conditions for the likelihood maximization problem do not have a simple closed-form solution. Below we discuss some specifics of maximum likelihood estimation in a more general framework.

A.1 The Likelihood Function

Let $\mathbf{Y} = \{y_1, y_2, ..., y_T\}$ represent the full population of possible outcomes for a random event. Each individual population outcome, indexed y_i, is drawn from a population probability density function $f(y_i|\mathbf{X}_i, \boldsymbol{\theta})$. For simplicity, we assume the distribution y_i are distributed independently and identically for all individuals in the population. The outcome is conditional on $\mathbf{X}_i$, a vector of individual specific characteristics, and $\boldsymbol{\theta}$, an unknown vector of distributional parameters. Now suppose we observe a random sample of N outcomes $(\mathbf{Y}_N)$ from the set of population outcomes $\mathbf{Y}$. If the population distribution $f(y_i|\mathbf{X}_i, \boldsymbol{\theta})$ were known, the probability of observing the set of outcomes $\mathbf{Y}_N$ would be

$$P(\mathbf{Y}_N) = \prod_{y_i \in \mathbf{Y}_N} f(y_i|\mathbf{X}_i, \boldsymbol{\theta}). \tag{A.3}$$

This result relies on the assumption that the individual observations of y_i are stochastically independent; otherwise, the probability would be the joint probability of observing the N outcomes simultaneously.

Equation (A.3) assumes that the distribution parameters $\boldsymbol{\theta}$ are known. Suppose now, that the population parameters are unknown, so that equation (A.3) is a function of the unknown parameter vector and conditioned on the sample observations of y_i and $\mathbf{X}_i$

$$L(\boldsymbol{\theta}|\mathbf{Y}_N, \mathbf{X}) = \prod_{y_i \in \mathbf{Y}_N} f(y_i|\mathbf{X}_i, \boldsymbol{\theta}). \tag{A.4}$$

For a given value of θ, equation (A.4) represents the likelihood of observing the exact sample of outcomes $\{\mathbf{Y}_N, \mathbf{X}\}$.This is a simple reinterpretation of the probability statement in equation (A.3).

A.2 Maximization

The question now becomes, what is a reasonable criterion for choosing the values for the unknown population parameter vector $\boldsymbol{\theta}$? Because the likelihood function as defined in equation (A.4) represents the likelihood of observing the sample outcomes $\{\mathbf{Y}_N, \mathbf{X}\}$ for a given value of $\boldsymbol{\theta}$, it makes sense to choose the value $\widehat{\boldsymbol{\theta}}$ that maximizes the likelihood of observing the specific sample of outcomes. That is, choose the value of $\boldsymbol{\theta}$ that maximizes $L(\boldsymbol{\theta}|\mathbf{Y}_N, \mathbf{X})$:

$$\widehat{\boldsymbol{\theta}} = \left\{ \boldsymbol{\theta} | \max_{\boldsymbol{\theta}} L(\boldsymbol{\theta}|\mathbf{Y}_N, \mathbf{X}) \right\}.$$

Assuming an interior solution, local concavity of the likelihood function and the existence of a global maximum, maximization of the likelihood function is accomplished by finding the solution to the system of first-order conditions:

$$\frac{\partial L(\boldsymbol{\theta}|\mathbf{Y}_N, \mathbf{X})}{\partial \boldsymbol{\theta}} = 0. \tag{A.5}$$

Because the probability density function is strictly positive, and the natural logarithm of $f(y_i|\mathbf{X}_i, \boldsymbol{\theta})$ is a monotonically increasing transformation of $f(y_i|\mathbf{X}_i, \boldsymbol{\theta})$, one can maximize the natural logarithm of the likelihood function which is made easier by the independence of the observations:

$$\ln L(\boldsymbol{\theta}|\mathbf{Y}_N, \mathbf{X}) = \sum_{y_i \in \mathbf{Y}_N} \ln (f(y_i|\mathbf{X}_i, \boldsymbol{\theta})) \tag{A.6}$$

yielding the system of first-order conditions:

$$\frac{\partial \ln L(\boldsymbol{\theta}|\mathbf{Y}_N, \mathbf{X})}{\partial \boldsymbol{\theta}} = \sum_{y_i \in \mathbf{Y}_N} \frac{1}{f(y_i|\mathbf{X}_i, \boldsymbol{\theta})} \frac{\partial f(y_i|\mathbf{X}_i, \boldsymbol{\theta})}{\partial \boldsymbol{\theta}} = 0. \tag{A.7}$$

The values of the parameters that solve the system in equation (A.7) will be identical to the solution to equation (A.5). Given the non-linear nature of most probability distributions, it is rarely the case that the likelihood maximization problems defined in equations (A.5) and (A.7) will have a closed form solution for $\widehat{\boldsymbol{\theta}}$. It is therefore necessary to rely on numerical optimization algorithms to approximate the maximum likelihood values for $\widehat{\boldsymbol{\theta}}$.

A.2.1 Maximum Likelihood Algorithms

There are numerous algorithms for solving systems of equations like (A.7). With the growth in computer power ML methods requiring numerical solution of equations play a much more central role in estimation than 20 years ago. Our intent here is not to give a detailed exposition of the numerous algorithms for finding maximum likelihood estimates.

Instead, we give the flavor for maximum likelihood algorithms and refer the reader to standard econometrics texts for more details on these algorithms (see, for example, Greene (1997), or Ruud (2000)). Before proceeding, it is useful to define the gradient and Hessian of a likelihood function. The gradient vector is simply the vector of first derivatives of the likelihood (or log-likelihood) function with respect to the parameters to be estimated. At a global maximum, the gradient will be zero with respect to all parameters. The Hessian matrix is the matrix of second derivatives of the likelihood (or log-likelihood) function with respect to the parameter vector. To ensure an algorithm has reached at least a local maximum, the Hessian should be negative definite. Ideally, the log-likelihood function will be globally concave and the Hessian will be negative definite at any value of the parameter vector. This holds for a number of commonly estimated models, such as logit models.

The basic idea behind typical maximum likelihood algorithms is:

1. Choose a starting value for the parameter vector: $\boldsymbol{\theta}_0$. The starting values are an initial guess as to the correct maximum likelihood parameter values. Often OLS parameters prove to be good starting values.

2. Evaluate the log-likelihood function, the gradient and Hessian at the starting values.

3. Update the parameter vector based on an updating rule (typically found by taking a Taylor-series approximation to the true parameter vector around the start values). Depending on the algorithm, the updating rule may be a function of the likelihood gradient, the Hessian and a step length that determines the size of the adjustment made to the parameter estimates.

4. Evaluate the log-likelihood function at the new parameter values.

5. Compare the log-likelihood function values to see if the likelihood function has increased. If it has, proceed to step 6. If the log-likelihood function has not increased, adjust the updating rule (or step length) and go to step 3.

6. Check the convergence criteria. If the new parameter vector meets the convergence criteria, then stop. The criteria might be the change in the likelihood function, the change in the parameter vector or the size of the first derivatives. Otherwise, go to step 3 and repeat until convergence is achieved.

Most maximum likelihood algorithms follow this basic procedure. Algorithms differ in how the Hessian is computed, how the updating rules are defined, and how the convergence criteria are defined. Most statistical packages have these algorithms pre-programmed and can be implemented with very simple calls to the likelihood maximization routines.

A.3 Properties of Maximum Likelihood Estimates

Maximum likelihood parameter estimates have a number of desirable statistical properties. The derivation of these properties depends on a series of regularity conditions described in detail in Ruud (2000). In brief, the regularity conditions are: (1) the assumed distribution is correctly specified; (2) a global maximum to the likelihood function with respect to the parameter vector exists and is identified, and (3) the parameter space is a closed and bounded set. Assuming these regularity conditions hold, the properties of the maximum likelihood parameter estimates $\widehat{\boldsymbol{\theta}}$ are:

A.3.1 Consistency

$\widehat{\boldsymbol{\theta}}$ is a consistent estimate of $\boldsymbol{\theta}$. Consistency implies that in the limit, the maximum likelihood parameter vector converges in probability to the true parameter vector. Among the appealing implications of consistency is Slutsky's theorem which states:

Slutsky's Theorem

$$p\lim f\left(\widehat{\boldsymbol{\theta}}\right) = f\left(p\lim \widehat{\boldsymbol{\theta}}\right)$$

if $f\left(\widehat{\boldsymbol{\theta}}\right)$ is continuous and independent of the sample size. Slutsky's theorem is valuable because it allows us to compute functions of parameter estimates. In general, the expected value of a function of random variables is not equal to the function of the expectation of the random variables. However, Slutsky's theorem implies that a function evaluated at a consistent estimate is a consistent estimate of the function itself.

A.3.2 Asymptotic Normality

$\widehat{\boldsymbol{\theta}}$ is distributed asymptotically as a normal random vector with mean $\boldsymbol{\theta}$ and variance-covariance matrix $V\left(\widehat{\boldsymbol{\theta}}\right)=-E\left[\frac{\partial^2 \ln L(\boldsymbol{\theta}|\mathbf{Y}_N,\mathbf{X})}{\partial\boldsymbol{\theta}\partial\boldsymbol{\theta}'}\right]^{-1}$. The mean of the asymptotic distribution follows from consistency of the maximum likelihood estimator. The matrix $E\left[\frac{\partial^2 \ln L(\boldsymbol{\theta}|\mathbf{Y}_N,\mathbf{X})}{\partial\boldsymbol{\theta}\partial\boldsymbol{\theta}'}\right]$ is often referred to as the Fisher information matrix. The variance-covariance matrix $-E\left[\frac{\partial^2 \ln L(\boldsymbol{\theta}|\mathbf{Y}_N,\mathbf{X})}{\partial\boldsymbol{\theta}\partial\boldsymbol{\theta}'}\right]^{-1}$ is the Cramer-Rao lower bound on the variance of $\widehat{\boldsymbol{\theta}}$, implying that the maximum likelihood estimator is asymptotically efficient.

A.4 Diagnostic Statistics and Tests for Maximum Likelihood

A.4.1 Likelihood Ratio Statistic

Consider an unrestricted log-likelihood function $\ln L_u\left(\boldsymbol{\theta}|\mathbf{Y}_N,\mathbf{X}\right)$. Define $\widehat{\boldsymbol{\theta}}_u$ as the vector of maximum likelihood parameter estimates obtained from the maximization log-likelihood function without restrictions on the parameters. Suppose we want to test a set of restrictions on the parameter estimates. For example, suppose a subset of the parameters is thought to be equal to zero. Define $\ln L_r\left(\boldsymbol{\theta}|\mathbf{Y}_N,\mathbf{X}\right)$ as the log-likelihood function evaluated with the imposed restrictions, and $\widehat{\boldsymbol{\theta}}_r$ as the resulting maximum likelihood parameter estimates. Under the null hypothesis that the parameter restrictions hold, the likelihood ratio statistic:

$$LR=-2\left[\ln L_r-\ln L_u\right]$$

is asymptotically distributed as a Chi-squared random variable with degrees of freedom equal to the number of parameter restrictions when the likelihood function is $\ln L_r$. Intuitively, if the parameter restrictions are true, that is, the parameters are actually zero, then imposing the restrictions will not significantly decrease the log-likelihood function value relative to the unrestricted version. In this case, $\ln L_r$ will be close to $\ln L_u$ and LR will be small. As the restrictions become more binding, $\ln L_r$ and $\ln L_u$ will diverge and LR will be large (leading to rejection of the null hypothesis).

A.4.2 A Special Case: $\widehat{\boldsymbol{\theta}}_r = 0$

As a special case, consider the hypothesis that all estimated parameters are equal to zero (for models that include a constant, the constant is not restricted to zero, but all other parameters are restricted to zero). Define $\ln L_0$ as the maximum value of the log-likelihood function under the null-hypothesis that all parameters are equal to zero. As before, $\ln L_u$ is the maximum log-likelihood function value when all parameters are free to vary to maximize the likelihood function. The parameter restrictions here are the maximum likelihood equivalent of restricting all slope parameters to be equal to zero in a standard linear regression model. This set of restrictions can be used to evaluate the model goodness of fit. Three candidate measures of model goodness of fit will be mentioned here: model Chi-squared statistic, pseudo-R^2 and McFadden's R^2. Each measure has relative advantages and disadvantages that will not be debated here. Maddala discusses the properties of these three measures. Note that only three pieces of information are necessary to calculate these three measures: the unrestricted log-likelihood function value ($\ln L_u$), the restricted log-likelihood function value ($\ln L_0$) and the sample size (N).

Model Chi-Squared Statistic

The model Chi-squared statistic is a special case of the likelihood ratio statistic from the previous section with all relevant parameters restricted to be equal to zero

$$LR_{Model} = -2\left[\ln L_r - \ln L_u\right].$$

The statistic is distributed as a Chi-squared with degrees of freedom equal to the number of parameters restricted to be equal to zero.

Pseudo-R^2

Various measures based on the likelihood ratios attempt to recreate an analogue to the traditional R^2 used in linear regression models. The difficulty is that the maximum of the likelihood value is one, so that the upper bound of the likelihood measures will typically be less than one.

The pseudo-R^2 measure is defined as

$$pseudo\ R^2 = \frac{\ln L_u^{2/N} - \ln L_r^{2/N}}{1 - \ln L_r^{2/N}}$$

where N is the number of observations. Similar to the likelihood ratio statistic, if the restriction is non-binding, then $\ln L_0$ will be close to $\ln L_u$ and *pseudo* R^2 will be close to zero.

McFadden's R^2

McFadden's R^2 is a simpler measure of model goodness of fit that does not rely on the sample size, but simply on the relative decrease in the likelihood function induced by the parameter restrictions

$$McR^2 = 1 - \frac{\ln L_u}{\ln L_r}$$

This measure of goodness of fit has a lower bound of zero when $\ln L_r = \ln L_u$ and goes to one when $\ln L_r$ gets very large or L_u goes to one.

In the presentation of statistics within the text, we report the likelihood value and the likelihood ratio, as well as the number of observations. We do not report any of the approximate $R^{2\prime}s$ though we report sufficient information to compute these measures if one wishes.

Percent Correctly Predicted

Often one will find the percent correctly predicted as a measure of goodness of fit in discrete choice models. For example, in a logit model, the prediction of alternative j for a choice set of J alternatives would be

$$\Pr(j) = \frac{e^{\mathbf{x}_j \hat{\boldsymbol{\beta}}}}{\sum_{k \in J} e^{\mathbf{x}_k \hat{\boldsymbol{\beta}}}}$$

where the $\hat{\boldsymbol{\beta}}$ are the estimated parameters. The typical rule for a prediction is to find the highest of the predicted probabilities and assign one to that alternative and zero to the others. If the individual actually chooses the alternative with the highest predicted probability, it will be a correct prediction. This measure can fail in two ways. If a model is quite skewed, say in a dichotomous choice, 95% choose alternative one, and the model predicts roughly the same for everyone, at 55%, then the percent correctly predicted will be 95%, even though the model doesn't really do very much. On the other hand, consider a multiple choice with four alternatives. Suppose the actual probabilities are $\langle 0.4, 0.3, 0.2, 0.1\rangle$ and the predictions are roughly 40% for the first alternative and 45% for the second alternative. The percent correctly predicted will give no credit for being close on the first alternative, and consequently can be quite low.

Appendix B

Some Useful Results

B.1 Basic Probabilistic Relations

This section summarizes some results of probability distributions that are well known but used periodically throughout the book.

B.1.1 $Pr(x > a)$

Consider a random variable x. By definition of a valid distribution function, $\Pr(x \leq a) + \Pr(x > a) = 1$. Rearranging yields:

$$\Pr(x > a) = 1 - \Pr(x \leq a). \tag{B.1}$$

This is useful because an assumed distribution function is often defined in terms of a cumulative distribution function such that $\Pr(x \leq a) = F(a)$. For example, for a variable that is distributed $N(\mu, \sigma^2)$ the cumulative distribution function (CDF) is

$$\Phi(a) = \int_{-\infty}^{a} \frac{1}{\sqrt{2\pi\sigma^2}} e^{-\frac{(x-\mu)^2}{2\sigma^2}} dx.$$

To find $\Pr(x > a)$, where x is normally distributed with mean μ and variance σ^2, use the definition of the normal CDF and relation B.1:

$$\Pr(x > a) = 1 - \Phi(a).$$

B.1.2 $Pr(x > -a)$

For a random variable x, distributed according to an arbitrary CDF $F(x)$, $\Pr(x \leq -a) + \Pr(x > -a) = 1$. Rearranging yields

$$\begin{aligned} \Pr(x &> -a) = 1 - \Pr(x \leq -a) \\ &= 1 - F(-a). \end{aligned}$$

This relationship can be seen in Figure B.1, where $f(x)$ is the probability density function associated with the CDF $F(x)$.

For simplicity it is drawn as a triangular distribution. Assume further that the CDF is valid such that the area under $f(x)$ is one. The area

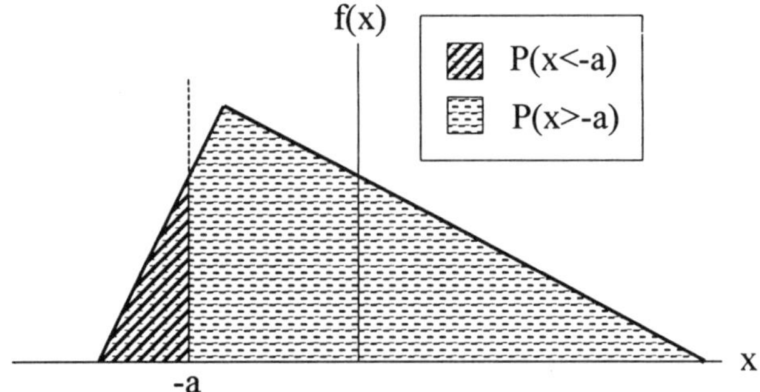

FIGURE B.1. Probability Relationship

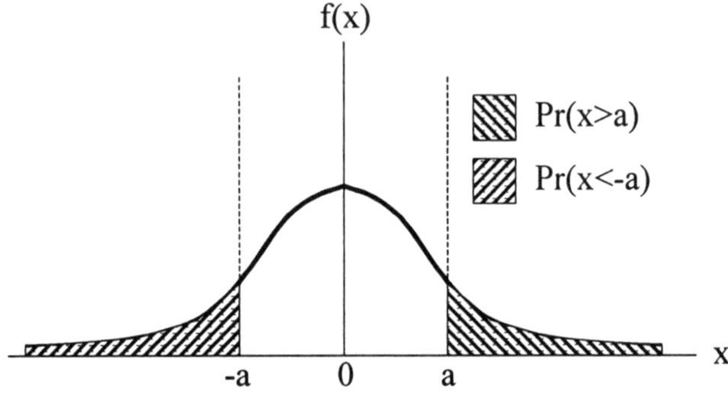

FIGURE B.2. Probability for Symmetric Distribution

$\Pr(x > -a)$ is the area to the right of $-a$ under $f(x)$. The area $F(-a)$ is the area to the left of $-a$ under $f(x)$. Because the total area under $f(x)$ must equal one, the area to the right of $-a$ is one minus the area to the left of $-a$.

B.1.3 Symmetry

If the distribution of a random variable x is symmetric with mean zero, then $\Pr(x \leq a) = \Pr(x > -a)$. Also, $\Pr(x \leq -a) = \Pr(x > a)$. Figure B.2 illustrates this. Because the distribution is symmetric about zero (a mirror image), the area below $-a$ under $f(x)$ is equal to the area above a under $f(x)$. If the distribution of x is symmetric about a non-zero mean, μ, then this result generalizes to: $\Pr(x - \mu \leq -a) = \Pr(x - \mu > a)$.

B.1.4 Summary of Results on Probabilities

The results of the previous section are summarized in Table B.1:

TABLE B.1. Summary of Basic Probability Relations

Distribution	Relation
Arbitrary CDF $F(x)^a$	$\Pr(x \leq a) + \Pr(x > a) = 1$
	$\Pr(x \leq -a) + \Pr(x > -a) = 1$
	$\Pr(x > a) = 1 - F(a)$
	$\Pr(x > -a) = 1 - F(-a)$
	$\Pr(x \leq a) = F(a)$
	$\Pr(x \leq -a) = F(-a)$
Symmetric about 0 Dist.[b]	$\Pr(x \leq a) = \Pr(x > -a)$
	$\Pr(x \leq -a) = \Pr(x > a)$
	$\Pr(x \leq -a) = 1 - F(a)$
Symmetric about μ Dist.[c]	$\Pr(x - \mu \leq a) = \Pr(x - \mu > -a)$
	$\Pr(x - \mu \leq -a) = \Pr(x - \mu > a)$
	$\Pr(x - \mu \leq -a) = 1 - F(a - \mu)$

a. These results carry over to symmetric distributions
b. Results do not hold in general, only mean zero symmetric distributions
c. Results do not hold in general, only mean μ symmetric distributions

B.2 Exponential Logistic Distribution

In this section we are concerned with the distribution of a positive valued random variable e^{η} where η is distributed logistically over the infinite range with mean zero and variance $\frac{\pi^2\sigma^2}{3}$. The moment generating function for a mean zero logistic random variate η is

$$E(e^{t\eta}) = \Gamma(1 - \sigma t)\,\Gamma(1 + \sigma t)\,, \tag{B.2}$$

where

$$\Gamma(a) = \int_0^{\infty} y^{a-1} e^{-y} dy. \tag{B.3}$$

For $\sigma t \leq 1$

$$E(e^{t\eta}) = \frac{\pi\sigma t}{\sin(\pi\sigma t)}$$

where $\sin(\pi\sigma t)$ is measured in radians. Evaluating at $t = 1$ yields

$$E(e^{\eta}) = \sigma\pi / \sin(\sigma\pi).$$

The restriction $\sigma t \leq 1$ implies $\sigma \leq 1$ if $t = 1$. The necessity of the restriction is evident for two reasons:

1. The gamma function $\Gamma(a)$ is only defined for $a \geq 0$. Substituting $1 - \sigma t = a$ implies $\sigma t \leq 1$.

2. Assuming $\sigma \geq 0$, $E(e^{\eta_j}) > 0$ if and only if $\sin(\sigma\pi) > 0$. This is true if $\sigma\pi \leq \pi$ which implies $\sigma \leq 1$. If $\sigma\pi > \pi$ then $\sin(\sigma\pi) < 0$ and $E(e^{\eta_j})$ would be less than zero. This is logically inconsistent as e^{η_j} is a positive valued random variable and cannot have a negative mean. If $\sigma > 1$ then the expected value of the exponential logistic random variable e^{η} is undefined.

The variance of e^{η} can be found in a similar fashion. By definition,

$$V(e^{\eta}) = E\left[(e^{\eta} - E(e^{\eta}))^2\right]$$

which simplifies to:

$$\begin{aligned} V(e^{\eta}) &= E\left[(e^{\eta})^2\right] - \left[E(e^{\eta})\right]^2 \\ &= E\left(e^{2\eta}\right) - \left[E(e^{\eta})\right]^2 \end{aligned}$$

Using the moment generating function from above, the variance of e^{η} becomes:

$$V(e^{\eta}) = \frac{2\pi\sigma}{\sin(2\pi\sigma)} - \left(\frac{\pi\sigma}{\sin(\pi\sigma)}\right)^2.$$

B.3 Properties of Truncated Normal

Suppose x is a normally distributed random variable with mean μ and variance σ^2, $\phi(z)$ is the standard normal density function, and $\Phi(z)$ is the standard normal distribution function. Define $x^* = \frac{x-\mu}{\sigma}$, $a^* = \frac{a-\mu}{\sigma}$. Then the expectation for the truncated x is

$$E(x|x > a) = \mu + \sigma\frac{\phi(a^*)}{1 - \Phi(a^*)}, \tag{B.4}$$

where $\frac{1}{\sigma}\phi\left(\frac{x-\mu}{\sigma}\right) = (2\pi\sigma^2)^{-\frac{1}{2}}e^{-\frac{1}{2}\left(\frac{x-\mu}{\sigma}\right)^2}$ is the density function of x. The distribution function of x, $\Phi\left(\frac{x-\mu}{\sigma}\right) = \int_{-\infty}^{\frac{x-\mu}{\sigma}} \sigma\phi(z)\,dz$ and the lower truncated density (truncated from below a) for x is

$$f(x|x>a) = \frac{1}{\sigma}\phi\left(\frac{x-\mu}{\sigma}\right) / \left[1-\Phi\left(\frac{a-\mu}{\sigma}\right)\right].$$

By definition,

$$E(x|x>a) = \int_a^\infty x f(x|x>a)\,dx. \tag{B.5}$$

Substituting in the expression for the truncated normal density function gives:

$$E(x|x>a) = \int_a^\infty x\frac{1}{\sigma}\phi(x^*(x)) / [1-\Phi(a^*)]\,dx, \tag{B.6}$$

where $x^* = \frac{x-\mu}{\sigma}$. For simplicity, let $P = [1-\Phi(a^*)]$ and rewrite the truncated expectation as

$$E(x|x>a) = \frac{1}{P}\int_a^\infty x\frac{1}{\sigma}\phi(x^*(x))\,dx. \tag{B.7}$$

To integrate this expression, we can transform the variable of integration from x to x^*. We substitute the function $x^*(x) = \frac{x-\mu}{\sigma}$ where it occurs and solve for x. To do this, we must rewrite the expression as an implicit function of $x(x^*) = x^*\sigma+\mu$. Note that $\lim_{x\to\infty} x^*(x) \to \infty$ and when $x = a$, $x^*(a) = \frac{a-\mu}{\sigma} = a^*$. The integral becomes

$$\frac{1}{P}\int_{x^*(a)}^{x^*(\infty)} x(x^*)\frac{1}{\sigma}\phi(x^*)\,x'(x^*)dx^* = \frac{1}{P}\int_{a^*}^\infty (x^*\sigma+\mu)\frac{1}{\sigma}\phi(x^*)\,\sigma dx^*$$

because $x'(x^*) = \sigma$. Expanding the right hand side and simplifying yields

$$E(x|x>a) = \frac{1}{P}\int_{a^*}^\infty (\sigma x^*\phi(x^*))\,dx^* + \frac{\mu}{P}\int_{a^*}^\infty \phi(x^*)\,dx^*. \tag{B.8}$$

The second integral is straightforward since by definition: $\phi(x^*) = \frac{d\Phi(x^*)}{dx^*}$, implying

$$\begin{aligned}
\frac{\mu}{P}\int_{a^*}^\infty \phi(x^*)\,dx^* &= \frac{\mu}{P}\int_{a^*}^\infty \frac{d\Phi(x^*)}{dx^*}dx^* \qquad \text{(B.9)}\\
&= \frac{\mu}{P}\left[\Phi(x^*)\right]_{x^*=a}^{x^*=\infty}\\
&= \frac{\mu}{P}\left[1-\Phi(a^*)\right]\\
&= \mu.
\end{aligned}$$

The first step follows from the definition of a cumulative distribution function, the final step follows from the definition of P.

To find an expression for $\frac{1}{P}\int_{a^*}^{\infty}(\sigma x^*\phi(x^*))\,dx^*$, note that $d\phi(x^*)/dx^* = d\frac{1}{\sqrt{2\pi}}e^{-\frac{x^{*2}}{2}}/dx^* = -x^*\phi(x^*)$. Substituting into the integral expression

$$\frac{1}{P}\int_{a^*}^{\infty}(\sigma x^*\phi(x^*))\,dx^* = -\frac{1}{P}\int_{a^*}^{\infty}\left(\sigma\frac{d\phi(x^*)}{dx^*}\right)dx^*$$

which upon evaluation becomes

$$\frac{1}{P}\int_{a^*}^{\infty}(\sigma x^*\phi(x^*))\,dx^* = -\frac{\sigma}{P}\left[\phi(x^*)\,|_{x^*=a^*}^{x^*=\infty}\right].$$

Because $\phi(\infty)=0$, this expression becomes

$$\frac{1}{P}\int_{a^*}^{\infty}(\sigma x^*\phi(x^*))\,dx^* = \sigma\frac{\phi(a^*)}{P}. \tag{B.10}$$

Substituting the expressions from equations (B.10) and (B.9) into equation (B.8) and substituting $P=[1-\Phi(a^*)]$ proves the proposition:

$$E(x|x>a) = \mu+\sigma\frac{\phi(a^*)}{1-\Phi(a^*)}. \tag{B.11}$$

Consequently in the model $y=\mathbf{z}\boldsymbol{\beta}+\varepsilon$, for $\varepsilon\sim N(0,\sigma^2)$, $E(\varepsilon|y\geq 0)=E(\varepsilon|\varepsilon\geq-\mathbf{z}\boldsymbol{\beta})=\sigma\frac{\phi(\mathbf{z}\boldsymbol{\beta}/\sigma)}{1-\Phi(-\mathbf{z}\boldsymbol{\beta}/\sigma)}$, the term found in truncated and censored regression models.

B.4 The Poisson and Negative Binomial

The Poisson probability of observing a non-negative integer outcome x is

$$\Pr(x)=\frac{e^{-\lambda}\lambda^x}{x!}, x=0,1,2,..$$

where λ is the Poisson mean. The negative binomial probability is:

$$\Pr(x)=\frac{\Gamma\left(x+\frac{1}{\alpha}\right)}{\Gamma(x+1)\,\Gamma\left(\frac{1}{\alpha}\right)}\left(\frac{\frac{1}{\alpha}}{\frac{1}{\alpha}+\lambda}\right)^{\frac{1}{\alpha}}\left(\frac{\lambda}{\frac{1}{\alpha}+\lambda}\right)^{x} \tag{B.12}$$

where

$$\Gamma(z)=\int_0^{\infty}y^{z-1}e^{-y}dy. \tag{B.13}$$

If z is a non-negative integer, then $\Gamma(z+1) = z!$. In Chapter 7 we assert that as $\alpha \to 0$, the negative binomial distribution collapses to the Poisson distribution. To see this, note that

$$\frac{\Gamma\left(x+\frac{1}{\alpha}\right)}{\Gamma\left(\frac{1}{\alpha}\right)} = \prod_{j=0}^{x-1}\left(j+\frac{1}{\alpha}\right).$$

We can also write $\left(\frac{1}{\frac{1}{\alpha}+\lambda}\right)^x = \prod_{j=0}^{x-1}\left(\frac{1}{\frac{1}{\alpha}+\lambda}\right)$. Rewrite the last parenthetical term on the right hand side of equation (??) as

$$\left(\frac{\lambda}{\frac{1}{\alpha}+\lambda}\right)^x = \lambda^x \prod_{j=0}^{x-1}\left(\frac{1}{\frac{1}{\alpha}+\lambda}\right).$$

Substitution and simplification gives

$$\Pr(x) = \frac{1}{x!}\left(\frac{\frac{1}{\alpha}}{\frac{1}{\alpha}+\lambda}\right)^{\frac{1}{\alpha}} \lambda^x \prod_{j=0}^{x-1}\left(\frac{j+\frac{1}{\alpha}}{\frac{1}{\alpha}+\lambda}\right). \tag{B.14}$$

Multiply the parenthetical terms by $\frac{\alpha}{\alpha}$ such that

$$\Pr(x) = \frac{1}{x!}\left(\frac{1}{1+\alpha\lambda}\right)^{\frac{1}{\alpha}} \lambda^x \prod_{j=0}^{x-1}\left(\frac{\alpha j+1}{1+\alpha\lambda}\right).$$

As $\alpha \to 0$

$$\begin{aligned} \left(\frac{1}{1+\alpha\lambda}\right)^{\frac{1}{\alpha}} &\to e^{-\lambda} \\ \prod_{j=0}^{x-1}\left(\frac{\alpha j+1}{1+\alpha\lambda}\right) &\to 1 \end{aligned}$$

So as $\alpha \to 0$

$$\lim_{\alpha\to 0}\Pr(x) = \frac{e^{-\lambda}\lambda^x}{x!}.$$

This is the Poisson probability.

B.5 The Type-I Extreme Value (Gumbel)

Let x be a Type-I extreme value random variable defined over the infinite range. The probability density function for x is

$$f_{EV}(x) = Be^{-B(x-A)}e^{-e^{-B(x-A)}} \tag{B.15}$$

where B is the scale parameter and A is the location parameter. The distribution function for x is

$$F_{EV}(x) = 1 - e^{-e^{-B(x-A)}} \tag{B.16}$$

The expected value of x is

$$E_{EV}(x) = A + \frac{1}{B}\frac{d\Gamma(t)}{dt}|_{t=1} \tag{B.17}$$

where $\frac{d\Gamma(t)}{dt}|_{t=1}$ is the first derivative of the incomplete gamma function $\Gamma(t) = \int_0^\infty z^{t-1}e^{-z}dz$ evaluated at $t = 1$. $\frac{d\Gamma(t)}{dt}|_{t=1}$ is referred to a Euler's constant

$$\frac{d\Gamma(t)}{dt}|_{t=1} \approx -0.57722. \tag{B.18}$$

The expectation of x is approximated as

$$E_{EV}(x) = A - \frac{0.57722}{B}. \tag{B.19}$$

The variance of x is

$$V_{EV}(x) = \frac{\pi^2}{6B^2}. \tag{B.20}$$

B.5.1 The McFadden RUM Probability

In Chapter 8, we define $u_{jk} = v_{jk} + \varepsilon_{jk}$ as the indirect utility of choice sequence k, j in a two-level nested choice structure. v_{jk} is the deterministic portion of utility and ε_{jk} is a random error term. $\Pr(j,k)$ represents the probability of choosing alternative j, k from among all possible combinations. As such, $\Pr(j,k)$ is the probability that the indirect utility from choice sequence k, j exceeds the indirect utility from any other choice sequence. In general

$$\Pr(j,k) = \Pr(u_{jk} > u_{lm} \ \forall \ lm \neq jk). \tag{B.21}$$

Substituting for the form of the indirect utility function

$$\begin{aligned} \Pr(j,k) &= \Pr(v_{jk} + \varepsilon_{jk} > v_{lm} + \varepsilon_{lm} \ \forall \ lm \neq jk) \\ &= \Pr(\varepsilon_{lm} < v_{jk} - v_{lm} + \varepsilon_{jk} \ \forall \ lm \neq jk). \end{aligned} \tag{B.22}$$

Define $f(\boldsymbol{\varepsilon})$ as the multivariate density function for the vector of errors $\boldsymbol{\varepsilon} = \{\boldsymbol{\varepsilon}_{J_1}, \boldsymbol{\varepsilon}_{J_2}, ..., \boldsymbol{\varepsilon}_{J_K}\}$, where $\boldsymbol{\varepsilon}_{\cdot k} = \{\varepsilon_{1k}, \varepsilon_{2k}, ..., \varepsilon_{J_k k}\}$. Equation (B.22) is a $\sum_{k=1}^{K} J_k$ dimension integral of the form

$$\Pr(j,k) = \int \cdots \int f(\boldsymbol{\varepsilon})\, d\varepsilon_{11} ... d\varepsilon_{J_K K} \tag{B.23}$$

where the bounds of integration are $(-\infty, v_{jk} - v_{lm} + \varepsilon_{jk})\ \forall\ \varepsilon_{lm} \in lm \neq jk$ and $(-\infty, \infty)$ for ε_{jk}. This integral can be reduced to a single integral of the form

$$\Pr(j,k) = \int_{\varepsilon_{jk}=-\infty}^{\varepsilon_{jk}=\infty} \Pr(\varepsilon_{lm} < v_{jk} - v_{lm} + \varepsilon_{jk}\ \forall\ lm \neq jk | \varepsilon_{jk})\, d\varepsilon_{jk} \tag{B.24}$$

using the following:

B.5.2 Conditional Probability Relation

Consider two jointly distributed random variables, x_1 and x_2, with joint distribution function $F(x_1, x_2)$. Let F_j denote the derivative of the joint distribution function with respect to the jth argument. The conditional probability of $x_1 < z$ given a particular value of x_2 is

$$\begin{aligned} \Pr(x_1 < z | x_2) &= \frac{dF(x_1, x_2)}{dx_2}|_{x_1=z} \\ &= F_2(z, x_2). \end{aligned}$$

Generalizing this result, $\Pr(j,k)$ becomes

$$\Pr(j,k) = \int_{\varepsilon_{jk}=-\infty}^{\varepsilon_{jk}=\infty} F_{jk}(v_{jk} - v_{11} + \varepsilon_{jk}, ...v_{jk} - v_{J_K K} + \varepsilon_{jk},)\, d\varepsilon_{jk}. \tag{B.25}$$

To derive a closed-form expression for $\Pr(j,k)$, we need the distribution of the random error terms in the indirect utility function. Kotz, Balakrishnan and Johnson provide an overview for multivariate extreme value distributions. McFadden utilized a special case of the multivariate extreme value distribution to derive the nested logit model. McFadden's generalized extreme value distribution is written in our notation as:

B.6 Generalized Extreme Value Distribution

$$F(\varepsilon) = \exp\left[-\sum_{m=1}^{K} a_m \left[\sum_{j=1}^{J_m} \exp\left(-\frac{\varepsilon_{jm}}{\theta_m}\right)\right]^{\theta_m}\right] \tag{B.26}$$

where $a_m > 0$ and $\theta_m \leq 1\ \forall m$ are parameters.

Equation (B.26) represents one form of the multivariate extreme value distribution. Other forms exist, but the generalized extreme value distribution has some desirable properties (namely a closed form solution for the expected maximum).

B.6.1 Probability Derivation

If ε is distributed generalized extreme value then

$$\Pr(j,k)=\frac{a_k e^{\frac{v_{jk}}{\theta_k}}\left[\sum_{l=1}^{J_k} e^{\frac{v_{lk}}{\theta_k}}\right]^{\theta_k-1}}{\sum_{m=1}^{K} a_m\left[\sum_{l=1}^{J_m} e^{\frac{v_{lm}}{\theta_m}}\right]^{\theta_m}}. \tag{B.27}$$

The proof for this proposition is as follows: First differentiate $F(\varepsilon)$ with respect to an arbitrarily chosen ε (we'll use ε_{11} for simplicity):

$$\begin{aligned} F_{11}(\varepsilon) &= F(\varepsilon)(-a_1\theta_1)\left[\sum_{l=1}^{J_1}\exp\left(-\frac{\varepsilon_{l1}}{\theta_1}\right)\right]^{\theta_1-1} \\ &\quad \times\exp\left(-\frac{\varepsilon_{11}}{\theta_1}\right)\left(-\frac{1}{\theta_1}\right) \\ &= a_1 F(\varepsilon)\left[\sum_{l=1}^{J_1}\exp\left(-\frac{\varepsilon_{l1}}{\theta_1}\right)\right]^{\theta_1-1}\exp\left(-\frac{\varepsilon_{11}}{\theta_1}\right) \end{aligned} \tag{B.28}$$

Substituting into equation (B.25):

$$\Pr(1,1)=\int_{\varepsilon_{11}=-\infty}^{\varepsilon_{11}=\infty} F_{11}\left(\varepsilon_{11}, v_{11}-v_{21}+\varepsilon_{11}, \ldots v_{11}-v_{J_K K}+\varepsilon_{11},\right) d\varepsilon_{11}$$

$$=\int_{-\infty}^{\infty}\left[\begin{array}{c} a_1 F\left(\varepsilon_{11}, v_{11}-v_{21}+\varepsilon_{11}, \ldots v_{11}-v_{J_K K}+\varepsilon_{11}\right) \\ \times\left[\sum_{l=1}^{J_1}\exp\left(-\frac{v_{11}-v_{l1}+\varepsilon_{11}}{\theta_1}\right)\right]^{\theta_1-1}\exp\left(-\frac{\varepsilon_{11}}{\theta_1}\right) \end{array}\right] d\varepsilon_{11}$$

$$=\int_{-\infty}^{\infty}\left[\begin{array}{c} a_1\exp\left[-\sum_{m=1}^{K} a_m\left[\sum_{l=1}^{J_m}\exp\left(-\frac{v_{11}-v_{lm}+\varepsilon_{11}}{\theta_m}\right)\right]^{\theta_m}\right] \\ \times\left[\sum_{l=1}^{J_1}\exp\left(-\frac{v_{11}-v_{l1}+\varepsilon_{11}}{\theta_1}\right)\right]^{\theta_1-1}\exp\left(-\frac{\varepsilon_{11}}{\theta_1}\right) \end{array}\right] d\varepsilon_{11}$$

$$=\int_{-\infty}^{\infty}\left[\begin{array}{c} a_1\exp\left[\begin{array}{c} -\sum_{m=1}^{K} a_m\left(\exp\left(-\frac{v_{11}+\varepsilon_{11}}{\theta_m}\right)^{\theta_m}\right) \\ \times\left[\sum_{l=1}^{J_m}\exp\left(\frac{v_{lm}}{\theta_m}\right)\right]^{\theta_m} \end{array}\right] \\ \times\exp\left(-\frac{v_{11}+\varepsilon_{11}}{\theta_1}\right)^{\theta_1-1} \\ \times\left[\sum_{l=1}^{J_1}\exp\left(\frac{v_{l1}}{\theta_1}\right)\right]^{\theta_1-1}\exp\left(-\frac{\varepsilon_{11}}{\theta_1}\right) \end{array}\right] d\varepsilon_{11}$$

$$= \int_{\varepsilon_{11}=-\infty}^{\varepsilon_{11}=\infty} \left[\begin{array}{c} a_1 \exp \left[\begin{array}{c} -\exp(-v_{11}) \exp(-\varepsilon_{11}) \\ \times \sum_{m=1}^{K} a_m \left[\sum_{l=1}^{J_m} \exp\left(\frac{v_{lm}}{\theta_m}\right) \right]^{\theta_m} \end{array} \right] \\ \times \exp\left(-\frac{v_{11}(\theta_1-1)}{\theta_1}\right) \exp\left(-\frac{\varepsilon_{11}(\theta_1-1)}{\theta_1}\right) \\ \times \left[\sum_{l=1}^{J_1} \exp\left(\frac{v_{l1}}{\theta_1}\right) \right]^{\theta_1-1} \exp\left(-\frac{\varepsilon_{11}}{\theta_1}\right) \end{array} \right] d\varepsilon_{11}$$

$$= \int_{\varepsilon_{11}=-\infty}^{\varepsilon_{11}=\infty} \left[\begin{array}{c} a_1 \exp \left[\begin{array}{c} -\exp(-v_{11}) \exp(-\varepsilon_{11}) \\ \times \sum_{m=1}^{K} a_m \left[\sum_{l=1}^{J_m} \exp\left(\frac{v_{lm}}{\theta_m}\right) \right]^{\theta_m} \end{array} \right] \\ \times \exp\left(-\frac{v_{11}(\theta_1-1)}{\theta_1}\right) \exp\left(-\frac{\varepsilon_{11}(\theta_1-1)}{\theta_1} - \frac{\varepsilon_{11}}{\theta_1}\right) \\ \times \left[\sum_{l=1}^{J_1} \exp\left(\frac{v_{l1}}{\theta_1}\right) \right]^{\theta_1-1} \end{array} \right] d\varepsilon_{11}$$

$$= \int_{-\infty}^{\infty} \left[\begin{array}{c} a_1 \exp \left[\begin{array}{c} -\exp(-v_{11}) \exp(-\varepsilon_{11}) \\ \times \sum_{m=1}^{K} a_m \left[\sum_{l=1}^{J_m} \exp\left(\frac{v_{lm}}{\theta_m}\right) \right]^{\theta k} \end{array} \right] \\ \times \exp\left(-\frac{v_{11}(\theta_1-1)}{\theta_1}\right) \exp(-\varepsilon_{11}) \\ \times \left[\sum_{l=1}^{J_1} \exp\left(\frac{v_{l1}}{\theta_1}\right) \right]^{\theta_1-1} \end{array} \right] d\varepsilon_{11}. \quad \text{(B.29)}$$

Let

$$C_1 = a_1 \exp\left(-\frac{v_{11}(\theta_1-1)}{\theta_1}\right) \left[\sum_{l=1}^{J_1} \exp\left(\frac{v_{l1}}{\theta_1}\right) \right]^{\theta_1-1} \quad \text{(B.30)}$$

and

$$C_2 = \exp(-v_{11}) \sum_{m=1}^{K} a_m \left[\sum_{l-1}^{J_m} \exp\left(\frac{v_{lm}}{\theta_m}\right) \right]^{\theta_m}. \quad \text{(B.31)}$$

Then

$$\Pr(1,1) = C_1 \int_{\varepsilon_{11}=-\infty}^{\varepsilon_{11}=\infty} \left[e^{-\varepsilon_{11}} e^{-C_2 e^{-\varepsilon_{11}}} \right] d\varepsilon_{11}. \quad \text{(B.32)}$$

The integrand is closely related to the density function for a Gumbel (extreme-value) distributed random variable (see equation (B.15)). From equation (B.15), the density function for a Gumbel distributed random variable (denoted f_{EV}) with unit scale and location parameter $\ln C_2$, is:

$$f_{EV}(\varepsilon_{11}) = C_2 e^{-\varepsilon_{11}} e^{-C_2 e^{-\varepsilon_{11}}} \quad \text{(B.33)}$$

so that $\int_{-\infty}^{\infty} f_{EV}(\varepsilon_{11})\, d\varepsilon_{11} = 1$. Substituting into equation (B.32) yields:

$$\begin{aligned}\Pr(1,1) &= C_1 \int_{-\infty}^{\infty} \frac{f_{EV}(\varepsilon_{11})}{C_2} d\varepsilon_{11} \\ &= \frac{C_1}{C_2} \int_{-\infty}^{\infty} f_{EV}(\varepsilon_{11})\, d\varepsilon_{11} = \frac{C_1}{C_2}. \end{aligned} \quad \text{(B.34)}$$

Hence we have

$$\Pr(1,1) = \frac{C_1}{C_2}. \quad \text{(B.35)}$$

This derivation holds for any choice combination j, k. Substituting back in the definitions of C_1 and C_2 proves the proposition in Chapter 8:

$$\begin{aligned}\Pr(j,k) &= \frac{a_k \exp\left(-\frac{v_{jk}(\theta_k - 1)}{\theta_k}\right)\left[\sum_{l=1}^{J_k} \exp\left(\frac{v_{lk}}{\theta_k}\right)\right]^{\theta_k - 1}}{\exp(-v_{jk}) \sum_{m=1}^{K} a_m \left[\sum_{l=1}^{J_m} \exp\left(\frac{v_{lm}}{\theta_m}\right)\right]^{\theta_m}} \\ &= \Pr(j,k) = \frac{a_k e^{\frac{v_{jk}}{\theta_k}} \left[\sum_{l=1}^{J_k} e^{\frac{v_{lk}}{\theta_k}}\right]^{\theta_k - 1}}{\sum_{m=1}^{K} a_m \left[\sum_{l=1}^{J_m} e^{\frac{v_{lm}}{\theta_m}}\right]^{\theta_m}}. \end{aligned} \quad \text{(B.36)}$$

B.6.2 Expected Maximum Utility

In chapter 8, we define $\mathbf{u}_{\cdot k} = \{u_{1k}, u_{2k}, ..., u_{J_k k}\}$ as the vector of utilities for upper level choice k in a two-level nested choice structure, and $\mathbf{u} = \{\mathbf{u}_{\cdot 1}, \mathbf{u}_{\cdot 2}, ..., \mathbf{u}_{\cdot K}\}$ as the concatenation of the error vectors across all upper and lower level choices. Max($\mathbf{u}$) is the maximum indirect utility attainable (largest element among all possible $u_{jk} = v_{jk} + \varepsilon_{jk}$).

If the error vector $\boldsymbol{\varepsilon}$ is distributed as generalized extreme value as in equation (B.26), then

$$E(max(\mathbf{u})) = \ln\left(\sum_{m=1}^{K} a_m \left[\sum_{l=1}^{J_m} e^{\frac{v_{lm}}{\theta_m}}\right]^{\theta_m}\right) - 0.57722. \quad \text{(B.37)}$$

The proof is as follows. Let

$$\max(\mathbf{u}) = \arg\max(v_{11} + \varepsilon_{11}, ... v_{J_K K} + \varepsilon_{J_K K}).$$

If alternative j, k is chosen, then $\max(\mathbf{u}) = v_{jk} + \varepsilon_{jk}$. For a given value of ε_{jk} this occurs with probability

$$\Pr(v_{jk} + \varepsilon_{jk} > v_{lm} + \varepsilon_{lm} \ \forall \ lm \neq jk | \varepsilon_{jk})$$

$$= F_{jk}(v_{jk} - v_{11} + \varepsilon_{jk}, v_{jk} - v_{21} + \varepsilon_{jk}, ...v_{jk} - v_{J_K K} + \varepsilon_{jk}) \quad \text{(B.38)}$$

where F_{jk} is the derivative of $F(\boldsymbol{\varepsilon})$ with respect to argument j, k. Multiplying by the realization of $\max(\mathbf{u})$, integrating over all possible values of ε_{jk}, and summing over all possible choice outcomes, the expected maximum utility is $E(max(\mathbf{u})) =$

$$\sum_{m=1}^{K}\sum_{l=1}^{J_m}\int_{\varepsilon_{lm}}(v_{lm} + \varepsilon_{lm}) F_{lm}\begin{pmatrix} v_{lm} - v_{11} + \varepsilon_{lm}, \\ ..., v_{lm} - v_{J_K K} + \varepsilon_{lm}\end{pmatrix} d\varepsilon_{lm}. \quad \text{(B.39)}$$

Define $z_{lm} = v_{lm} + \varepsilon_{lm}$ then

$$E(max(\mathbf{u})) = \sum_{m=1}^{K}\sum_{l=1}^{J_m}\int_{z_{lm}} zF_{lm}(z - v_{11}, ..., z - v_{J_K K})\, dz. \quad \text{(B.40)}$$

Assume $F(\boldsymbol{\varepsilon})$ is the GEV cumulative distribution function as defined in equation (B.26). >From equation (B.28)

$$F_{lm}(\boldsymbol{\varepsilon}) = a_m F(\boldsymbol{\varepsilon})\left[\sum_{l=1}^{J_m}\exp\left(-\frac{\varepsilon_{lm}}{\theta_m}\right)\right]^{\theta_m - 1}\exp\left(-\frac{\varepsilon_{lm}}{\theta_m}\right). \quad \text{(B.41)}$$

Substituting $F(\boldsymbol{\varepsilon})$,

$$C_1 = a_m \exp\left(-\frac{v_{lm}(\theta_m - 1)}{\theta_m}\right)\left[\sum_{j=1}^{J_m}\exp\left(\frac{v_{jm}}{\theta_m}\right)\right]^{\theta_m - 1}$$

and

$$C_2 = \exp(-v_{lm})\sum_{k=1}^{K} a_k\left[\sum_{j=1}^{J_k}\exp\left(\frac{v_{jk}}{\theta_k}\right)\right]^{\theta_k}$$

from equation (B.32), $F_{lm}(\boldsymbol{\varepsilon})$ becomes

$$F_{lm}(\boldsymbol{\varepsilon}) = C_1 e^{-\varepsilon_{lm}} e^{-C_2 e^{-\varepsilon_{lm}}}. \quad \text{(B.42)}$$

Transforming random variables from ε_{lm} to z_{lm}

$$F_{lm}(z - v_{11}, ..., z - v_{J_K K}) = e^{v_{lm}} C_1 e^{-z_{lm}} e^{-e^{v_{lm}} C_2 e^{-z_{lm}}}.$$

Now define

$$C_3 = e^{v_{lm}} C_1 \tag{B.44}$$
$$= a_m \exp\left(\frac{v_{lm}}{\theta_m}\right) \left[\sum_{j=1}^{J_m} \exp\left(\frac{v_{jm}}{\theta_m}\right)\right]^{\theta_m - 1}$$

and

$$C_4 = e^{v_{lm}} C_2 \tag{B.45}$$
$$= \sum_{k=1}^{K} a_k \left[\sum_{j=1}^{J_k} \exp\left(\frac{v_{jk}}{\theta_k}\right)\right]^{\theta_k}.$$

Expected maximum utility can now be written as $E\,(max\,(\mathbf{u}))$

$$= \sum_{m=1}^{K} \sum_{l=1}^{J_m} \int_{z_{lm}} z F_{lm} \left(z - v_{11}, ..., z - v_{J_K K}\right) dz \tag{B.46}$$
$$= \sum_{m=1}^{K} \sum_{l=1}^{J_m} \int_{z_{lm}} z C_3 e^{-z} e^{-C_4 e^{-z}} dz$$
$$= \sum_{m=1}^{K} \sum_{l=1}^{J_m} C_3 \int_{z_{lm}} z e^{-z} e^{-C_4 e^{-z}} dz.$$

A couple of notes are important here. The last line above follows because C_3 is independent of z. Also, C_4 is a constant and as such independent of the summations. Further, because the GEV distribution is defined over the infinite range, the range of integration for is z_{lm} infinite. Hence we can write

$$E\,(max\,(\mathbf{u})) = \int_{z_{lm}} z e^{-z} e^{-C_4 e^{-z}} dz \sum_{m=1}^{K} \sum_{l=1}^{J_m} C_3. \tag{B.47}$$

Now consider the summation term. Differentiating C_4 with respect to

$e^{v_{lm}}$ will provide a useful result (note that $\exp\left(\frac{v_{jk}}{\theta_k}\right) = (e^{v_{lm}})^{\frac{1}{\theta_m}}$)

$$\frac{dC_4}{de^{v_{lm}}} = a_m \left(e^{v_{lm}}\right)^{\frac{1}{\theta_m}-1} \left[\sum_{j=1}^{J_m} \exp\left(\frac{v_{jm}}{\theta_m}\right)\right]^{\theta_m - 1} \tag{B.48}$$

$$= e^{-v_{lm}} a_m \left(e^{\frac{v_{lm}}{\theta_m}}\right) \left[\sum_{j=1}^{J_m} \exp\left(\frac{v_{jm}}{\theta_m}\right)\right]^{\theta_m - 1}$$

$$= e^{-v_{lm}} C_3.$$

Substituting this result into the summation term in equation (B.47) yields

$$\sum_{m=1}^{K} \sum_{l=1}^{J_m} C_3 = \sum_{m=1}^{K} \sum_{l=1}^{J_m} e^{v_{lm}} \frac{dC_4}{de^{v_{lm}}}. \tag{B.49}$$

Relying on Euler's Theorem for homogeneity of a function, if C_4 is homogeneous of degree 1 in $\mathbf{e}^{\mathbf{v}}$, where $\mathbf{e}^{v} = e^{v_{11}}, \ldots e^{v_{KJ_K}}$ is the full vector of possible $e^{v_{jk}}$, then

$$C_4 = \sum_{m=1}^{K} \sum_{l=1}^{J_m} e^{v_{lm}} \frac{dC_4}{de^{v_{lm}}}. \tag{B.50}$$

Is C_4 homogeneous of degree 1 in all $e^{v_{jk}}$? From above,

$$C_4\left(\mathbf{e}^{v}\right) = \sum_{k=1}^{K} a_k \left[\sum_{j=1}^{J_k} \exp\left(\frac{v_{jk}}{\theta_k}\right)\right]^{\theta_k}. \tag{B.51}$$

Notc that since

$$a_k \left[\sum_{j=1}^{J_k} \left(r \exp\left(v_{jk}\right)\right)^{\frac{1}{\theta_k}}\right]^{\theta_k} = r a_k \left[\sum_{j=1}^{J_k} \left(\exp\left(v_{jk}\right)\right)^{\frac{1}{\theta_k}}\right]^{\theta_k}$$

is homogeneous of degree one, C_4 is the sum of homogeneous of degree one functions and hence is homogeneous of degree one itself. This establishes the validity of equation (B.50). Combining equations (B.50) and (B.49) gives

$$\sum_{m=1}^{K} \sum_{l=1}^{J_m} C_3 = C_4. \tag{B.52}$$

Substituting this result into equation (B.47), expected maximum utility now becomes

$$E\left(max\left(\mathbf{u}\right)\right) = \int_{z_{lm}} ze^{-z}e^{-C_4e^{-z}}dzC_4 = \int_{z_{lm}} zC_4e^{-z}e^{-C_4e^{-z}}dz. \quad \text{(B.53)}$$

The integrand is the expected value of a Type-I extreme value (Gumbel) random variable with unit scale and location parameter $\ln\left(C_4\right)$ (see equation (B.15)). From equation (B.19), expected maximum utility is therefore:

$$E\left(max\left(\mathbf{u}\right)\right) = \ln\left(C_4\right) - 0.57722 = \ln\left(\sum_{m=1}^{K} a_m \left[\sum_{l=1}^{J_m} \exp\left(\frac{v_{lm}}{\theta_m}\right)\right]^{\theta_m}\right) - 0.57722. \quad \text{(B.54)}$$

This is the expected maximum utility that serves as the indirect utility function when calculating welfare effects for the nested logit model, and when the parameters a_m and θ_m are appropriately restricted, for the conditional logit.

Index